UNIFYING HINDUISM

SOUTH ASIA ACROSS THE DISCIPLINES

SOUTH ASIA ACROSS THE DISCIPLINES

◈ ◈ ◈

EDITED BY DIPESH CHAKRABARTY, SHELDON POLLOCK, AND SANJAY SUBRAHMANYAM

Funded by a grant from the Andrew W. Mellon Foundation and jointly published by the University of California Press, the University of Chicago Press, and Columbia University Press

Extreme Poetry: The South Asian Movement of Simultaneous Narration by Yigal Bronner (Columbia)

The Social Space of Language: Vernacular Culture in British Colonial Punjab by Farina Mir (California)

Everyday Healing: Hindus and Others in an Ambiguously Islamic Place by Carla Bellamy (California)

South Asia Across the Disciplines is a series devoted to publishing first books across a wide range of South Asian studies, including art, history, philology or textual studies, philosophy, religion, and the interpretive social sciences. Series authors all share the goal of opening up new archives and suggesting new methods and approaches, while demonstrating that South Asian scholarship can be at once deep in expertise and broad in appeal.

UNIFYING HINDUISM

PHILOSOPHY AND IDENTITY IN INDIAN INTELLECTUAL HISTORY

Andrew J. Nicholson

COLUMBIA UNIVERSITY PRESS *NEW YORK*

Columbia University Press
Publishers Since 1893
New York Chichester, West Sussex

Paperback edition, 2014

Library of Congress Cataloging-in-Publication Data
Nicholson, Andrew J.
Unifying Hinduism : philosophy and identity in Indian
intellectual history / Andrew J. Nicholson.
p. cm. — (South Asia across the disciplines)
Includes bibliographical references and index.
ISBN 978-0-231-14986-0 (cloth)—ISBN 978-0-231-14987-7 (pbk. : alk. paper)—
ISBN 978-0-231-52642-5 (e-book)
1. Hinduism—History. 2. India—Intellectual life. I. Title. II. Series.
BL1150.N53 2010
294.509—dc22
2010027458

Columbia University Press books are printed on permanent and durable acid-free paper.

Printed in the United States of America

c 10 9 8 7 6
p 10 9 8 7 6 5 4 3 2 1

Cover image: Artist unknown, The Churning of the Ocean of Milk
(from The Song of the Herdsman or Dark Lord*), ca. 1785.*
Edwin Binney 3rd Collection, 1990:1271. San Diego Museum of Art
Cover designer: Milenda Nan Ok Lee

CONTENTS

ACKNOWLEDGMENTS

THERE ARE many people who deserve thanks for helping me to write this book. Sheldon Pollock has been with me through every stage of this project, from my first inchoate thoughts on late medieval Sāṃkhya through the most recent round of revisions. His willingness to let me follow my own path, even when that path sometimes led to a dead end, is what made this book possible in its current form. Matthew Kapstein has consistently challenged me to rethink my basic presuppositions about Indian intellectual history, doxography, and periodization; and Jonardon Ganeri has offered encouragement, guidance, and philosophical perspective from across the ocean. Most recently, Johannes Bronkhorst and Edwin Bryant have been generous with their time and have offered many suggestions that have improved this book. Wendy Lochner, Christine Mortlock, Anne McCoy, and Roy Thomas with Columbia University Press have been invaluable in their guidance and prompt answers to my many questions. A grant from the Columbia University Seminars enabled me to hire Hamsa Stainton, who expertly proofread the Sanskrit passages in this book. I give special thanks to Cynthia Garver, who painstakingly copyedited the first nine chapters of this book but suddenly and tragically passed away before we had completed our work together.

The funding for the initial research in India for this book was provided through a U.S. Department of Education Fulbright-Hays Fellowship and fellowships from the University of Chicago Committee on Southern Asian Studies. My daily tutorials reading Sanskrit texts with Shree Narayan Mishra, Professor Emeritus of Sanskrit at Benares Hindu University, formed the core of my research in India. Without his erudite instruction, my knowledge of Sanskrit and Indian philosophy would be much poorer, and those sessions are some of my fondest memories from my times in India. Kanshi Ram of Hans Raj College, Delhi University, was extremely helpful in giving a second opinion on various perplexing passages. Unless otherwise noted, however, all Sanskrit translations in this book are my own.

I have presented parts of this book in several scholarly forums. I thank audiences at the University of Chicago South Asia Workshop, 13th World Sanskrit Conference, Columbia University Seminar on South Asia, University of Pennsylvania South Asia Colloquium, American Academy of Religion Buddhism Section, and Worldview and Theory in Indian Philosophy Conference for their spirited and insightful reactions. Some of the many conversation partners who have enriched the thoughts I present here are Dan Arnold, Purushottama Bilimoria, Arindam Chakrabarti, Christopher Chapple, Malcolm David Eckel, Vincent Eltschinger, Jonathan Gold, Hiroshi Marui, John Nemec, Hugh Nicholson, Parimal Patil, Ajay Rao, T. S. Rukmani, Stuart Sarbacker, Audrey Truschke, Milind Wakankar, and Ian Whicher. The encouragement and collegial atmosphere provided by my colleagues in the Department of Asian and Asian American Studies and the Center for India Studies at Stony Brook University have also facilitated my work in recent years. Parts of this book were originally published as articles in the *Journal of Indian Philosophy*, *Journal of Vaishnava Studies*, and *Internet Encyclopedia of Philosophy*, and I thank them for allowing me to reprint them here.

Finally, I thank Norman and Marlene Nicholson for their unflagging faith in my abilities, and I thank Claudia Misi and Silvia Nicholson for keeping a smile on my face during the long months and years that this book has been in preparation.

ABBREVIATIONS

Bh. Pu.	*Bhāgavata Purāṇa*
BhG	*Bhagavad Gītā*
Bṛh. Up.	*Bṛhadāraṇyaka Upaniṣad*
BS	*Brahmasūtras of Bādarāyaṇa*
BSB	*Brahmasūtrabhāṣya*
Ch. Up.	*Chāndogya Upaniṣad*
Kai. Up.	*Kaivalya Upaniṣad*
Kaṭha Up.	*Kaṭha Upaniṣad*
Kūrma Pu.	*Kūrma Purāṇa*
Manu.	*Manusmṛti (Mānavadharmaśāstra)*
Mbh	*Mahābhārata*
MHK	*Madhyamakahṛdayakārikā* of Bhāviveka
MMK	*Mūlamadhyamakakārika* of Nāgārjuna
Mokṣ.	*Mokṣadharma Parvan*
MS	*Mīmāṃsāsūtras* of Jaimini
PMS	*Pūrvamīmāṃsāsūtras*
SDS	*Sarvadarśanasaṃgraha* of Mādhava
SK	*Sāṃkhyakārikā* of Īśvarakṛṣṇa
SPB	*Sāṃkhyapravacanabhāṣya* of Vijñānabhikṣu
SS	*Sāṃkhyasūtras* of Kapila
Śvet. Up.	*Śvetāśvatara Upaniṣad*
Tai. S.	*Taittirīya Saṃhitā*
Tai. Up.	*Taittirīya Upaniṣad*
TK	*Tattvakaumudī* of Vācaspati Miśra
TSS	*Tattvasamāsasūtras*
TV	*Tattvavaiśāradī* of Vācaspati Miśra

VAB	*Vijñānāmṛtabhāṣya* of Vijñānabhikṣu
Viṣ. Pu.	*Viṣṇu Purāṇa*
Yaj. Smṛ.	*Yajñavalkya Smṛti*
YD	*Yuktidīpikā*
YS	*Yogasūtras* of Patañjali
YSS	*Yogasārasaṃgraha* of Vijñānabhikṣu
YV	*Yogavārttika* of Vijñānabhikṣu

UNIFYING HINDUISM

[1] INTRODUCTION

CONTESTING THE UNITY OF HINDUISM

The word "Hinduism" is loaded with historical and political resonances. Like such comparable terms as Buddhism, Sikhism, Confucianism, and Taoism, this word is a site of contestation, with proponents and detractors, open to varied interpretations. In this introduction I briefly sketch two opposing and influential contemporary interpretations of Hinduism, both of which I believe have significant weaknesses.

The first, often enunciated by Hindus themselves, is that Hinduism is the modern term for what was known in earlier times as the eternal religion (*sanātana dharma*) described in such texts as the *Bhagavad Gītā* and the Vedas.[1] Properly speaking, it has no history. Although historians today attempt with some degree of success to chronicle the poets and philosophers who found new ways of expressing the truths of Hinduism, the essence of this religion has remained the same since the very beginning of Indian civilization, thousands or even tens of thousands of years ago. In this regard, Hinduism is different from Christianity and Islam, two traditions founded relatively recently by single individuals which have undergone extensive changes in response to world-historical events.

In the second, partly as a response to this portrayal, some scholars of modern history, anthropology, and postcolonial studies have argued that a unified set of beliefs and practices known as Hinduism did not exist before the nineteenth century. According to this narrative, British scholars closely aligned with Britain's imperial project looked for an Indian analogue to the Western religions that they already knew. But after arriving in India and finding a multitude of popular rites without any unifying philosophical or theological framework, "the first British scholars of India went so far as to invent what we now call 'Hinduism,' complete with a mainstream classical tradition consisting entirely of Sanskrit philosophical texts like the Bhagavad-Gita and the Upanishads."[2] This invention was internalized by the English-educated Indians of the so-called Hindu renaissance, who were in fact elaborating on an entirely new religion that had little to do with the self-understanding of their own ancestors. According to this interpretation, the invention of Hinduism is one particular instance of the widespread tendency toward "the invention of tradition" that was so common among the Victorians.[3] Hinduism, far from being the oldest religion in the world, is one of the youngest, if it can really be said to exist at all.

These two stories about the provenance of Hinduism could hardly be more starkly opposed. Critics of the first narrative argue that it is simply an ahistorical fabrication. It is based on a selective reading of ancient texts that ignores the great variety of opposed contradictory beliefs and practices and the complete lack of any notion of a "Hindu unity" that existed before the arrival of the British in India. Conversely, many Hindus see the "modern invention of Hinduism" hypothesis as a slap in the face, the final culmination of Western imperialist scholarship on India, portraying faithful Hindus as passive dupes and Hinduism as nothing more than a fraud perpetrated by the imperialists themselves. I argue that these two general approaches, admittedly introduced here only in broad outline, are tendentious readings based on a modern tendency to homogenize and oversimplify premodern Indian history. The idea of Hindu unity is neither a timeless truth nor a fiction wholly invented by the British to regulate and control their colonial subjects.

The thesis of this book is that between the twelfth and sixteenth centuries CE, certain thinkers began to treat as a single whole the diverse philosophical teachings of the Upaniṣads, epics, Purāṇas, and the schools known retrospectively as the "six systems" (*ṣaḍdarśana*) of mainstream Hindu philosophy.[4] The Indian and European thinkers in the nineteenth century who developed the term "Hinduism" under the pressure of the new explanatory category of "world religions" were influenced by these earlier philosophers and doxographers, primarily Vedāntins, who had their own reasons for arguing the unity of Indian philosophical traditions. Before the late medieval period, there was little or no systematic attempt by the thinkers we now describe as Hindu to put aside their differences in order to depict themselves as a single unified tradition. After this late medieval period, it became almost universally accepted that there was a fixed group of Indian philosophies in basic agreement with one another and standing together against Buddhism and Jainism.

In pre-twelfth-century India, many thinkers today labeled "Hindu" went to great efforts to disprove one another's teachings, including use of *ad hominem* attacks, straw man arguments, and other questionable means. There was no understanding then that all of these thinkers were part of a shared orthodoxy. Nor was there an idea that schools such as Sāṃkhya and Mīmāṃsā had commonalities that differentiated them from the non-Hindu philosophies of the Jainas and Buddhists. Kumārila Bhaṭṭa, the influential seventh-century Mīmāṃsaka, wrote that "the treatises on righteousness and unrighteousness that have been adopted in Sāṃkhya, Yoga, Pāñcarātra, Pāśupata, and Buddhist works . . . are not accepted by those who know the triple Veda."[5] Likewise, Sāṃkhya and Yoga philosophers faulted Vedāntins and Mīmāṃsakas for their uncritical acceptance of Vedic authority, which included the performance of what they considered immoral animal sacrifices.[6] One author of this period, the eleventh-century Śaiva author Somaśambhu, even asserts that Vedāntins, Mīmāṃsakas, and those who worship other gods such as Viṣṇu will be reborn in hells unless they undergo a complicated conversion ritual designed to make them full-fledged Śaivas.[7]

Later codifiers of Indian traditions sought to depict the "six systems of philosophy" (*ṣaḍdarśanas*) as sharing a fundamental commitment to the authority of the Veda that unified them as Hindus and made them understand themselves as fundamentally different from Jainas and Buddhists. However, no single, well-demarcated boundary between "affirmers" (*āstikas*) and "deniers" (*nāstikas*) existed before the late medieval period. But by the sixteenth century, most Mīmāṃsakas and Vedāntins did understand themselves united in their shared commitment to the Vedas over and against other groups they designated as *nāstikas.* In this book, I tell the story of this remarkable shift, arguing that the seeds were planted for the now-familiar discourse of Hindu unity by a number of influential philosophers in late medieval India. I give particular attention to one such philosopher, Vijñānabhikṣu, a sixteenth-century polymath who was perhaps the boldest of all of these innovators. According to him, it was not just that all of the philosophies of the *āstikas* agreed on the sanctity of the Veda. He claimed that, properly understood, Sāṃkhya, Yoga, Vedānta, and Nyāya were in essence different aspects of a single, well-coordinated philosophical outlook and their well-documented disagreements were just a misunderstanding.

Because of Vijñānabhikṣu's bold rethinking of the relationship between the schools of Indian philosophy, Western scholars have regarded him with suspicion. The nineteenth-century translator and historian Richard Garbe expressed the opinion of many of his colleagues when he wrote that "Vijñānabhikṣu mixes up many . . . heterogeneous matters, and even quite effaces the individuality of the several philosophical systems."[8] Nonetheless, Garbe considered Vijñānabhikṣu's works too important to be written off as the idiosyncratic ramblings of a fringe thinker. He describes Vijñānabhikṣu's commentary on the *Sāṃkhyasūtras* as "not only the fullest source we have of the Sāṃkhya system, but also one of the most important."[9] More recently, scholars of Yoga have found Vijñānabhikṣu's subcommentary on Patañjali's *Yogasūtras* similarly indispensable for a detailed understanding of the Yoga system of philosophy.[10]

All of the previous scholarly treatments on Vijñānabhikṣu have had in common an approach that understands him only from a single perspective, through the lens of Sāṃkhya, Yoga, or Vedānta.[11] They either sidestep the question of the relationship between the three parts of Vijñānabhikṣu's corpus or are openly hostile to Vijñānabhikṣu's efforts toward a concordance of philosophical systems. This attitude is based on an uncritical acceptance of a particular model of the relationship between the philosophical schools of India. According to this model, the schools of Indian philosophy are well established and distinct. Most commonly, they list six *āstika darśanas* (commonly translated "orthodox schools"), without exploring the provenance of this list.[12] On the other side are the *nāstika* schools, the most well known of which are the Buddhists, Jainas, and Cārvāka materialists. Any attempt to blur the divisions between these discrete philosophical schools is condemned as syncretism, an illicit mixture of irreconcilable philosophies.

It is surprising how widespread and influential this understanding of the schools of Indian philosophy remains today. This picture comes from the writings of Indologists of the eighteenth and nineteenth centuries, although these early Indologists did not invent these ideas by themselves. Rather, they adopted for their own purposes the classificatory schemes they found in reading medieval catalogues of doctrines, or doxographies. These doxographies, composed at a relatively late date by authors who were themselves partisan adherents of one or another of the schools they sought to catalogue, were widely accepted by eighteenth- and nineteenth-century

Orientalists as objective depictions of a fixed state of affairs. Orientalists extrapolated from these texts the notion that the Indian philosophical schools arose as separate and distinct in ancient times and have remained stable and essentially unchanged for centuries. By comparison, they understood Western philosophical schools as arising, adapting, and going out of existence in historical time, sometimes portrayed as the unfolding of a larger historical dialectic. Much like Marx's depiction of traditional Indian social life as "undignified, stagnatory, and vegetative," Orientalists often understood Indian philosophy as existing outside of history. Unlike Marx, however, they understood this ahistoricity as one of the positive features of Oriental wisdom, in contrast to the changeable fads of European intellectuals.[13] Hindu reformers of the modern period picked up the Orientalist narrative of premodern India as a timeless realm of philosophical contemplation to serve their own ends. Although modern Hindus continue to take the great antiquity of Indian intellectual traditions as a source of national pride, many have denied the incompatibility of the *āstika* philosophical schools, instead arguing for a common essence at the heart of all *āstika* schools.

One of the ironies of the Orientalists' use of medieval doxographies to show that the schools of philosophy were distinct and logically incompatible is that it was these same doxographies that began to question earlier assumptions about the logical incompatibility of philosophical schools. Vijñānabhikṣu was only one of a number of late medieval intellectuals in India who sought to find unity among the apparent differences of the philosophical schools of the *āstikas.* Śaṅkara, the influential eighth-century Advaita Vedāntin, issued scathing attacks on *āstika* and *nāstika* alike, hardly distinguishing between the two.[14] Yet Śaṅkara's self-proclaimed followers of the late medieval period rehabilitated the same *āstika* schools that early Vedāntins had scorned, most notably the Sāṃkhya and Yoga schools. The medieval Advaita doxographers Mādhava and Madhusūdana Sarasvatī suggest that such non-Vedāntic schools are useful as partial approximations of a truth only fully enunciated by Advaita Vedānta. Although his allegiances were to a different school of Vedānta, Vijñānabhikṣu is the most outstanding example of this late medieval movement to find unity among the apparent diversity of philosophical schools. None of these unifiers would have described themselves as "Hindus," a term that was still uncommon in sixteenth-century Sanskrit usage. But it was their unification of *āstika* philosophies that nineteenth- and twentieth-century reformers drew on when they sought to enunciate a specific set of beliefs for a world religion called "Hinduism." While some recent scholars have argued that the vision of Hinduism as a single, all-embracing set of beliefs is wholly a modern fabrication, such assertions ignore the historical developments of the late medieval period. In unifying the *āstika* philosophical schools, Vijñānabhikṣu and his contemporaries made possible the world religion later known by the name Hinduism.

VIJÑĀNABHIKṢU AND HIS LATE MEDIEVAL MILIEU

Like many premodern Indian authors, Vijñānabhikṣu offers little in his works to help identify his time and place. He makes no mention of his teachers or family, nor does he comment on political or historical events. Although there is consensus among historians that he lived in the latter half of the sixteenth century, this dating is itself based on meager evidence.[15] Scholars have estimated Vijñānabhikṣu's dates based on the dates of his disciples, in particular one disciple named Bhāvāgaṇeśa.[16] Since Bhāvāgaṇeśa identifies himself as an immediate disciple of Vijñānabhikṣu, and since Bhāvāgaṇeśa's life span has been estimated from the late sixteenth to the early seventeenth century, it follows that Vijñānabhikṣu's dates would be slightly earlier, suggesting that he flourished sometime after 1550.[17] Scholars have also attempted to locate Vijñānabhikṣu in time based on perceived influences on his philosophy. So, for instance, S. C. Śrīvāstavya puts Vijñānabhikṣu after Sadānanda Vyāsa, author of the *Vedāntasāra,* and T. S. Rukmani argues that Vijñānabhikṣu was influenced by the Navya-Naiyāyika Raghunātha Śiromaṇi.[18] Since Vijñānabhikṣu neither refers to these authors by name nor quotes their works directly, these, too, are admittedly conjectures. Śrīvāstavya also attempts to determine Vijñānabhikṣu's place of residence based on his occasional references to Prayāga (modern-day Allahabad) and claims based on his analysis of Vijñānabhikṣu's Sanskrit usage that he was a Hindi speaker.[19] Reviewing all the evidence collectively, there is enough to suggest that he lived in northern India in the late medieval period. Tentatively accepting Gode's arguments regarding Bhāvāgaṇeśa's identity, I will assume for the purposes of this study that Vijñānabhikṣu lived in approximately the late sixteenth century, perhaps in the vicinity of what is now Uttar Pradesh.

Vijñānabhikṣu is primarily known to modern scholars for his commentaries on texts from the Sāṃkhya and Yoga schools, especially for his commentary on the *Sāṃkhyasūtras* (the *Sāṃkhyapravacanabhāṣya*) and his subcommentary on the *Yogasūtras* (the *Yogavārttika*). However, his works on Sāṃkhya and Yoga were written after his Vedāntic works, which make up the majority of Vijñānabhikṣu's extant corpus.[20] These works include Vijñānabhikṣu's commentary on the *Brahmasūtras* (the *Vijñānāmṛtabhāṣya*), his commentaries on numerous Upaniṣads (collectively known by the name *Vedāntāloka*), and his commentary on the *Īśvara Gītā* section of the *Kūrma Purāṇa* (entitled *Īśvaragītābhāṣya*). Vijñānabhikṣu considers these three texts to be his *prasthānatrayī*, the trilogy of commentaries obligatory for Vedāntins. It is this he has in mind when he remarks at the beginning of the *Īśvaragītābhāṣya* that his commentary on the *Īśvara Gītā* makes up for the lack of a commentary on the *Bhagavad Gītā*, since there is no difference in meaning between the two.[21]

These Vedāntic writings have been largely neglected by modern scholars. Although editions of Vijñānabhikṣu's four works on Sāṃkhya and Yoga have been published both in Sanskrit and in English translations, only one of Vijñānabhikṣu's Vedāntic texts has been published in Sanskrit, and none have been translated in full.[22] Yet an understanding of these earlier works is necessary to comprehend the metaphysical foundations of his later writings on Sāṃkhya and Yoga. Vijñānabhikṣu himself makes this clear by referring the reader time and again to his *Vijñānāmṛtabhāṣya* when discussing metaphysical issues in the *Sāṃkhyapravacanabhāṣya* and *Yogavārttika*. This is also clear evidence that Vijñānabhikṣu conceives of all of his writings as presenting a single comprehensive philosophical position. Unlike other thinkers who commented on texts of multiple schools, Vijñānabhikṣu is not content to see his comments on a single text as merely applying to that school and no other. He sees the dualism of Sāṃkhya and Yoga's *puruṣa* (consciousness) and *prakṛti* (primal matter) as valid at a certain level of analysis, and he refrains from positing a higher, overarching unity in his works on Sāṃkhya and Yoga. But by his references to the *Vijñānāmṛtabhāṣya,* he clearly maintains that this higher unity exists—in his work on Sāṃkhya and Yoga, he never retracts statements from his earlier Vedantic writings. In most cases, he instead tactfully skims over issues about which Vedānta, Sāṃkhya, and Yoga disagree.[23]

In his Vedāntic works, Vijñānabhikṣu only hints at the coordination of various doctrines found in his later Sāṃkhya and Yoga commentaries. It is likely that he had not yet fully worked out the details of this concordance, and at times he criticizes Sāṃkhya and Yoga for their shortcomings. But the Bhedābheda (Difference and Non-Difference) metaphysical foundation he lays out in these earlier works is well adapted to accommodate the realist and dualistic aspects of Sāṃkhya and Yoga. Like Sāṃkhya and Yoga commentators, most Bhedābhedavādins accept some form of the view that the world is a real transformation (*pariṇāma*) of Brahman, and not merely an illusory manifestation (*vivarta*). Using Bhedābheda interpretive strategies, Sāṃkhya's teaching of the multiplicity of individual selves (*puruṣas*) can also easily be reconciled with the statements from the Upaniṣads apparently expressing the ultimate unity of the self. Although Vijñānabhikṣu understands non-separation (*avibhāga*) to be the fundamental relation of the individual selves and Brahman, during the period of the world's existence selves become separated from Brahman and from each other and therefore exist as described in the *Sāṃkhyasūtras*. Similarly, the fundamental dichotomy described in Sāṃkhya between consciousness and matter, *prakṛti* and *puruṣa*, can be explained as real from a certain perspective by the Bhedābhedavādin, although originally both must be understood to come from Brahman, the material cause (*upādānakāraṇa*) of the entire world.

My approach to Vijñānabhikṣu in this book proceeds from the premise that he was not the willfully perverse and arbitrary thinker that his critics make him out to be. When understood in proper historical context, even his most controversial claims make sense. Vijñānabhikṣu's claim that Kapila, the mythical founder of the Sāṃkhya system, was not an atheist must be understood in light of the influence of Pūraṇic Sāṃkhya in the medieval period. The *Bhāgavata Purāṇa*, for instance, contains a lengthy section in which Kapila teaches the value of devotion to God to his mother, Devahūti.[24] Modern advocates of Advaita Vedānta have portrayed Vijñānabhikṣu's realist Vedānta as nonsensical and his claims of defending an older form of Vedānta from the more recent Advaita school as historically baseless. The attitudes of critics generally stem from their own lack of knowledge of the complexity within the philosophical traditions of Sāṃkhya and Vedānta. In the case of Sāṃkhya, this includes their arbitrary insistence on the canonical status of Īśvarakṛṣṇa's *Sāṃkhyakārikā*, paired with an ignorance of early commentaries on this same work that are theistic in their outlook. In the case of Vedānta, the hegemony of Advaita Vedānta in the modern period has blinded most modern authors to the diversity of opinions among the Vedānta schools. The realist tradition of Bhedābheda Vedānta predated Śaṅkara's school of Advaita Vedānta, and in the late medieval period Bhedābheda experienced a renaissance in northern India. Vijñānabhikṣu's corpus was a part of that renaissance. Although his philosophy contains its own internal tensions, as any comprehensive philosophical system must, it can almost never be as lightly dismissed as his critics maintain.

DOXOGRAPHY AND METHOD

Vijñānabhikṣu's assertions about the concordance of the *āstika* schools must be understood in the context of his late medieval intellectual milieu. His contemporary, the sixteenth-century doxographer Madhusūdana Sarasvatī, argues that since all of the sages who founded the *āstika* philosophical systems were omniscient, it follows that they all must have shared the same beliefs.[25] The diversity of opinions expressed among these systems is only for the sake of its hearers, who are at different stages of understanding. Madhusūdana, who understood the highest truth of these sages to be the monistic doctrine of Advaita Vedānta, not Vijñānabhikṣu's Bhedābheda Vedānta, shared with Vijñānabhikṣu a concern for reconciling the diverse systems of the *āstikas.* According to Madhusūdana, the sages taught these various systems in order to keep people from a false attraction to the views of *nāstikas* such as the Buddhists and Jainas. Even Mādhava's well-known fourteenth-century doxography *Sarvadarśanasaṃgraha* (Compendium of All Schools) can be read as an attempt to show that all of the *āstika* philosophical schools exist in a complementary logical hierarchy. Although Vijñānabhikṣu's project is more ambitious than these other authors and based on Bhedābheda instead of Advaita notions of ultimate truth, his basic problematic is common to a number of other late medieval thinkers. Vijñānabhikṣu never wrote a doxography, but his entire corpus is motivated by doxographic concern, the need so typical among late medieval Vedāntins to organize, classify, and rank different philosophies in order of their truth and efficacy.

"Doxography" is, of course, not a native Sanskrit category. Scholars of Indian philosophy have adopted the term from scholars of Western philosophy only recently to distinguish a genre of Indian texts often labeled using the Sanskrit terms *saṃgraha* ("compendium") or *samuccaya* ("collection").[26] The word "doxography" was a neologism coined by the classicist Hermann Diels in 1879 for his collection entitled *Doxographi Graeci.* Since Diels, historians of Western philosophy have applied this term, sometimes quite loosely, to refer to works by authors such as Cicero, Plutarch, and Diogenes Laërtius that present the philosophical views of a number of different thinkers or schools.[27] There are differences between

Sanskrit doxography and doxography written in Greek and Latin, but they have enough in common to justify the use of a single term to refer to both groups of texts. The study of doxography in India is still quite new, and scholars of Indian doxography can look to the recent work of Jaap Mansfeld and David Runia on European doxography for an example of how to proceed.

Richard Rorty, in his essay "The Historiography of Philosophy: Four Genres," nicely encapsulates an important feature that Indian and Western doxographies share. In Rorty's use of the term, doxography is "the attempt to impose a problematic on a canon drawn up without reference to that problematic, or, conversely, to impose a canon on a problematic constructed without reference to that canon."[28] For Diogenes Laërtius, this means asking the question "what did X think the good was?" for a disparate group of philosophers who may or may not have directly addressed this question. Similar problems occur for the eighth-century Jaina doxographer Haribhadra when he seeks to classify the philosophical schools according to deity (*devatā*). When confronted with schools that have no deity, he stretches his definition in such a way to serve his needs as a comprehensive cataloguer of philosophical views: he ascribes to Buddhists a deity known as Sugata (i.e., the Buddha), and Jinendra, the supreme Jaina patriarch, becomes the deity of the Jainas. This way of approaching Buddhism and Jainism serves Haribhadra's classificational needs as a doxographer, but it does so by distorting the actual views of the two schools.

Rorty is more interested in "doxography" in the modern period than in the ancient, and David Runia has censured him for unnecessarily stretching the term and turning it into a pejorative.[29] Rorty expands the category of doxography to include more recent works that share the feature he considers essential, the doxographer's imposition of a problematic on a given canon of thinkers. Examples include many common works with the title "A History of Philosophy," such as those by Frederick Copleston and Bertrand Russell. It is not difficult to find modern "histories of Indian philosophy" that suffer from the same defects. Of these, there is sometimes a direct link to the medieval doxographies of Mādhava and Pseudo-Śaṅkara.[30] Often authors of works on Indian philosophy seem uncertain of the precise purpose of their writing and end up with works that neither are faithful enough to the original Sanskrit text to be described as translations nor analyze arguments in any depth. Such writings involve lists of conclusions, skipping over the dialectics that led to these conclusions. These "histories" are neither historical nor philosophical—they are doxographies, in the broadest literal sense of a text that records the opinions (*doxai*) of philosophers. From the reader's perspective, the most immediate problem of such works is boredom. Lists of other people's beliefs do not make for exciting reading, especially when there is no effort to give context or show the wider relevance of these beliefs to contemporary philosophical debates. When the problem is compounded by the jargon and stilted language that are typical of many books on Indian philosophy, even the most motivated students are driven to despair.

It is no wonder, then, that educated readers with a good general knowledge of Western philosophy are so often ignorant about even the most basic aspects of Indian philosophy. While the near-total exclusion of Indian philosophy from departments of philosophy in North American universities is primarily due to lingering Eurocentric biases, some responsibility must also be accepted by Anglophone authors on Indian philosophy. We have for too long been content to repeat these same lists of doctrines, devoid of serious philosophical analysis or historical examination of their claims (such as the time-worn belief that the true Sāṃkhya is atheistic). Such presentations have led readers to conclude that the beliefs of Indian philosophers were derived from private mystical experiences, operating entirely outside the realm of warrant and rational argument. Hence the widespread idea that Indian religions are mystical rather than rational.[31] Public intellectuals like Freeman Dyson can proclaim in the *New York Review of Books* that "Hinduism and Buddhism . . . have no theology" and are "poetical, rather than analytical."[32] None of Dyson's editors caught the mistake, as they surely would have with such a massive error about Western intellectual traditions.

Books titled "The History of Indian Philosophy" rarely deal with history. The "historical" portion of such books is generally limited to a few sentences at the beginning of each section listing the philosopher's dates and (optionally) in which part of India he lived. The theory of history presupposed in these books typically conforms to a perennial philosophy/great books model. A small group of great minds was able to rise above the petty squabbles that concerned their contemporaries, to address the same timeless, universal philosophical concerns that we grapple with today. By studying the answers to these perennial questions provided by such great men side by side, we ourselves become culturally literate. Such a minds-floating-in-the-ether model of the history of philosophy led in the late twentieth century to a spate of comparative works mixing and matching Derrida, Wittgenstein, Śaṅkara, Bhartṛhari, and Nāgārjuna.[33] These articles generally avoid the messy complexities of textual analysis and rely on the Davidsonian premise that any linguistic differences can be readily bridged with a good translation, so knowledge of primary languages is unnecessary.[34]

The lingering effects of this discourse have had disastrous effects on the discipline of the history of Indian philosophy. Modern histories of Indian philosophy generally offer depictions quite similar to their premodern Indian doxographic counterparts, including discussions of a fixed number of philosophical schools (typically, the aforementioned six systems: Mīmāṃsā, Vedānta, Sāṃkhya, Yoga, Vaiśeṣika, and Nyāya).[35] Such histories deemphasize the disagreements and historical shifts that occurred within these philosophical schools, along with the contradictions and ambiguities within the bodies of work of individual authors. The reason earlier generations of scholars were attracted to simple generalizations and classificatory schemes is clear. Early authors on Indian philosophy, such as T. H. Colebrooke (1765–1837) and A. E. Gough (1845–1915), faced the daunting task of making a map of an intellectual world hitherto uncharted. Taking seriously the classificatory schemes provided by Indian authors was an important first step, enabling Western scholars for the first time to make out the outlines of the various thinkers and schools in Indian philosophy. But in our current situation, approximately two hundred years after the pioneers in the history of Indian philosophy made these first attempts, such simplistic schemes as the "six systems" do more harm than good. Confronting this situation, the philosopher and historian Daya Krishna remarked,

> [The schools of Indian philosophy] are treated as something finished and final. No distinction, therefore, is ever made between the thought of an individual thinker and the thought of a school. A school is, in an important sense, an abstraction. It is a logical construction springing out of the writings of a number of thinkers who share a certain similarity of outlook in tackling certain problems. Sāṃkhya, for example, is identified too much with Īśvarakṛṣṇa's work, or Vedānta with the work of Śaṅkara. But this is due to a confusion between the thought of an individual thinker and the style of thought which he exemplifies and to which he contributes in some manner. All that Śaṅkara has written is not strictly Advaita Vedānta. Nor all that Īśvarakṛṣṇa has written, Sāṃkhya. Unless this is realized, writings on Indian philosophy will continuously do injustice either to the complex-

ity of thought of the individual thinker concerned, or to the uniqueness of the style they are writing about.[36]

The philosophy of Vijñānabhikṣu flies in the face of the reified conception of discrete philosophical schools championed by nineteenth-century Orientalists, and it is this that accounts for much of the hostility directed toward him. Hence, an examination of Vijñānabhikṣu's entire oeuvre offers not just the opportunity to rehabilitate the reputation of a maligned thinker; his work also forces us to turn our gaze back on ourselves, the historiographers of Indian philosophy. Like Daya Krishna, I believe that we must overcome the facile overreliance on "schools" that still informs much writing on Indian philosophy. At the same time, when understood to be a construction of the historian instead of a pre-given entity, the notion of "school" has value as a heuristic device, in pointing out the similarities between thinkers. The danger of the notion of schools, however, is the tendency to concentrate on the similarities between thinkers classified under the rubric of a single school and to gloss over significant differences.

Just as the concept of the philosophical school overemphasizes similarity between thinkers within the school, it has also frequently led to the assumption that the doctrines of separate schools are contradictory and irreconcilable and that thinkers of separate schools are natural enemies, competing for adherents to their philosophies. In the west, our understanding of Indian philosophical schools (as the word *darśana* is generally translated) has been colored by our own history. The default model for the relationship between these schools is often unwittingly based on models derived from Western religious history: the hostilities between the three religions of the Book, the modern relationship of the various Christian denominations, or even the relation between orthodox and heterodox sects in early Christianity. But other familiar models can also be deployed as a corrective to models emphasizing conflict above concordance. One is the relationship between the natural sciences in contemporary academia. Biologists, chemists, physicists, and astronomers typically see their work as complementary, not in direct conflict. The biologist assumes the laws of chemistry and physics to be true, and it is with these laws in the background that he undertakes his own experiments. In India, this model of complementarity predated Vijñānabhikṣu, and he extends it even farther. He portrays all of the *āstika* schools in this way, saying that when the schools of philosophy are understood in terms of their proper scope, they are complementary and not at all contradictory.[37] This claim has some plausibility, since the various schools of Indian philosophy do have different central foci: Mīmāṃsā focuses on exegesis of Vedic ritual injunctions, Vedānta on the nature of Brahman, Nyāya on logical analysis, Vaiśeṣika on ontology. Yet there are also many apparent contradictions between the *āstika* schools, as a student with even the most cursory knowledge of Indian philosophical polemics will show. Vijñānabhikṣu's challenge is to show that the complementarity model he espouses is superior to other models emphasizing conflict and contradiction. Even his detractors must admit that he often shows extraordinary philosophical and interpretive ingenuity, whether or not all his arguments to this end are ultimately persuasive.

PREMODERN PHILOSOPHY IN A POSTCOLONIAL WORLD

After Richard Rorty impugned what he described as "modern doxographies," he registered his support of another genre of writing about philosophers, called "intellectual history." Included in this genre is one particular subcategory:

> I should want to include under "intellectual history" books about all of those enormously influential people who do not get into the canon of the great dead philosophers, but who are often called "philosophers" . . . people like Erigena, Bruno, Ramus, Mersenne, Wolff, Diderot, Cousin, Schopenhauer, Hamilton, McCosh, Bergson and Austin. Discussion of these "minor figures" often coalesces with thick description of institutional arrangements and disciplinary matrices.[38]

Had Rorty concerned himself with the Indian intellectual sphere, he would have certainly included Vijñānabhikṣu in his list. Like those thinkers, Vijñānabhikṣu exists somewhere at the fringes of the philosophical canon. Unlike Śaṅkara and Rāmānuja, he did not found a lasting intellectual lineage, nor were hagiographies composed about his life. There was little time for that—he lived during the final flourishing of the Sanskrit intellectual tradition, just a few years before the Mughal Emperor Jahangir officially recognized the British East India Company in 1617, part of a series of events that would lead to British political dominance of the subcontinent. By indications such as the small number of his manuscripts available in Indian archives, Vijñānabhikṣu's influence among Sanskrit intellectuals was not as great as the enormous impact of the Bhedābheda Vedāntins

Caitanya and Vallabha, whose lineages continue to thrive in modern-day India and elsewhere.[39]

Vijñānabhikṣu's greatest fame began in the eighteenth century, when Orientalists seeking to catalogue the doctrines of the Hindus looked to his treatment of the Indian philosophical schools in his commentary on the *Sāṃkhyasūtras* as a possible set of guidelines for understanding the relationship between Vedānta, Sāṃkhya, Yoga, and Nyāya. Also in question was the authenticity of the Advaita Vedānta interpretation of the Vedas, which H. T. Colebrooke argued was a recent departure from an older tradition. By the late nineteenth century, the Indological controversies surrounding Vijñānabhikṣu had died down. Some rejected his model for the concordance of schools in favor of other concordances that portrayed Advaita as the pinnacle of *āstika* philosophies. Other scholars, like Garbe, insisted on the irreducibility of the six ancient schools of Indian philosophy. Vijñānabhikṣu's name, if not his Bhedābheda philosophy, has been recognizable to subsequent generations of scholars, often with a whiff of controversy. His works today appear in scholarly footnotes and from time to time as optional reading in Indian university curricula. Meanwhile, the hegemonic narrative established in the nineteenth century of Advaita Vedānta as the essence and culmination of Indian philosophical systems has drowned out competing counternarratives, especially at the popular level of appreciation for Indian philosophy.

The recovery of the history of Indian philosophy is a difficult project, given the few chronological markers left by authors writing in Sanskrit and the difficulty in settling on even the most minimal biographical details about these thinkers. Is it also a misguided project, a philological flight from real human concerns in the postcolonial era? This is a logical conclusion that might be drawn from the "modern invention of tradition" hypothesis with regard to Hindu philosophy and religion. If the Indian encounter with European colonialism was truly a rupture in which all traditional institutions for the transmission of knowledge were uprooted, replaced with new regimes of knowledge and power by the British, then the study of precolonial India has little or no significance for understanding the current postcolonial situation. Whether or not this attitude toward premodern Indian intellectual life has been fully articulated by scholars of modern India, it is impossible to deny the disciplinary chasm between scholars of premodern and modern India.

Perhaps it is surprising that the uselessness of the attempt to recover premodern Indian intellectual history is the one area where more extreme advocates of the "invention of Hinduism" hypothesis tend to agree with those who understand Hinduism as eternal and essentially unchanging. For the first group, premodern history has nothing to tell us about the present, making it the sole province of those who seek imaginative escape from their current situations and from human life, the class of philological footnote-scribblers. For the second group, premodern intellectual history is a waste because it has no ability to shed light on the perennial, universal aspects of Indian philosophical traditions. The truth of Hindu philosophy transcends space and time, and therefore any attempt for a historically grounded study of Indian philosophy is doomed from the outset. Time would be better spent studying the other thinkers East and West whose thought transcends history (e.g. Meister Eckhart, Plotinus), instead of being distracted by the accidental sociopolitical conditions in which these thinkers lived and worked.

Such portrayals of a timeless, otherworldly, spiritual Orient have been ably critiqued by Edward Said and other critics of Orientalism, including many scholars of South Asia. However, Said's model of the relationship between Orientalist and Orient has also contributed to the neglect of the study of premodern Asian intellectual traditions. Said, a scholar of European literature by training, emphasizes the irrelevance of knowledge of a "real" Orient when it comes to studying the phenomenon of Orientalism. In the book *Orientalism* he is ambivalent about whether such a real place exists. Sometimes he seems to suggest that the Orient is nothing more than a "production" of European culture. At other times he shies away from this constructivist language and acknowledges that there is a real Orient.[40] But Said is insistent that knowledge of the real Orient, whatever its ontological status, is irrelevant to the understanding of the wholly European phenomenon of Orientalism.[41]

If Said is correct that the Orient is little more than a blank screen on which Orientalists projected their fantasies of a spiritual, exotic, timeless Other, it follows that knowledge of the texts that the Orientalists were reading and the non-Western interlocutors with whom they were speaking is of little use to the study of Orientalism. But, of course, to know whether Said's model is correct requires us to know something about these texts and peoples, to ascertain whether or not there is such an absolute disconnect between the discourses of the Orientalists and the objects of their study. I believe that this is not the case. We require an alternative model that sees Orientalists as engaged in a project of interpretation, albeit one whose prejudices often distorted the object of study completely beyond recognition. Instead of understanding the phenomenon of Orientalism as a one-way projection, we should approach it as a two-way relationship. This relationship was one in which there was a vast imbalance of power. Yet the "Oriental" objects of the Orientalists' studies did have a part in shaping the Orientalist stereotypes that became prevalent in the eighteenth and nineteenth centuries. In the words of Chinese historian Arif Dirlik, Orientalism is "the product of an unfolding relationship between Euro-Americans and Asians, that required the complicity of the latter in endowing it with plausibility."[42] In the case of the history of Indian philosophy, the Orientalists' primary living interlocutors were Brahmin pundits, who themselves had a particular understanding of their own intellectual traditions and who did their best to portray themselves as essential to any Orientalist project to govern according to native customs and laws. They were also eager to give these Western scholars of Indian philosophy what they wanted, specifically to point them to the types of texts that would confirm the European stereotype of Indians as quietistic, impractical idealists who doubted or denied the very existence of the physical world. It is in this way that Vedānta, especially the "idealist" Advaita Vedānta, gained its modern reputation as the essence of the Indian mind.

The backlash against traditional Orientalism since the late 1970s has also had the consequence of delaying further advances in the study of Vedānta, particularly in those parts of the Western world that have been most influenced by postcolonial and post-Orientalist thought. Recent studies have made enormous advances in the understanding of realist intellectual traditions that had been largely neglected by Orientalist historiography, such as Mīmāṃsā and Nyāya. It is ironic, however, that our picture of Vedānta has not been updated to the same extent and that many of these Orientalist discourses have continued to hamper our ability to appreciate the diversity of Vedānta philosophical schools. In this book, I show that most of these schools bear scant resemblance to the stereotype of Vedānta as an idealist monism unconcerned with ethical action and being in the world.

Recent trends in academia have moved away from Orientalist biases, which is a good thing, but in doing so have also moved away from the study of premodern India, especially by marginalizing the study of the "elite" Sanskrit knowledge systems in favor of more practical orientations toward India as an emerging economic and political superpower.[43] Indologists today tend to argue against this trend by invoking the importance of pure knowledge and of study of the past as itself having intrinsic value. But another argument can be made, once we better appreciate the importance of Sanskrit knowledge systems toward the making of the modern world, through their influence on both the European Orientalists and Indian intellectuals in the modern period. No one can deny the importance of these intellectuals, including Ram Mohan Roy, Swami Vivekananda, Sri Aurobindo, Sarvepalli Radhakrishnan, and Mohandas Gandhi, in shaping Indians' self-understanding and the political formation of India as a modern nation-state. Once the theory of the British invention of almost everything in modern India has been properly debunked, we can look realistically at the ways that such thinkers creatively appropriated some Indian traditions and rejected others. This is not the only reason to study premodern India, but it is one of the most important. Sanskrit intellectual traditions should be approached not as a rarefied sphere of discourse hovering above everyday life and historical time but, rather, as a human practice arising in the messy and contingent economic, social, and political worlds that these intellectuals occupied.

Although scholars are nowadays at great pains to avoid perpetuating stereotypes about the essential otherness of the consciousness of modern Indians, discourses about otherness persist when dealing with the mindset of the *premodern* Indian. Medieval historian Jeffrey Cohen has observed that "postcolonial theory in practice has neglected the study of this 'distant' past, which tends to function as a field of undifferentiated alterity against which modern regimes of power have arisen."[44] So it is, according to the hypothesis of the modern invention of Hinduism, that Indian self-consciousness underwent an absolute transformation at the beginning of the so-called Hindu renaissance. At the hands of the British, the Indians became modern for the first time and in this process became completely alienated from their own traditions. Recapitulating the rupture that occurred with the renaissance in sixteenth-century Europe, the Indians received the gift and the burden of modernity from their British colonizers.

Since Edward Said's book *Orientalism,* published in 1978, scholars of Asia have bent over backward to avoid "Orientalizing" the peoples and texts of their studies: that is, positing Orientals as an ontological other wholly distinct from Europeans. According to the Orientalist discourses prevalent during the eighteenth, nineteenth, and most of the twentieth centuries, Oriental peoples are not like Europeans. Europeans are historical, while Orientals have no historical consciousness. Europeans (especially modern Europeans) are secular, while Orientals have a fundamentally religious outlook that provides all the norms by which they live their lives.[45] Europeans are rational, while the lives of Orientals are superstitious. Contemporary scholars of Asian studies have rejected these pernicious stereotypes, yet they live on in latent forms in a variety of ways. For some historians of modern Asia, the stereotypes have just been pushed back several centuries. Modern Asians, this thinking goes, are quite a bit like us—how could they not be, since their entire conceptual universe was determined by the discourses of their European colonial oppressors? For this reason, Asians have no real understanding of their own histories, just a vague idea of cultural superiority employed to the ends of identity politics and nationalist ideologies. The lives and the thought-worlds of their ancestors four hundred years earlier are just as foreign to them as they are to the European scholars who study them.

We sometimes forget that the stereotypes earlier generations of Orientalists used to "Orientalize" the peoples of Asia were not invented by them. In fact, they were largely recycled from the discourses about premodern Europe propagated by historians in the nineteenth century. For instance, one influential historian of the renaissance, Jacob Burckhardt, wrote in 1860:

> In the Middle Ages, both sides of human consciousness—that which was turned within as well as that which was turned without—lay dreaming and half aware beneath a common veil. The veil was woven of faith, illusion, and childish prepossession, through which the world and history were seen clad in strange hues. Man was conscious of himself only as a member of a race, people, party, family, or corporation—only through some general category.[46]

With a few alterations (replacing "Middle Ages" with "Asia" and changing verbs from past to present tense), this confident statement by a romantic historian about the European past would be quite at home in the description of the Hindus from James Mill's *History of British India*. Present here are statements about the dreamlike, passive state of the medieval European consciousness. Also here is the idea that medievals had no individual consciousness but, instead, were only aware of themselves as "dividuals," mere parts in the larger whole of society.[47]

Contemporary medieval studies has rejected this "medievalism," the treating of the European middle ages as the ontological other of the modern era, lacking all constitutive features of modernity.[48] So, too, have scholars of Asia rejected Orientalism in its most blatant forms. But the Oriental medieval is still often depicted by default using these familiar ideas from European scholars centuries ago. So it becomes possible to oppose "traditional Hinduism" with "Neo-Hinduism"—the first being the authentic mindset of premodern Hindus, the second the Westernized consciousness of modern ersatz Hindus.[49] Both of the assumptions at work here are problematic: the first that there was a single traditional way of being Indian or Hindu, and the second that, due to the shock of colonialism, the traditional way of being is no longer available to Westernized Indians. Instead of taking our cue from Orientalist periodizations that posit three eras in Indian history—Hindu, Muslim, and British (which were themselves inspired by the periodization of European history into ancient, medieval, and modern periods)—we must instead recognize the ruptures and discontinuities within each of these supposed epochs, along with the ideologies of those historians who created these periodizations.[50] Even further, we must recognize that human subjectivities in the contemporary world are complex and contradictory, bearing the contemporaneous imprint of the "premodern," "modern," and "postmodern." This is not only the case in India, where the cliché of "ancient faiths meet modern democracy" is invoked by the Western media every time an Indian election occurs, but also in the west and particularly in North America, where the once–seemingly inevitable triumph of secularism and the withering away of atavistic belief systems has shown itself to be an illusion. We postmoderns are more medieval than we care to admit.

Some avenues opened by the postcolonial critique of European cultural hegemony have yet to be fully explored. One of these is what Dipesh Chakrabarty terms the "provincializing" of Europe. Virtually all of the work done in contemporary literary theory and continental philosophy is overwhelmingly Eurocentric.[51] Even the work of postcolonial and post-Orientalist thinkers remains almost exclusively devoted to a European canon of French and German intellectuals. As Chakrabarty puts it:

> Faced with the task of analyzing developments or social practices in modern India, few if any Indian social scientists or social scientists of India would argue seriously with, say, the thirteenth-century logician Gaṅgeśa or with the grammarian and linguistic philosopher Bhartṛhari (fifth to sixth centuries), or with the tenth- or eleventh-century aesthetician Abhinavagupta. Sad though it is, one result of European colonial rule in South Asia is that the intellectual traditions once unbroken and alive in Sanskrit or Persian or Arabic are now only matters of historical research for most—perhaps all—modern social scientists in the region. They treat these traditions as truly dead, as history.[52]

The Eurocentrism of the institutional structures that have excluded thinkers from the curricula of graduate programs in philosophy, literary theory, and the social sciences has not yet given way to the pressure of post-Orientalist critique. Students of literary theory today, whether in Calcutta or Cambridge, take more inspiration from Aristotle than from Abhinavagupta. If they are acquainted with Indian philosophy at all, it is regarded only as a historical curiosity, not as a vital philosophical tradition. This entrenched historicist attitude, in which the works of premodern thinkers can only be approached as symptoms of a certain historical epoch, has long since fallen by the wayside in works on the history of philosophy in European antiquity. Yet when we approach the history of Indian philosophy, there is an unspoken taboo against raising questions of truth and falsity. Contemporary historians of philosophy are willing to fully engage with and criticize European philosophers: perhaps to say that Plato was mistaken in his positing on a realm of pure forms, that Descartes' mind-body dualism is untenable, or that Kant's distinction between analytic and synthetic propositions cannot pass muster. Out of a lingering sense that premodern Indian philosophers are somehow fundamentally "other" in a way that the philosophers of European antiquity are not, historians of Indian philosophy in Europe and North America have refrained from approaching these thinkers with a properly critical—that is to say, philosophical—attitude. Yet whether or not we acknowledge it, historians of philosophy are not just writing history. We are also doing philosophy. Even when this is not explicit, there are always implicit philosophical commitments that the historian of philosophy brings to bear on her subjects, including philosophical commitments about the nature of history itself. The very act of choosing which philosophers' works are of sufficient value to include in a philosophical canon and which are only of marginal importance is both a historical and a philosophical judgment.

Although at times in this book I do critique premodern Indian philosophers, I am generally more concerned with critiquing the claims of those Western Indologists who sought, for instance, to marginalize the works of realist Vedāntins in arguing for an authentic, originally monist Vedānta orthodoxy. I employ to this end a "hermeneutics of charity." As I understand it, this means giving the benefit of the doubt to premodern thinkers such as Bhāskara and Vijñānabhikṣu whose works have been dismissed as philosophically incoherent. When confronted with an idea, an argument, or a block of text that appears problematic, instead of assuming that the premodern thinker is childish, guilty of a philosophical solecism, or a victim of false consciousness, I begin with the assumption that I as the interpreter am the one with the problem. This does not mean that the premodern author is always right. Instead, it is an assumption of innocence until proven guilty. This principle of charity is not the same as that expounded by Donald Davidson, in which any apparent philosophical mistake an earlier philosopher makes is to be read in such a way to impute to him the correct answer established by later generations. It is, rather, an attempt to identify and preserve ideas that seem so different, wrongheaded, or strange that they appear to require immediate correction.[53] Once this project of hermeneutic recovery has been provisionally accomplished, these thinkers' works can become potential participants in twenty-first-century philosophical conversations.

Instead of approaching these premodern Indian philosophers in terms of an ontological other, as earlier Orientalists and some current scholars are wont to do, I believe that the language of "difference" is much more productive.[54] This approach avoids the false dilemma of (1) if the premodern philosopher is truly other, then we have no real access to his ideas since they arise in such a different conceptual universe that they will have no meaning to us in our current situation and (2) if the premodern philosopher is the same as we are, then we have nothing to learn from him since the things he says we have already heard.[55] Using the language of "difference," however, we can recognize both that a philosopher might have something relevant to say to us that has not yet been said in our European philosophical tradition and that, with some effort, these different ideas are recoverable in spite of obvious historical and linguistic obstacles. Philosophers in medieval India do have something to teach those of us living in the twenty-first century to help us out of the apparent philosophical impasse between the sovereign, universal subject of the European Enlightenment and the fragmented, localized subjectivities of post-Enlightenment critique.[56] To that end, in this book I attempt to create a clearing for future attempts at constructive engagement with medieval Indian philosophy. My hope here is that I can point to possible modes of self-understanding and self-transformation that fall between such binaries as religious/secular, rational/mystical, and Hindu/non-Hindu—alternative possibilities that have been overlooked by most philosophers in the modern West.

This book is structured to give an overview of certain philosophical currents in the *Wirkungsgeschichte* of premodern India. I also feel it necessary to go into some depth presenting specific arguments in the works of Indian philosophers, especially those whose core philosophies have been widely misinterpreted or misrepresented in the modern period. Although readers looking for a general history may be somewhat less interested in these close readings of Vijñānabhikṣu and other medieval philosophers, they are necessary to fully understand the interpretive tendencies and philosophical rigor of those thinkers who attempted to establish unity of Indian *darśanas.* In chapters 2 and 3, I present Bhedābheda Vedānta, first by uncovering the history of Bhedābheda Vedānta and its relation to other schools (chapter 2) and then by presenting three of Vijñānabhikṣu's characteristically Bhedābheda arguments in some detail (chapter 3). In chapters 4 through 6, I take a similar approach to Sāṃkhya and Yoga philosophy. Chapter 4 is a historical exploration of Sāṃkhya and Yoga, with particular reference to the relation between these two schools (if, indeed, they are two separate schools) and to the question of God's existence in each. In chapter 5, I analyze Vijñānabhikṣu's reading of the *Sāṃkhyasūtras,* especially his attempt to find a place for God in Sāṃkhya in the context of theistic Sāṃkhya traditions. In chapter 6, I focus on Vijñānabhikṣu's works on Yoga, showing his understanding of Yoga as both a specific philosophical system and a practice of self-transformation open to varying philosophical interpretations.

In chapters 7 through 10, I look at questions surrounding the classification of philosophical schools, expanding the focus of this study to understand the early history of the formation of these boundaries and the influence of medieval Indian classifications on modern scholars. I do this in chapter 7 by taking the controversies surrounding Vijñānabhikṣu's concordance of schools in his reception by eighteenth- and nineteenth-century Orientalists as an opportunity to reflect on the historiography of Indian philosophy. In chapter 8, I analyze tendencies in the forms of Indian doxography, from their earliest examples through to the late medieval period. In chapter 9, I deal extensively with the distinction of *āstika* and *nāstika* throughout a variety of texts, as well as looking more generally at modes of "othering" in Indian philosophical discourse. I conclude in chapter 10 by arguing that Vijñānabhikṣu and his contemporaries formulated a proto-Hindu identity. This identity was later elaborated by Hindu reformers in the nineteenth and twentieth centuries and transformed into the basis of the world religion known today as Hinduism.

{2} AN ALTERNATIVE HISTORY OF VEDĀNTA

VEDĀNTA AND ORIENTALIST HISTORIOGRAPHY

One reason to focus on the late medieval period in general, and on the sixteenth-century philosopher Vijñānabhikṣu specifically, is in order to reframe common assumptions about the history of Indian philosophy. According to standard Orientalist accounts, the history of India can be divided into three periods: Hindu, Muslim, and British.[1] During the Muslim period, from the eleventh to the eighteenth century, Indian culture went into a decline, only to be revived in the British period by the efforts of Western Indologists to rediscover and help Indians recover the genuine achievements of Indian civilization and to filter out the lesser cultural accretions of the medieval period in India. Historians of Indian philosophy have taken this to mean that all that was greatest in Indian philosophy was already present in the Upaniṣads. The achievement of classical Indian philosophers such as Śaṅkara was to systematize the mystical insights of the Upaniṣadic seers, and by the fourteenth century, the ancient insights of the Vedic seers had been almost irrecoverably lost, covered over by the pedantry of medieval scholasticism and the effusive superstitions of devotional Hindu sects.

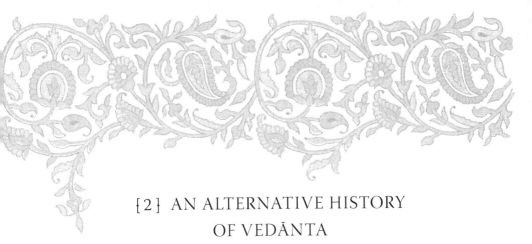

Powerfully influential narratives such as this one do not die without a struggle. Thanks to the influence of postcolonial studies and the critique of Orientalism, the motives of Indologists and the British colonialists have been put under a critical microscope. However, in some corners of the academy, the Orientalists' understanding of premodern Indian history has so far escaped thorough reexamination. In the backwater that is the history of Indian philosophy, this narrative of cultural degeneration is still often accompanied by the idea that the authentic philosophy of the Upaniṣads was Advaita Vedānta and the unfortunate movement away from the Upaniṣads' pure monism toward dualism and theism was the result of the cultural degeneration of the medieval period.[2] Until quite recently, this led to the scholarly neglect of realist schools of Vedānta, not to mention philosophical schools like Nyāya and Vaiśeṣika, whose commonsense realism did not jibe with the Orientalist depictions of India as the land of mystical otherworldliness.[3] The rise of Bhedābheda Vedānta is understood in this hegemonic narrative as a symptom of the decline of the true monistic Vedānta of the Upaniṣads, along with its replacement by theistic forms based on non-Vedic texts such as the Purāṇas. Such an Orientalist reading of the history of Indian philosophy has also been co-opted by Hindu reformers such as Dayananda Saraswati, who argued that what was needed was a return to the true beliefs of the Vedas and a turning away from medieval superstitions such as *bhakti* and animal sacrifice.

In this chapter, I present a counternarrative to the Advaita-centric histories of Vedānta that have been so influential. Rather than seeing Advaita as the authentic, timeless philosophy of the Hindus, textual evidence suggests that it was a relatively recent development in the long-term intellectual history of India. The teachings of Śaṅkara, the most well-known thinker in Advaita Vedānta, were in part a reaction against earlier Bhedābheda interpretations of the *Brahmasūtras* and the Upaniṣads. It is also not fair to say that the early Upaniṣads were themselves propounding a pure monistic or idealistic philosophy. As recent scholarship has shown, the philosophical themes presented by the *Bṛhadāraṇyaka* and the *Chāndogya Upaniṣads* were quite varied, and by no means uniformly monistic, as Paul Deussen and other Advaita apologists maintained.[4]

In this chapter, I have chosen to foreground Bhedābheda and push to the background other forms of Vedānta, including the Viśiṣṭādvaita (Qualified Non-Dualist) and Dvaita (Dualist) schools. There are doubtless many other histories of Vedānta and histories of Indian philosophy waiting to be written from the differing standpoints of other neglected philosophical traditions. While this brief history of Bhedābheda Vedāntic realism is only one of these many possible alternative histories, it can serve as at least a partial counterbalance. The other function of this chapter is to serve as a necessary historical introduction to the philosophy of Vijñānabhikṣu, the sixteenth-century philosophical polymath whose innovations in Bhedābheda Vedānta, Sāṃkhya, and Yoga I investigate in subsequent chapters. His works on Sāṃkhya were discovered by Indologists in the eighteenth and nineteenth centuries, and growing interest in yoga and all things associated with it in the late twentieth century has led to new interest in Vijñānabhikṣu's *Yogavārttika* and *Yogasārasaṃgraha.* But still today, his earliest works, on Bhedābheda Vedānta, are widely ignored, despite their enormous influence on his later works in Sāṃkhya and Yoga. In this brief historical overview, I locate Vijñānabhikṣu's early works in their proper context and clear up some persistent misconceptions about the history of Vedānta philosophy in India.

EARLY BHEDĀBHEDA VEDĀNTA

Numerous Indologists, including Surendranath Dasgupta, Paul Hacker, Hajime Nakamura, and Mysore Hiriyanna, have described Bhedābheda as the most influential school of Vedānta before Śaṅkara (eighth century).[5] Nakamura and Dasgupta even claim that the author of the *Brahmasūtras* was himself a Bhedābhedavādin.[6] The *Brahmasūtras* are a collection of terse aphorisms (*sūtras,* or literally "threads"). Bādarāyaṇa is traditionally regarded as their author, a figure who was in later times conflated with the sage Vyāsa, legendary author of the *Mahābhārata.* From a historical perspective, the *Brahmasūtras* are best understood as a group of sūtras composed by multiple authors over the course of hundreds of years, most likely compiled in its current form between 400 and 450 BCE.[7] The earliest stratum of sūtras in the *Brahmasūtras* is concerned with the interpretation of the Upaniṣads, especially the attempt to harmonize the apparent differences between the teachings of the *Chāndogya, Bṛhadāraṇyaka,* and *Taittirīya Upaniṣads.* In later periods, the *Brahmasūtras* were revised and expanded, and new sūtras were added to refute the doctrines of rival philosophical schools. The majority of these attacks were directed against the Sāṃkhya school, although Vaiśeṣika, Buddhist, Jaina, Pāśupata, and Bhāgavata teachings were also subject to critique.

Even in comparison with other sūtra compilations such as the *Yogasūtras* of Patañjali and the *Nyāyasūtras* of Gautama, the aphorisms of the *Brahmasūtras* are unusually laconic. For that reason, the *Brahmasūtras* are unintelligible without reference to a commentary (*bhāṣya*). The cryptic quality of the aphorisms would have assured that those without the proper qualifications, *śūdras* and outcastes in particular, had little access to the philosophical content of the *Brahmasūtras.*[8] It is this same quality that eventually led to the proliferation of competing schools in later Vedānta, as there were few textual restraints on later commentators to keep them from reading into the *Brahmasūtras* later ideas, such as the concept of *bhakti,* that were beyond the purview of the *Brahmasūtras'* fifth-century compiler. From the perspective of the history of ideas, it is possible to reconstruct probable meanings of the original sūtras by careful comparison of the different extant commentaries and by paying close attention to the terminology of the sūtras themselves. This project should in no way be seen as a disproof of later developments in Vedānta. Rather, it should lead us to a new appreciation of the ingenuity of later Vedāntins, who often show even more creativity and philosophical sophistication than the *Brahmasūtras'* original authors.

All commentators, following *Brahmasūtra* 1.1.2, agree that Brahman is the cause of the world. But the precise nature of this causality has been a source of contention among Vedāntins. Medieval Vedāntins distinguished two basic positions. One theory, Pariṇāmavāda, states that the world is a real transformation (*pariṇāma*) of Brahman. Just as clay is transformed into the multiple forms of pots, saucers, cups, and so forth, Brahman is the material cause, transforming itself into the many real entities visible in the world. The alternative to this model is Vivartavāda, the theory that the world is merely an unreal manifestation (*vivarta*) of Brahman. Vivartavāda states that although Brahman appears to undergo a transformation, in fact no real change takes place. The myriad of beings are essentially unreal, as the only real being is Brahman, that ultimate reality which is unborn, unchanging, and entirely without parts. The most visible advocates of Vivartavāda are the Advaitins, the followers of Śaṅkara who went on to establish a powerful network of monastic schools across India. In the Pariṇāmavāda camp we find the majority of other schools of Vedānta, who see the phenomenal world as real.

The *Brahmasūtras* themselves espouse the realist Pariṇāmavāda position, which appears to have been the view most common among early Vedāntins.[9] For the *Brahmasūtras,* the world is a real transformation of Brahman from one form to another. Brahman is the material cause of the world (*BS* 1.4.23, 2.1.18–20). This causal process should be seen as analogous to the process by which milk turns into curds (*BS* 2.1.24), transforming itself without any outside agent or the existence of some type of lower Brahman that engages in creative activity while the higher Brahman remains unchanged. *BS* 2.3.43 defines the individual self as being both different and non-different from Brahman. This is because it is a part (*aṃśa*) of Brahman: "[the individual self is] a part [of Brahman], on account of the declaration of difference [between the two] and also the opposite."[10] This passage has been seen as problematic since elsewhere, in *BS* 2.1.26, Brahman is described as "partless" (*niravayava*). The latter supports the monistic position of Śaṅkara and other Advaitins, who mention that Brahman is absolutely without parts and that each individual self exists in a relation of identity with Brahman. So, when confronted with the definition of the individual self as being a part at *BS* 2.3.43, Śaṅkara chooses to explain this passage away using a figurative interpretation: "'Part' means 'like a part' (*aṃśa iva*), since a thing that is free from parts (*niravayava*) cannot literally have parts (*aṃśa*)."[11] By contrast, the commentators Bhāskara and Rāmānuja read this *sūtra* literally. Although apparently contradictory, the terminological difference in the two passages allows some interpretive leeway for commentators who wish to uphold the relation part and whole between individual self and Brahman. Although Brahman is free from one type of part (*avayava*), it is nonetheless correct to say that it possesses another kind of part (*aṃśa*). Nor, according to the *Brahmasūtras*, is the individual self completely dissolved into Brahman at the time of its liberation. Although *BS* 4.2.16 describes the liberated self as "non-separate" (*avibhāga*) and indistinguishable from Brahman, there nonetheless remains a trace of individuality. Unlike a person in a state of deep sleep or unconsciousness, the liberated self retains volition and discriminative awareness (*BS* 4.4.8, 4.4.16). The *Brahmasūtras*' basic understanding of individual self and Brahman as part and whole influenced many early Vedāntins, including the Bhedābheda Vedāntin Bhartṛprapañca.

One of the challenges of reconstructing the intellectual world of the early Bhedābheda Vedāntins is that the works of many important figures such as Bhartṛprapañca (sixth century) are only available secondhand. Bhartṛprapañca follows the general outlook of the *Brahmasūtras*, upholding Pariṇāmavāda and his own distinctive version of Bhedābheda Vedānta. But his extant works illustrate how even at this early stage, Vedānta commentators elaborated on and expanded the meanings they found in the *Brahmasūtras* and Upaniṣads, claiming the authority of tradition while transforming it through strong misreading of authoritative texts. It is only thanks to Bhartṛprapañca's later enemies, the Advaitins Śaṅkara, Sureśvara, and Ānandagiri, that his views are available to us at all. Śaṅkara's commentary on the *Bṛhadāraṇyaka Upaniṣad* repeatedly attacks Bhartṛprapañca's interpretations, and Śaṅkara's followers Sureśvara and Ānandagiri flesh out these disagreements, sometimes repeating direct quotations from Bhartṛprapañca's commentary on the same Upaniṣad. These attacks indicate the major split between the Advaitins and the Bhedābheda interpreters that came before them.

According to Bhartṛprapañca, Brahman is that "whose nature is dual and non-dual."[12] He claims that both duality and non-duality are absolutely real and it is not appropriate to subordinate one to the other. He cites the example of a turbulent ocean: both the water and the waves are real, and it is not appropriate to claim that waves are somehow less real than water. Bhartṛprapañca shares this view with the later Vedāntins Yādavaprakāśa (eleventh century) and Nimbārka (thirteenth century?). But not all Bhedābheda Vedāntins embrace his position that ultimate reality is in its nature both dual and non-dual (Svābhāvika Bhedābheda). The majority position in later times was the view of Bhāskara (ninth century), who held that Brahman in itself is non-dual and duality in the world is only due to limiting conditions (*upādhis*) that are extrinsic to Brahman's absolute nature. While Bhāskara still maintains that the world of duality is real, his theory suggests that there are different grades of reality, proceeding from the ultimate reality of non-dual Brahman to the mundane reality of the phenomenal world. Bhāskara's philosophical position of difference and non-difference merely due to limiting conditions (Aupādhika Bhedābheda) is much closer to Advaita than is Bhartṛprapañca's uncompromising insistence that duality and non-duality are equally real.

Bhartṛprapañca's acceptance of the world's absolute reality creates an opportunity for increased reliance on rational inference (*anumāna*) in understanding Brahman. Traditional Indian logic maintains that *anumāna* depends on perception (*pratyakṣa*) for its data. The five-step logical syllogism developed by the Nyāya school requires a real-world example (*udāharaṇa*). So, in the common Naiyāyika example, after seeing smoke somewhere, we can only infer that there is fire if we have seen smoke accompanied by fire in other places. Rational inference is therefore not independent of worldly experiences, as it is in the formal logic of Aristotle. This limits the scope of rational inference for those philosophers who deny that everyday objects are real. If Brahman is transcendent, completely other than the world of lived experience, it follows that the types of reasoning useful in worldly interactions will not be helpful in understanding Brahman. This explains the tendency among Advaita Vedāntins to criticize perception, which provides us with a dualistic understanding of the world, and rational inference, which takes this erroneous dualism as its basis.

Bhartṛprapañca teaches us that our senses do not deceive. There really are many things in the world, not just in a conventional sense but in an ultimate sense—the pots, towels, and cows of our everyday experiences have the same ontological status as Brahman. Accepting this, new possibilities open up in the application of *a posteriori* reason. Since we see

Brahman's effects firsthand, we can investigate the nature of these effects in order to understand the nature of their cause. No longer are we solely dependent on Vedic authority for knowledge of Brahman. According to Bhartṛprapañca, the universal proposition we abstract from all of our experiences in the world is this: "All things are in their nature both different and non-different."[13] For Bhartṛprapañca, there are four categories of difference and non-difference relations:

1. Cause (*kāraṇa*) and effect (*kārya*), such as clay and pot.
2. Whole (*bhāgin*) and its parts (*bhāga*), such as a chariot and its hub.
3. The subject of a state (*avasthāvat*) and the state itself (*avasthā*), such as sea water and foam.
4. Universal (*sāmānya*) and particular (*viśeṣa*), such as a cow and its dewlap.[14]

Bhartṛprapañca's general interest in rational inference and his concern with the relation of universal and particular show similar concerns to the Nyāya school of logic. The Naiyāyikas' stock example of the universal-particular relation is the cow. On Bhartṛprapañca's interpretation, an individual cow possesses the universal property of "cowness." Without this property, we would not be able to understand her as a member of a species of animals. Yet she also possesses particular characteristics that belong to her alone—a certain pattern of markings, a slight tilt to one of her horns, and so forth—that allow us to distinguish her from the other members of her class. Both aspects of the cow are real and necessary, and neither aspect can be subordinated to the other. We look around and find that everything possesses this dual aspect, both different (as particular) and non-different (as universal). And Bhartṛprapañca maintains that every entity, including Brahman, is in some sense a "thing." It therefore follows that Brahman, like the cow, has a nature that is both dual (*dvaita*) and non-dual (*advaita*). In this way, Bhartṛprapañca uses *a posteriori* reasoning, examining the phenomenal world to make conclusions about Brahman, the ultimate cause.

BHEDĀBHEDA VEDĀNTA AFTER ŚAṄKARA

Although the Advaita school has been widely understood as propounding the theory of *vivarta,* or the world as an unreal manifestation of Brahman, there are some questions regarding where Śaṅkara himself stood on this issue. Paul Hacker, for instance, sees considerable ambiguity in Śaṅkara on this point. Hacker points in particular to a metaphor from one passage of an early work of Śaṅkara, the *Upadeśasāhasrī.* There Śaṅkara likens the creation of unevolved name-and-form from Brahman to the creation of dirty foam from clear water. Śaṅkara's own explanation of this metaphor suggests that he had in mind a relation of difference and non-difference between the cause and its effect:

> Originally unmanifest name and form, manifesting from this very self (*ātman*), took on the name "space" (*ākāśa*). In this way, the element named space was created from the highest self in the same way that dirty foam is created from pure water. Foam is not water, nor is it completely different (*atyantaṃ bhinnaṃ*) from water, since it is never seen in the absence of water. But water is pure and different from foam, whose form (*rūpa*) is dirt.[15]

Śaṅkara uses the language of difference and non-difference in his discussion of the relation between the world of name and form and the highest self. Furthermore, there is no suggestion in this passage that the world has an ontological status any different from that of the highest self. The metaphor of "dirty foam" suggests impurity rather than unreality. Hacker therefore took this passage as evidence that Śaṅkara's views on the reality of the world and the precise causal relationship between Brahman and world went through a "transitional stage" before finally reaching the full-blown theory of unreal manifestation (*vivarta*) found in his commentary on the *Brahmasūtras.*[16] Hacker saw Śaṅkara as an innovator who took the earlier theory of the real transformation (*pariṇāma*) of Brahman and eventually developed it into a theory of an illusory phenomenal world. More recently, Srinivasa Rao has contended that Śaṅkara never argued for the unreality of the phenomenal world and that this view was projected onto him by his later followers.[17] This would mean that Śaṅkara fully supported the theory of *pariṇāmavāda.* Whether or not Rao's interpretation is correct, such ambiguities in Śaṅkara's works are further evidence of the deep influence of the early theory of the real transformation (*pariṇāma*) of Brahman across a wide spectrum of schools and thinkers. Although there were also *vivartavādins* such as Gauḍapāda writing during the early Vedāntic period, the majority position seems to have been some variety of *pariṇāmavāda.*

The first Bhedābhedavādin widely recognized as such by the later tradition is Bhāskara (eighth/ninth century).[18] He was either a younger contemporary of Śaṅkara or perhaps lived slightly after Śaṅkara. Besides his commentary on the *Brahmasūtras*, he also commented on the *Bhagavad*

Gītā. His commentary on the *Brahmasūtras* is expressly written in order to defend the earlier claims of Bhedābhedavādins against Śaṅkara's interpretation. Although he never mentions Śaṅkara by name, he makes it clear from the beginning that his primary intention in commenting on the *Brahmasūtras* is to oppose some predecessor: "I am writing a commentary on this sūtra in order to obstruct those commentators who have concealed its ideas and replaced them with their own."[19] Bhāskara is the earliest in a long line of Vedāntic authors concerned to refute Advaita (including Rāmānuja and Madhva, not to mention numerous Bhedābhedavādins). Many of the stock arguments used against the Advaita originated with Bhāskara, if indeed he did not borrow them from an even earlier source.[20] The Advaita tradition also seems to have collectively remembered him as a thorn in its side. So, for instance, in the fourteenth-century hagiography of Śaṅkara, *Śaṅkaradigvijaya,* Mādhava depicts one "Bhaṭṭa Bhāskara" as a haughty and famous Bhedābhedavādin whom Śaṅkara defeats in a lengthy debate.[21]

Besides insistence that the phenomenal world is a real transformation of Brahman, another view shared by all Bhedābhedavādins is the need for ritual acts in combination with knowledge (*jñānakarmasamuccayavāda*) in order to obtain liberation. This seems to have been a particular concern of Bhāskara. He devotes much of the beginning of his commentary on the *Brahmasūtras* to a critique of the view that knowledge alone is sufficient for the attainment of Brahman, as long as one has fulfilled one's ritual requirements at an earlier stage. Although polemics between Vedāntins are usually depicted in solely philosophical or theological terms, this suggests that perhaps above all, Śaṅkara's new teachings were seen by other Vedāntins of the time as a serious threat to the ritual and social order. Śaṅkara argues that knowledge alone leads to liberation. However, that is not to say that ritual acts have no place in Śaṅkara's thought. Śaṅkara agrees that ordinary people should perform ritual activities throughout their entire lives. Vedic study and ritual activity are both necessary before embarking on higher instruction in the meaning of the Upaniṣads. Performance of obligatory (*nitya*) and contingent (*naimittika*) rites leads to the purification of the mind, and without a pure mind no understanding of the nature of Brahman is possible. However, optional (*kāmya*) rites, preceded as they are by the fulfillment of worldly desires, actually militate against purity of mind, and for this reason they should be abandoned. Bhāskara and others who follow *jñānakarmasamuccayavāda* also agree with Śaṅkara that such optional rites should not be performed.

The controversy arises with the Advaitins' argument that after the mind is cleansed by means of such activities, ritual can be completely abandoned. After the mind is purged of defilements and the four prerequisite virtues (*sādhanas*) necessary for the reception of Vedāntic instruction are cultivated, the practitioner moves on to the next stage of spiritual development. In this next stage, ritual activity is superfluous—or even worse than superfluous, since Advaitins point out that it can distract the adept from hearing, reflection, and meditation on the Upaniṣads. Bhāskara and the rest of the Bhedābhedavādins take exception to this and cite *BS* 3.4.26, "And there is requirement of all, according to the scripture beginning 'sacrifice'" as evidence that ritual activity must be performed throughout one's entire life.[22] Non-activity, they argue, always leads to the generation of mental impurity, and therefore there is no stage at which the practitioner can completely abandon ritual activity. One particularly high-profile forum in which these arguments are played out is in commentaries on the *Bhagavad Gītā*. The performance of action without concern for its results, and the unacceptability of non-action, is often depicted as the central teaching of the *Bhagavad Gītā*.[23] Because this message seems to be more in keeping with Bhāskara's and Rāmānuja's views, this work is a particular challenge for Śaṅkara and his followers, as his commentary on the *Bhagavad Gītā* frequently reveals.[24]

Śaṅkara's position with regard to ritual is much more modest than sometimes portrayed by his opponents. It is not a complete abandonment of ritual duties, but only an abandonment of ritual duties for those rare few who have been able to become completely free of impurity through the previous performance of ritual duties. Nonetheless, his view has the potential for an enormous destabilization of previous social norms, since it gives those who are lazy or subversive an easy excuse for abandonment of traditional ritual responsibilities. This practical argument as such is never presented against the Advaita position, and instead its opponents' critiques are arguments from scripture and inference. Nonetheless, I believe we should see Bhāskara's lengthy argumentation on this topic as indication of a real concern for the social effects of apparently abstract controversies in scriptural interpretation.[25] Many modern interpreters have tried to depict Advaitins and their opponents as purely philosophical in their focus. Yet by the amount of space they devote in their writings, it is clear that the Vedāntins, like the Pūrva Mīmāṃsakas, were acutely concerned with issues revolving around ritual practice and its implications.

Perhaps one of the reasons that Bhedābheda is not a widely known school of Vedānta is that the term *bhedābheda* eventually took on a negative connotation, while *advaita* was a term that thinkers of many different types wanted to associate with their own thought. One case in point is Rāmānuja's (eleventh/twelfth century) system of Viśiṣṭādvaita (Qualified Non-Dualism), often depicted in textbooks as the second major school of Vedānta after the Advaita. Rāmānuja's complicated relationship with Bhedābhedavāda thinkers is rarely discussed. It is clear from Rāmānuja's writings that he is widely conversant with Bhāskara's works, and many of his attacks on Advaita echo the words of Bhāskara's *Brahmasūtrabhāṣya*. Yamunācārya, perhaps Rāmānuja's main intellectual influence, mentions Bhartṛprapañca and Bhāskara in his writings.[26] Furthermore, Rāmānuja's own teacher Yādavaprakāśa was a Bhedābhedavādin. In spite of (or perhaps because of) this, Bhedābhedavāda is one of the central targets of opprobrium for Rāmānuja and his followers, suggesting that the very affinity of many of his ideas led Rāmānuja to try to differentiate himself from what was still clearly an influential Vedāntic tradition.[27] The vilification of Yādavaprakāśa becomes complete in some later hagiographies of Rāmānuja. They depict Yādavaprakāśa as so angered by Rāmānuja's impertinence for challenging his interpretations of the Upaniṣads that he arranges a plot to assassinate his pupil by drowning him in the Ganges during a pilgrimage to Allahabad.[28]

Yādavaprakāśa's works have been lost, and therefore almost all of what we know of his ideas comes from Rāmānuja and one of Rāmānuja's commentators, Sudarśanasūri. However, it is possible from these numerous hints to draw a sketch of Yādavaprakāśa's basic views.[29] Rāmānuja depicts Yādavaprakāśa as an exponent of Svābhāvika Bhedābhedavāda, the view that Brahman is both different and non-different than the world in its very nature, and that difference is not simply due to difference of artificial limiting conditions (*upādhis*).[30] He shares this basic viewpoint with the Bhartṛprapañca and Nimbārka (thirteenth century?), and disagrees with the Aupādhika Bhedābhedavāda of Bhāskara, who maintains that the difference of the world and Brahman is due to limiting conditions. Although differing in this respect, Bhāskara, too, can maintain that the world is real, since for him the limiting conditions are themselves real and not ultimately unreal as in the Advaita tradition. Another characteristic of Yādavaprakāśa's thought is his repeated insistence that Brahman has the substance of pure existence (*sanmātradravya*). The relationship between Brahman and the world is not merely one of class (*jāti*) and individual (*vyakti*); rather, both are existent entities, standing in the relationship of cause (*kāraṇa*) and effect (*kārya*).[31]

In the late medieval period, the doctrine of Bhedābheda became increasingly associated with devotional (*bhakti*) movements in North India. It is largely on the basis of their reputations as the founders of religious sects, and not as philosophers per se, that thinkers such as Vallabha (1479–1531) and Caitanya (1485–1533) became widely known. Among the former's most influential works are a commentary on the *Brahmasūtras* entitled *Anubhāṣya* and his commentary on the *Bhāgavata Purāṇa*, entitled the *Subodhinī*. Vallabha founded the Vaiṣṇava sect of the *puṣṭimārga* ("path of grace") popular with the Gujarati merchant caste, now based in Nathdwara, Rajasthan. His philosophical system, called Śuddhādvaita (Pure Non-Dualism), takes its name from his view that there is no dualism whatsoever between a real Brahman and an unreal world. Since both are completely real, he denies that there can be any sort of ontological dualism of real and unreal between the two—therefore it is a "pure" non-dualism.[32] Obviously, this refers to the Advaita school's view that the phenomenal world is not real in an ultimate sense, and is a clever attempt at reappropriating the valued label *advaita* for his own school. Yet in this regard, all Bhedābhedavādins equally deserve the name *śuddhādvaita*, since all schools assert the reality of the phenomenal world. Vallabha is also notable for maintaining, like Bhāskara, that the soul is atomic in size and not omnipresent as maintained by most Vedāntins.

Caitanya was also a Vaiṣṇava theologian, famous for a school of thought known as Acintyabhedābheda (Inconceivable Difference and Non-difference). No works remain that were written by Caitanya. However, he had numerous followers who wrote works inspired by his teachings, such as Jīva Gosvāmin, author of a well-known commentary on the *Bhāgavata Purāṇa*.[33] This system's notion of "inconceivability" (*acintyatva*) is a central concept used to reconcile apparently contradictory notions, such as the simultaneous oneness and multiplicity of Brahman and the difference and non-difference of God and his powers. This notion has also led some philosophers to accuse all Bhedābhedavādins of being irrationalists. However, this notion of *acintyatva* appears nowhere in the works of Bhāskara, Nimbarka, or Vijñānabhikṣu. In fact, it is precisely the rational resolution of such apparent contradictions that motivates so much of the writings of Vijñānabhikṣu and other Bhedābhedavādins.

It is not a coincidence that Bhedābhedavāda has historically been associated with theism. Like the schools of Rāmānuja and Madhva,

Bhedābhedavāda is a realist tradition. Whereas in the Advaita school, even God (*īśvara*) has to be understood as ultimately unreal, since he, too, is merely Brahman limited the artificial condition of lordliness (*aiśvarya*), certain types of Bhedābheda philosophy can accommodate a God who is real in his qualified (*saguṇa*) form. Although on a certain level, an Advaitin can profess a belief in God, he or she knows that ultimately God is merely a crutch, a heuristic to enable human beings to go one step closer to that ultimate Brahman devoid of qualities. Such a God is ultimately unsatisfying for those whose primary interest is devotion—in any system of Advaita, devotion must occupy a lower position than pure knowledge. Still, many worshippers will also be unsatisfied with the Dvaita school's uncompromising notion that they themselves are completely separate from God and that ultimate unification with the Godhead is impossible. Both Bhedābhedavāda and Viśiṣṭādvaita offer the possibility to bridge these two alternatives, by offering the alternative of both a real God possessing qualities and the possibility of personal participation in that Godhead. However, this attempt to have it both ways, to bridge apparently contradictory opposites, also presents philosophical puzzles.

Scholars sometimes refer to Bhedābheda as a "school" of philosophy, but this term has to be defined and qualified in certain ways. Vijñānabhikṣu and his earlier predecessors were clearly aware of and had read the works of earlier Bhedābhedavādins, borrowing certain central ideas and metaphors (the ocean and its waves, the sun and its rays) as part of their own philosophies. However, the Bhedābheda tradition does not trace itself back through a single lineage of teachers and pupils to earlier figures such as Bhāskara. Although such lineages have no doubt existed, they were regional and limited in scope. This contrasts markedly with the Advaita and Viśiṣṭādvaita traditions, whose founders not only set down a certain philosophical viewpoint but also established a set of institutions designed for the continuation and propagation of these philosophical ideas. The most clear and influential example of this type of institutionalization occurs with the Advaita school, and its establishment of five *maṭhas* (monasteries) at Sringeri, Dwaraka, Badrika, Puri, and Kanchipuram. Something similar occurs among the Viśiṣṭādvaitins, although their influence outside of their base in Tamil Nadu has not been as great as the widespread, pan-Indian appeal of Advaita. The most similar example of such institutions among Bhedābheda philosophers occurs in the case of Vallabha, whose sect in Rajasthan has a formalized institutional hierarchy with a single appointed leader similar to those of the Advaitins and

Viśiṣṭādvaitins. Therefore, it might be better to refer to a loose Bhedābheda "tradition" of scholars who, although separated by space and time, hold certain essential views in common such as the reality of the world and the difference and non-difference of the soul and Brahman. Within this overarching tradition there are also more localized schools, such as those of Vallabha and Caitanya. Even Vijñānabhikṣu might be said to have founded a "school" in a very limited sense, as his teachings are clearly reflected in the works of his disciples Bhāvāgaṇeśa and Divyasiṃha Miśra.

To be sure, philosophers outside the tradition of Bhedābheda Vedānta have also characterized certain relations in terms of "difference and non-difference." For instance, the Mīmāṃsaka Kumārila Bhaṭṭa characterizes the relation between the universal (*sāmānya*) and the particular (*viśeṣa*) as one of difference and non-difference.[34] But this alone is not enough to qualify Kumārila as a Bhedābhedavādin.[35] The defining characteristic of all Bhedābheda Vedāntins is the affirmation of a *bhedābheda* relation between Brahman and the individual self (*jīvātman*). This relation is commonly portrayed as a relation of cause (*kāraṇa*) and effect (*kārya*), or a relation of part (*aṃśa*) and whole (*aṃśin*). But each Bhedābhedavādin stakes out his separate view by his individual interpretation of the precise meaning of these philosophical terms. Bhāskara, for instance, takes the view that when the individual self (*jīva*) is termed a "part" (*aṃśa*) in philosophy and scripture, it is not a part in its normal sense but, rather, has a technical meaning: it is limited by the artificial conditions of mind (*antaḥkaraṇopādhyavacchinna*).[36] Vijñānabhikṣu also understands the important Bhedābheda term "part" (*aṃśa*) in a specialized way. Because of the extraordinary flexibility of these philosophical concepts, there are often substantial disagreements among Bhedābheda Vedāntins.

THE FUTURE OF BHEDĀBHEDA VEDĀNTA

Although in the modern period Bhedābheda Vedānta has been eclipsed in popularity by neo-Vedantic interpretations of Advaita Vedānta philosophy, its lineage continues today among traditional scholars in Puṣṭimārga and Gauḍīya Vaiṣṇava religious communities. And, for the first time in the late twentieth and early twenty-first century, Bhedābheda is finally beginning to receive the attention it deserves from researchers in Europe and North America.[37] Yet much more work remains to be done, particularly on pivotal but little-understood figures such as Nimbārka, whose century has not even been agreed on by historians. The precise nature of the

Bhedābheda renaissance of the late medieval period is also unclear. Did Bhedābheda Vedānta go into decline between the ninth and thirteenth centuries, or were there other important figures such as Rāmānuja's teacher Yādavaprakāśa, whose influence has been elided due to the predominance of Advaita and Viśiṣṭādvaita during that period? What were the formative Bhedābheda philosophical influences on Vallabha and Caitanya? While these questions are beyond the scope of the present study, they are just a few of the issues that future attempts to recover the history of Bhedābheda Vedānta will have to address. In chapter 3, I turn to one late medieval example of Bhedābheda Vedānta, the philosophy of Vijñānabhikṣu. Fully aware of the earlier challenges to Bhedābheda from other philosophical schools, Vijñānabhikṣu offers ingenious solutions to a number of philosophical puzzles that had concerned the Bhedābheda Vedāntins who preceded him.

[3] VIJÑĀNABHIKṢU'S "DIFFERENCE AND NON-DIFFERENCE" VEDĀNTA

THE MEANING OF "BHEDĀBHEDA"

Does the term *bhedābheda* present a logical impossibility? It is a *dvandva* compound, consisting of the words *bheda* (difference) and *abheda* (non-difference).[1] Therefore, Bhedābheda philosophy would be the philosophy of "difference and non-difference," holding out the promise of bridging the apparently unbridgeable disagreements between philosophers who subscribe to the theory of difference (or dualism, *dvaita*) and complete, unqualified non-difference (non-dualism, *advaita*). In the few places in Western secondary literature on Indian philosophy where Bhedābhedavāda is mentioned, it is typically translated as "Difference-in-Identity" philosophy, presumably in an attempt to make it seem more familiar by linking it with the Western tradition of "Difference-in-Identity" typified by thinkers like Bonaventure, Spinoza, and Hegel. Although there are meaningful similarities between these Western thinkers and Indian Bhedābhedavādins, purely on the basis of Sanskrit grammar, "difference-in-identity" cannot be the translation of *bhedābheda*.[2] A preferable translation is the more literal "difference and non-difference," since linguistically it leaves open the question of whether difference is ultimately subsumed under non-difference, or vice versa.

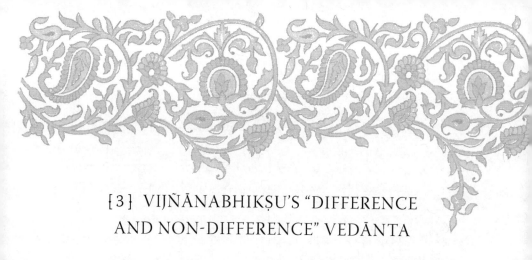

Since basing a philosophical system on both difference and non-difference appears to be the equivalent of arguing both "*p* and not-*p*," one possible explanation of the doctrine of *bhedābhedavāda* might involve a denial or suspension of the principle of contradiction, "*p* and not-*p* cannot both be true." Some critics have understood the meaning of *bhedābhedavāda* in just this way and for this reason have identified it with the Jaina theory of perspectivism (*anekāntavāda*). The Viśiṣṭādvaitin Vedānta Deśika, for instance, labels Bhāskara a "Vedantin who smells like a Jaina" (*jainagandhivedāntin*).[3] But just as it is a mistake to portray the Jainas as denying the law of contradiction, so, too, it is clearly a misunderstanding to accuse Bhedābhedavāda of holding that *p* and not-*p* can simultaneously be true.[4] In the late medieval period, it was the Navya-Nyāya school that most emphatically upheld the validity of logical principles such as the law of contradiction and for this reason was one of the most emphatic in condemning the apparent paradox of simultaneous *bheda* and *abheda*. Throughout his works, Vijñānabhikṣu takes pains to illustrate his understanding of the Navya-Nyāya technical terminology. Not only does Vijñānabhikṣu try to show his anticipated Naiyāyika critics that *bhedābheda* does not involve any logical contradiction, he also employs Navya-Nyāya terms while explicating his own philosophical ideas. This tendency is even more marked in the writings of Vijñānabhiksu's disciple Bhāvāgaṇeśa, author of the *Sāṃkhyatattvayāthārthyadīpana*, suggesting that Vijñānabhikṣu's students understood the defense of Bhedābheda and Sāṃkhya concepts using the language of Navya-Nyāya as an essential part of Vijñānabhikṣu's project.[5] To illustrate the rigor of his own ideas, Vijñānabhikṣu is careful to note precisely the places where he sees his difference from the Naiyāyikas as merely resulting from arbitrary differences in terminology. One paradigmatic example is his explanation of the multiple meanings of the terms *bheda* and *abheda*.

To begin to understand the advantages the Bhedābheda Vedānta tradition has over its competitors, the Dvaita and Advaita schools, one must keep in mind that Vedānta itself is as much a school of scriptural interpretation as it is a school of philosophy per se. Vedāntins of almost all affiliations see scripture (*śabdapramāṇa*) as a more important source of knowledge than inference (*anumāna*).[6] Although both arguments from scripture and arguments on the basis of inference are frequently cited, the former is primary. The name "Vedānta" as referring to one particular school is itself a relatively uncommon usage in Sanskrit texts. More typically, *vedānta* simply means the "end of the Vedas," referring to the Upaniṣads themselves. Often the Vedānta school is called Brahma Mīmāṃsā (Exegesis of Brahman) or Uttara Mīmāṃsā (Later Exegesis), these epithets obviously alluding to the school of the Pūrva Mīmāṃsā (Prior Exegesis). Both schools' primary concern is the interpretation of the Veda. What distinguishes the two is that the later school is concerned with the exegesis of the

Upaniṣads, those portions of the Veda that describe the nature of Brahman (*brahmakāṇḍa*), while the prior school concentrates on the parts of the Veda that describe the performance of rituals (*karmakāṇḍa*).[7]

Although the two schools do have significant differences in the content of their interpretations, the Uttara Mīmāṃsā, or Vedānta, nonetheless accepts most of the interpretive principles developed by the earlier school for the interpretation of the Veda. One of these is the principle that the entire Veda itself is a single extended sentence (*ekavākyatā*) and hence can never be self-contradictory. This principle has many significant consequences, but perhaps the most important is that it forced schools of Vedic interpretation to interpret the entire Veda as being a unitary text with a single message. Discarding parts of the text because of their apparent contradiction with other, more celebrated passages was not an acceptable option. Instead, this principle encouraged creativity on the part of interpreters, to use whatever means they had at their disposal to show that anomalous passages did not disagree with what they took to be the main message of the Vedas.

Vijñānabhikṣu believes that Bhedābheda Vedānta is superior because it is the only Vedāntic school capable of making sense of all of the statements found in the Upaniṣads. Two types of passages are most significant for him: statements of difference (*bhedavākyas*) and statements of non-difference (*abhedavākyas*). For Vijñānabhikṣu, the primary flaw of Advaitic interpretive strategies is that they subordinate statements of difference to statements of non-difference. For instance, the eighth-century Advaita Vedāntin Śaṅkara dubbed four Upaniṣadic sentences as "great statements" (*mahāvākyas*): "You are that" (*tat tvam asi*), "I am Brahman" (*ahaṃ brahmāsmi*), "This self is Brahman" (*ayam ātmā brahma*), and "Brahman is consciousness" (*prajñānaṃ brahma*). Each of these statements seems to suggest strongly that the individual self (*jīvātman*) is identical to Brahman. Yet there are statements elsewhere in the Vedas that state the difference between Brahman and the individual self. Because of the principle that the Vedas are a single complex sentence, these statements cannot simply be ignored or rejected as fallacious. There are a number of strategies for making sense of these statements of difference without acknowledging that they have the same weight as statements of non-difference. Often these involve resorting to secondary, or figurative, interpretation (*lakṣaṇā*). Vijñānabhikṣu summarizes one of these interpretive strategies of the Advaitins, whom he dismissively labels as "modern thinkers":

> However, modern thinkers claim that due to the complete undividedness of the self and Brahman, the primary meaning of the word "Brahman" is also "self," just as the primary meaning of the word "space" is also "space inside of a pot."[8]
>
> On the other hand, the notion that the self is not Brahman is brought about by ignorance. Furthermore, they say, there are hundreds of revealed texts of non-difference, such as "You are that," "I am Brahman," "Having entered by means of this, the self, name and form are differentiated," and "There is no perceiver other than he." From these they claim that the self simply is Brahman, since pure consciousness is uniform and also since lordliness and bondage are merely a pair of limiting conditions.
>
> They say that of the hundreds of statements of difference—including "Two birds who are friends and companions perch on the selfsame tree" [*Śvet. Up.* 4.6]; "Changeless among the changing, sentient among the insentient, the one, who grants the desires among the many, the wise perceive him residing in themselves. For them, and not for others, there is eternal peace" [*Śvet. Up.* 6.13]; "He who resides in the self, but is other than the self, should know, 'the self belongs to me.'" "In the three abodes, whatever might be an object of enjoyment, an enjoyer, or enjoyment, I, pure consciousness, witness, and always munificent, am different from them"—there cannot be claimed a logical incongruity. For the statements [of difference] make sense insofar as they reiterate difference with regard to artificial conditions.[9]

While Advaitins accept that the referents of the statements of non-difference like "I am Brahman" are the individual self (*jīvātman*) and Brahman, they resort to figurative interpretation to deny that the referent of statements of difference is Brahman in its highest form, even in cases where the word "Brahman" is used. So, for instance, "He who resides in the self, but is other than the self" cannot possibly refer to Brahman in itself, since the Advaitin maintains the view that there is complete undividedness (*akhaṇḍatā*) or identity (*tādātmya*) of the individual self and highest Brahman. Advaitins would therefore commonly argue that the referent of the pronoun "he" in this sentence is not Brahman in its absolute form but only in a lower form, limited by artificial conditions (*upādhi*). This is because the Advaitins take it as axiomatic that the Upaniṣadic statements of non-difference express complete identity of the self and Brahman. However, Vijñānabhikṣu argues that this is only one possible interpretation of statements of non-difference, and by no means the best one:

With regard to this, we reply: You claim that the statements of difference contradict statements of non-difference only because they refer to difference regarding artificial conditions. But why not claim that the statements of non-difference contradict statements of difference because they refer to non-difference in the form of non-separation, etc. [and not complete identity]? Both are logically consistent.[10]

Here Vijñānabhikṣu lays out his basic strategy for reconciling the statements of difference and non-difference that appear in the Vedas, and likewise for logically accommodating both difference and non-difference in a way that the Naiyāyikas will find logically rigorous. According to Vijñānabhikṣu, the terms difference (*bheda*) and non-difference (*abheda*) can each be understood in at least two ways. In Naiyāyika terminology, non-difference is understood as identity (*tādātmya*) while difference is the negation of identity, called "mutual absence" (*anyonyābhāva*).[11] However, these two terms, difference and non-difference, so central to discussions of the relation between the self and Brahman, can also be understood to mean separation (*vibhāga*) and non-separation (*avibhāga*). By adopting this alternate interpretation, it is possible to explain both the statements of difference and the statements of non-difference that appear in the Vedas without arbitrarily subordinating one to the other. Although Vijñānabhikṣu introduces this suggestion in response to an Advaita *pūrvapakṣin,* the argument could equally well appear in response to a Dvaita Vedāntin, since the Dvaitin engages in the same reductive project, only reversed: he is forced to explain away statements of non-difference after taking statements of the difference between Brahman and the individual self as axiomatic. From the point of view of the Bhedābhedavādin, both Advaitin and Dvaitin share the mistake of always interpreting the words "non-difference" and "difference" in the Upaniṣads as univocal, not understanding their equivocality.

After introducing these alternate meanings for the two words, Vijñānabhikṣu has to show that they are logical ways of characterizing the relation between Brahman and the individual self. He does this by appealing to quotes from revealed texts (*śruti*) and traditional texts (*smṛti*) that refer to the self being "divided" or not "divided":

Non-difference in the form of non-separation is also heard in revealed texts such as: "In which way pure water poured into the pure [water] is like that, in that way, O Gautama, is the self of the learned seer. But it is not a second,

> different from that, divided (*vibhakta*)." And in the traditional texts: "And undivided within beings, He stands as if divided. Whether manifestly or unmanifestly, He is truly the supreme *puruṣa*."
>
> We understand this passage to mean that ultimately, there is non-difference [from that Brahman] in the form of non-separation, etc. But we do not understand this passage to mean that there is a difference due to artificial conditions (*upādhi*) which are ultimately false (*mithyā*).[12]

Vijñānabhikṣu remarks that in the opinion of the Advaita Vedāntins, half of the statements of scripture are false—those statements expressing difference between the individual self and Brahman. The advantage of being able to understand difference and non-difference in terms of separation and non-separation is that it allows us to understand all of the statements that refer to Brahman as being true, instead of having to explain them as merely referring to the artificial conditions that appear to limit Brahman in the world.

Following this, Vijñānabhikṣu has to give linguistic justification to argue that "separation" (*vibhāga*) and "non-separation" (*avibhāga*) are legitimate ways of glossing the words difference and non-difference. He does this by appealing to authority of the grammatical *Dhātupāṭha,* which sets down the meanings of Sanskrit verbal roots:

> And it is not the case that when there is the word "non-difference" (*abheda*) in the sense of "non-separation" (*avibhāga*) there is a figurative usage, due to the rule of the root *bhid: "bhid,* in the sense of splitting (*vidāraṇa*)," meaning also in the sense of separation (*vibhāga*).[13]

Vijñānabhikṣu takes pains to emphasize that "separation" is a primary meaning of the word "difference," not a figurative meaning. Establishing this allows him to argue that understanding difference as "separation" is just as legitimate as understanding it as mutual absence (*anyonyābhāva*). Any Naiyāyika or Vedāntin who insists on the latter meaning instead of the former is merely arguing from the verbal conventions of his own school, not from any fundamental principles of the Sanskrit language.

Of course, Vijñānabhikṣu is not arguing that in all scriptural passages difference should be understood as "separation" and not as "mutual absence." To maintain this would be just as arbitrary as a Naiyāyika's insistence that the opposite should be the case. It would also violate the law of contradiction, since the relationship between Brahman and the individual self is alternately described as "difference" and "non-difference" in the Upaniṣads. Accepting simultaneous separation and non-separation would be no less incoherent than accepting simultaneous difference and non-difference. Both would entail a statement of the form *p* and not-*p*, which Vijñānabhikṣu agrees is logically invalid. Instead, these readings have to be coordinated based on context to allow for logical continuity. For instance, in passages where the Upaniṣads reject difference, this difference must be understood as separation, not as mutual absence (*anyonyābhāva*). This is because mutual absence, the denial of complete identity, is permanent. Separation, however, is an ephemeral state, and the fundamental relation between Brahman and the self is the state of non-separation. Vijñānabhikṣu illustrates the logic behind his interpretive method in a polemical exchange with an Advaita *pūrvapakṣin*:

> Objection: In revealed texts (*śruti*) there are statements such as: "He who makes a cavity, a fissure in this, he has fear" (*Tait. Up.* 2.7.1); and in traditional texts (*smṛti*): "His knowledge with regard to bodies apart from the self as in reality being only one, that is the highest truth. The dualists are those whose views are false" (*Viṣ. Pu.* 2.14.31). Since the traditional texts reject difference, it is not possible for the revealed texts to have difference as their primary meaning.
>
> Response: No, this is not the case. For the statements of non-difference (*abheda*) are concerned with non-separation (*avibhāga*), and the statements that reject difference (*bheda*) have as their concern "difference" (*bheda*) in the sense of separation (*vibhāga*). For that which is contrary to the topic under discussion must be rejected. Otherwise, in revealed texts such as, "By the mind alone this is to be obtained—here there is no difference whatsoever. He who sees difference here obtains death upon death" (*Kaṭha Up.* 4.11), due to the rejection of difference, there would be non-difference with the classes of insentient beings.[14]

Vijñānabhikṣu sees the fundamental relationship between Brahman and the individual self as non-separation (*avibhāga*). This obtains before God's creation and after his destruction of the world. However, during the world's existence, the individual self exists in a state of separation (*vibhāga*) from Brahman, until it achieves the state of liberation. Liberated selves, too, exist in a state of non-separation (*avibhāga*). Since at various times the self undergoes both the state of separation and non-separation, this allows Vijñānabhikṣu to make sense of both statements of separation and non-separation. This appeal to differences of time is yet another strategy that Vijñānabhikṣu employs to reconcile the apparent contradiction of difference and non-difference.[15] If difference and non-difference occur at different times, and not simultaneously, then there is no problem:

> The difference and non-difference of the part and whole, in the form of separation and non-separation, is not a contradiction since it refers to differences at different times. But the mutual non-existence (*anyonyābhāva*) of the self and Brahman is permanent, and the non-separation of the power and the power-possessor is permanent.[16]

Because the state of identity (*tādātmya*) never obtains between the self and Brahman, every passage of scripture that affirms the relation of non-difference between the two means non-separation, never identity. The fundamental error of Advaita Vedānta is a failure to understand this. Therefore, the relation between the self and Brahman can be understood correctly as a permanent state of mutual absence (*anyonyābhāva*). This is simply another way of saying that there is never complete identity (*tādātmya*) between the two. Understanding these four terms correctly, it is possible to make logical sense of any passage expressing difference or non-difference, without appeal to mystical paradox or denial of the law of contradiction. Vijñānabhikṣu never attempts to uphold a statement in the form "*d* and not-*d*." Instead, he understands "difference and non-difference" to be a case of "d_1 and not-d_2." "D_1" might stand for "difference" in one sense, such as mutual absence, while in "not-d_2," d_2 refers to "difference" as separation. By mixing the different definitions of difference and non-difference in such ways, Vijñānabhikṣu can avoid logical contradiction entirely.

Vijñānabhikṣu understands these two pairs of terms to have precise philosophical definitions. One stock example for the relation of identity ("*A* is *B*") in the Indian logical tradition is "The pot is the pot." This is a complete denial of difference. In the sphere of Navya-Nyāya logic that Vijñānabhikṣu presupposes, to say "*A* is *B*" is to say that these two things are the very same individual.[17] The negation of the previous statement of identity, "*A* is not *B*" is given the technical name "mutual absence" (*anyonyābhāva*) as in the example "The pot is not the cloth." Note that this is merely a denial of the relation of identity between two individual entities; it implies nothing further. The pot in question can share many properties with the cloth (e.g., blueness, handsomeness, being a product, being ephemeral) and still have the relation of mutual absence. For that matter, there can be two pots sitting side by side, indistinguishable in shape, size, color, and texture. But as long as they are not the very same individual pot, they can still be referred to as having the relation of mutual absence.

Identity and mutual absence are familiar concepts from the Nyāya tradition. Vijñānabhikṣu's technical definitions of separation and non-separation, however, are his own innovation. Non-separation refers to a state in which two entities are perceptually indistinguishable from one another, while nonetheless not having the relationship of identity (*tādātmya*). Vijñānabhikṣu sees the relation of non-separation expressed in statements like "In which way pure water poured into the pure [water] is like that, in that way, O Gautama, is the self of the learned seer. But it is not a second, different from that, divided (*vibhakta*)." Other examples he cites include the mixing of sugar into milk and of salt into water. In both these examples, the two substances, although mixed, remain separate things. Another logical example of the relation of non-separation is the relation between a power and power-possessor, or between a property and a property-possessor. In the example of a blue cloth, "blueness" and the cloth are not identical; conceptually, they can still be distinguished. Yet they are conjoined in a relationship of non-separation in the blue cloth itself.

But the previous definitions of separation and non-separation only apply to everyday examples; in a philosophical context, Vijñānabhikṣu establishes technical definitions: "'Separation' (*vibhāga*) in its technical sense means difference in characteristics, and more specifically difference in characteristics that are manifest. 'Non-separation' means absence of difference in characteristics."[18] Separation (*vibhāga*) does not mean total disjunction, as the Nyāya-Vaiśeṣika school maintains. Rather, it means a manifest difference in properties (*abhivyaktadharmabheda*). Therefore, although Vijñānabhikṣu is quite happy to use examples from everyday life as metaphors to describe separation, these metaphors, generally based on spatiality, cannot literally apply to Brahman and the selves. Since Brahman and selves are both omnipresent, there can be no physical-spatial "detachment" of the selves from Brahman. Rather, when a self separates from Brahman, that means that it manifests differences in properties from Brahman. So, for instance, bound selves are characterized by limited knowledge (*alpajñatva*), while Brahman is characterized by omniscience (*sarvajñatva*). It is on the basis of such factors that we can describe selves as "separate" from Brahman.

Vijñānabhikṣu is also careful not to claim that these two pairs of concepts—identity and mutual absence, non-separation and separation—are as exhaustive as the meanings of the terms "difference" and "non-difference" found in the Upaniṣads. Another important meaning of the word "non-difference" is non-difference of essential attributes (*avaidharmya*). In the example of the two indistinguishable pots, they are neither identical (as they are two distinct individuals) nor are they non-separate in the everyday sense (since they are not connected in space). They are two tokens of the same type. Although there is more than one, they are not different because they lack differences of their essential attributes. This meaning of non-difference is particularly important in the context of the Sāṃkhya school, which teaches that there are multiple *puruṣas*. Even though these *puruṣas* are multiple in number, and therefore not identical in the Naiyāyikas' sense of the term, they are non-different in the sense of not having a difference of essential attributes (*avaidharmya*). This is how Vijñānabhikṣu understands the well-known passage, "One only, without a second" (*Chānd. Up.* 6.2.1).[19]

Although this state of non-separation exists, Vijñānabhikṣu recognizes that the relationship between salt and water, self and Brahman, and blueness and cloth are not characterized by permanent inseparability. These things can be separated over time. As the color blue is bleached out of the cloth, or water is evaporated in order to become separate from the salt, so does the self become separate from Brahman in certain conditions (i.e., manifests different qualities). But Vijñānabhikṣu claims that unlike the first two examples, in the example of the self and Brahman, non-separation is fundamental and can even be termed to be real in a way that the relation of separation cannot:

> Therefore, difference and non-difference in the form of separation and non-separation is established, by the relation of part and whole between the self and God. And between those two, only non-separation is true (*satya*), due to its being available at the beginning and the end of creation, due to its being the natural state (*svābhāvika*), and due to its being eternal. But separation, since it is only for a limited time between the beginning and end of creation, is conditional (*naimittika*). Like other changes (*vikāra*), it is merely verbal (*vācārambhaṇamātra*). This is its particular characteristic.

In this way the non-dual self is explained in general, and we will explain the statements of the non-dual Brahman in the commentary on the third sūtra. And defining difference as mutual non-existence (*anyonyābhāva*), God, the referent of the word Brahman, can be said to be completely different from the self.[20]

Vijñānabhikṣu's assertion that the *natural* state of Brahman is non-separation seems to align him with Bhāskara's Conditional Difference and Non-Difference (Aupādhika Bhedābheda), and separates him from Nimbarka and Yādavaprakāśa, who hold that difference and non-difference are both essential to Brahman. But Vijñānabhikṣu goes even further—in the language of the first paragraph, he comes extremely close to adopting the Advaitins' description of the world as unreal. He even uses the same epithet from the *Chāndogya Upaniṣad* that Vācaspati Miśra uses to apply to the unreal status of the effects of Brahman, "merely verbal" (*vācārambhaṇamātra*). However, we must take this passage from Vijñānabhikṣu in the context of his frequent assertions, in the *Vijñānāmṛtabhāṣya* and elsewhere, of the reality of the phenomenal world. Instead of a strict binary relationship between the real and unreal, we should understand a theory of different grades of reality. On the one hand, non-separation is the most real because it is the natural state of the self and Brahman. It is even described as eternal (*nitya*), although this, too, seems to contradict Vijñānabhikṣu's previous statements. Although non-separation is the fundamental state from which the world originates and to which everything will return after the world's dissolution, there is an in-between period when separation exists.

Non-separation can therefore only be understood as "eternal" if we understand that, at the time of the phenomenal world's existence, non-separation exists in a latent state. It is also important to note that this notion of the gradations of reality itself appears in a slightly different form in the mainstream Advaita tradition. Although Brahman in its unqualified form is the ultimate reality, there are *two* other stages of reality below that which is ultimately real. The lowest is the state of that which is completely unreal (*prātibhāsika*), which includes illusions, physical impossibilities like a sky-lotus, and logical impossibilities like the son of a barren woman. Above this is the level of the phenomenal world, intersubjectively understood as real by normal people. This world, although ultimately unreal (*mithyā*), is phenomenally real, and for that reason important. The Advaitins use the epithet "inexplicable" (*anirvacanīya*) to describe its ontological state, which is neither totally real (like Brahman) nor totally unreal (like illusory objects). Vijñānabhikṣu rejects the Advaitins' formulation as nonsensical and elsewhere argues that the phenomenal world is real (*sat*). But at times he uses terminology that edges him surprisingly close to the standard Advaita position.

SELF AND BRAHMAN AS PART AND WHOLE

One problem that the Bhedābheda Vedāntic tradition faces comes from its claim that the individual selves and Brahman exist in a relation of part (*aṃśa*) and whole (*aṃśin*). The stock analogies used by Bhedābhedavādins to illustrate the part/whole relation between the two include a fire and its sparks, the ocean and its waves, the sun and its rays. This relation is made explicit in Bhedābheda commentaries on the *Brahmasūtras* since Bhāskara, especially in reference to one particular sūtra: "A part, due to being stated as different. And otherwise also, as some people study it as servant, lord, etc." (*BS* 2.3.43).[21] It is partly on the basis of this sūtra that Hajime Nakamura reaches the conclusion that the author of the *Brahmasūtras* was a Bhedābhedavādin: "According to one sūtra, the individual self is clearly defined as being a part (*aṃśa*) of *Brahman* (2.3.43). . . . [The] *sūtra* states that the individual self is different (*nānā*) from Brahman but at the same time not different. From this we see that the *Brahma-sūtra* took the standpoint of what was called *Bhedābheda* by later thinkers."[22]

However, a serious interpretive problem arises. In *BS* 2.1.26, the author refers to Brahman as "partless" (*niravayava*). Furthermore, as most commentators point out (including Vijñānabhikṣu and Śaṅkara), there are passages in the Upaniṣads that also say that Brahman is "partless," such as *Śvet. Up.* 6.19: "partless (*niṣkala*), inactive, peaceful, faultless, spotless." Reconciling these two passages is a fundamental problem for anyone who wishes to comment on the *Brahmasūtras.* Not surprisingly, Bhedābhedavādins and Advaitins take drastically different steps to resolve this contradiction in the text—this might even be described as the central interpretive difference between the two schools. Advaita Vedāntins accept the Upaniṣadic statements of the complete partlessness of Brahman at face value, and describe Brahman as a single, undifferentiated mass that is totally indivisible (*akhaṇḍa*). This leads them to interpret *BS* 2.3.43, where Brahman is described as a "part," in a purely figurative way. Śaṅkara writes:

> He [Bādarāyaṇa] says, "it is a part (*aṃśa*)." The self (*jīva*) should be understood as part of the Lord (*īśvara*), just as the spark is [a part] of the fire.

"Part" means "like a part" (*aṃśa iva*), since a thing that is free from parts (*niravayava*) cannot literally have parts (*aṃśa*).[23]

Śaṅkara goes on to remark that when the sūtra says "and otherwise also," it refers to the many statements where the so-called parts are described as non-different from their whole. These statements of non-difference, according to Śaṅkara, should be taken to refer to the ultimate state of identity between the so-called parts and the whole, while difference is merely due to difference in artificial limiting conditions. It is clear that Advaitins simply cannot make literal sense of *BS* 2.3.43, and hence they employ interpretive strategies to make the passage conform to the standard Advaita reading. But Advaitins have good reasons for making this interpretive move, since the Upaniṣads attest that Brahman is a partless whole. The Advaitins have not only scriptural authority (*śabdapramāṇa*) on their side but also inference (*anumāna*). It is inconceivable that Brahman could be made up of parts, for things that are made up of parts are dependent on those parts and impermanent. When the parts are separated from that thing, it is diminished. For instance, when a table is separated from one of its legs, it no longer functions well as a table. Anyone who hopes to argue plausibly for the part/whole relation pertaining to the self and Brahman must show that it is meaningful to speak of a different sort of part/whole relation, in which the whole is completely independent of its parts.

At the beginning of his defense of the logical coherence of the part/whole relation, Vijñānabhikṣu asserts that it is the best of all alternatives. His critique of the Advaita includes a critique of the metaphors by which the Advaitins theorize the relation between Brahman and the individual self (*jīva*). The most influential analogies for theorizing the complete unity and partlessness of Brahman are those of the sun and its reflection in pools of water, and of space (*ākāśa*) and space as limited by a pot. These two metaphors correspond to two major schools of thought within post-Śaṅkara Advaita, reflectionism (*pratibimbavāda*) and limitationism (*avacchedavāda*).[24] Vijñānabhikṣu tries to show through a process of elimination that when both of these metaphors break down, the only adequate way to represent the relation between Brahman and the self are metaphors expressing the doctrine of part and whole (*aṃśavāda*), such as the fire and its sparks. So, for instance, the metaphor of space and the space limited by a pot expresses the view that the self is identical with Brahman but merely limited by artificial conditions (*upādhi*)—just as the pot is an artificial condition that limits space. But, Vijñānabhikṣu argues,

> if it [Brahman] were a single, partless whole, then there might again be the undesirable occurrence of bondage for someone who has been previously liberated. For although the liberated part is disjoined from one internal organ (*antaḥkaraṇa*), there is the possibility of union with another internal organ. In the same way, the space that is limited by one pot, even when that pot is broken, eventually comes back into relation with another pot.[25]

This is a variation on the familiar criticism of Advaita that it cannot account for liberation. The limitationists' model can account for the conventional appearance of difference between various selves, one self apparently being liberated while another is bound, since liberation just means that the artificial limiting condition (*upādhi*) has been destroyed. But it cannot account for the permanent liberation of selves—on the model of the pots and space, there would be the constant possibility of the self's backsliding and ceasing to be liberated. That is because any given section of space might be surrounded by a new pot, even after the previous one is broken.

After advancing numerous arguments for the inadequacy of the limitationist and reflectionist models, on the basis of both scripture and inference, Vijñānabhikṣu suggests that his own doctrine of part and whole should be accepted as the last one standing:

> We have seen the examples of the moon and the moon's reflection in the water, space and the space limited by a pot, fire and its sparks, shade and heat, woman and man. All these correspond to viewpoints like reflectionism, limitationism, the doctrine of part and whole (*aṃśavāda*), and so forth. Because they conflict, it is impossible for all of these views to be true—only one can be accepted. The rest of the examples should be understood as only partially expressing that which is intended everywhere. This being the case, it is appropriate to accept just the doctrine of part and whole.[26]

Vijñānabhikṣu does not completely reject the other metaphors for the relation between Brahman and the self. To the extent that these other views have similarities with his own, they might be regarded as partially true. To argue that the doctrine of part and whole is the only one that can be completely accepted he repeatedly cites *BS* 2.3.43: "a part, due to being stated as different . . ." However, simply to cite this sūtra is not enough. To make his case that this sūtra should be read literally, not figuratively as the Advaitins do, Vijñānabhikṣu understands that he has to show that the doctrine of part and whole is logically coherent. To do this, he makes a subtle distinction between two different Sanskrit words that are both typically translated as "part": *aṃśa* and *avayava*. While the selves are the *aṃśas* of Brahman, they are not the *avayavas* of Brahman. Vijñānabhikṣu wishes to make this distinction by saying that an *avayava* can be understood in the everyday sense of the word "part." However, an *aṃśa* has a specific technical meaning in the *Brahmasūtras* and in his philosophical writings:

> To be a part (*aṃśa*), something must be of the same class (*sajātīya*) as the whole (*aṃśin*) and be the adjunct of non-separation (*avibhāgapratiyogin*). The whole is the subjunct of non-separation (*tadanuyogin*). When referring to the part as being of the same class as the whole, one must be consistent with regard to the property under discussion. For instance, when discussing the part being a self, one should say it falls under the class of selfhood (*ātmatva*). When discussing the part as existent, etc., one should refer to it as falling under the class of existence (*sattva*), etc. Following this procedure, there will be no confusion.[27]

In this passage, Vijñānabhikṣu employs two relational terms from Navya-Nyāya, subjunct (*anuyogin*) and adjunct (*pratiyogin*).[28] In the Naiyāyikas' stock example, "there is absence of the pot in the ground," the pot is the adjunct in the relation, while the ground is the subjunct. It is important to see that the relation of absence only goes one way: to say that there is absence of the pot in the ground is not the same thing as to say that there is absence of the ground in the pot. Likewise, although it is possible to say that the selves are parts of Brahman, it is quite something else to say that Brahman is the part of the selves. Therefore, to avoid the possibility that Brahman could also be called a "part" and the selves called the "whole," Vijñānabhikṣu must argue that separation is a one-way relation, not a two-way relation as it might appear at first glance. In the relation of separation or non-separation, the *anuyogin* is the locus, while the *pratiyogin* is that which separates from the locus. In the example of leaves falling from a tree, the leaf would be the *pratiyogin* of separation, while the tree is the *anuyogin*. In the case of the selves and Brahman, it is the selves that separate from Brahman at the time of creation and reattach to Brahman at the time of the world's dissolution. Throughout this entire process, however, Brahman, the whole, remains unchanged.[29] One way of expressing such a one-way relation of separation is by paradoxical statements of difference and non-difference, such as one of Vijñānabhikṣu's favorite passages from the *Viṣṇu Purāṇa*: "There is nothing different from it, yet it is different from everything" (*Viṣ. Pu.* 1.16.78). Less enigmatically, one might gloss this to mean that, although all of the selves are its parts, Brahman is not dependent on, or affected by, the states of bondage and liberation of those very same selves.

The other half of Vijñānabhikṣu's technical definition of a part (*aṃśa*) stipulates that a part must be of the same class (*sajātīya*) as the whole. Vijñānabhikṣu offers examples of two such properties that Brahman and the selves share: selfhood (*ātmatva*) and existence (*sattva*). Another property that Brahman and selves have in common is consciousness (*cittva*).[30] For Vijñānabhikṣu, however, being bliss (*ānandatva*) does not qualify as a shared property. This is because, he argues, the term "bliss" or "happiness" when applied to the liberated self or Brahman can only refer to a complete absence of suffering. It therefore does not refer to a positive state, as the word does in everyday statements such as "Devadatta is happy." Vijñānabhikṣu borrows this argument from the Sāṃkhyas and in arguing the position cites the *Sāṃkhyasūtras* in support of his view.[31] Vijñānabhikṣu also emphasizes here that properties like selfhood and existence must not be conflated. This is a rejection of Śaṅkara's view that the consciousness, existence, and bliss of Brahman are in fact one and the same. Furthermore, according to Śaṅkara, they are not properties of Brahman—they are identical with Brahman. Vijñānabhikṣu also differs from Rāmānuja on this issue, since Rāmānuja holds that bliss is a property of Brahman. Vijñānabhikṣu believes that Brahman possesses multiple properties but bliss is not among them. Strictly speaking, bliss exists only in the realm of *prakṛti,* and therefore it cannot be a property of Brahman.[32]

In his commentary on the *Brahmasūtras,* Vijñānabhikṣu seeks to justify all of the traditional metaphors he has inherited from other Bhedābhedavādins, in spite of their apparent dissimilarities and inconsistencies. An ocean and its waves, fire and its sparks, the sun and its rays, and a father and his son are all different in their specific details. The father is clearly the cause of his son (along with the mother, of course), but it seems implausible to modern sensibilities that a son can be described as a part of his father. Likewise, in the case of a fire and its sparks, the sparks cease to be parts of the fire as soon as they are distinguishable as sparks. Furthermore, with all of these metaphors except for the first, there appears to be no eventual reabsorption of the parts back into their whole—only the ocean creates waves that manifest as distinct parts of the ocean as a whole and then reabsorbs those same waves. Recognition of the inadequacy of these metaphors is implicit when the Advaita objector in the *Vijñānāmṛtabhāṣya* asks, "How do we know that the relation of part and whole as in the examples of the fire and sparks, father and son, etc., is intended?"[33]

The common characteristic in all of these metaphors is showing the possibility for a whole to exist that is completely independent of its parts. In an example that Vijñānabhikṣu does not use, the parts of a human body, loss of a limb greatly diminishes the proper functioning of the body as a whole; loss of certain parts of the body will result in the whole's complete termination. But the fire can continue to be separated from its sparks without thereby being diminished; the same holds for the father, who is in no way lessened by the production of a son. This difference gets to the heart of Vijñānabhikṣu's distinction between the two different Sanskrit words for "part." While a part in its everyday sense (*avayava*) describes a relationship where the whole is dependent on, and constituted by, its parts, a loss of a part in its specialized sense (*aṃśa*) is not responsible for the diminishing of the whole:

> Objection: Since Brahman is devoid of parts (*niravayava*), how could it possess a "part" (*aṃśa*) in a primary sense?
>
> Reply: We have seen that it possesses a "part" (*aṃśa*) as according to the technical definition given previously, although it does not possess any "part" in the popular sense of the word (*avayava*). Likewise, the hair is referred to as a "part" (*aṃśa*) of the body. A single unit is called a "part" of the group. The son is called a "part" of the father. Like the possessions of the son that upon his death go to the father, at the time of the dissolution of the universe, the selves give up their own characteristic of illumination of only the sense-object and take on unity (*ananyatva*) with the characteristic of Brahman, the pure consciousness, which constantly illuminates everything.[34] And at the time of the creation of the universe, just due to the Lord's own desire, the selves, after attaining effective consciousness, become manifest just as the sons of the father become manifest.[35] Therefore, selves can be called the parts (*aṃśa*) of Brahman. By the *śruti*, "he himself is manifested as the son," there is non-difference characterized by non-separation of the father with the son. In the same way, by the *śruti*, "Let me be manifest as many" (*Ch. Up.* 6.2.3), the non-difference characterized by non-separation of Brahman with the self is established. Hence, the selves have as their primary meaning "parts of Brahman."[36]

The specifics of Vijñānabhikṣu's analogy of the son and the father is unclear in its details, in part possibly due to textual corruption. Either Vijñānabhikṣu means that the father inherits his son's possessions (*vetanāḥ*) when the son dies, or his consciousness (*cetanāḥ*) is absorbed into his father's at death. The first seems irrelevant, while the second is simply false. The basic problem with this metaphor is that although the father can certainly be said to be responsible for the manifestation of his son, it is hard to see how he might reabsorb his son at the time of his son's death. Nonetheless, the basic cosmological picture that Vijñānabhikṣu presents is clear. The world is divided into three periods: origin, existence, and dissolution. Before the origin of the world, the individual consciousnesses of the selves are latent, not in use. Only after the world's creation do the consciousnesses of the selves become manifest, or effective. Once again after the selves are reabsorbed into Brahman, they return to their original latent state. This threefold chronological division appears in most commentaries on *BS* 1.1.2.[37] This basic cosmological picture of an undifferentiated stuff being differentiated and then reabsorbed at the end of the world is depicted in virtually all of the Purāṇas. It also has obvious parallels to the activity of *prakṛti* in the Sāṃkhya-Yoga system. However, it seems slightly more problematic in the Vedāntic context, since Brahman, unlike *prakṛti*, is changeless.

BRAHMAN'S CAUSALITY IN ADVAITA AND BHEDĀBHEDA VEDĀNTA

One of the primary differences between Bhedābheda Vedānta and its better-known rival is its doctrine of real transformation (*pariṇāmavāda*), as opposed to the doctrine of unreal or apparent manifestation (*vivartavāda*) maintained by the Advaita. According to the Bhedābhedavādins, the world of multiplicity that most normal people believe to be real is in fact just that: although there may be an underlying, unitary cause from which the universe evolves, the results of this evolution (tables, chairs, books, individual human beings, etc.) are also real. This is denied by Advaita Vedāntins.[38] Although Advaitins will admit that the world can be said to be conventionally real (*vyavahārasat*), they insist that the only absolutely real entity is Brahman, which is unitary, free from qualities, and the cause of this apparent phenomenal world.[39]

Providing these two different answers to the question of the reality of the phenomenal world takes the Advaitins and the Bhedābhedavādins in quite different directions and leads to two different sets of problems for each to resolve.[40] To illustrate some of Vijñānabhikṣu's philosophical tendencies, I wish to discuss just one such problem confronting the Bhedābhedavādins:

How can Brahman, which is universally accepted to be eternally unchanging, be the material cause (*upādānakāraṇa*) of the universe? This is a problem that many Advaitins claim they do not have to confront, since in their theory the world is merely an unreal manifestation (*vivarta*) of Brahman. Furthermore, Śaṅkara does not address this, implying that he simply did not consider it to be a problem. Although neither Śaṅkara nor Bhāskara mentions this issue, however, late medieval Advaitins and Bhedābhedavādins recognize it as a central problem.

Indian logicians name things like "clay" and "copper" as real-world examples of material causes. The potter (or instrumental cause, *nimittakāraṇa*) transforms the clay (the material cause) into its various forms: a pot, a plate, and so on. Although the forms (*rūpas*) of the clay have changed, the essence (*svarūpa*) of the clay, its clay-ness, remains the same throughout all of these transformations. Perhaps the most well known description of what it means to be a material cause comes from the dialogue between Śvetaketu and his father Āruṇi in *Ch. Up.* 6.1.4–5. This is the *locus classicus* of the doctrine that the effect preexists in the cause (*satkāryavāda*):

> "It is like this, son. By means of just one lump of clay one would perceive everything made of clay—the transformation is a verbal handle, a name—while the reality is just this: 'It's clay.'"
>
> "It is like this, son. By means of just one copper trinket one would perceive everything made of copper—the transformation is a verbal handle, a name—while the reality is just this: 'It's copper.'"[41]

Of course, the unstated subject of this metaphor is Brahman. Brahman is the material cause of the world, just as clay is the material cause of pots, plates, and other sorts of things. Although frequently cited, this passage itself is a source of controversy between the two different types of Satkāryavādins. Sāṃkhyas and realist Vedāntins such as Bhedābhedavādins belong to the school of Pariṇāmavāda, which maintains that the world is a real transformation (*pariṇāma*) of Brahman. Just as a lump of clay changes, undergoing a real transformation when it assumes the form of a pot, so does Brahman undergo some real change in form when it becomes the phenomenal world. However, because the clay's essence does not change, the lump of clay can also be described as being the same as the pot. For Pariṇāmavādins, the material cause and its effects are both different and non-different: different with regard to form, but non-different with regard to essence.[42] Advaita Vedāntins are usually described as subscribing to the other school of Satkāryavāda, called Vivartavāda.[43] On the interpretation of the Advaitin Vācaspati Miśra, for instance, Brahman undergoes no real transformation. Its apparent manifestation (*vivarta*) in the world has a merely verbal existence (*vācārambhaṇamātra*). Therefore, Brahman itself does not change in any way.

It seems clear that if the Bhedābhedavādins understand Brahman to be the material cause of the universe in the same way that clay is the material cause of a pot, this will involve some real change in form of Brahman itself. Bhāskara even uses the metaphor of milk changing into curds to describe Brahman's transformation into the world. On this model, Brahman's causality would be similar to the causality of the original, undifferentiated *prakṛti* of the Sāṃkhya school. The Sāṃkhya's cosmological dualism maintains that there are two eternal, fundamental principles, one the *puruṣa,* the other *prakṛti.* The difference between the two is that the *puruṣa* is eternal and unchanging (*kūṭasthanitya*), while *prakṛti* is changing, albeit nonetheless eternal in its changing form (*pariṇāminitya*). On the Sāṃkhya model, *prakṛti* begins in an undifferentiated, quiescent form, transforms into twenty-three other principles (*tattvas*) during the period of creation of the world, then returns to its original quiescent state after the world's dissolution.[44] One option for the Bhedābhedavādin would be to accept that Brahman is eternal yet changing, just like the Sāṃkhya *prakṛti.* However, this was generally not an option. In spite of the many differences among Vedāntins in their interpretations of the Upaniṣads, there seems to have been agreement that the Upaniṣadic statements asserting Brahman's eternality also assert its unchangeability. Since the rejection of Brahman as unchanging was not a possibility, the other available option was to reinterpret the precise nature of the causality of Brahman.

If Vedāntins were hesitant to reject the unchanging nature of Brahman, then rejection of Brahman as cause of the universe was even more of a problem. After all, the second aphorism of the *Brahmasūtras,* "From which there is the origin, etc., of this"(*BS* 1.1.2), is interpreted by the entire tradition to mean that Brahman is that "from which there is the origin" of this world (*jagat*): that is, Brahman is the cause of the world. In his commentary on the second sūtra, Vijñānabhikṣu attempts to resolve the problem of explaining an unchanging cause of the world by reinterpreting material causality to include what he calls "locus causality" (*adhiṣṭhānakāraṇatva*).[45] Vijñānabhikṣu makes his case by arguing that the term "material cause" (*upādānakāraṇa*), frequently used to describe Brahman, can be of two sorts. One sort is a changing cause (*vikārikāraṇa*), such as the example of the clay, which undergoes changes when it is transformed into various effects. However, Vijñānabhikṣu asserts that the term *upādānakāraṇa* can also refer to an unchanging cause (*avikārikāraṇa*), also known as a root cause (*mūlakāraṇa*) or a locus cause (*adhiṣṭhānakāraṇa*). By this he is not saying that the locus can be said to be a cause in a figurative, or secondary, sense. Rather, he insists that one of the primary meanings of "material cause" is "locus cause." To make this claim, he offers a definition of material causality that can apply equally to a changing cause or a locus cause: "The general definition of material cause is 'that which is a substratum, non-separate from its effect.'"[46] This allows Vijñānabhikṣu to claim that an unchanging locus such as Brahman is no less deserving of the appellation "cause" than a changing cause like the potter's clay. But what precisely does it mean to call something a "locus cause"?

Vijñānabhikṣu's technical definition of a locus cause is "that from which the [changeable] material cause is not separated, and by which the [changeable] material cause is fully supported."[47] To make this more tangible, Vijñānabhikṣu offers an example of one such locus cause from Sāṃkhya cosmology. According to the Sāṃkhyas, each of the five gross elements has its origin in a corresponding subtle element, which is too small for the human sense organ to perceive. But Vijñānabhikṣu suggests that for the subtle element of earth to successfully evolve into the gross element earth, water is necessary as a locus cause: "For example, at the time of world creation, there are minute parts of the earth, known as subtle elements and not separate from the water. These subtle elements change into the form of earth due to the support of water, so water is the locus cause of the gross element earth."[48]

In other words, Vijñānabhikṣu portrays this causal relation as having three terms: unchangeable locus cause, changeable cause, and effect. The changeable cause is both non-separate with the effect and also inheres in the effect (i.e., the stuff that the effect is made up of is the same as the stuff of the material cause). The locus cause, although non-separate (*avibhakta*) from both the changeable cause and the effect, does not inhere in either the changeable cause or the effect. Without the locus cause, no change can take place in the changeable cause, and in that sense the locus can itself be described as a cause. Nonetheless, the locus cause itself undergoes no change in form. The effect simply arises because of the presence of the locus cause, not because of any action taken by the locus cause. As we saw, this relationship between locus cause and changeable cause is verbally complicated by the fact that both can equally be called "material cause" (*upādānakāraṇa*). This has the potential for great confusion, especially since Vijñānabhikṣu commonly refers to a material cause without elaborating which type. But it also allows a great deal of interpretive flexibility. It allows Vijñānabhikṣu to make sense of apparently nonsensical passages that refer to something unchanging as a "cause," while still accepting that stock examples like clay and copper are also correctly described as material causes.

I suggested before that Vijñānabhikṣu's positing of a type of causality called locus causality was in order to solve a problem specific to Bhedābheda Vedanta and its theory of real transformation (*pariṇāmavāda*). However, the lines between the doctrines of *pariṇāmavāda* and *vivartavāda* are considerably blurrier than what is usually depicted in histories of Indian philosophy. First, evidence I cited in chapter 2 suggests that the development of the theory of unreal manifestation of Brahman was actually a gradual development out of the earlier theory of the real transformation of Brahman. Paul Hacker believes that the early Śaṅkara held a position on this question somewhere between the realist *pariṇāmavāda* of the author of the *Brahmasūtras* and the *vivartavāda* of the later Advaitic tradition. Srinivasa Rao has argued even more radically that the Śaṅkara of the *Brahmasūtrabhāṣya* does not regard the empirical world as *mithyā*, by implication placing Śaṅkara squarely in the camp of the *pariṇāmavādins*.[49] Further complicating matters, Vijñānabhikṣu claims that he himself is neither a *pariṇāmavādin* nor a *vivartavādin*.[50] This is because he understands *pariṇāmavādin* to mean one who believes that Brahman is a changeable material cause, precisely what he tries to avoid with his two-fold distinction of material causes. Nonetheless, it is clear that Vijñānabhikṣu's position comes out of the tradition of *pariṇāmavāda*, more widely construed, in which the world is a real effect of Brahman. And there is no ambiguity about Vijñānabhikṣu's vitriol toward the *vivartavāda* position of the later Advaitins.

In spite of his emphatic rejection of Advaitic views, however, Vijñānabhikṣu's concept of locus cause has some remarkable affinities with at least one of the conceptions of causality prevalent among Advaitins in the late medieval period. In this regard, he is much closer to his sixteenth-century Advaita contemporaries than to early Bhedābhedavādins such as Bhāskara, since these earlier Vedāntins did not appear to see any inherent contradiction in describing Brahman as material cause and therefore did not formulate any concept similar to locus causality.[51] By the late medieval period, it seems, consensus held that Brahman could not possibly be a material cause in the familiar sense without undergoing some change. Therefore, Advaitins, too, adopted a host of theories to sidestep this apparent aporia.

Appaya Dīkṣita's sixteenth-century catalogue of the various Advaita views, the *Siddhāntaleśasaṃgraha* (Brief Compendium of Doctrines), lists numerous opinions on the question of Brahman's causality. Typically, these later Advaitins saw ignorance (*avidyā*) or illusion (*māyā*) themselves as having some part in creating the world.[52] By reifying such terms and giving these entities autonomous causal power, they were likely quite far from the original position of their school's putative founder, Śaṅkara, with regard to the origin of the world. This was in part because Śaṅkara himself was silent or ambiguous on certain puzzling issues regarding Brahman's causality.[53] Therefore, these thinkers apportion the causal duties in various ways. Appaya Dīkṣita lists a few of these alternatives:

1. According to the author of the *Padārthatattvanirṇaya* [attributed to Ānandānubhava or Gaṅgāpurī Bhaṭṭāraka], both Brahman and illusion (*māyā*) are material causes. Brahman's being material cause is not just a technical term, in the sense of "locus of apparent manifestation (*vivarta*)." Brahman itself undergoes apparent manifestation, while illusion undergoes real transformation.
2. Some [unidentified] others say that both Brahman and illusion are material causes. But they say that being material cause simply means "having effects that are non-different from that cause." With respect to the world's existence, it is non-different from Brahman with regard to existence, and non-different from illusion with regard to insentience.
3. According to the author of the *Saṃkṣepaśarīraka* [Sarvajñātman], Brahman is the material cause. However, because it is unchanging, it cannot be a cause by itself. Therefore illusion (*māyā*) is a subordinate cause (*dvārakāraṇa*).
4. According to Vācaspati Miśra, Brahman alone is the material cause, and is apparently manifested into the form of the world because it is made an object by the illusion (*māyā*) situated in the self (*jīva*). Illusion is merely an assistant (*sahakārin*), not a subordinate cause (*dvārakāraṇa*).
5. According to the author of the *Siddhāntamuktāvalī* [Prakāśānanda], the power of illusion (*māyāśakti*) is the material cause, not Brahman. Brahman can only be described as material cause in a secondary sense, as it is the locus of illusion.[54]

This last suggestion is the view of Prakāśānanda, a late sixteenth-century Vedāntin who authored the *Vedāntasiddhāntamuktāvalī* (Pearl-String of Vedānta Doctrines).[55] He may or may not be the same person as the scholar of Advaita named Śrīpāda Prakāśānanda Sarasvatī, who is immortalized in a section of Caitanya's biography. There, Caitanya takes on a *sannyāsin* who is a leader of the Advaitin community in Varanasi and shows him the error of his ways for rejecting *bhakti*. Although the actual encounter is likely a later fabrication (Caitanya died in 1533, while Prakāśānanda probably lived in the second half of the century), it may offer evidence that Prakāśānanda was based in Varanasi, and that he was well known among both Advaitins and non-Advaitins.

Since Prakāśānanda was influential in sixteenth-century northern India and had numerous disciples, it is likely that Vijñānabhikṣu was aware of his views. So it is not surprising that Prakāśānanda's view that Brahman is the locus of the material cause, and not directly the cause of the world, has similarities with Vijñānabhikṣu's concept of locus cause (*adhiṣṭhānakāraṇa*). Prakāśānanda regards *māyā* as the direct material cause of world creation. He uses the same term for locus (*adhiṣṭhāna*) that Vijñānabhikṣu uses to refer to Brahman. However, he takes a slightly different tack than Vijñānabhikṣu. Vijñānabhikṣu habitually avoids appealing to figurative or metaphorical meanings of words unless there is absolutely no other way to make interpretive sense of the passage in question. We saw this previously in his rejection of the Advaitins' figurative interpretations of Upaniṣadic passages expressing non-difference, as well as in his rejection of Śaṅkara's figurative interpretation of the word "part" in *BS* 2.3.43. Unlike Prakāśānanda, Vijñānabhikṣu argues that the true definition of material cause, "that which is a substratum, non-separate from its effect," is broad enough to include a locus. Hence there is no need to appeal to figurative usage, and referring to a "locus cause" itself presents no contradictions. Prakāśānanda, however, freely admits to using figurative interpretation. He believes that strictly speaking, Brahman is not a cause at all. But we can make sense of Bādarāyaṇa's clear statement in *BS* 1.1.2 that Brahman is cause of the world by understanding that a locus can be understood as a material cause (*upādāna*) in a figurative sense. Prakāśānanda sees this as the best way to reconcile scriptural passages that seem to disagree about the world's causality:

> It is not true that there is a contradiction between the two sets of scriptural passages, one that declares ignorance to be the cause of the world and the other that declares Brahman to be cause of the world:

> 38. Brahman is said to be cause of the world only out of ignorance, since Brahman has nothing to do with causality. Brahman is only declared to be "cause" because it is the locus.
>
> Ignorance, which is indescribable and beginningless, is cause of the world, which is indescribable and established by means of being visible, and so on. Brahman is not its cause. For Brahman, which is changeless, is neither cause nor effect, as stated by the scriptural passage, "This Brahman has no cause, no effect, no interior, no exterior. This self is the omniscient Brahman."[56] So how is it that in the scripture, Brahman is widely declared to be the cause of the world? By being the locus of the cause of the world, Brahman is the cause in a figurative sense.[57]

The most significant difference between Vijñānabhikṣu and Prakāśānanda is in their positions concerning the reality or unreality of the world. Vijñānabhikṣu believes that the world is the real effect of Brahman. Prakāśānanda is extreme even among Advaitins in his defense of the doctrine of *dṛṣṭisṛṣṭivāda*—that the existence of objects is nothing more than their perception.[58] In this, he is at odds with the two largest sub-schools in the later Advaita tradition, the Bhāmatī and Vivaraṇa, and is closer to Yogācāra Buddhism.[59] While mainstream Advaitins such as Vācaspati Miśra understand the phenomenal world to have some sort of temporary independent existence that sets it apart from purely subjective cognitive mistakes like hallucinations, Prakāśānanda denies this. In so doing, he reduces the Advaitins' normal threefold ontological division to two, making the Vedantic technical term "indescribable" (*anirvacanīya*) synonymous with "completely unreal" (*tuccha*).[60] More than most others, Prakāśānanda deserves the appellation "crypto-Buddhist" (*pracchannabauddha*) that Vijñānabhikṣu indiscriminately applies to all Advaitins. Prakāśānanda's thought illustrates a general historical trend in Advaita philosophy itself, which begins in Śaṅkara's earliest works with a view close to the realism of the Bhedābheda, moves on to a position in the works of Vācaspati and Prakāśātman in which the world is phenomenally real although ultimately unreal, and then with Prakāśānanda's thought in the late medieval period becomes thoroughly illusionistic in its outlook.

In spite of the thoroughgoing illusionism of Prakāśānanda on the one hand and Vijñānabhikṣu's realism on the other, both thinkers saw a fundamental contradiction in the concept of a "changeless material cause." This contradiction remains, regardless of whether the effect of such a cause is real or illusory. While recognized as a problem by many medieval Advaitins, however, some Advaita apologists claim that there is no problem precisely because the effect of Brahman is unreal. One of the most common ways Advaita apologists of the Bhāmatī school attempt to defend the possibility of Brahman being a cause while nonetheless being unchanging is to take the position that Brahman does not undergo any real change, only apparent change. That is because the world is ultimately unreal (*mithyā*). To the extent that it undergoes any change whatsoever, that is only change on a phenomenal or conventional (*vyāvahārika*) level. Because its effect is itself ultimately unreal, therefore on the ultimate level Brahman is not really a cause and hence undergoes no change. But this argument fails to distinguish between two separate statements regarding a cause and its effect:

S1. *X* is the cause of the unreal effect *Y*.
S2. *X* appears to be, but is not the real cause of the effect *Y*.

What we actually have in the case of a real Brahman as the cause of an unreal world is S1. In this statement, Brahman really is the cause, although its effect is merely apparent. Take as an example an illusionist who saws his assistant in half. He is the cause of the appearance that the assistant is sawed in half; without his activity, the assistant would not appear to be sawed into two separate parts. Although the state of the assistant is illusory, the illusionist is the real cause of such an illusory state. This is clearly a different situation from S2, where *X* is not the real cause of the effect *Y*. One example of S2 would be a man who believes that the religious rites he performs before dawn each morning cause the sun to come up. Whether the sun's rising is illusory or real is irrelevant (if we like, we can call it illusory, insofar as the earth revolves around the sun, and not vice versa); the important thing here is that there is no real relation of cause and effect between his morning prayers and the sun's rising.

Faced with S2, the question inevitably arises: If *X* is not the real cause of *Y*, then what is *Y*'s cause? It is axiomatic that every effect must have a corresponding cause. In the specific context of Advaita philosophy: if Brahman is not really the cause of the world, then what is? Mere appearances, too, must have their causes. Otherwise the world would not exist in any form, whether real (as Bhedābhedavādins hold) or unreal (*mithyā*, as mainstream Advaitins hold). This is where the later Advaitins' talk of a separate cause, *māyā* or *avidyā*, comes into play. And what is the cause of illusion? Late medieval Advaitins hold that, like Brahman, illusion is not an effect—it is beginningless (*anādi*).[61] Therefore, also like Brahman, it itself has no other cause. Without positing some other entity that plays an important part in world-creation, Brahman would undergo change.

BHEDĀBHEDA AND THE UNITY OF PHILOSOPHIES

Although Vijñānabhikṣu is a self-described Bhedābhedavāda Vedāntin in his earliest works, he is eager to show his familiarity with the details of the other systems of thought that were prevalent in late medieval North India. His involvement with the Naiyāyikas is generally one of appropriating logical concepts and terminology that he believed would allow him to present his own philosophy more rigorously or persuasively. There is also an apologetic function in his use of Navya-Nyāya concepts, since by "translating" Bhedābheda Vedānta into a terminology that Naiyāyikas can understand, he hopes to show the viability of a philosophical tradition that by the late medieval period had been savaged by Advaita, Viśiṣṭādvaita, and Dvaita polemics. Vijñānabhikṣu shows his familiarity with Advaita, the other dominant philosophical school, primarily through constant critiques of its teachings. But I have shown that, just as in the case of the Nyāya, he is also open to taking concepts that he finds in Advaita works (like Brahman as locus, *adhiṣṭhāna*), and recontextualizing them for use in a realist philosophical setting. In some ways, Vijñānabhikṣu's general worldview is actually closer to sixteenth-century Advaitins than it is to eighth-century Bhedābhedavādins in spite of his shared doctrinal affiliation with the latter. He, like other late medieval Vedāntins, sees the changelessness of Brahman, the cause of the world, as a problem that needs to be explained. Śaṅkara and Bhāskara did not, perhaps because for them, "changelessness" simply meant changelessness of essence, not changelessness of external form.[62] Vijñānabhikṣu, Prakāśānanda, and their contemporaries do not understand it in this way.

Another similarity between Vijñānabhikṣu and his sixteenth-century Advaitin opponents is a more tolerant attitude toward non-Vedāntic schools, most notably Sāṃkhya and Yoga. Vedāntins in the eighth century spent a great deal of energy critiquing Sāṃkhya and Yoga, particularly the notion of *prakṛti*. Bhāskara was just as concerned as Śaṅkara with defeating these philosophical enemies, who appear to have been a dominant school at the time.[63] The early Vedāntic commentators sought to show that Sāṃkhya had no basis whatsoever in logical inference or revealed scripture (*śruti*). This was not just a denial of Sāṃkhya's claim that primordial *prakṛti* was insentient and uncreated but also included the rejection of apparently more benign Sāṃkhya teachings, such as the theory of the three *guṇas*.[64]

By the sixteenth century, Sāṃkhya had ceased to be an independent intellectual force to rival the Vedānta. In his own commentary on the *Sāṃkhyasūtras*, Vijñānabhikṣu describes it as a very old school, "devoured by the sun of time," and sees his project as a rehabilitation of Sāṃkhya.[65] Yet while it had virtually ceased to exist at all as an independent school, it triumphed in a different way: its influence had permeated many different philosophical traditions and texts. So, for instance, the term *prakṛti* in medieval Advaita becomes accepted as a synonym for *māyā*. As long as it is understood that *prakṛti* is not ultimately real, Advaitins see no contradiction in adopting the notion of a *prakṛti* divided into three *guṇas*. Medieval Advaitins begin to see Sāṃkhya and Yoga as valuable and complementary teachings to Vedānta. In the context of medieval Vedānta, Vijñānabhikṣu's acceptance of Sāṃkhya teachings on a conventional (*vyāvahārika*) level in his commentary on the *Brahmasūtras* is not at all surprising. But Vijñānabhikṣu goes further than that. In his post-Vedāntic works, he ceases to identify himself exclusively as a Vedāntin and ambitiously attempts to show the fundamental unity among the apparent differences of the Vedānta, Sāṃkhya, and Yoga schools. In chapter 4, I turn to his complicated relationship with Sāṃkhya and Yoga traditions, along with the tangled history of God in Sāṃkhya and Yoga.

[4] A HISTORY OF GOD IN SĀṂKHYA AND YOGA

SĀṂKHYA: AN ATHEIST PHILOSOPHY?

Although Vijñānabhikṣu's works on Sāṃkhya and Yoga have earned him most of his fame in the modern period, they have also been the objects of some controversy. This ambivalence is encapsulated in the Indologist Richard Garbe's relationship to Vijñānabhikṣu's commentary on the *Sāṃkhyasūtras,* the *Sāṃkhyapravacanabhāṣya.* Garbe was almost single-handedly responsible for the notoriety of this work, as it was he who edited the Sanskrit text and first translated it. Yet Garbe considered the text to be an inauthentic expression of the Sāṃkhya philosophy in several ways. The most important of Vijñānabhikṣu's divergences from the true Sāṃkhya doctrine was his affirmation of God's existence, in spite of the *Sāṃkhyasūtras*' clear rejection of God. Garbe writes: "In order to bridge over the chasm between the Sāṃkhya system and his own theism (which he is pleased to style Vedāntic), Vijñānabhikṣu resorts to the strangest means to do away with one of the fundamental doctrines of the genuine Sāṃkhya, which is the denial of God."[1] But for Garbe, Vijñānabhikṣu also fails as a representative of Vedānta philosophy. Demonstrating a bias in favor of the Advaitic interpretation of the Upaniṣads, Garbe writes of Vijñānabhikṣu:

> Some kindred spirit had already identified the *māyā* of the Vedānta with the *prakṛti* of the Sāṃkhya, namely in the Śvetāśvatara Upaniṣad, 4.10; and accordingly our commentator does not scruple to make the most of this identification as a scriptural one; and repeats in divers places of his work . . . the explanation that by *māyā* in Scripture is meant naught else than real matter.

> In view of all of this we can hardly be surprised to find that Vijñānabhikṣu mixes up many other heterogeneous matters, and even quite effaces the individuality of the several philosophical systems. . . . Nevertheless in spite of all of the false assumptions and the errors of which Vijñānabhikṣu is undoubtedly guilty, his commentary on the Sāṃkhya Sūtras must be declared to be not only the fullest source that we have for a knowledge of the Sāṃkhya system, but also one of the most important of such sources.[2]

This mixing up of heterogeneous matters, which is frequently given the name "syncretism," is ultimately what led Indologists to label Vijñānabhikṣu as an unreliable representative of his own cultural heritage. Yet Garbe's statement contains a number of unwarranted assumptions about the history of Indian philosophy. The most obvious of these is a barely veiled hostility toward the realist schools of Vedānta philosophy. As I suggested in the preceding chapters, such an attitude is based primarily on the supremacy and antiquity of the Advaita school in the Orientalist imagination. However, a preponderance of historical evidence identifies the realist schools as older than Advaitic antirealism. Therefore, if one wishes to define the authentic Vedānta as the school closest to the original views of the *Brahmasūtras*' author, then realism, and not idealism, wins out. Even within the Advaita school, there are a variety of views falling at different points on the realist/idealist spectrum. At one end are doctrines such as the extreme illusionism of the sixteenth-century Advaitin Prakāśānanda; at the other are the realist or nearly realist positions expressed in the early works of Śaṅkara.

One assumption in Garbe's statement that has received less attention is that the Sāṃkhya school is unambiguously atheistic in its outlook, and hence therefore Vijñānabhikṣu's views are illegitimate. This assumption is less obviously problematic only because the conventional wisdom expressed by Garbe in the late nineteenth century is still the conventional wisdom in the early twenty-first. Yet it, too, is based on oversimplifications and on the arbitrary privileging of certain "classical" texts over others that Indologists have not deemed fit to include in the Sāṃkhya canon. This conventional wisdom has been repeated again and again in the secondary literature without critical scrutiny or crosschecking of the Sanskrit texts themselves. Therefore, before embarking on an analysis of Vijñānabhikṣu's argumentative strategies in his Sāṃkhya works, it is necessary to provide an overview of Sāṃkhya history, especially vis-à-vis the question of the existence of God.

THEISM IN EARLY SĀṂKHYA AND THE PURĀṆAS

Although philosophers typically begin their accounts of Sāṃkhya with the "classical" Sāṃkhya of Īśvarakṛṣṇa's *Sāṃkhyakārikā* (fourth to fifth century CE), when talking about the question of God in Sāṃkhya, it is necessary to go back to the very beginning, to the earliest occurrences of the word *sāṃkhya* and the allusions to Sāṃkhya concepts in the Upaniṣads, *Arthaśāstra*, and *Mahābhārata*.[3] For instance, the *Śvetāśvatara Upaniṣad* (fourth to second century BCE) makes statements that, although allegorical, almost certainly refer to Sāṃkhya concepts like *prakṛti, puruṣa,* and the three *guṇas:*

> One [unborn] billy goat, delighting, lies with one [unborn] she-goat, who is colored red, white, and black, and who gives birth to many offspring with the same colors. Another [unborn] billy goat leaves her after she has taken enjoyment.[4]

Although Sāṃkhya authors, unlike their Vedāntic counterparts, do not habitually argue on the basis of scriptural authority, this is the passage that comes closest to the status of a Sāṃkhya "great statement" (*mahāvākya*). It appears in the benedictory verses to Vācaspati Miśra's *Sāṃkhyatattvakaumudī* and three times in Vijñānabhikṣu's *Sāṃkhyapravacanabhāṣya*. It also seems to have been used by the Sāṃkhyas in defense of their own doctrines in the eighth century CE and earlier. Śaṅkara attributes such a scripturally based argument to a Sāṃkhya adversary and spends a fair amount of time arguing that the "[unborn] she-goat" (*ajā*) does not refer to *prakṛti* and that her three colors do not refer to the three *guṇas*.[5] The *Śvetāśvatara Upaniṣad* also contains the earliest mention of the name Kapila, the mythical founder of the Sāṃkhya school.[6] As with the other apparent references to Sāṃkhya in this Upaniṣad, Śaṅkara must argue this allusion away, by saying that the text in fact refers to Vāsudeva, who is sometimes called Kapila.[7] Śaṅkara is not alone in making these arguments. Sāṃkhya seems to have been one of the principal adversaries of the early Vedānta, and Bhāskara makes similar arguments to counter what were apparently Sāṃkhya's appeals to scriptural authority.[8] It is quite likely that earlier Vedāntic commentators did the same, as refutations of Sāṃkhya claims are written into the *Brahmasūtras* themselves.[9]

What is most notable about these frequent allusions to what are now known as distinctively Sāṃkhya concepts, however, is their general context in the *Śvetāśvatara Upaniṣad.* Besides being known as a heavily Sāṃkhya-influenced Upaniṣad, it is also one of the most theistic. This Upaniṣad makes frequent reference to a powerful personal deity, known by terms such as Lord (*īśa*), God (*deva*), Rudra, and Hara. Nor are references to a personal deity kept separate in the text from allusions to Sāṃkhya concepts—on the contrary, this Upaniṣad integrates these Sāṃkhya concepts with the idea of a powerful God.[10] The same is the case for the other main source for early Sāṃkhya, the *Mahābhārata.* The *Mokṣadharma Parvan* and the *Bhagavad Gītā* sections of this epic contain frequent allusions to Sāṃkhya, but yet they are thoroughly theistic. It is a peculiar position to conclude from this that the Sāṃkhya taught in the Upaniṣads and the epics are therefore confused or corrupted. Nonetheless, this claim is frequently made by historians of philosophy writing about this early phase of Sāṃkhya.[11] In making this claim, they project back from a later phase of (allegedly) atheistic Sāṃkhya to conclude that earlier Sāṃkhya is somehow impure. Often the assumption is that there existed a separate atheistic school of Sāṃkhya at a very early period. Although no writings survive from this school, some of its basic teachings somehow found their way into texts like the Upaniṣads and the epics, where they were thoroughly confused and compromised by theism. Yet there is absolutely no historical or textual evidence to support such a claim; indeed, there is some fairly strong evidence to the contrary. It is more likely that to the extent Sāṃkhya existed at all in the Upaniṣadic and epic periods, it existed as part of a wider theistic worldview.

Often the position that there was an early school of purely atheistic Sāṃkhya is argued on philosophical grounds. Commentators frequently allege that God is *logically* superfluous in the Sāṃkhya system.[12] For God has nothing to do in the Sāṃkhya cosmology. He is not needed to effect the union of *prakṛti* and *puruṣa,* since the attraction between the two is automatic, like the attraction between a magnet and iron. The Sāṃkhya system is a purely mechanistic one, and the superfluity of God is attested to by his uncomfortable situation in Patañjali's *Yogasūtras.* There the existence of God is taught, but as a God who has little positive role to play other than to be an object of devotion and meditative contemplation. Surely, proponents of this picture of the early Sāṃkhya suggest, the introduction of God in the Sāṃkhya of the Upaniṣads and epics, and in the school of Yoga philosophy, is merely an attempt to appeal to popular prejudices and not supported philosophically in any way.

This argument of the logical superfluity of God in Sāṃkhya also rests on certain assumptions that seem self-evident only due to the historical acceptance of authentic Sāṃkhya as atheistic by modern scholars. Another compelling philosophical argument is that *prakṛti* and *puruṣa* themselves must have some superintendent (*adhiṣṭhātṛ*), an intelligent being, to set their union in motion. This is because before the union of these two entities, *prakṛti* exists in a state of total equilibrium, in which the three *guṇas* are all present in equal measure. It is in a state of complete stasis, and without some external agent to set it into motion to begin its series of transformations, such a union of these two entities would be impossible. *Puruṣa* cannot effect this change because it is eternally inactive, and *prakṛti* cannot because it is inactive in its primordial state. This is not, of course, the position of the *Yogasūtras,* in which God has no role in the creation of the world. But it is precisely this view that is enunciated in Purāṇic Sāṃkhya, as in *Viṣṇu Purāṇa* 1.2.29: "Having entered into *prakṛti* and *puruṣa* by his own desire, at the time of creation Hari shakes the manifest and unmanifest."[13] We can put this argument in terms of the metaphor of the magnet and iron: both magnet and iron require a third party to set their attraction into motion. A piece of iron at one end of the room and a magnet at the other end do not have any effect on one another; only when they are brought into proximity by some external force can the magnet attract the piece of iron.

This argument for the necessity of God in Sāṃkhya would have seemed even more compelling, given the generally theistic environment in which these texts were composed.[14] One of the reasons that modern commentators have been so insistent on the atheism of the true Sāṃkhya school is that for them, Sāṃkhya functions as something like an early Indian analogue to Darwin's theory of evolution. For Garbe, Sāṃkhya is proof that even in the earliest times of Indian philosophical speculation, rigorous and tough-minded philosophies coexisted with the more otherworldly focus of schools such as Advaita Vedānta. Marxist historians, such as Debiprasad Chattopadhyaya, have also given attention to Sāṃkhya, along with Cārvāka and Buddhist philosophies, in order to argue for a thriving atheist tradition in ancient India.[15] However, evidence for the atheism of the earliest Sāṃkhya (sometimes called "proto-Sāṃkhya" in order to contrast with the mature, atheistic form of "classical Sāṃkhya") is virtually nonexistent.[16]

Besides these frequent allusions to Sāṃkhya concepts in the Upaniṣads and in the *Mahābhārata,* we also find the terms *sāṃkhya* and *yoga* themselves, beginning with the *Śvetāśvatara Upaniṣad* and with great frequency in the epic literature. The two terms also occur in Kauṭilya's *Arthaśāstra,* verse 1.2, where Sāṃkhya, Yoga, and Lokāyata are described as constituting "investigation" (*anvīkṣikī*).[17] The question, therefore, is not whether these terms were used but, rather, what the meanings of the terms *sāṃkhya* and *yoga* were in the Upaniṣads and the epics. Another puzzle for translators has been the precise meaning of the compound word *sāṃkhyayoga* in preclassical Sāṃkhya, which occurs in the well-known passages of *Śvet. Up.* 6.13 and *BhG* 5.4.[18] The context of the word in the *Bhagavad Gītā* indicates that it should be understood as a *dvandva* compound, meaning "Sāṃkhya and Yoga." And based on the frequent use of the two terms to contrast with each other in the *Bhagavad Gītā*, neither of these two terms denoted a specific system of philosophy. Keeping with the general theme of renunciation versus action that is the subject of most of the *Bhagavad Gītā*, one common interpretation is that the terms *sāṃkhya* and *yoga* correspond with the way of knowledge and the way of action, respectively.[19] This is the usage in *BhG* 3.3, for instance: "I taught in ancient times that in this world there is a two-fold foundation: Of the Sāṃkhyas it is the *yoga* of knowledge (*jñānayoga*), and of the Yogins it is the *yoga* of action (*karmayoga*)."[20] There is no hint here that *yoga* refers to some settled set of philosophical doctrines. Furthermore, *sāṃkhya* does not seem to correspond to any particular philosophy but, rather, to any type of contemplation that can bring about salvation.[21] There are a great diversity of meanings of the words *sāṃkhya* and *yoga* in the epic, and even variation within specific sections.[22] But it is clear that nowhere in the *Bhagavad Gītā* are the two terms *sāṃkhya* and *yoga* understood in the way that they were generally understood by the medievals and moderns: Sāṃkhya as a particular philosophical system that teaches atheism and Yoga as a different but closely related system that teaches the existence of God.

To complicate matters further, there is an enigmatic occurrence of the two terms in Vātsyāyana's (fifth century CE) commentary on the *Nyāyasūtras* of Gautama. In his commentary on sūtra 1.1.29, Vātsyāyana cites some examples of the philosophical conclusions (*siddhāntas*) of various schools. According to him, the Sāṃkhyas believe that "the non-existent does not come into being; the existent cannot be destroyed; conscious souls are incapable of modification; there can be modification only in body, sense-organs, mind, objects of cognition, and in the causes of all these."[23] These four conclusions are characteristic of both Īśvarakṛṣṇa's *Sāṃkhyakārikā* and of Patañjali's *Yogasūtras*. However, Vātsyāyana goes on to list four conclusions of those whom he calls the "Yogas": "The creation of the world is due to the *karman,* etc., of the *jīva;* defects and activity are the causes of *karman;* conscious souls are qualified by their respective attributes; the non-existent comes into being and that which has come into being ceases to exist."[24] These four doctrines are not accepted by Patañjali. Furthermore, they are contrary to the most fundamental views of Sāṃkhya and Yoga—for instance, the doctrine of *satkāryavāda* is contradicted by the fourth conclusion, that "the non-existent comes into being and that which has come into being ceases to exist." In short, the four views described by Vātsyāyana as belonging to the "Yogas" are apparently the doctrines of Nyāya-Vaiśeṣika.[25]

The evidence from the *Mahābhārata* and the *Nyāyabhāṣya* of Vātsyāyana should introduce some doubt among those who would wish to understand the words *sāṃkhya* and *yoga* in *Śvet. Up.* 6.13 and Kauṭilya's *Arthaśāstra* 1.2.10 as referring to what are later known as Sāṃkhya and Yoga. Johannes Bronkhorst suggests that the first usage of the word *yoga* as referring to Patañjali's philosophy is not until Śaṅkara's *Brahmasūtrabhāṣya* (eighth century). Even after this, *pātañjaladarśana* and *seśvarasāṃkhya* were more common epithets for his system.[26] Therefore, when Kauṭilya writes in *Arthaśāstra* 1.2.10 that "investigation" (*anvīkṣikī*) is found primarily in the three systems Sāṃkhya, Yoga, and Lokāyata, it is quite unlikely that he understood Sāṃkhya and Yoga to refer to the systems of Kapila and Patañjali, respectively. It is much more likely, although by no means certain, that the *sāṃkhya* of the *Arthaśāstra* refers to some form of theistic Sāṃkhya. The word *yoga,* on the other hand, would have very likely referred to either Nyāya or Vaiśeṣika or both. Bronkhorst argues that "if Nyāya and Vaiśeṣika existed when this sentence was written, they would belong in the list. It is therefore wise to assume that they—or one of them—are represented by the word 'Yoga', rather than that our 'Yoga system' is meant."[27]

In light of these other occurrences, the usage of *sāṃkhyayoga* at *Śvet. Up.* 6.13 is more comprehensible: "Having known that cause, which is attainable by means of *sāṃkhyayoga,* as God, he is freed from all fetters." It should be understood more along the lines of the usage of *sāṃkhya* and *yoga* in the *Bhagavad Gītā* than their usage in the *Nyāyabhāṣya* of Vātsyāyana. Because the *Śvetāśvatara Upaniṣad*'s date of composition is from six hundred to one thousand years before the *Nyāyabhāṣya,* it is likely that the terms *sāṃkhya* and *yoga* did not refer to specific doctrinal systems but, instead, to contemplation and practice, respectively. The compound word at *Śvet. Up.* 6.13 could either be a *dvandva,* "philosophical investigation and spiritual praxis," or a *karmadhāraya*, "the spiritual praxis that is philosophical investigation." The first interpretation is favored by the tradition (e.g., Śaṅkara's commentary on the *Śvetāśvatara Upaniṣad*).[28]

Although many scholars nowadays agree that the early, prephilosophical tradition of Sāṃkhya, sometimes called "proto-Sāṃkhya," is generally theistic in its outlook, they claim that that all changes as Sāṃkhya matures as a philosophical doctrine, particularly in the *Sāṃkhyakārikā* of Īśvarakṛṣṇa. Sāṃkhya commentators treat three texts as fundamental: the *Sāṃkhyakārikā*, the *Tattvasamāsasūtras* (ascribed to Kapila), and the *Sāṃkhyasūtras* (also attributed to Kapila). The two sūtra texts are quite late, perhaps as late as the fourteenth century, although both texts seem to include some sūtras from earlier periods.[29] For that reason, most modern scholars take the *Sāṃkhyakārikā* (fourth to fifth century CE) to be the authoritative expression of the Sāṃkhya philosophy in its mature form. The *Sāṃkhyakārikā* and the *Tattvasamāsasūtras* make no mention of God (*īśvara*), while they do enumerate the twenty-five principles (*tattvas*), including *puruṣa*, *prakṛti*, and *prakṛti*'s twenty-three evolutes. Unlike the other two texts, the *Sāṃkhyasūtras* explicitly reject God. In *SS* 5.10–12, the author lists each of the three means of valid knowledge (*pramāṇas*) accepted by the Sāṃkhya school and shows that none can establish the existence of God. At *SS* 5.2–9, he advances a number of positive arguments refuting the possibility of the existence of God. On the basis of these three texts, most modern scholars have claimed that beginning with the *Sāṃkhyakārikā*, Sāṃkhya was a thoroughly atheistic school of thought.

Historians of philosophy interested in Sāṃkhya have tended to focus on the *Sāṃkhyakārikā*, *Tattvasamāsasūtras*, and *Sāṃkhyasūtras*. But the identification of these three texts as the authentic representatives of the Sāṃkhya school leaves out an enormous body of literature that claims to represent Sāṃkhya teachings. Most of these works are theistic in their outlook. By far the most influential of these are the Purāṇas, whose Sāṃkhya influences are widely acknowledged, if seldom taken seriously as philosophical works in their own right.[30] Much of the bias against the Purāṇas by Western scholars of Indian philosophy seems to be motivated by the idea that the Purāṇas are mythological or literary texts and therefore are not philosophically rigorous. This idea of the separation between poetry and philosophy seems to be an unwarranted influence from the Greek tradition on Western Indologists—it is demonstrably absent among premodern Indian thinkers. Authors of commentaries on Sāṃkhya texts and the texts of other philosophical schools readily introduce material from Purāṇic sources to elucidate the teachings of the philosophical text at hand, and in many cases quote from these Purāṇas themselves to lend scriptural support to their arguments. The *Bhāgavata Purāṇa* (tenth century), the most influential of all Purāṇas, has been the object of dozens of commentaries by philosophical authors and is treated by some Vedāntic schools, such as the followers of Caitanya, as an authority on a par with the Vedas themselves.

The *Bhāgavata Purāṇa* includes a lengthy section that purports to be an account of Kapila, the founder of the Sāṃkhya school, teaching its doctrines to his mother Devahūti.[31] Kapila himself is depicted as an incarnation of Nārāyaṇa and teaches a form of Sāṃkhya that is integrated both with the practice of *bhakti* and with a Vedāntic conception of Brahman. However, as Dasgupta has pointed out, the Vedāntic teachings presented in the Purāṇas are generally not compatible with the teachings of Śaṅkara and, instead, have more in common with Rāmānuja and Vijñānabhikṣu. He contrasts to the "semi-realistic interpretation" of the Upaniṣads that is found in the earliest Purāṇas with Śaṅkara's monism and suggests that it is the former that presents "the oldest outlook of the philosophy of the Upaniṣads and the *Brahma-sūtra*."[32] It should therefore not be surprising that Advaita Vedāntins less frequently quote the Purāṇas. For Vedāntins of other affiliations, however, the Purāṇas stand side by side with the *Bhagavad Gītā* as the most important *smṛti* texts.

Whatever we might make of the alleged lack of logical rigor of the Purāṇas, the historian of Indian philosophy can ignore Purāṇic Sāṃkhya only at his or her peril. Part of the dismissal of the Purāṇas by earlier scholars probably had something to do with their apparent disagreement with, and irrelevance to, the doctrines of the Advaita Vedānta school. Yet, given the strong influence of the Purāṇas on numerous philosophical authors, a complete historical account of the origins and development of the different philosophical systems requires that we take the Purāṇas into account. Vijñānabhikṣu himself wrote a commentary on the *Īśvaragītā* section of the *Kūrma Purāṇa* and believed that commenting on this text was tantamount to commenting on the *Bhagavad Gītā* itself. As I discuss in chapter 5, the techniques that Vijñānabhikṣu uses in his attempt to unify the apparently contradictory schools of *āstika* philosophy have much of their basis in portrayals of doctrinal conflict and resolution in Purāṇas such as the *Viṣṇu Purāṇa*.

ATHEISM AND THEISM IN "CLASSICAL" SĀṂKHYA

Although exponents of the view that the authentic Sāṃkhya is atheistic can freely admit that Purāṇic Sāṃkhya is theistic simply by saying that it represents a popularized or debased form of the real doctrines, more serious problems arise when the commentaries on the *Sāṃkhyakārikā* are read carefully. Johannes Bronkhorst has argued that all of the pre-second-millennium commentaries on the *Sāṃkhyakārikā* accept the existence of God (*īśvara*).[33] Although this does not necessarily imply that Īśvarakṛṣṇa himself accepted the existence of God, it nonetheless almost completely overturns the conventional wisdom regarding the history of the Sāṃkhya school. If true, it would mean that the majority of Sāṃkhya authors historically have been theistic, and only a few relatively late texts, like the *Sāṃkhyasūtras,* can be regarded as unambiguously atheistic in outlook.

Bronkhorst bases his argument for the theism of the Sāṃkhya school in the first millennium on a number of commentaries on the *Sāṃkhyakārikā:* primarily the *Yuktidīpikā,* but also the *Māṭharavṛtti* and *Gauḍapādabhāṣya.* All of these texts allow for the existence of some form of God (*īśvara*). However, this seems to have been overlooked by almost all modern scholars of Sāṃkhya because of the understated way that these texts talk about God. The *Yuktidīpikā,* apparently the oldest commentary on the *Sāṃkhyakārikā,* has frequently been mistaken as arguing an atheistic position. This interpretation is based on an inattentive reading of the text. The anonymous author of the *Yuktidīpikā* spends significant time arguing against the view that the world was created by God, a position he attributes to the Pāśupatas and Vaiśeṣikas.[34] However, close inspection of the text reveals that the author of the *Yuktidīpikā* does believe in some sort of God. In one passage, for instance, a theistic opponent makes the mistake of believing that the Sāṃkhya rejects God entirely. To this, the *Yuktidīpikā*'s author responds that Sāṃkhyas do accept the existence of God:

> Opponent: Furthermore, scripture teaches that he possesses a form, "wearing a skin," "Pināka bow in hand," "having a drawn bow," "black-crested," etc. If this is accepted, your view is refuted. From the language of the scriptures, a God who possesses a form is accepted, and therefore his existence is established. For it is impossible for a nonexistent thing to possess a form.

> Reply: This, too, is mistaken, since you do not understand our intended meaning. We do not completely reject the particular power of the Lord, since he assumes a majestic body and so forth. Our intended meaning is just that there is no being who is different from *prakṛti* and *puruṣa* and who is the instigator of these two, as you claim. Therefore, your view is refuted. The conjunction between *prakṛti* and *puruṣa* is not instigated by another being.[35]

The view expressed here seems similar to the view of Patañjali's *Yogasūtras.* God exists, but he does not have any part in the creation of the world. Furthermore, the *Yuktidīpikā*'s author clarifies that there is no need to posit a twenty-sixth principle over and above *prakṛti* and *puruṣa.* As in the *Yogasūtras,* God is a special *puruṣa,* one distinct from ordinary *puruṣas* in certain ways but nonetheless, like those *puruṣas,* is constituted by pure awareness. As Patañjali defines God in *YS* 1.24, he is a "special *puruṣa,* unaffected by defilements, actions, the results of actions, and unconscious traces."[36] According to the *Yuktidīpikā,* God is also capable of being embodied in some form, in the aforementioned "majestic body," and also quite possibly in bodies of supreme seers like Kapila.[37] This would explain why it is not necessary for the *Sāṃkhyakārikā* and the *Tattvasamāsasūtras* to describe a twenty-sixth principle named God (*īśvara*).

If the views of the *Yuktidīpikā* regarding God were an anomaly among commentaries on the *Sāṃkhyakārikā,* it might be possible to dismiss the text as influenced by the foreign views of another philosophical school, the Yoga school. However, acceptance of the existence of God was the rule rather than the exception among commentaries on the *Sāṃkhyakārikā* in the first millennium CE. Two other commentaries, the *Gauḍapādabhāṣya* and *Māṭharavṛtti,* also take for granted the existence of God in the Sāṃkhya system. Furthermore, they do so by drawing even more explicitly on the notion of God found in Patañjali. Both texts, in the context of discussing the purity of the intellect (*buddhi*) described in *SK* 23, explicitly draw on the lists at *YS* 2.30 and 2.32 where the abstentions (*yamas*) and observances (*niyamas*) are enumerated. And like the *Yogasūtras,* both list devotion to God (*īśvarapraṇidhāna*) among the observances. Both texts also explicitly deny the possibility that God himself could have created the world. According to the *Gauḍapādabhāṣya,* "God is free of the *guṇas,* and therefore it does not make sense that the world, which is made up of the *guṇas,* could be created by him."[38]

The most influential of all of the first-millennium commentaries on the *Sāṃkhyakārikā* is undoubtedly the *Tattvakaumudī* of Vācaspati Miśra (late tenth century). Like the *Sāṃkhyakārikā* itself, Vācaspati's commentary does not explicitly mention God, and hence neither affirms nor denies his existence. However, the *Tattvakaumudī* does implicitly accept God. Like the *Gauḍapādabhāṣya* and the *Māṭharavṛtti* when commenting on *Sāṃkhyakārikā* verse 23, Vācaspati refers readers to Patañjali's eight-limbed yoga when explaining specific techniques for purification of the intellect. So Vācaspati writes: "The virtue brought about by the performance of sacrifices, charity, etc. is the cause of good fortune. The virtue brought about by the practice of eight-limbed yoga is the cause of liberation."[39] Of course, Patañjali's eight-limbed yoga includes devotion to God (*īśvarapraṇidhāna*) among the observances (*niyamas*). Although Vācaspati never writes the word "God," he implies that devotion to God is part of the Sāṃkhya system by referring his readers to Patañjali's eight-limbed yoga.

Vācaspati occupies an intriguing place in the history of Indian philosophy because of his influence on a wide range of philosophical schools. He wrote commentaries on texts from the Vedānta, Sāṃkhya, Yoga, Nyāya, and Pūrva Mīmāṃsā traditions. The tradition characterizes him as *sarvatantrasvatantra*, "a master of all systems, yet dependent on none." For instance, thanks to his well-known subcommentary on Śaṅkara's *Brahmasūtrabhāṣya*, the *Bhāmatī*, Advaitins typically claim him as one of their own, and one of the two most influential schools of post-Śaṅkara Advaita is named after this work. Vācaspati did not just repeat the views of others—in many of these commentaries, he refined and improved theories or even offered new ones. Yet unlike Vijñānabhikṣu, Vācaspati endeavored to keep the strands of thought in his various commentaries separate. In spite of the apparent contradictions between the Advaitic teachings of the *Bhāmatī* and the Sāṃkhya and Yoga of the *Tattvakaumudī*, he makes no attempt to resolve these contradictions by underpinning Sāṃkhya's dualism with a Vedāntic metaphysics, as Vijñānabhikṣu does. This might lead some readers to ask the question: What were Vācaspati's actual views concerning issues like the plurality or unity of souls and the ontological status of the phenomenal world? As discussed here, the Sāṃkhya and Advaita Vedānta are at odds on these and many other issues.

Besides his Sāṃkhya commentary, the *Tattvakaumudī*, Vācaspati also authored a commentary on the *Yogasūtras*, entitled *Tattvavaiśāradī* (Learned Treatise on the Principles). Unlike the *Tattvakaumudī*, the *Tattvavaiśāradī* makes explicit reference to God, especially in those sūtras where Patañjali mentions God (*īśvara*): *TV* 1.23, 1.24, and 2.45. Like Vijñānabhikṣu and the *Yuktidīpikā,* Vācaspati sees God as something more than a passive entity whose place in the universe is simply to be an object of meditation or devotion. Instead, God is active in helping Yogins achieve liberation through his grace (*anugraha*). Although modern scholars frequently insist that Patañjali's God is purely passive, this conclusion goes against the commentarial traditions on Patañjali's work. I suspect several factors are at work in the insistence by these modern scholars on God's passivity in Patañjali. First, they confuse being creator of the world (which God in the *Yogasūtras* is surely not) with bestowing grace.[40] Although God is not the cause of the world, it is nonetheless possible that he has some causal relation to entities in the world. While God is described in *YS* 1.24 as "unaffected by defilements, actions, the results of actions, and unconscious traces," it is an open question whether this implies that he can have no active role in the world. As the *Yuktidīpikā*'s depiction of the God of Sāṃkhya suggests, it may be possible for God to be embodied and active in the world without being affected by the four types of impurities listed in *YS* 1.24. The insistence on God's complete passivity might also be an attempt to keep the role of God in the Yoga system as small as possible, based on the assumption that God is actually out of place in both the Sāṃkhya and Yoga systems. From a historical standpoint, it is this antitheistic impulse that is out of place. Contrary to popular belief, most Sāṃkhyas and Yogins did not see a problem with including God in their system.

SĀṂKHYA AND YOGA

The history of Sāṃkhya is inextricably intertwined with the history of what is now called the Yoga school of philosophy. The most common understanding of the difference between Sāṃkhya and Yoga by modern scholars is that one is atheistic while the other accepts God. But once it is established that the early commentaries on the *Sāṃkhyakārikā* accepted the existence of God, there seems little basis for differentiating between Sāṃkhya and Yoga. As discussed in the preceding section, these early Sāṃkhya commentaries themselves quote the *Yogasūtras* with approval regarding the existence of God. Even Vācaspati Miśra, a scholar who was not prone to mixing up doctrines from separate systems, refers to Patañjali's eight-limbed Yoga in order to elucidate a point on the question of the intellect (*buddhi*) as taught by the Sāṃkhyas.[41] Perhaps it is entirely mistaken to think that from early times, two separate philosophical schools existed, one named

Sāṃkhya and the other Yoga. As Johannes Bronkhorst has provocatively claimed:

> We must conclude that there never was a separate Yoga philosophy. This is saying more than that the "Yoga philosophy" is closely related with Sāṃkhya, or even an old school of the latter. It entails that the early history of the Yoga school of Sāṃkhya cannot be written, not because there is not sufficient material available, as Frauwallner maintains, but simply because it has no early history and can have none.[42]

Even in the *Yogasūtras* themselves, there is no evidence that *yoga* is understood to refer to a distinct philosophical school. Vyāsa's commentary on the *Yogasūtras,* the earliest available to us, refers to Patanjali's work as "Patañjali's authoritative book on Yoga, expository of Sāṃkhya."[43] Therefore, Vyāsa seems to think he is commenting on a text that belonged to the Sāṃkhya school—otherwise, why refer to it as "expository of Sāṃkhya"?[44] The widely used name "Yogasūtras" is not a label Patañjali gives to his own text but one that came later. It is presumably on the basis on *YS* 1.1: "Now, an exposition of Yoga."[45] Yoga is clearly the topic of the text. But this does not mean that *yoga* should be taken as the name of a philosophical school. The foundational text of the Mīmāṃsakas, for instance, Jaimini's *Mīmāṃsāsūtras,* begins, "Now, an inquiry into Dharma,"[46] and Bādarāyaṇa's *Brahmasūtras,* the foundational text of the Vedānta school, begins "Now, an inquiry into Brahman."[47] The first line of these sūtras simply establishes the topic of investigation, without necessarily referring to any particular school.

The preponderance of evidence suggests that the *Yogasūtras* and *Sāṃkhyakārikā* were not understood by their early commentarial traditions as being the foundational texts of two separate and at times conflicting schools of thought. Instead, the *Yogasūtras* were themselves considered to be a text belonging to the Sāṃkhya philosophical tradition, albeit one with a particular focus. While the *Sāṃkhyakārikā* is primarily interested in enumeration of the twenty-five metaphysical principles (*tattvas*) and their relation to each other, the *Yogasūtras* proceeds from this metaphysical backdrop to describe the practical means to liberation. The focus on the practical means to liberation and particularly on the acquisition of superhuman powers (*vibhūtis*) is not found in the *Sāṃkhyakārikā.* But with regard to philosophical doctrines, there is little that differentiates one text from the other. The commentarial traditions on both texts generally accept God, albeit a God who had no part in the creation of the universe. Commentators believed that God is capable of bringing about change in the world, both by temporarily assuming bodily form in the world (as according to the *Yuktidīpikā*) and by bestowing grace upon Yogins striving for liberation (as according to Vācaspati's commentary on the *Yogasūtras*, the *Tattvavaiśāradī*).

Although this general picture holds for most of the first millennium CE, gradually the idea that Yoga and Sāṃkhya represent two separate schools became increasingly widespread. Bronkhorst traces the notion that there are two different but related philosophical schools to Śaṅkara's commentary on *BS* 2.1.3. There Śaṅkara writes that "by the rejection of the Sāṃkhya tradition, the Yoga tradition has also been rejected."[48] However, Śaṅkara makes no mention of what distinguishes the Yoga school from the Sāṃkhya school, and he makes most of his polemical exertions for the sake of refuting the school he calls Sāṃkhya. Around the same time, the notion that there are two schools, one with God (*seśvara*) and one without God (*nirīśvara*) begins to take shape, not in Sāṃkhya works themselves but in the accounts of their opponents. The Jaina doxographer Haribhadra (eighth century), for instance, was one of the first to categorize the schools (*darśanas*) into six categories in his *Ṣaḍdarśanasamuccaya*. Unlike later lists, however, Haribhadra does not mention the Yoga as a separate group apart from the Sāṃkhya. Instead, his six schools are the Buddhists, Naiyāyikas, Sāṃkhyas, Jainas, Vaiśeṣikas, and Mīmāṃsakas. But Haribhadra remarks in verse 35 that "Some Sāṃkhyas are atheists, while others have Īśvara as their deity. But for all of them, there are 25 principles."[49] Note that nowhere in this text is the notion of a Yoga school of philosophy introduced; Haribhadra here is simply talking about the Sāṃkhya school.

Haribhadra's discussion of Sāṃkhya seems to go against Bronkhorst's thesis, since Bronkhorst maintains that there was no school of atheistic Sāṃkhya in the eighth century. One possibility is that Haribhadra was reading the *Sāṃkhyakārikā* independent of its commentaries, or did not read them carefully. The *Sāṃkhyakārikā* is, of course, "without God" in a very literal sense—God is never mentioned. A more likely explanation is one advanced by Bronkhorst with reference to two eighth-century Buddhist texts, Śāntarakṣita's *Tattvasaṃgraha* and its commentary, Kamalaśīla's *Pañjikā*. Both texts give a description of the doctrine of "Sāṃkhya with God." Kamalaśīla describes this God as "the unborn one who controls creation, existence, and destruction."[50] Although this passage clearly cannot describe the doctrines of Patañjali (who denies that God creates the world), it could refer to any number of other groups or texts. The *Viṣṇu* and *Kūrma Purāṇas* frequently depict God as being responsible for the world's creation and the activation of the principles of *prakṛti* and *puruṣa*, as do the texts of the Pāñcarātras. Therefore, by *nirīśvara sāṃkhya,* Haribhadra might more precisely mean "Sāṃkhyas without a creator God," and by *seśvara sāṃkhya,* "Sāṃkhyas with a creator God."

Although Haribhadra may not have had Patañjali in mind when referring to "Sāṃkhya with God," later thinkers explicitly identify it as the philosophy of Patañjali. The most influential of the later texts that make this identification is the *Sarvadarśanasaṃgraha* of the Advaita Vedānta doxographer Mādhava (fourteenth century). He devotes one section to the Sāṃkhya with God and another to the Sāṃkhya without God, which he identifies as the view of Īśvarakṛṣṇa. And he is clear in what he means by "Sāṃkhya without a God." According to Mādhava, the *Sāṃkhyakārikā* and its followers reject God completely. The followers of Patañjali, he suggests, are "Sāṃkhya with God" because they accept God, albeit a God who does not have any role in the creation of the world. Even at such a late date, however, Mādhava does not identify Patañjali's school as "Yoga." It is only in two later texts, Mādhavasarasvatī's *Sarvadarśanakaumudī* and Vijñānabhikṣu's *Sāṃkhyapravacanabhāṣya,* where "Yoga" is first used to denote the school of Patañjali.[51]

The primary purpose of the foregoing discussion was to show that belief in God was widespread among Sāṃkhya authors throughout most of the history of Indian philosophy. While the relationship between Sāṃkhya and Yoga is a complex and much-argued topic, there is substantial evidence to suggest that before the eighth century CE there was little or no understanding of the two as distinct schools holding conflicting philosophical theories. However, most medieval authors did perceive Sāṃkhya and Yoga as two separate schools, one preaching atheism and the other preaching theism. This presents a particular interpretive challenge for Vijñānabhikṣu, a medieval commentator who argued for the unity of Sāṃkhya, Yoga, and Vedānta. How can there be any such unity when one of the schools rejects a basic tenet of the other two, the existence of God? This question is a challenge that Vijñānabhikṣu addresses in his commentary on the *Sāṃkhyasūtras,* the *Sāṃkhyapravacanabhāṣya.* Of course, he does not do so by historically contextualizing the texts of these three schools, as I have done in this chapter. In chapter 5, I show how he adopts an ingenious interpretive strategy based on an appeal to the intention of each text's author and on an understanding of the "proper scope" of each of the *āstika* philosophical schools.

{5} READING AGAINST THE GRAIN OF THE *SĀṂKHYASŪTRAS*

ATHEISM IN THE *SĀṂKHYASŪTRAS*

In chapter 4, I addressed the oft-repeated notion that the fundamental difference between the Sāṃkhya and Yoga schools is on the existence of God: Yoga is theistic and Sāṃkhya is an atheist school. Like many other truisms in the history of Indian philosophy, this statement falls apart when examined closely. But there is one text, the late medieval *Sāṃkhyasūtras,* that reverses historical trends by offering a sustained and systematic disproof of the existence of God. Although this work is traditionally ascribed to the mythic teacher Kapila, evidence internal to the text suggests that it came long after the *Sāṃkhyakārikā* of Īśvarakṛṣṇa, perhaps as late as the fourteenth century. The *Sāṃkhyasūtras* also contain repetitions from other texts, Sāṃkhya and otherwise. Richard Garbe pointed out that, among the Vedāntic influences on the text, *SS* 4.3 is a word-for-word repetition of *BS* 4.1.1.[1] Yet the *Sāṃkhyasūtras* are hardly friendly toward Advaita Vedānta, and they devote many sūtras (e.g., *SS* 1.150–57) to the refutation of the theory of absolute non-dualism.

For our immediate purposes, the *Sāṃkhyasūtras* are most notable because they are the only Sāṃkhya source-text that explicitly argues for the nonexistence of God. Both the *Sāṃkhyakārikā* and *Tattvasamāsasūtras* are silent on the subject. This allows commentators on these earlier two texts three options: to read Sāṃkhya as affirming God's existence, to read it as rejecting God's existence, or to remain silent on the topic. The *Sāṃkhyasūtras* do not allow as much commentarial leeway on the issue of God as those other texts. Aniruddha, the author of the only extant commentary on the *Sāṃkhyasūtras* earlier than Vijñānabhikṣu's, contents himself with a brief and fairly straightforward exposition of the sūtras. Vijñānabhikṣu's commentary, the *Sāṃkhyapravacanabhāṣya,* takes on a much bigger challenge, arguing against the grain of the *Sāṃkhyasūtras.* Vijñānabhikṣu claims that in spite of Kapila's apparent arguments to the contrary in the *Sāṃkhyasūtras,* Kapila was actually a believer in the existence of God.

One of the *Sāṃkhyasūtras'* uses for Vijñānabhikṣu is as corroborating evidence for the existence of a plurality of individual selves (*jīvas*). This is something he earlier insisted on in his commentary on the *Brahmasūtras* and is an obvious attack on Advaita Vedānta. He begins this attack in his introductory verses to the text: "That which is expressed in hundreds of scriptural passages such as 'You are that; that is you,' the non-difference in essential properties between all the selves, is the topic of this text."[2] This is a continuation of his attempt in the *Vijñānāmṛtabhāṣya* to expand the definition of "difference" and "non-difference" to present a logically consistent philosophy. Therefore, he adds "non-difference of essential qualities" (*avaidharmya*) to the list of possible meanings of *abheda* (non-difference), along with the non-separation (*avibhāga*) and complete identity (*akhaṇḍatā*) presented at length in his earlier works (see chapter 3). In the context of the *Sāṃkhyasūtras,* however, this particular form of non-difference pertains not to the relation between the individual selves (*jīvas*) and Brahman but to the mutual relations of all of these different selves. In the *Sāṃkhyapravacanabhāṣya,* Vijñānabhikṣu uses the word *brahman* sparingly, not because he is no longer interested in questions regarding Brahman but because it lies outside the scope of the Sāṃkhya. Likewise, in the *Sāṃkhyapravacanabhāṣya,* he indiscriminately uses the Sāṃkhya term *puruṣa* alongside the term for individual self common in the schools of Vedānta, *jīva.* Here and elsewhere, he seems to consider the terms *puruṣa* and *jīva* to be equivalent.

In his lengthy introduction to the *Sāṃkhyasūtras,* Vijñānabhikṣu expresses his overall philosophical-commentarial project to illustrate the harmony of the major *āstika* schools more explicitly than anywhere else in his corpus. The schools in play for Vijñānabhikṣu are those he identifies as Nyāya-Vaiśeṣika, Sāṃkhya, Yoga, and Brahma Mīmāṃsā (also called Vedānta). Although he generally treats the Nyāya-Vaiśeṣika as one system, he acknowledges that the prima facie understanding of Sāṃkhya and Yoga is as two separate systems. Vijñānabhikṣu states in the *Sāṃkhyapravacanabhāṣya* and the *Yogavārttika* that the most notable difference between the Sāṃkhya and Yoga schools is on the question of the existence of God.[3] Therefore, unlike Gauḍapāda and other earlier Sāṃkhya commentators who noted no difference between Sāṃkhya and Yoga on the existence of God, for Vijñānabhikṣu the apparent disagreement between the two schools is a given that has to be explained away by philosophical and exegetical means.

Vijñānabhikṣu regards the Sāṃkhya as a very old school and himself as effecting a sort of Sāṃkhya renaissance. In one of his introductory verses to the *Sāṃkhyapravacanabhāṣya*, he states, "The Sāṃkhya teaching, of which only a small part remains, is a moon full of nectar, devoured by the sun of time. I will fill it once again with the nectar of my words."[4] However, there is certainly no notion in Vijñānabhikṣu that the *Sāṃkhyasūtras* themselves are a part of this renaissance—he considers them to be the ancient, authentic work of Kapila, founder of the Sāṃkhya school, whom Vijñānabhikṣu identifies as an incarnation of Nārāyaṇa.[5] By contrast, Vijñānabhikṣu never suggests that the Vedānta, Nyāya, or Yoga schools exist only as fragmentary relics of a hoary past, an indication that the lineages of these schools were more active than those of the Sāṃkhya, if such a thing as a Sāṃkhya lineage existed at all in the late sixteenth and early seventeenth centuries. At the same time, however, Vijñānabhikṣu clearly values antiquity and is suspicious of newness. This is especially evident in his favorite epithet for the Advaita Vedāntins, "moderns" (*ādhunikas*). In spite of the great number of doctrinal innovations in his own works and the works of other schools of his era like the Navya-Nyāya (literally, the "New" Nyāya), Vijñānabhikṣu sees more rhetorical benefit in emphasizing the antiquity of his ideas than their novelty.

Vijñānabhikṣu addresses the question of God in Sāṃkhya directly in his introduction and once again his commentary on *SS* 1.92 and 5.12. He is aware that, along with his argument for the multiplicity of selves, his argument for the existence of God is his most controversial statement in the *Sāṃkhyapravacanabhāṣya*. However, these two statements are controversial in two different ways. Vijñānabhikṣu's argument for the multiplicity of selves is not out of place in a Sāṃkhya text, where it functions as an attack on the competing school of Advaita Vedānta, one of the most powerful schools of philosophy in late medieval India. The existence of God is uncontroversial insofar as it is something that almost all philosophers of his era would have agreed on, with the exception of the Jainas. The controversy here is the context in which he presents the argument, in a commentary on the *Sāṃkhyasūtras*. Sāṃkhya was widely accepted as being an atheistic school by the sixteenth century, following the influence of a medieval doxographic tradition that depicted the difference between Sāṃkhya and Yoga as one between atheism and theism. So Vijñānabhikṣu might strain credulity in upholding theism in his commentary on an atheistic text. This example of commenting against the grain of the text is unusually extreme, even in the context of the creative commentarial practices so common in premodern India.

Vijñānabhikṣu first establishes the place of the Nyāya-Vaiśeṣika in his hierarchy of schools. The inclusion of this school is not mere lip service. Vijñānabhikṣu frequently uses philosophical terminology developed by the Navya-Nyāya school in his own apologetics for Bhedābheda Vedānta and Sāṃkhya-Yoga, and he appears to have some anxiety about establishing his philosophical positions against the powerful influence of its exponents. According to his *Yogasārasaṃgraha* (Compendium of the Essence of Yoga), he even wrote a treatise on the Nyāya school, which unfortunately has never been found.[6] To clear a space for the Nyāya-Vaiśeṣika among the *āstika* schools, Vijñānabhikṣu employs the concepts of conventional (*vyāvahārika*) and ultimate (*pāramārthika*) truth developed by the Advaitins (and before them the Buddhists):

> Objection: There is contradiction between the arguments of the Nyāya-Vaiśeṣikas, who teach that the self possesses qualities, and the arguments found here in the Sāṃkhya, that the self is free from qualities. Therefore, both sets of arguments lack authority.
>
> Vijñānabhikṣu: No, this is not the case. There is no contradiction, and both schools' teachings are established, since one is concerned with conventional truth, the other with ultimate truth. From the common experience of pleasure and pain, the Nyāya-Vaiśeṣikas distinguish the self from the body by means of inference at the first level, yet are unable to enter immediately into that which is extremely subtle. Their knowledge, rejecting the notion that the body is the same as the self, is certainly correct knowledge at the conventional level. . . . Nyāya and Vaiśeṣika are authoritative, since their intended meaning is not contradicted. This is because of the rule, "the meaning of the word is that which is intended."[7]

The teaching of the Nyāya-Vaiśeṣika is that the self is the agent (*kartṛ*) and the one who experiences sensations like pleasure and pain (*bhoktṛ*). It is correct, according to Vijñānabhikṣu, insofar as its intention is to differentiate the self from the body and to teach that there must be something beyond the body, different from it, known as the self. However, it is not able to rise to the level of Sāṃkhya, which teaches that the self is ultimately pure, changeless, and free of all qualities. Because the Nyāya-Vaiśeṣika's intention is simply to teach that there is something different from the body known as the self, it cannot be considered a defect of the Nyāya-Vaiśeṣika that it does not penetrate to the higher level of knowledge. By means of this argumentative strategy, Vijñānabhikṣu is able to say both that (1) Nyāya-Vaiśeṣika is a lower teaching than Sāṃkhya and (2) this does not mean that Nyāya-Vaiśeṣika is defective. This ploy, and the appeal to the rule that "the meaning of the word is that which is intended," is one that he also uses to find a place for the Sāṃkhya denial of God. Just as it is not the Nyāya-Vaiśeṣika's project to teach ultimate truths about the nature of the self, Sāṃkhya is unconcerned with the topic of the existence or nonexistence of God. Although a Naiyāyika would certainly take umbrage at the suggestion that he is simply unconcerned about the true nature of the self, there is some historical plausibility to the second claim that the Sāṃkhyas are simply not very interested in God, as there is little or no discussion of God in the *Sāṃkhyakārikā* and its commentaries. But in the text at hand, the *Sāṃkhyasūtras,* there is explicit rejection of God's existence. This is once again explained by Vijñānabhikṣu in terms of conventional (*vyāvahārika*) versus ultimate (*pāramārthika*) truths:

> Here too, on the question of the existence of God, there is the relation of conventional and ultimate truth. "They say that the world is without truth, without foundation, and Godless" (*BhG* 16.8). In such scriptures, atheism is rejected. In the *Sāṃkhyasūtras,* the conventional rejection of God is mentioned only for the sake of indifference to lordliness. For if the eternal God had not been rejected just as the materialists do, the practice of discrimination would be hindered by desire after seeing perfect lordliness. This is what Kapila intended.[8]

Theories of meaning in premodern India were unabashedly intentionalist, and Vijñānabhikṣu is no exception. The rule "the meaning of the word is that which is intended" implies that knowledge of a statement's meaning requires knowledge of the speaker's intent. The limitations and problems of such theories have been well documented in twentieth-century hermeneutics.[9] But in the Indian context, it presents some interesting puzzles. For instance, how can the Pūrva Mīmāṃsakas, who believe that the Veda is literally authorless, interpret the Veda? If the author or speaker's intention determines the meaning of his words, then it seems that when there is no author, there can be no meaning.[10] The problems are not quite as great when interpreting the non-Vedic texts that have a human author (*smṛti*), such as the *Sāṃkhyasūtras* of Kapila. Those interpreters who fail to account for what Kapila meant to do with his words when he denied the existence of God will be misled. Vijñānabhikṣu suggests that worshippers might be so distracted with thoughts of God—particularly with the possibilities of the God-like powers (*aiśvaryas*) that they themselves might attain—that knowledge of God can potentially be detrimental to the attainment of liberation.[11] In the *Yogasūtras,* meditation on God is described as a means to spiritual advancement. But here Vijñānabhikṣu suggests that there is a downside to knowledge of God as well. Presumably for certain followers who would be prone to be distracted by God's powers rather than benefit from meditation on him, Kapila taught the doctrine of the nonexistence of God, knowing that it was ultimately untrue. Therefore, at times one can say that ignorance is preferable to knowledge on the path to liberation. In such cases, the disinterested quest for truth collides with the common Indian notion that philosophy is primarily an instrument for attaining the state of ultimate release.

Vijñānabhikṣu insists that Sāṃkhya doctrines cannot be considered defective because they have no flaws when discussing their intended topics, such as discrimination of the self from the material world. Yet he is also forced to admit that the Sāṃkhya is limited in some ways that Yoga and Vedānta are not. This is clear in his exegesis of two passages from the *Mahābhārata* that praise Sāṃkhya:

> "There is no knowledge equal to Sāṃkhya. There is no power equal to yoga." "Let there be no doubt in this regard: Sāṃkhya is considered the highest knowledge." Passages such as these prove the superiority of the Sāṃkhya to all other doctrines only with regard to the discrimination of the self from other things. The Sāṃkhya is not superior to all other doctrines with regard to its rejection of God.[12]

The first of the two quotes cited from the *Mokṣadharma Parvan* of the *Mahābhārata* seems to express the difference between Sāṃkhya and Yoga in the sense that Franklin Edgerton points out (see chapter 4). Sāṃkhya is considered the highest "knowledge" while Yoga is the highest "power," suggesting that the difference between Sāṃkhya and Yoga is the difference between theoretical knowledge and knowledge as the instrument of liberation. Vijñānabhikṣu, however, understands the two terms to refer to two separate schools: one that teaches the existence of God, and one that does not. To reconcile the differing views of the different schools, he does not deny that these differences exist but, rather, denies that the differences are significant. Each school has a certain proper scope of topics, and within that scope it is authoritative. Outside of that scope, however, its teachings should not be heeded. The scope of the Nyāya does not involve topics having to do with the precise nature of the true self. Sāṃkhya's scope does not include teachings involving God. By limiting each doctrine's proper range of functioning, he is able to reconcile these doctrines. However, for at least two of the schools he discusses, Yoga and Vedānta, there appears to be no limiting of scope—these two schools are authoritative on any topic. In a significant way, that puts them at a higher level in the hierarchy of schools than Nyāya and Sāṃkhya.

KAPILA'S "BOLD ASSERTION" AS SPEECH ACT

Vijñānabhikṣu's overall philosophical-commentarial project to illustrate the harmony of the major *āstika* schools is clearly evident in his lengthy introduction to the *Sāṃkhyasūtras.* In particular, he wishes to show that the text is compatible with the Bhedābheda (Difference and Non-Difference) Vedānta that he himself champions in his earliest writings. All the other textual evidence that Vijñānabhikṣu has on hand—the *Bhagavad Gītā;* the Upaniṣads; the Purāṇas; and the philosophical treatises of the Nyāya-Vaiśeṣika, Yoga, and Vedānta schools—is unanimous in its acceptance of God. The Sāṃkhya, an anomaly among the *āstika* systems, therefore needs to be brought back into line with the clear majority of *āstika* viewpoints. Furthermore, it is inconceivable that Kapila, the omniscient seer who is portrayed in the *Bhāgavata Purāṇa* as an incarnation of the god Nārāyaṇa, could differ in opinion so greatly with other authoritative texts on the question of God's existence. But the sheer number of times the *Sāṃkhyasūtras* repeat their denial of God makes it impossible to say that no such denial exists. Some other strategy is required to reconcile Kapila's assertion with the theism of the other *āstika* schools and with Kapila's own assertions elsewhere.

Vijñānabhikṣu therefore shifts the discussion away from what it was that Kapila taught in the *Sāṃkhyasūtras* and toward what his intention or purpose was in teaching those things. Using J. L. Austin's well-known terminology, what is at stake is not the content of Kapila's words, the locutionary act.[13] Kapila said that God does not exist; no one disputes that. Nor is there much controversy concerning the illocutionary force of Kapila's statement: that is, what he was doing *in saying* those words. Kapila was asserting something, not questioning or promising or wondering out loud. Instead, the real interest lies in Kapila's perlocutionary act: What was it that Kapila brought about or achieved *by saying* that God does not exist? Unlike illocutionary acts, perlocutionary acts are part of a chain of effects that follow after the initial utterance. They succeed or fail depending on whether they manage to bring about a certain effect in the listener. Perlocutionary acts are thus tied up with the intentionality of the speaker. In Kapila's assertion that God does not exist, he wished to convince his listeners of something that was ultimately untrue. This, according to Vijñānabhikṣu, was the perlocutionary effect he had in mind.

Although he has nothing but the highest praise for its author, Kapila, Vijñānabhikṣu admits that the Sāṃkhya doctrines as presented are limited. But what precisely were Kapila's intentions in teaching this limited set of doctrines? Are there precedents for this sort of benign deception? Vijñānabhikṣu expands on these issues in an important and controversial passage from the *Sāṃkhyapravacanabhāṣya:*

> As a temporary concession (*abhyupagamavāda*), a bold assertion (*prauḍhivāda*), etc., the Sāṃkhya's intention is the rejection of God on a conventional level. Hence, there is no contradiction with the Yoga and Vedānta. Temporary concession also appears in the śāstras, e.g., in the *Viṣṇu Purāṇa* (1.17.83): "O demons, I have explained the notions of those who see God as separate from themselves, making a temporary concession regarding those views (*kṛtvā 'bhyupagamaṃ tatra*). Hear my summary."[14]

Alternatively, it may be that in order to impede the knowledge of the wicked, even in parts of the believers' systems (*āstikadarśana*) there is presentation of views that are contrary to the Veda. Only those parts lack authority. But on their main topics, which are not opposed to revealed scripture or traditional texts, they are authoritative. Only on this ground is the criticism of all schools other than the Vedānta and Yoga justified in the *Padma Purāṇa*.

The first alternative Vijñānabhikṣu presents is the one suggested previously: namely, the denial of God is actually for the benefit of the worshipper, since without any knowledge of God, the worshipper cannot be distracted with thoughts of Godlike powers he might attain. Vijñānabhikṣu labels this type of assertion as a "temporary concession" (*abhyupagamavāda*) or a "bold assertion" (*prauḍhivāda*). Of the two terms, the former is the one Vijñānabhikṣu generally uses in the commentary on the *Sāṃkhyasūtras,* perhaps because it is a more precise description of how the denial of God's existence functions in the *Sāṃkhyasūtras.*[15] To understand these two terms of art and their relation to one another, it is necessary to turn to the Nyāya school's analysis of the "temporary tenet" (*abhyupagamasiddhānta*).

The *Nyāyasūtras,* the foundational text of the Nyāya school of logic and argumentation, enumerate four different types of "established tenets" (*siddhāntas*). *NS* 1.1.27 lists them as (1) a tenet accepted by all philosophical systems (*sarvatantrasiddhānta*), (2) a tenet that is particular to a specific system (*pratitantrasiddhānta*), (3) a tenet that is implied by the topic (*adhikaraṇasiddhānta*), and (4) a tenet that is accepted temporarily (*abhyupagamasiddhānta*). It is this fourth category from which Vijñānabhikṣu derives his idea of a "temporary concession" (*abhyupagamavāda*). The context of these four types of tenets for the Naiyāyikas is clearly formal philosophical debate; by understanding classifications such as the four types of *siddhāntas,* a participant will avoid breaking the rules and losing the competition to his opponent. All four of these classifications received considerable attention from commentators on the *Nyāyasūtras,* and the details of each were also the topics of some controversy. For my brief explanation of the fourth classification, *abhyupagamasiddhānta,* I rely primarily on the interpretation of Jayanta Bhaṭṭa (ninth century CE) in his *Nyāyamañjarī.*[16]

In the course of philosophical debate, it is not always possible or desirable to call attention to every point about which one disagrees with one's opponents. At times, it will be necessary for a debater to temporarily grant points to his opponent that he does not actually accept, to let certain assertions of the opponent pass unremarked. For example, a Naiyāyika might try to prove in debate with a Mīmāṃsaka that sound (*śabda*) is not eternal. The two debaters will differ in other details about the specifics of sound. According to Nyāya texts, sound is categorized as a quality (*guṇa*), while Mīmāṃsakas consider sound to be a substance (*dravya*). But during debate, the Naiyāyika may choose to temporarily allow his opponent's assertion that sound is a substance stand, as the Naiyāyika is primarily interested in establishing sound's non-eternality. He calculates that even if he concedes this minor point, he will still be able to win the argument about whether sound is eternal.[17] It is clear from this example that employing the "temporary tenet" (*abhyupagamasiddhānta*) is not something for amateurs.

A debater must be confident and experienced to fight with a handicap, since conceding what may at first appear a minor point may end up losing him the entire competition. Hence in his discussion of *NS* 1.1.31, Jayanta repeatedly refers to the person who employs the acceptance of temporary tenets as a "bold debater" (*prauḍhivādin*): "Therefore, the meaning of the sūtra is that the *abhyupagamasiddhānta* is the temporary acceptance of something not examined, done by the bold debater in order to examine its specific property. This is often precisely how philosophers argue with one another."[18]

Vijñānabhikṣu would quite likely have been acquainted with Jayanta's account of the *prauḍhivādin* in the *Nyāyamañjarī*. Even if he did not derive his particular usage from this text itself, this Naiyāyika understanding of the one who employs a temporary thesis as being a confident or bold debater is almost certainly where Vijñānabhikṣu's term "bold assertion" (*prauḍhivāda*) originates. It is obvious that Vijñānabhikṣu's use of the term *abhyuypagamavāda* has much in common with Jayanta Bhaṭṭa's definition of the "temporary tenet." Kapila's acceptance of the nonexistence of God is merely a temporary acceptance of the views of others (implicitly, an acceptance of *nāstika* views). This temporary acceptance is done keeping in mind the greater ends that can be achieved. In the example between the Naiyāyika and the Mīmāṃsaka, it is the eventual disproving of the opponent's argument. In the acceptance of atheism in the *Sāṃkhyasūtras,* it is the enabling of the Sāṃkhya practitioner to achieve enlightenment without distraction. Vijñānabhikṣu brings something new to the discussion by transposing the Nyāya notion of *abhyupagama* from the context of formal philosophical debate to the wider sphere of rhetoric. The "temporary concession" for Vijñānabhikṣu is primarily about persuasion rather than truth or falsity.[19] In fact, for him the primary purpose of the temporary concession is not to lead his listeners to the truth but, rather, to lead them to self-transcendence. According to Vijñānabhikṣu in the *Sāṃkhyapravacanabhāṣya,* knowledge of God is not a precondition for liberation.[20]

The example of "temporary concession" Vijñānabhikṣu cites in his previous quote comes from the section of the *Viṣṇu Purāṇa* that tells the story of Prahlāda, the demon prince who becomes one of Viṣṇu's foremost devotees. Prahlāda gives a sermon in which he tries to convince his demonic brethren to give up their hatred and violence. He first formulates a series of arguments designed to appeal to dualists, those who understand God to be wholly other than themselves. Although this conception of the relationship between Viṣṇu and the individual worshipper is a false one, for the purposes of ending violence, he formulates arguments to appeal to those with such a mindset. He then goes on to explain the higher truth—that the entire world is a manifestation of Viṣṇu—and offer a new set of arguments for nonviolence based on this insight. For this reason, translations of Vijñānabhikṣu sometimes render *abhyupagamavāda* as "concession to popular views." But it is more than this. Any acceptance of an untruth for the sake of a higher purpose can be termed an *abhyupagamavāda.*

The doctrine of the "temporary concession" or the "bold assertion" may have even earlier roots than the Purāṇas. Ironically, it may originate with the *nāstikas* themselves, in the form of the Buddhist doctrine of skillful means (*upāya*). An early example of the practice of the Buddha skillfully tailoring his speech to suit the understanding of his audience occurs in the Pali Canon, where he addresses two young Brahmins on how to attain union with the god Brahmā:

> And he lets his mind pervade one quarter of the world with thoughts of love, and so the second, and so the third, and so forth. And thus the whole wide world, above, below, around and everywhere, does he continue to pervade with a heart of love, far reaching, grown great, and beyond measure. . . . Verily this . . . is the way to the state of union with Brahmā.[21]

Rather than teach these Brahmins to immediately abandon their worship of the god Brahmā and instead follow the noble eightfold path, the Buddha gives them a teaching that will appeal to their level of spiritual development. In this case, he suggests that the way to union with Brahmā is by means of Buddhist loving-kindness meditation. This is quite similar to Prahlāda's bold assertion or temporary concession to the dualists in the *Viṣṇu Purāṇa,* where he speaks using dualistic theological assumptions in order to convince the demons to abandon violence.

Skillful means was later developed farther and more explicitly in the *Upāyakauśalyasutras,* which deal not only with skillful speech acts but also with physical acts that the Buddha performs to alleviate the suffering of other people, sometimes using means that seem out of keeping with the teachings of the eightfold path. In one instance, a young woman was so in love with the Buddha that she would have killed herself if she could not have him. The Buddha's skillful response was to have a sexual affair with the woman, as that was the most skillful way to keep her from suffering. In another story from the *Upāyakauśalyasūtras,* the Buddha in one of his former lives murders a man to prevent him from killing five hundred other people in the future. According to this line of thought, in theory a Buddha or Bodhisattva can do anything, no matter how contrary to Buddhist restrictions on verbal or bodily action, if he knows that it will alleviate suffering.[22]

Early Buddhist hermeneutics was highly aware of the confusions that can result when listeners do not take into account the intentions of the speaker, usually in this case the Buddha himself. Therefore, early Buddhist thinkers developed a distinction between *nītārtha* and *neyārtha* teachings. The *nītārtha* sūtra is one whose meaning is clear and can be taken literally since it was spoken without any ulterior motive. However, the *neyārtha* sūtra's meaning is not so straightforward because it is intentional (*ābhiprāyika*), based on some specific motivation on the Buddha's part.[23] This twofold distinction of *nītārtha/neyārtha* served simply as a way of classifying different teachings of the Buddha. However, the Mādhyamika philosopher Nāgārjuna (second century CE) developed this hermeneutical distinction into the epistemological doctrine of the "two truths," conventional and ultimate, which went on to have enormous influence not only on Mahāyāna Buddhist philosophy but also on the Advaita Vedānta school.[24] In spite of his hostility toward both Buddhism and Advaita Vedānta, Vijñānabhikṣu also invokes the two levels of "conventional" and "ultimate" in justifying his own reading of the Sāṃkhya denial of God as merely a conventional teaching.[25] Although Vijñānabhikṣu's reading of the denial of God in the *Sāṃkhyasūtras* has often been portrayed as highly idiosyncratic, in fact he is tapping into an interpretive tradition that predated him by over fifteen hundred years.

Just as the Buddha tries to aid the worshippers of Brahmā by telling them to practice loving-kindness meditation in order to get closer to him, Vijñānabhikṣu argues that Kapila is denying God's existence to keep the concept of God from those who would find him more of a hindrance than a boon to liberation. Indeed, as Johannes Bronkhorst has observed, the sage Kapila is something like a Sāṃkhya Bodhisattva. According to Bronkhorst's reading of the *Māṭharavṛtti,* an early commentary on the *Sāṃkhyakārikā,* "God is the light of Kapila . . . the self which resides, shines, in Kapila."[26] Much as Purāṇic Sāṃkhya takes Kapila to be an incarnation of Nārāyaṇa, early (pre-tenth-century) commentaries on the *Sāṃkhyakārikā* take Kapila to be an embodiment of Īśvara, the God mentioned in the *Yogasūtras,* who is also frequently mentioned in Sāṃkhya commentaries. As an incarnation of God, Kapila has a superhuman knowledge of future events and of the dispositions of the people he encounters. Just as the Mahāyāna Bodhisattva tailors his message and actions keeping in mind the best interests of those around him, Kapila, too, might wish to change his message based on his audience. This explanation certainly helped Vijñānabhikṣu make sense of the atheistic teachings of the *Sāṃkhyasūtras,* which are completely contrary to his other major Sāṃkhya sources, the Upaniṣads, the *Mahābhārata,* and the Purāṇas.[27]

DEGREES OF DECEPTION IN SĀṂKHYA AND THE PURĀṆAS

To explain the rampant atheism of the *Sāṃkhyasūtras,* Vijñānabhikṣu's most common strategy is to characterize Kapila's teaching as an intentional use of indirect speech in order to appeal to the level of spiritual sophistication of his listeners. In other words, it is for their own good that Kapila deceives the members of his audience. However, he entertains another possibility. The second alternative Vijñānabhikṣu suggests, the one that Richard Garbe describes as a "monstrous idea," is that Kapila taught the false doctrine of atheism to keep knowledge from the wicked: "Alternatively, it may be that in order to impede the knowledge of the wicked, even in parts of the affirmers' systems (*āstikadarśanas*) there is presentation of views that are contrary to the Veda."[28]

This explanation comes only once in the *Sāṃkhyapravacanabhāṣya,* as a brief suggestion immediately after his mention of the "bold assertion" hypothesis. These two explanations are not necessarily exclusive of one another. It is possible that, among one group of audience members, Kapila determined that withholding knowledge of God would be beneficial in enabling discrimination of the self to evolve; faced with a demonic audience, he determined that withholding knowledge would be the best means for preventing his audience from acquiring dangerous powers based on knowledge of correct doctrines. In this second scenario, unlike the first explanation for Kapila's deception, knowledge leads to power and ignorance to ruin.

This suggestion by Vijñānabhikṣu shows once again a Purāṇic influence, harking back to a well-known story at *Viṣ. Pu.* 4.18.[29] In order to defeat the demons (*daityas*) who had succeeded in obtaining great powers through religious austerities, Viṣṇu came down to earth disguised as an ascetic and began teaching doctrines contrary to the Vedas. First, disguising himself as the founder of the Jaina school, he taught the doctrine of *anekāntavāda* (perspectivism or "non-one-sidedness") to the group of demons. Then, moving on to another group, he changed his outfit and, appearing as the Buddha, taught that animal sacrifices are immoral and so forth. By this means, the demons lost all of the powers they had attained, and were summarily massacred by the gods. This story is remarkable because it accomplishes two goals simultaneously. First, it manages to subsume Buddhism and Jainism under orthodox Brahmanism, by demonstrating that both Mahāvīra (if that is indeed who is portrayed—he is nameless in the *Viṣṇu Purāṇa*) and the Buddha were incarnations of Viṣṇu. Second, it completely discredits the actual content of the doctrines of these two sects, by suggesting that the teachings of Buddhism and Jainism are intentionally false and nonsensical. The dupes are the Buddhists and Jainas, who do not understand that the source of all of the teachings they defend so vehemently is a divine trick.[30]

After making his claim that Kapila taught atheism in order to keep knowledge from the wicked, Vijñānabhikṣu cites a passage from the *Padma Purāṇa* in which Śiva gives a long list of the *tāmasa śāstras,* the teachings that have been made in order to confuse rather than illuminate their hearers. Unlike the story from the *Viṣṇu Purāṇa,* most of the teachings he enumerates are considered to be among the *āstika* systems by Indian doxographers. Śiva explains that "merely by the hearing of these *tāmasa śāstras,* even the wise are brought low."[31] According to the passage from the *Padma Purāṇa* that Vijñānabhikṣu cites, these *tāmasa śāstras* comprise the following:

1. The Śaiva teachings—for example, the Pāśupata teachings and the like, taught by Śiva himself.
2. The "great" (*mahat*) Vaiśeṣika teachings of Kaṇāda.
3. The Nyāya of Gautama.
4. The Sāṃkhya of Kapila.
5. The Pūrva Mīmāṃsā of the twice-born Jaimini, which deals with the Veda.
6. The despised Cārvāka system, taught by Dhiṣaṇa.
7. The false doctrine of Buddhism, taught by Viṣṇu in the form of the Buddha in order to destroy the demons; Buddhism consists of those who are naked and those clad in blue.[32]
8. The false doctrine of Illusionism (*māyāvāda*), which is Buddhism in disguise; Śiva taught this in the *kali yuga* disguised as a Brahmin. This doctrine incorrectly interprets the Vedas. It teaches that ritual activity

> should be abandoned. Śiva has taught the unity of the highest self and the individual self, and that Brahman in its highest form is free from qualities. Śiva taught the non-Vedic doctrine of Illusionism in the *kali yuga* in order to destroy the entire world, while purporting to be teaching the meanings of the Veda.[33]

Vijñānabhikṣu cites this passage from the *Padma Purāṇa* as scriptural support for his suggestion that the teachings of the Sāṃkhya, or some other *āstika* school, could exist for the sake of misleading its hearers. But Vijñānabhikṣu realizes how outrageous such a claim might sound and therefore is careful in trying to qualify the apparent wholesale rejection of the systems listed in the *Padma Purāṇa.* Each of the rejections of the *āstika* systems in this passage is not a complete rejection of an entire system. Certain parts of these systems were taught in order to confuse the wicked, and it is only these parts that are false. He says that "on their main topics, which are not opposed to revealed scripture or traditional texts, they are authoritative. Only on this ground is the *Padma Purāṇa* justified in its criticism of all schools other than Vedānta and Yoga."[34]

The list from the *Padma Purāṇa* is said by the speaker, Śiva, to be "in order" (*yathākrama*).[35] The organizing principle of this ordering appears to be the progressively more egregious philosophical mistakes made by the each of the systems. While some of the first systems mentioned are described in value-neutral language (or even positively, as when the Vaiśeṣika is called "great"), by the time the reader arrives at the end of the list, it is clear who the whipping-boy of the *Padma Purāṇa* is. The worst of all doctrines is the Advaita (only described as "Illusionism"), which is so wrongheaded that it will eventually succeed in destroying the world. Vijñānabhikṣu himself points out that two doctrines have been left off this list, Vedānta and Yoga. These two schools are implicitly free from defects in any part and therefore have no place there. By Vijñānabhikṣu's account, Advaita is not a real form of Vedānta. Nor is it even an *āstika* system. According to Vijñānabhikṣu and the *Padma Purāṇa,* it is secretly a type of Buddhism, and in fact, its doctrines are even more awful than Buddhism's. Buddhist doctrines were only capable of deluding a group of demons and depriving them of their powers. Advait doctrines are weapons of mass destruction.

Vijñānabhikṣu concludes his interpretation of the passage from the *Padma Purāṇa* by suggesting that he has said more on this topic in his commentary on the *Brahmasūtras.*[36] This statement recurs over and over in the *Sāṃkhyapravacanabhāṣya,* often in places where it makes obvious sense. For instance, since Vijñānabhikṣu takes the Sāṃkhya "person" (*puruṣa*) to be synonymous with the "individual self" (*jīva*) of the Vedāntins, reading his lengthy analysis of the self and its relation to Brahman in the commentary on the *Brahmasūtras* will aid understanding of the use of the term *puruṣa* in the *Sāṃkhyasūtras.* However, where his commentary on the *Brahmasūtras* does have explicit discussion of the relationship between Vedānta, Sāṃkhya, and Yoga, it is often to disparage Sāṃkhya and Yoga at the expense of Vedānta. Examples include the following:

> This knowledge of Brahman as the self is superior to the knowledge of the solitary self (*viviktajīva*) taught by the Sāṃkhyas. There is no knowledge superior to the knowledge of Brahman as the self.[37]

> Here we explain the essential difference between our teaching and theirs. According to the Sāṃkhya and Yoga, two schools that believe in the independence of *prakṛti,* the transformation (*pravṛtti*) that is directed towards the ends of man is just by itself united with the *puruṣa,* the very first self. They assert that it is just like the way in which iron is united with a magnet. But according to us the union of *prakṛti* and *puruṣa* is made by the Lord.[38]

Although there is talk of the relationship between Sāṃkhya, Yoga, and Vedānta in the *Vijñānāmṛtabhāṣya,* it is just as often to point out differences as it is to point out agreement. Furthermore, there is nowhere a suggestion that the Sāṃkhya and Yoga are on the same level as Vedānta, even if one takes into account their different topics of inquiry. In the *Vijñānāmṛtabhāṣya,* unlike the *Sāṃkhyapravacanabhāṣya,* Vedānta is presented as unambiguously superior to Sāṃkhya and Yoga on any number of points of doctrine. By the time he wrote the *Sāṃkhyapravacanabhāṣya,* Vijñānabhikṣu has come to a more nuanced understanding of the relationship of these schools: "None of the *āstika* teachings are unauthoritative or contradictory, since with regard to their respective topics none are obstructed or contradicted."[39] Although Sāṃkhya and Yoga are important influences throughout his early career, only in his later works does Vijñānabhikṣu come to accept the full value of these schools alongside the Vedānta.

In the *Sāṃkhyapravacanabhāṣya,* Vijñānabhikṣu sees the relationship of Sāṃkhya and Yoga as they are portrayed by most modern textbooks that enumerate six *āstika* systems without problematizing their history and origins: Sāṃkhya and Yoga are separate schools, albeit closely related. The most noteworthy difference between the two schools, according to Vijñānabhikṣu in the *Sāṃkhyapravacanabhāṣya,* is that the latter accepts this existence of God, while the former rejects him: "The Yoga system, however, avoids the deficiency by explaining God, while God is denied by the two [Sāṃkhya texts, the *Sāṃkhyasūtras* and *Tattvasamāsasūtras*] because of their temporary concession."[40] Therefore, Vijñānabhikṣu's implicit hierarchy of teachings based on their levels of truth and completeness begins with Vedānta at the top, followed by Yoga (which teaches that God exists, while failing to detail his role in world-creation), Sāṃkhya, and Nyāya-Vaiśeṣika. The other *āstika* schools presumably fall somewhere below these four. The Advaita Vedānta, however, is not an *āstika* school at all. Vijñānabhikṣu simultaneously insists that none of the *āstika* schools is defective (since they all are correct with regard to each of their main topics) while nonetheless being able to hold that the Vedānta alone is complete—that is, it is correct with regard to every one of the statements it makes, on all topics. The *nāstika* schools are left out of this harmonizing strategy. Presumably, the Jaina, Buddhist, Cārvāka, and Advaita Vedānta schools are completely false, or at least false on so many different topics that their entire teaching is compromised and worthy of derision. Each of the *āstika* schools, in contrast, is largely correct in its teachings and worthy of respect.

DISPROVING GOD IN THE *SĀṂKHYASŪTRAS*

Although this technique of avoiding direct doctrinal conflict between Sāṃkhya, Yoga, and Bhedābheda Vedānta on the question of God can be sustained, it requires difficult decisions for Vijñānabhikṣu in his commentary on the *Sāṃkhyasūtras.* This is nowhere more the case than the fifth chapter, which begins with an extended disproof of the existence of God. There, arguments are presented to show that it is logically indefensible to maintain the existence of a being called God (*īśvara*) who is unlike the other *puruṣas.* Clearly, Vijñānabhikṣu does not agree with these arguments, nor does he even think such arguments are presented as valid by the *Sāṃkhyasūtras*' author. So should he go along with the text fulfilling the normal duties of a commentator, or should he immediately state his objections to the arguments as presented? His choice is a compromise: although he presents a straightforward gloss of the arguments presented at *SS* 5.1–11, at 5.12 he can no longer hold his pen in check and essentially takes back everything he has said to that point, presenting a terse counter-argument supporting God's existence.

Vijñānabhikṣu explains that chapter 5 of the *Sāṃkhyasūtras* is devoted to the destruction of opponents' viewpoints, since the views of the Sāṃkhya have been thoroughly proven in the first four chapters. The existence or nonexistence of God is the first topic addressed in this chapter, since it is the topic where the *Sāṃkhyasūtras* are most at odds with the other *āstika* schools.[41] The argument against God begins at *SS* 5.2, in a discussion on the law of karma and its results. Specifically, what is the mechanism underlying the connection between an act and its final karmic result? The Nyāya philosophical school argues that God must exist, since without a superintendent, the law of karma could not function. Because actions (*karma*) and matter (*prakṛti*) are themselves insentient, they cannot originate any operation on their own. Furthermore, it would be incomprehensible for a present action to be the cause of a result in the distant future without positing some sort of sentient being superintending the entire process.[42] In response to the Naiyāyika view, *SS* 5.2 claims that no such positing of a God to superintend this process is necessary. Vijñānabhikṣu introduces and elucidates this sūtra:

> Certain opponents say that the sūtra "due to the non-establishment of God" (*SS* 1.92) does not make sense, since God is established as the one who bestows the results of actions. The author of the sūtra refutes these opponents:
>
> > 5.2 It is not that when [the cause] is supported by God there is the attainment of results, since there is proof that the result is by means of the action.
>
> "When the action is superintended by God, then there is attainment of the consequence, in the form of the action's result." This assertion is not appropriate. For there is the possibility of the attainment of the result by the necessary action alone. This is the meaning.[43]

Vijñānabhikṣu here suggests that the Naiyāyikas' positing the existence of God in order to explain the law of karma is unnecessarily complex. It is possible to account for the arising of effects without recourse to the concept of God. The Naiyāyikas think that the arising of the effect from the action is on the model of the potter—the clay (the cause) cannot automatically give rise to the pot (the effect) without an intelligent being as superintendent. However, the author of the sūtra contends that the Naiyāyikas' causal model is faulty. In this case, no supervising being is necessary to bring about the cause, as is the case with many other things in the world (the seed giving rise to the sprout, for example). Vijñānabhikṣu is uncharacteristically terse in commenting on this passage, and indeed in all *SS* 5.2–11. This is likely because he does not consider the arguments to be valid. Nonetheless, he goes through the motions necessary as a responsible commentator by fleshing out the syntax of the sūtras to give the reader a better understanding of the author's meaning.[44]

Not only is it unnecessary to posit God to explain the functioning of karma; there are also reasons that God *cannot* be a joint cause along with the action of the effect, in the way that the potter and the clay both cause the pot. Here the author of the *Sāṃkhyasūtras* goes beyond mere denial that God's existence can be proven. In fact, he argues that a creator God cannot exist, for the very definition of God given by the Nyāya and other theistic schools is self-contradictory.[45] Unlike a normal human potter, God has none of his own ends to serve, since he is all-powerful and always already fulfilled: he lacks nothing. The human potter creates the pot because he has a certain want. He needs a receptacle to hold water, or he needs to make pots in order to earn his livelihood. God has no desire (*upakāra*) analogous to the desires of the potter and therefore will not cause anything. The opponent might respond: "Very well, let us posit a God who, like the potter, has desires and needs." *SS* 5.4 functions as a response to this. If you posit a God who possesses his own desires, he will be just like a worldly lord (*laukikeśvara*). This is because, as Vijñānabhikṣu points out, "If it is admitted that God too has needs, then he would be just like a worldly lord, subject to *saṃsāra*. And since His desires have not been fulfilled, there would be the unwanted implication of pain, and so forth."[46] In other words, by altering the definition of God to include his wants and needs, God will simply be an extremely powerful being among beings, not a unique being who is all-powerful, omniscient, and free from all suffering.

Following from this, *SS* 5.5 points out that the appellation of "God" (*īśvara*) would simply be a technical term referring to the first *puruṣa* at the beginning of creation, and not referring to God as commonly understood by the philosophical systems. The author of the *Sāṃkhyasūtras* is perfectly happy to concede that such a technical meaning of the word "God" is possible. In fact, it is a useful hermeneutic strategy for the Sāṃkhya to allow this interpretation of the word "God," since it gives them an opportunity to explain apparent references to God in scripture by reducing the word "God" to the first *puruṣa,* who is subject to *saṃsāra* and did not create the world.

SS 5.6–7 continue in this vein. Not only will a God who is the superintendent of karma have his own interests (*upakāra*); he will also be beset by desire (*rāga*), which is quite obviously inappropriate. For if it is admitted that God experiences desire, he will not be eternally free (*SS* 5.7). Anticipating another strategy by his opponent, the author states in *SS* 5.8, "If you claim that he attains the state of God due to his connection with the powers of *prakṛti,* there is the unwanted implication of his attachment."[47] Vijñānabhikṣu explains *SS* 5.8 in some detail. The problem here, as he sees it, is the flaw of mutual dependence (*anyonyāśraya*) between God and *prakṛti:*

> Moreover, it is not possible that lordliness is directed toward *prakṛti* by desire, etc. which are transformations of *prakṛti.* For then there would be a mutual dependence: the activation of *prakṛti* would occur before the arising of desire, and the arising of desire, etc. would occur before the activity of *prakṛti.* Nor does it make sense to say that desire exists eternally in *prakṛti.* That is impossible, since the *śruti* and *smṛti* teach that *prakṛti* exists in a state of equilibrium before the creation of the world.[48]

Although *prakṛti* exists eternally, it exists in a changing, evolving state. Before the creation of the world, it exists in a state of pure equilibrium, in which the three *guṇas*—agitation, lethargy, and purity—all exist in equal measure. If the opponent claims that God possesses desires merely through his association with *prakṛti,* and not inherently in himself, then a paradox arises. God is the one, according to the theistic opponent, who sets in motion the evolution of *prakṛti.* To do so, however, he has to possess some desire to do so. Yet strictly speaking, desire is an evolute of *prakṛti;* before *prakṛti's* evolution, desire does not exist. Desire can develop in *prakṛti* only when the *guṇa* of agitation is predominant, which is not the case when the three *guṇas* are in equilibrium. This is why Vijñānabhikṣu sees this as an example of mutual dependence. *Prakṛti* depends on God in order to evolve, but before God can activate *prakṛti,* he himself requires that *prakṛti* is already evolved. Therefore, the desire to create can neither exist for God in himself, as proven in *SS* 5.3–7, nor can such desire be a part of *prakṛti,* since it would not be available to God before the time of creation.

Finally, in *SS* 5.9, the author entertains the possibility that the condition of being God might somehow arise automatically by the mere proximity of *prakṛti* to the *puruṣa,* without any real attachment between the two. Vijñānabhikṣu uses the analogy of the iron and magnet to explore this possibility. Sāṃkhya accepts the possibility that two entities can have an effect on each other without any direct association. Most famously, this metaphor of iron and magnet is used to explain the attraction of the *puruṣa* to *prakṛti.* In the *Sāṃkhyakārikā,* it is this automatic attraction of the *puruṣa* to *prakṛti* that begins the process of evolution, and not the intervention of any God. Likewise, the opponent suggests that perhaps the proximity of *prakṛti* to the *puruṣa* creates some sort of automatic development of the qualities of God in the *puruṣa* itself. But, if this were the case, the *Sāṃkhyasūtras* point out that all *puruṣas* would be God, instead of only one. Having explored all of the possibilities, the author of the sūtra has shown that there is no way for God to exist. The complex of related arguments in *SS* 5.2–9 is, in essence, a *reductio ad absurdum.* Assume that such a God exists who possesses all of the desires and capabilities necessary for superintending the law of karma and creating the world. If that were the case, these very desires would preclude him from being God, all-powerful and free from worldly attachments.

The basic thrust of the arguments in *SS* 5.2–9 is that desire is a precondition for the creation of anything. Because God is by definition free from desire or any other want, he cannot be the creator of the universe. To rebut the Sāṃkhya argument, the first option would be to contest its initial premise, that desire is necessary for creation. The most well-known attempt among theistic schools to do just this is by relying on the concept of play (*līlā*). According to some theists, there is one sort of creation that is not preceded by any desire or want on the part of the creator. That is the sort of creation that occurs as the result of the free, purposeless play of the creator himself. The *Sāṃkhyasūtras* do not address this argument, although it might be interesting to see how such a theory of play would be rejected by an atheist school. A second option also remains open for a theist. The author of the *Sāṃkhyasūtras* has disproved the existence of a God who is the superintendent of karma and who creates the world by setting *prakṛti* into motion. It is possible, however, to conceive of a God who does neither of these things. In fact, this is one interpretation of the account of God given in the *Yogasūtras,* especially among modern rationalizing interpreters of Patañjali.[49] God is an omniscient, all-powerful being who is completely passive, because he has no interest or desire to act. He functions purely as an object of meditation and an inspiration for the yogin, who aspires to the state of complete detachment from desire that God has already attained. This is not the picture of God portrayed in the *Yuktidīpikā* or the other early commentaries on the *Sāṃkhyakārikā*. There, although God is not depicted as the creator of the world, he is an active being who affects the world. This is explicit in the *Yuktidīpikā*'s discussions of the "bodies of dignity" (*mahātmyaśarīra*) that God assumes. That he should desire to take such bodies, and that he presumably goes on to act in the world, indicates that he does have some particular interests of his own to pursue. This possibility would be disallowed by the arguments of the *Sāṃkhyasūtras*.

There are three possible accounts for God in the Sāṃkhya and Yoga systems: (1) a God who is completely passive, (2) a God who is not creator of the world but is an active agent in the world, and (3) a God who is creator of the world. The arguments of *SS* 5.2–12 are designed to prove the nonexistence of the third type of God and would also seem to apply to the second, since any action by God would require some prior desire. However, these arguments are not targeted at the first sort of God, a completely passive God. This suggests that the existence of a completely passive God remains a theoretical possibility for the Sāṃkhya, albeit not one that Vijñānabhikṣu and other late medieval thinkers found particularly compelling or attractive. While the earliest commentaries on the *Sāṃkhyakārikā* seem to endorse the second possibility, Vijñānabhikṣu opts for a God who is fully responsible for the creation of the world, and he makes arguments to show that this was the true position of Kapila, the founder of the Sāṃkhya system.

Vijñānabhikṣu chooses to finally state his objections to these disproofs of God's existence in his commentary on *SS* 5.12. Notably, *SS* 5.12 is where the sūtra's author switches to the topic of the scriptural evidence for God's nonexistence. Up until now, Vijñānabhikṣu has remained a faithful commentator, glossing the *Sāṃkhyasūtras* and at times adding arguments in support of their assertion that God does not exist. However, after supplying a rather halfhearted gloss of *SS* 5.12's contention that scriptural authority fails to prove the existence of God, Vijñānabhikṣu abruptly reverses course. He essentially takes back everything he has said over the course of commenting on the sūtras denying the existence of God, *SS* 5.2–12. Once again, he appeals to the idea from his introduction that Kapila denies the existence of God in the *Sāṃkhyasūtras* merely in order to keep its readers indifferent to the Godlike powers they might attain:

> And this denial of God is for the sake of indifference with regard to lordliness, as well as for the sake of explaining the possibility of liberation without knowledge of God. It is merely a bold assertion (*prauḍhivāda*), as previously explained. Otherwise, there would be excessive complexity resulting from the acceptance of a secondary meaning of God's eternality, which does not belong to individual selves. The rejection of God must be abandoned because the eternality of God is consistent with my view that the eternal knowledge, desire, etc. of God belong to his limiting conditions, and are modifications of the intellect (*buddhi*), and so forth. This can be seen in the *Vedāntasūtra*s.[50]

After a long silence in which Vijñānabhikṣu appears to accept the sūtras' assertions rejecting God's existence, he finally counters with what he considers to be the correct view—in fact, the true view of the Sāṃkhya sage Kapila. Besides reiterating his earlier claim that it invokes indifference to lordliness among hearers, he adds one more reason for Kapila's apparent rejection of God. We see certain instances where men have been liberated without any apparent worship of, meditation on, or aid from God. In fact, it is perfectly possible to achieve liberation without any conception of God, as the Sāṃkhya teaching shows. At least in certain cases, it seems, acceptance of God is a hindrance to enlightenment, and rejection is a boon. The nonexistence of God, although false, is sometimes "good to think." However, as we will see, this suggestion is contradicted by certain passages in Patañjali's *Yogasūtras* and Vyāsa's commentary on that text, the *Yogabhāṣya*. Patañjali depicts God as an important meditative object for yogins seeking liberation. Furthermore, Vyāsa's commentary implies that without God, there can be no liberation. Although God is acknowledged to have no hand in world-creation, in Patañjali and Vyāsa he has an essential role to play in the drama of individual human liberation.

While the first half of the preceding quotation from the *Sāṃkhyapravacanabhāṣya* is straightforward, the brevity of the argument in the second half has caused perplexity among the few scholars who have attempted to make sense of it.[51] I follow Garbe's interpretation, which understands the passage to be an argument for the rejection of the apparent Sāṃkhya denial of God. If God is not accepted, then all of the passages that speak of God's eternality and omnipotence will have to be understood in some secondary sense and therefore will suffer from the defect of complexity (*gaurava*). As I discussed in chapter 3, Vijñānabhikṣu strongly resists use of secondary interpretation of scriptural passages if there is any possibility of understanding the passage in question in a primary sense—this is his central argument for the rejection of Advaita interpretations of the Upaniṣads. Here, he applies the same argument to the *Sāṃkhyasūtras'* rejection of God. If we understand the epithet "God" to refer simply to the first *puruṣa,* then we will also have to use secondary interpretation to understand references to this first *puruṣa*'s "eternality," "omnipotence," and so forth. The much simpler course is simply to take passages from the Upaniṣads such as "Then it thought, let me become many" (*Ch. Up.* 6.2.3) in a literal, and not a figurative sense. The creator of the world is a sentient being, not blind, insentient *prakṛti.* Vijñānabhikṣu's emphasis on scriptural proofs for God's existence is itself uncharacteristic of a Sāṃkhya commentary, where rational inference takes priority over scriptural authority. By basing his refutation of Sāṃkhya's apparent atheism on interpretation of the Upaniṣads rather than on an argument from natural theology, Vijñānabhikṣu exposes his Bhedābheda Vedānta roots. And, at the end of his commentary on *SS* 5.12, Vijñānabhikṣu once again refers the reader back to his commentary on the *Brahmasūtras* for further elucidation of the relation between the individual self and Brahman at the time of the world's dissolution and re-creation. That text remains the key for understanding the metaphysical relations that serve as the ground for the evolution of *prakṛti* in the Sāṃkhya worldview.

Vijñānabhikṣu's commentary on the *Sāṃkhyasūtras* is his most unusual work. He has to reconcile the text's clear denial of God with his own theism and the theism of his readers, most of whom would have been believers in God's existence, proponents of some variety of Vedānta or Nyāya theism. Faced with this difficult situation, in his paean to Sāṃkhya in the introduction to his commentary, he tactfully hints that Sāṃkhya does not present the ultimate teachings. It stops at the level of difference and fails to posit explicitly the overarching unity (or non-separation, *avibhāga*) between the individual self and Brahman. As I will show in chapter 6, he also subordinates Sāṃkhya to Yoga. Not only is Yoga more complete than Sāṃkhya in its acknowledgment of God, it is also the highest practical teaching. According to Vijñānabhikṣu's subcommentary on the *Yogasūtras,* Patañjali's eight-limbed path of Yoga presents a more potent technique for liberation than the purely theoretical exercises of discrimination between *prakṛti* and *puruṣa* presented by Sāṃkhya.

[6] YOGA, PRAXIS, AND LIBERATION

THE EXCELLENCE OF THE YOGIC PATH

Vijñānabhikṣu's *Yogavārttika,* a subcommentary on Patañjali's *Yogasūtras,* is currently his best-known work. But historical trends, not anything inherent in Vijñānabhikṣu's philosophy, have mostly determined which of his works was most popular in a given era. At the beginning of the twentieth century, his most well-known work was his commentary on Sāṃkhya, largely thanks to Richard Garbe's Sanskrit edition and German translation of that work. At the beginning of the twenty-first century, T. S. Rukmani has made the *Yogavārttika* available to practitioners of yoga in India, Europe, and North America thanks to her translation. Rukmani has strong opinions concerning the relationship between the Vedānta, Sāṃkhya, and Yoga strands of Vijñānabhikṣu's philosophy. She believes that in his heart of hearts, Vijñānabhikṣu was truly a Yogin:

> Vijñānabhikṣu was active at a time when, on the one hand, in the philosophical field, Vedānta was at its height and on the other hand, in the religious field, bhakti was gaining supremacy. Vijñānabhikṣu himself was an uncompromising yogī, both by conviction and practice. In the *Yogavārttika* he argues for Yoga being the philosophy par excellence for attaining liberation. As such, in order to establish Yoga in a Vedāntic atmosphere, it was his first duty to write commentaries on the Prasthānatrayī as was the practice amongst the Vedāntācāryas. . . .
>
> Coming to Vijñānabhikṣu's yogic beliefs it must be remarked that Vijñānabhikṣu is first and foremost a yogī. His interpretation of Vedānta

> and Sāṃkhya have mainly been from the yogic angle. Other commentators like Vācaspati Miśra have been able to comment on the different schools of philosophy objectively. But in Vijñānabhikṣu one finds an intense commitment to his personal philosophy which he tries to fit into the other kindred systems like Vedānta and Sāṃkhya. That he considers yoga superior to both Sāṃkhya and Vedānta has already been pointed out.[1]

Two major pieces of evidence from the *Yogavārttika* appear to support Rukmani's claim. First, she points out that Vijñānabhikṣu makes laudatory statements about Yoga that imply its superiority to all other schools. Second, Vijñānabhikṣu asserts that Yoga is a more effective means to liberation than any other system. Of course, in the earlier history of Sāṃkhya-Yoga there is quite a bit of ambiguity concerning whether Sāṃkhya and Yoga consisted of two systems or were just one. The historical evidence supports the conclusion that at the time the *Yogasūtras* were written, there was no separate "Yoga" system and that Patañjali's text is an "exposition of Sāṃkhya" (*sāṃkhyapravacana*).[2] However, Vijñānabhikṣu is one of the many late medieval commentators who does seem to regard the two schools as having different teachings, as indicated by passages in both the *Sāṃkhyapravacanabhāṣya* and the *Yogavārttika*. It is, therefore, a legitimate question to ask: Did Vijñānabhikṣu consider himself a Yogin (i.e., an adherent of a separate Yoga school of philosophy) and not a Sāṃkhya or a Vedāntin? Did he consider the Yoga school of philosophy superior to those two other schools? Just as in the discussion of God's existence and nonexistence (chapter 5), it was necessary to remain sensitive to the many different possible meanings of the word "God," so, too, we have to be careful to keep from conflating the many meanings of the word *yoga*. At stake here is a doctrinal affiliation to a distinct school known as "Yoga," not simply the practice of certain techniques described by the *Yogasūtras* or Vijñānabhikṣu's celebratory remarks in reference to something called "yoga."

As is traditional in Indian philosophical texts, Vijñānabhikṣu begins each of his three commentaries on Vedānta, Sāṃkhya, and Yoga with laudatory comments directed toward the philosophical tradition on which he is commenting. As I discussed in the previous chapter, these remarks are ambiguous in his commentary on the *Sāṃkhyasūtras*. Although he celebrates the Sāṃkhya sage Kapila, he also tactfully admits that there are some parts of Kapila's text that are not completely accurate. In his introductions to the Vedānta and Yoga commentaries, however, no such caveats are given. In his *Yogavārttika,* as Rukmani has pointed out, he refers to Yoga as the highest teaching, the ocean into which all of the other teachings flow:

> 2. The commentary on Patañjali's work, the treasure-house of jewels in the form of knowledge, excavated by the great sage Vyāsa, is an ocean of milk. In it is the nectar that is fit for the great Yogins to drink. So that knowledgeable Brahmins here on earth can churn out the nectar from Vyāsa's commentary, the *Vārttika* is offered as the Mandara mountain, the great churning stick.
>
> 3. There [in his commentary] Vyāsa declares the essence of the meaning of all of the Vedas, disguised as a commentary on Yoga. Hence it is the path for those who desire liberation.
>
> 4. Just as all the rivers, beginning with the Ganges, exist as parts of the ocean, so too the philosophical systems, beginning with the Sāṃkhya, exist entirely as parts of this Yoga system.[3]

Vijñānabhikṣu once again uses the language of disguise (*miṣa*) and deception to describe a philosophical teaching. Although Vyāsa's commentary appears simply to be a work on Yoga, it is, in fact, a distillation of all the Vedas and therefore is the way to liberation. Vijñānabhikṣu also describes it as an "ocean of milk." The metaphor of the nectar churned out of the ocean of milk harks back to the famous story from the *Mahābhārata* and the Purāṇas of the gods and demons vying for the nectar of immortality.[4] Of course, his Vedāntic commentary, the *Vijñānāmṛtabhāṣya* (Commentary on the Nectar of Knowledge) takes its name from that same myth. Vijñānabhikṣu deploys the myth in similar ways in both commentaries. At the beginning of the *Vijñānāmṛtabhāṣya* he writes:

> 3. This nectar of knowledge, drawn out by churning of the sea of milk that is the speech of revealed texts, remembered texts, and reasoning, I offer to Brahmins to please the teacher.
>
> 4. Having distributed the nectar and used the Mohinī that is discriminative wisdom to cheat the demons who are bad arguments, let those who desire nectar drink this.
>
> 5. After Brahmins have drunk this and become strong, conquering the leaders of the troops of demons who are the infidels (*pākhaṇḍa*), may they reach the abode of the great teacher through knowledge and ritual action.[5]

Vijñānabhikṣu extends the metaphor even farther in the *Vijñānāmṛtabhāṣya* , alluding to Mohinī, the attractive female form taken on by Viṣṇu in order to distract the demons from seizing the nectar that they and the gods had churned from the ocean using the Mandara mountain as a churning-rod and the giant serpent Vāsuki as a rope. This is not the only similarity between the introductions of the two texts. Just as the *Yogavārttika* presents yoga as the path for those who seek liberation, so, too, knowledge of Brahman is the path to liberation, according to the *Vijñānāmṛtabhāṣya:*

> "The knower of Brahman obtains the highest," "One who knows Brahman becomes Brahman," "Only knowing that, he reaches beyond death." In these and other passages of revealed scripture there is injunction regarding knowledge of Brahman, which has been proven the instrument for the attainment of the highest human end. "One should meditate on just the self." "The wise Brahmin, just knowing that, should perform knowledge of Brahman." Such is the form of the injunction. In these statements, what is Brahman? What are the group of qualities that prove that it is Brahman? What sort of thing is the knowledge of it? What sort of thing is its result? These kinds of questions are precisely what those seeking liberation wish to know, due to apparently contradictory meanings in scripture caused by the differences among the Vedic lineages. Hence, in order to settle these issues, the discipline of Brahma-Mīmāṃsā is required.[6]

This account from the *Vijñānāmṛtabhāṣya* is similar in its depiction of knowledge of Brahman as indispensable for liberation. It differs from the account in the *Yogavārttika,* however, in its absence of inclusivist rhetoric. At the time of the writing of the *Vijñānāmṛtabhāṣya,* Vijñānabhikṣu did not feel the larger rhetorical need to argue that all of the *āstika* philosophical systems are ultimately a single unified body of doctrine. Instead, he portrays the various philosophical systems as having frequent disagreements and portrays himself an exponent of the Vedānta. Although the commentary is rife with Sāṃkhya and Yoga influences, and Vijñānabhikṣu even feels comfortable quoting Kapila for support on occasion, nonetheless, he portrays other systems of philosophy as frequently defective.

The *Yogavārttika* and *Sāṃkhyapravacanabhāṣya* are the work of a more mature scholar than the *Vijñānāmṛtabhāṣya,* as others have remarked.[7] One piece of evidence for this is the more nuanced attitude that

Vijñānabhikṣu takes in treating the various non-Yoga systems as parts of a greater Yogic whole. In principle, there was nothing to prevent him from treating Vedānta the same way in his earlier works. In many ways, Bhedābheda Vedānta is even more amenable to this type of treatment than Yoga, since its central concept is that of a metaphysical unity that underlies phenomenal difference. But Vijñānabhikṣu never explicitly thematizes the unity of all of the schools in the language of *bhedābheda.* Very likely, such an application of *bhedābheda* never occurred to him. *Bhedābheda* operates on a metaphysical plane different from the social-historical plane of doxographic organization, and the relation of the different schools is not a topic of inquiry in the same way that the nature of Brahman is. Vijñānabhikṣu certainly does have a systematic understanding of the relationship and relative worth of philosophical schools, but it has to be inferred by the reader from his discussions on topics such as Brahman, the individual self, the multiplicity of *puruṣas,* the existence of God, the nature of and means to liberation, and so forth.

Of course, it is one thing to celebrate a school of philosophy in the benedictory verses at the beginning of a text. It is quite another thing to say precisely why one set of doctrines is superior to another. In the *Yogavārttika,* Vijñānabhikṣu gives some hints concerning the precise reasons for Yoga's superiority by bringing into play another connotation of the word *yoga.* Although he clearly understands Yoga to be a body of philosophical doctrines distinct from Sāṃkhya and Vedānta, Vijñānabhikṣu also sees the Yoga system as having a special concern with the practical means to liberation. And it is this special orientation, different from all other philosophical systems, that gives it its superiority. After listing several quotes from the Upaniṣads and Purāṇas that seem to allude to some particular yogic practices, he suggests that the Yoga system is uniquely capable of discussing such practices:

> There [in *smṛti* texts mentioned previously] those who desire liberation wish to know the nature of Yoga, what are the means to its attainment, how is it the cause of knowledge and liberation, etc. In the Vedānta, Sāṃkhya, etc., only knowledge is usually discussed, and Yoga is only discussed briefly as a means to knowledge. But the Yoga that arises from knowledge is not mentioned there, even briefly. Therefore, Patañjali, who desires to explain the two-fold Yoga at great length, in order to get the attention of students, introduces the text that is a teaching on Yoga by saying at the beginning, "Now, a teaching on Yoga."[8]

Vijñānabhikṣu here refers obliquely to an equation that he will later make explicit. Since Sāṃkhya and Vedānta are primarily concerned with the correct conceptualization of the individual self (*jīvātman* or *puruṣa*) in its relationship to the material world and (in the case of Vedānta) to Brahman, the highest state attainable to practitioners of these schools is meditation accompanied by conceptual objects (*samprajñātasamādhi*). In this form of meditation, the yogin has not yet completely transcended worldly conceptions of subject and object. There are multiple forms of this type of meditation, all involving the yogin's conscious unification with a meditative object.[9] So, to take one example, a yogin might meditate on the form of the god Kṛṣṇa, identifying completely with this god. Although he has attained a state of unification (*samāpatti*) with his object of meditation, that object is still conceptually available to him as a meditative object. While meditation accompanied by conceptual objects (*samprajñātasamādhi*) represents a high stage of yogic accomplishment, it is not the highest. The highest meditative state a yogin can attain is meditation free of conceptual objects (*asamprajñātasamādhi*). This is the state that Vijñānabhikṣu identifies closely with the Yoga system of philosophy. Although a follower of Yoga philosophy has access to both meditation accompanied by conceptual objects and meditation without conceptual objects, Sāṃkhyas and Vedāntins only have access to the lower stage of meditation. In this respect, specifically in terms of practice, Yoga can be described as superior to the systems of Sāṃkhya and Vedānta.

But what is the specific relation of these two meditative states to the highest goal of human life—liberation from the cycle of death and rebirth? Vijñānabhikṣu maintains that practitioners of all three schools, Vedānta, Sāṃkhya, and Yoga, are capable of achieving liberation. As discussed in chapter 5, Sāṃkhyas are even capable of reaching liberation without relying on any concept of God (*īśvara*). Just as in their system God is not a necessary precondition for liberation, so, too, meditation without conceptual objects (*asamprajñātasamādhi*) is not a necessary precondition. It is superior in that it is an express route to liberation, while meditation with conceptual objects (*samprajñātasamādhi*) takes more time. Specifically, meditation without conceptual objects allows a practitioner to skip entirely the state of embodied liberation (*jīvanmukti*) and to progress immediately to final liberation. To understand why this should be so according to Vijñānabhikṣu requires some background into philosophical controversies surrounding embodied liberation and the mechanics of the Indian theory of karma.

KARMA AND EMBODIED LIBERATION

One way of classifying actions has to do with the status of results. The theory of karma states, in essence, that every positive or negative act (*karman*) has a commensurate result (*phala*). In many cases, there is a substantial period of time between the act and the arising of its result. With this in mind, Vijñānabhikṣu refers to a threefold typology of acts commonly accepted by most traditions of Indian philosophy: (1) acts that have already begun to produce results (*prārabdhakarman*), (2) acts whose positive or negative effects have been collected but are not yet giving results (*saṃcitakarman*), and (3) acts that are currently being performed so therefore have not as yet given results (*anāgatakarman*). The third sort of acts are the ones most amenable to change, since the actor is currently performing those acts. Acts whose effects have been collected but not yet come to fruition (*saṃcitakarman*) also hold out the possibility that the results can be avoided.

Vijñānabhikṣu and most other theorists of karma hold that by means of knowledge of the sort attained in the Sāṃkhya and Vedānta systems, it is possible to cut off such "collected" (*saṃcita*) acts before they come to fruition and to experience liberation. According to most Vedānta, Sāṃkhya, and Yoga thinkers, however, acts that have already begun to produce results (*prārabdhakarman*) cannot be avoided—their results must be experienced, even if the one who experiences these acts has already achieved liberation (*mokṣa*). They are karmic residue, which must be allowed to burn off before the enlightened one can achieve final release, which is characterized as the complete and permanent separation from the realm of *saṃsāra* and *prakṛti.* This period in which the liberated being waits for this residue to burn off is called "embodied liberation," or *jīvanmukti.* This is the state of all of those enlightened teachers who were able to remain in the world for a time to instruct their followers. Hence the possibility of *jīvanmukti* is important from a practical and pedagogical standpoint—without it, all worldly teachings would only be the testimonies of those who had not yet been liberated.

The topic of embodied liberation was itself at the center of frequent polemics, as the Pūrva Mīmāṃsakas rejected this possibility, while many Vedāntins, Sāṃkhyas, and Yogins accepted it.[10] *BS* 4.1.15 appears to support the existence of *jīvanmukti:* "But only those former works whose effects have not yet begun are destroyed by knowledge, because that death of the body is the term." In their commentaries on this sūtra, Vijñānabhikṣu and Śaṅkara also cite *Ch. Up.* 6.14.2 as scriptural support for the view that *jīvanmukti* is a human possibility: "There is delay here of him only as long as he is not freed, but then he will arrive." Both commentators understand this to mean that there is delay of the liberated one as long as he is not freed of his body, due to the necessity of burning off karmic residue. After the residue is exhausted, however, the sage is permanently free of embodiment. The commentators identify knowledge as that which destroys acts whose results have not yet begun to arise, and the same knowledge as being incapable of destroying results that have begun to arise (*prārabdhakarman*).

A reader only familiar with Vijñānabhikṣu's Vedāntic works would be led to believe that this is the last word in the matter. However, Vijñānabhikṣu revisits this same topic near the beginning of the *Yogavārttika.* Although he still maintains that knowledge of Brahman is incapable of cutting off acts that have already begun to produce results, he suggests that such acts can be cut off by another means:

> And in that way, by means of the destruction of karma, it is established that like knowledge, objectless yoga too is the cause of liberation. And there, by burning up all subconscious traces by means of objectless yoga, even previous acts that have already begun to produce results are left behind. This is how it is different from knowledge. Knowledge is unable to destroy acts that have already begun to produce results, as indicated in the statements such as, "There is delay here of him only until he is not freed, but then he will arrive" (*Ch. Up.* 6.14.2), and there are revealed scriptures and remembered texts on the topic of *jīvanmukti.* For [objectless] yoga, however, there is no inability to destroy acts that have already begun to produce results. On the contrary, "The yogin who has attained *samādhi* and burned up the heap of karma by means of the fire of yoga immediately attains liberation in that life" (*Viṣ. Pu.* 6.7.35). Hence even acts that have already begun to produce results are left behind, just as atonement is described [as destroying] the effects of acts. The result of [objectless] yoga is instantaneous liberation alone. Furthermore, when all mental traces are destroyed by the two yogas, due to the lack of an assisting mental trace of experience, even previous acts that have already begun to produce results become incapable of producing results. This too is a result of yoga. This is said in the *Mokṣadharma* section of the *Mahābhārata:* "There is no knowledge equal to Sāṃkhya; there

> is no power equal to Yoga." "Power" means that by leaving behind previous acts that have already begun to produce results, Yoga by itself is the cause of quick liberation.[11]

Vijñānabhikṣu had previously suggested that only Yoga can lead to the stage of objectless meditation. And it is only by means of objectless meditation that acts that have already begun to produce results (*prārabdhakarman*) can be destroyed. It follows that there are two paths to final liberation. The path of knowledge (*jñāna*), offered by the Sāṃkhya and Vedānta systems, can lead to meditation with objects and can be efficacious for enlightenment. But the follower of Sāṃkhya or Vedānta will have to endure the state of *jīvanmukti,* as suggested by *BS* 4.1.15 and *Ch. Up.* 6.14.2. However, *Viṣ. Pu.* 6.7.35 suggests that Yoga can cause immediate release, destroying *prārabdha* acts and bypassing *jīvanmukti* altogether. Yoga, according to Vijñānabhikṣu, is the fast track to complete liberation. Although Sāṃkhya, Vedānta, and Yoga can all lead to liberation, Yoga is the best of the three solely in terms of its efficiency.

Vijñānabhikṣu takes the statement from *Mokṣadharma* quite seriously that "There is no knowledge equal to Sāṃkhya. There is no power equal to Yoga."[12] This suggests a division of labor between the systems. The Yoga system is the most efficient means to enlightenment, but not the highest system in terms of true or ultimate doctrines. There is little or nothing in the *Yogasūtras* that would suggest that the ultimate relationship between the *puruṣa* and Brahman is difference and non-difference. Both Sāṃkhya and Yoga function on a lower theoretical level than the Vedānta; both are dualistic systems, primarily (or, a modern historian would say, exclusively) concerned with the level of difference. Yet, according to Vijñānabhikṣu's brand of Bhedābheda Vedānta, this level is ultimately sublated by the state of non-difference, or non-separation, between Brahman and the individual self. Vijñānabhikṣu even uses the terms "conventional" (*vyāvahārika*) and "ultimate" (*pāramārthika*) to describe these two levels in his commentary on the *Brahmasūtras.* For Vijñānabhikṣu, it would have been even more apt for the passage just quoted from the *Viṣṇu Purāṇa* to read, "There is no knowledge equal to Vedānta." Vedānta acknowledges God and teaches of an ultimate level that surpasses the duality of *prakṛti* and *puruṣa.*[13] But in spite of its philosophical ultimacy, it is inferior to Yoga on the level of practice.

The larger question at stake in this extremely technical discussion of the mechanisms that cause *jīvanmukti* and its cessation has do to with the relative superiority of the systems of Indian philosophy. Whether or not we accept Vijñānabhikṣu's arguments based on scripture and inference, his conclusion of Yoga's superior ability to bring speedy liberation means that it is proper to say that Yoga is superior to all other systems in at least this one regard. But does his argument for Yoga as the fastest road to the destination of liberation entitle us to say that Vijñānabhikṣu was a Yogin first and foremost? The answer is almost certainly that it depends on our definition of the words *yogin* and *yoga.* In spite of his apparent high regard for the Yoga system, it is not relevant to introduce questions of his personal practice of yoga into the discussion. At times, Vijñānabhikṣu offers descriptions of yogic states, claiming that he has experienced these states himself. Yet, like other medieval scholastics, he argues primarily from scriptural authority (*śabdapramāṇa*) and rational inference (*anumāna*), not on the basis of his personal mystical experiences as a yogin (*yogipratyakṣa*). It would seem consistent that he, as well as earlier commentators on the *Yogasūtras,* put into practice a system he held in such high regard. But there is no less reason to think that he practiced the discipline of inquiry into the nature of Brahman that is a central part of Vedānta, or the Sāṃkhya technique of intellectual discrimination (*viveka*) between *prakṛti* and *puruṣa.* All three systems are systems of contemplative practice. None are purely theoretical.[14] It would seem he practiced all three systems, Vedānta, Yoga, and Sāṃkhya. There is no indication from his writings that would allow us to make a distinction between the three systems based on his own personal practice or lack thereof.[15] And it is important to remember here that Vijñānabhikṣu considered the divisions between these three schools to be artificial when understood from the highest perspective. Any attempt to distinguish these three systems goes against the spirit of Vijñānabhikṣu's fundamental project itself. For him, all three are ultimately aspects of one and the same truth.

Vijñānabhikṣu is certainly not a Yogin if we take a Yogin to mean one who subscribes to all of the doctrines of Patañjali's *Yogasūtras.* Patañjali, unlike Vijñānabhikṣu, believed that God has no role in the creation of the world and that the activation of *prakṛti* and *puruṣa* is a mechanical process, like the attraction of iron filings to a magnet. Vijñānabhikṣu clearly states his belief that God is the one who activates *prakṛti* and *puruṣa* at the beginning of creation, citing Purāṇic verses such as "Hari enters into *prakṛti* and *puruṣa* according to his desire. When the time of creation is at hand, he agitates both the mutable and the immutable."[16] However, exclusively associating yoga and yogins with Patañjali's *Yogasūtras* is an arbitrary convention, established by some modern scholars who seek to privilege one moment in Indian intellectual history and use that to evaluate the authenticity of all earlier and later authors who claimed to be part of a tradition known as *yoga*. It is true that for many medievals and moderns, Patañjali's *Yogasūtras* function as the sourcebook for the authentic Yoga school. But thanks to the aphoristic ambiguities of the *Yogasūtras*, Vijñānabhikṣu can and does identify himself as an inheritor of the tradition of Patañjali's Yoga system. Furthermore, unlike Patañjali, Vijñānabhikṣu holds that there is a discrete Yoga school separate from the Sāṃkhya. Because the *Yogasūtras* mention God, yet do not clarify precisely what God's role is, Vijñānabhikṣu and most medieval yogins are free to understand the God of the *Yogasūtras* as none other than the God of Vedānta. According to Vijñānabhikṣu, that God is Viṣṇu, the omniscient, omnipotent creator of the universe.

THE UNITY OF YOGA AND VEDĀNTA SOTERIOLOGIES

The introductory section of Vijñānabhikṣu's *Sāṃkhyapravacanabhāṣya* offers ample evidence that at the time of its writing Vijñānabhikṣu saw Sāṃkhya, Yoga, and Vedānta as consisting of a single teaching. But some readers might argue that he had abandoned this notion by the time he wrote his works on Yoga. In this section, I dispute this claim by drawing from the final chapter of Vijñānabhikṣu's *Yogasārasaṃgraha* (Epitome of the Essence of Yoga). This work, probably Vijñānabhikṣu's last, functions as a summary of his much longer *Yogavārttika*.[17] He clearly states the purpose of the *Yogasārasaṃgraha* in its third benedictory verse: "After churning the ocean of yoga with the churning-rod that is *Yogavārttika*, I have extracted the essence of the nectar and deposited it into the pot that is this book."[18] Yet the *Yogasārasaṃgraha* is more than just a summary of the *Yogavārttika*. Its fourth and final section is also a summation of all of his works on Yoga, Vedānta, and Sāṃkhya, a brief final attempt to argue for the ultimate unity of the three systems.[19] In this section, he does so primarily by arguing for the unity of the end goal of the three systems—specifically, that the state of aloneness (*kaivalya*) taught as the final end of all human existence by the Sāṃkhya and Yoga is the same as the state of liberation (*mokṣa*) that Vedāntins strive to attain.

As discussed in chapter 3, Vijñānabhikṣu's early writings uphold a form of Bhedābheda Vedānta that can be described as *vibhāgāvibhāga*, or "separation and non-separation." He describes at length the relationship between the *jīvātman* (or individual self) and Brahman as one of separation and non-separation in his commentary on the *Brahmasūtras.* However, the concept of separation and non-separation also appears elsewhere in his philosophical corpus. This includes the two works that he probably wrote last, the *Sāṃkhyasāra* (Essence of Sāṃkhya) and *Yogasārasaṃgraha,* which is evidence that he never abandoned the Bhedābheda Vedāntic formulations of his earliest works. On the contrary, these *bhedābheda* concepts underlie his later work in Sāṃkhya and Yoga. Throughout his corpus, Vijñānabhikṣu understands the natural relation between the individual self and the absolute (or Brahman) to be non-separation. Non-separation is the relation that obtains between the two entities before the world's creation. It is also the relation between the *jīvātman* and Brahman after the *jīvātman* is liberated. Although we beings in the world are in a relation of separation (*vibhāga*) from Brahman before we are liberated, this current state of separation is adventitious and temporary. At the time of liberation, or *mokṣa,* we return to our natural state of non-separation (*avibhāga*).

Vijñānabhikṣu claims that all those passages in the Upaniṣads that express non-difference between the individual self and Brahman should be understood in the sense of non-separation. In this he differs fundamentally from Advaita Vedānta. He faults the Advaitins for their understanding of the relation between the *jīvātman* and Brahman as one of complete identity (*tādātmya*). Vijñānabhikṣu argues against the Advaita view both because it is inherently illogical and because he considers it a misreading of the Upaniṣads and the *Brahmasūtras.* Vijñānabhikṣu is also quite clear that the Advaita Vedānta is excluded from the concordance of philosophical schools. Like the Buddhists whose theories Advaita so closely resembles, Advaita Vedāntins are *nāstikas* and, according to him, therefore contrary to Sāṃkhya, Yoga, and true Vedāntic teachings.

Of course, it may seem that Vijñānabhikṣu's understanding of *mokṣa* as non-separation has just as little to do with the Yoga concept of aloneness (*kaivalya*) as does the Advaita understanding of *mokṣa* as complete oneness. The word *kaivalya* itself may conjure up the image of a *puruṣa* that is completely aloof and cut off from everything else in the universe—cut off not only from *prakṛti* but also from the other *puruṣas.* If this notion is correct, then what could Yoga possibly have in common with Vedāntic soteriologies that portray *mokṣa* as some sort of oneness or togetherness? The soteriology of isolation in the *Yogasūtras* and *Sāṃkhyakārikā* seems to go against the grain of most other Indian soteriologies. It also presents an obstacle for modern practitioners of yoga, who are often surprised at just how lonely the end destination described by Patañjali appears to be. Yet Vijñānabhikṣu understands the Vedāntic concept of *mokṣa* to be completely compatible with the concept of *kaivalya.* He says this explicitly in the fourth and final chapter of his *Yogasārasaṃgraha,* where he discusses the precise philosophical meaning of *kaivalya.* To understand his point, it is necessary to ascertain just what "aloneness" does and does not mean in its Yogic context.

Vijñānabhikṣu's *Yogasārasaṃgraha* quotes the well-known definition of *kaivalya* from the very last sūtra of Patañjali's *Yogasūtras. YS* 4.34 reads, "Isolation is the de-evolution of the *guṇas,* which serve no purpose for the *puruṣa.* Or it is the power of consciousness being established in its own nature."[20] Both in his *Yogasārasaṃgraha* and in his *Yogavarttika,* Vijñānabhikṣu offers an unusual reading of this aphorism that divides it into two. The "first *kaivalya,*" in Vijñānabhikṣu's terminology, is the de-evolution (*pratiprasava*) of the *guṇas.* This deevolution or dissolution of the *guṇas,* leads to the complete disjunction (*atyantaviyoga*) of the *puruṣa* and the *guṇas* of *prakṛti.* The *puruṣa* is completely alone, insofar as it is isolated from the *guṇas.* But Vijñānabhikṣu is careful to note that this does not mean that these *guṇas* have utterly ceased to exist. As far as the *puruṣa* who has become disjoined from the *guṇas* is concerned, the *guṇas* no longer exist. But the *puruṣas* are multiple, and for other *puruṣas,* union with *prakṛti* continues. He supports this position by citing another sūtra, *YS* 2.22: "Although *prakṛti* has ceased to exist for the one whose purpose has been attained, it has not ceased to exist completely, since it is the common experience of other beings as well."[21]

This is the first *kaivalya,* according to Vijñānabhikṣu, and it pertains primarily to *prakṛti.* He describes it as a property of *prakṛti* (*prakṛtidharma*). However, the second half of *YS* 4.34, describing the phenomenon of *kaivalya* from the standpoint of the *puruṣa* itself, is the part most important for the Vedāntic concordance with Yoga. Vijñānabhikṣu describes the second *kaivalya* as "the establishment of the *puruṣa* in its own nature" (*puruṣasya svarūpapratiṣṭhā*). But he points out that phenomenologically, the result is the same whether we are talking about the first or second *kaivalya.* Both entail the cessation of the experience of suffering. He finds common ground here between Sāṃkhya and Yoga, as he points out the assertion of *SS* 1.1 that the highest goal of the *puruṣa* is the complete cessation of suffering.

While this concordance with Sāṃkhya will not strike us as especially surprising, Vijñānabhikṣu's next statement in the *Yogasārasaṃgraha* is more controversial. There he seeks to establish common ground between Yoga and Vedānta:

> The Vedāntins speak of liberation, which is the dissolution (*laya*) of the individual self into the highest self. But there is no contradiction between our theory and theirs. Just as there is dissolution of the rivers into the ocean, there is dissolution of the individual selves into Brahman, by means of the dissolution of the limiting conditions. For the meaning of the word "dissolution" is simply "non-separation." It has also been determined that the individual self is not stable as something apart from Brahman.[22]

First note that Vijñānabhikṣu reintroduces the technical term "non-separation" (*avibhāga*), continuing the thread of Bhedābheda Vedāntic interpretation that began in his earliest works. This passage makes it clear that Vijñānabhikṣu does not consider it necessary to abandon his earlier positions in Bhedābheda Vedānta in order to embrace Sāṃkhya and Yoga. On the contrary, he still considers these three schools to be complimentary when understood correctly.

Vijñānabhikṣu believes that the word pair *puruṣa* and *jīvātman* are synonyms, as are the two words *kaivalya* and *mokṣa*. He accepts that the *jīvātmans* are many. This is one of the ways in which his Bhedābheda Vedānta is closer to Yoga than is Advaita Vedānta. At the beginning of his commentary on the *Sāṃkhyasūtras*, Vijñānabhikṣu makes the argument that when the *Chāndogya Upaniṣad* (6.2.1) declares "one only, without a second" (*āsīd ekam evādvitīyam*), it declares the *jīvātmans* to be one only insofar as they share the same nature: each is constituted by pure consciousness. However, they remain multiple in number, even after they are liberated. When Vijñānabhikṣu says in the final chapter of the *Yogasārasaṃgraha* that the word dissolution (*laya*) simply means non-separation, he resorts once again to his central concept from the commentary on the *Brahmasūtras:* after liberation, the individual selves are non-separate from Brahman, but they are not absorbed into a state of complete nondifferentiation with Brahman, the Advaita *tādātmya* relation that he rejects.

For Vijñānabhikṣu's Bhedābheda concordance, the complementarity of Vedānta and Yoga hinges on the second *kaivalya,* the "establishment of the *puruṣa* in its own nature." Note that nowhere in Patañjali's definition of *kaivalya* at *YS* 4.34 does he say that this aloneness means the complete isolation of the *puruṣas* from one another or, for that matter, from

Brahman. The disjunction, or isolation, in question is specifically the disjunction between *prakṛti* and *puruṣa.* But the other aspect of *kaivalya* is the abiding of the *puruṣa* in its own natural state (*svarūpapratiṣṭḥā*). No longer does the *puruṣa* exist in the adventitious, temporary state of separation from Brahman. When it reverts to its natural state, it reverts to the state of being non-separate from Brahman. Therefore, *kaivalya* is not just a turning away, as it often seems when translated. It is also a turning toward. While turning away from *prakṛti,* the liberated *puruṣa* is simultaneously turning toward Brahman, returning to its original relation of non-separation. Yet the relation of separation is also real for a certain amount of time. When the *puruṣa* is yoked to the *guṇas* in the phenomenal world, it is separate from Brahman. But Vijñānabhikṣu considers this state of separation to be characterized by instability (*apratiṣṭhatva*). Thus he says in the quote cited previously from the *Yogasārasaṃgraha:* "The individual self is not stable as something apart from Brahman." Note the contrast made by his choice of Sanskrit terms—at the time of liberation or *kaivalya,* the *puruṣa* is established in its own nature (*svarūpapratiṣṭha*). During its time in the world as separate from Brahman, the *puruṣa* is unstable (*apratiṣṭha*). Hence, there is an underlying mechanism to explain why *kaivalya* occurs from the Vedāntic standpoint as well as from the Yogic. All things tend to return to their natural state of equilibrium. For the *puruṣa,* that state is non-separation from Brahman.

In the state of *kaivalya,* the individual self becomes what it is, reverting to its natural state. In the *Yogasūtras,* one dimension of this natural state is described as disjunction from the *guṇas* of *prakṛti* and freedom from pain. Patañjali says nothing about Brahman or about the embodied self's relation to Brahman. For Vijñānabhikṣu, this is not surprising—as he says in his commentary on the *Sāṃkhyasūtras,* to understand each school correctly, one must understand its proper scope. The scope of the Sāṃkhya is the philosophical discrimination between that which is self and that which is not self. Yoga offers a detailed discussion of the practical means to the disunion of these two, of *puruṣa* and *prakṛti.* But only Vedānta describes the individual self's relation to the highest self, or Brahman. It is unnecessary to choose one of these three systems as correct and the other two as wrong, for the *darśanas* are complementary, not contradictory.

Vijñānabhikṣu regarded the practices of the Vedānta, Sāṃkhya, and Yoga schools to be different but complementary paths. While Yoga is the most direct of those paths, the contemplative practices of the Vedānta and Sāṃkhya schools are also means to the same end. He regards the goal of all three systems to be identical: it is the reuniting of the individual self with Brahman, in its natural state of non-separation. The attempts by modern scholars to portray Vijñānabhikṣu either as an apostate Sāṃkhya or as a Yogin who paid lip service to Vedānta and Sāṃkhya go against the fundamental tenet of Vijñānabhikṣu's late works, the unity of the philosophical systems.[23] Furthermore, these modern attempts are themselves based on historical assumptions about the proper ways of categorizing Indian philosophical systems and identifying the authentic doctrines of each of the schools. As shown in the brief historical survey of the relation between Yoga and Sāṃkhya presented in chapter 4, these classificatory schemes are by no means obvious or without their own set of problems. In chapter 7, I show how modern scholars fought over Vijñānabhikṣu's legacy in their own attempts to set down the precise relationship between the schools of Indian philosophy.

[7] VEDĀNTA AND SĀṂKHYA IN THE ORIENTALIST IMAGINATION

INDIAN PHILOSOPHY AND THE CRITIQUE OF ORIENTALISM

The period from 1550 to 1750 that directly preceded the British rule of the Indian subcontinent was enormously fertile for philosophical innovation.[1] Yet although he could not have known it, Vijñānabhikṣu's generation of Sanskrit intellectuals was one of the last that remained untouched by colonialism. Coming near the end of an ancient commentarial tradition, Vijñānabhikṣu's Difference and Non-Difference philosophical system had little lasting impact on Indian intellectual life. Unlike the medieval Bhedābhedavādins Vallabha and Caitanya, Vijñānabhikṣu's writings did not become the theological basis for a popular devotional sect. The demanding nature of his writings and the relatively small place he gives to *bhakti* made such a movement unlikely. Nor was he the founder of a major school of philosophical commentary, like Śaṅkara and Rāmānuja. There are records of three immediate disciples of Vijñānabhikṣu: Bhāvāgaṇeśa, Prasāda Mādhava, and Divyasiṃha Miśra.[2] Bhāvāgaṇeśa's *Sāṃkhyatattvayāthārthyadīpana* (Light on the True Meaning of the Sāṃkhya Principles), for instance, extends Vijñānabhikṣu's project by applying Navya-Nyāya terminology in a commentary on the *Tattvasamāsasūtras,* another influential sūtra collection in the Sāṃkhya tradition.[3]

Vijñānabhikṣu's final follower in the premodern period is Nāgojī Bhaṭṭa (early eighteenth century), whose *Laghusāṃkhyavṛtti* is a condensed version of the *Sāṃkhyapravacanabhāṣya.*[4] There is also at least one record of a follower of a different school citing Vijñānabhikṣu. Puruṣottama, an important commentator on the works of the Bhedābheda

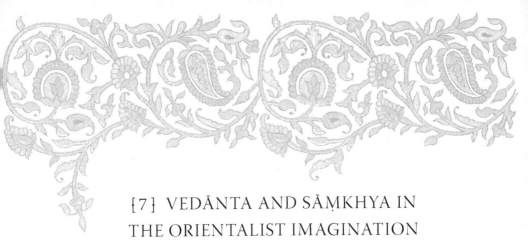

Vedāntin Vallabha, cites Vijñānabhikṣu's *Sāṃkhyapravacanabhāṣya* to elucidate the nature of renunciation (*tyāga*) in the Sāṃkhya school.[5] There may be yet other writings of the seventeenth and early eighteenth centuries that testify to the influence of Vijñānabhikṣu's ambitiously synthetic philosophical project in northern India. Historians have yet to analyze the great majority of Vedānta, Sāṃkhya, and Yoga texts of this period. When they finally do, the situation of these philosophical schools on the eve of British colonialism, and the extent of Vijñānabhikṣu's influence among Sanskrit intellectuals, will become substantially clearer.

One can imagine that if historical circumstances had been different, Vijñānabhikṣu's works could have been the beginning of a neo-Sāṃkhya commentarial tradition that accepted as established fact the concordance of Vedāntic, Sāṃkhya, and Yogic principles and enunciated a realist worldview as a counter to the increasingly illusionistic outlook of Advaitins such as Prakāśānanda. Due in part to external historical forces, however, Vijñānabhikṣu's most decisive influence was not on his countrymen but on the British and German Orientalists who read his commentary on the *Sāṃkhyasūtras*. For all of the nineteenth and most of the twentieth century, this work was Vijñānabhikṣu's most famous. Orientalists T. H. Colebrooke (1765–1837), A. E. Gough (1845–1915), Paul Deussen (1845–1919), and Richard Garbe (1857–1927) were also in a meaningful way the intellectual inheritors of Vijñānabhikṣu's thought. Beginning with Colebrooke's 1823 essay "On the Philosophy of the Hindus," the *Sāṃkhyapravacanabhāṣya* was regarded as an indispensable source text for one of the central controversies of nineteenth-century Indology, the true relationship between the Sāṃkhya and Vedānta systems.[6] Perhaps surprisingly, Vijñānabhikṣu stood at the center of the Orientalists' dispute over the true essence of Indian philosophy. While his general importance among his philosophical contemporaries might be a matter of dispute, there can be no disputing the strong feelings about Vijñānabhikṣu held by these early historians of Indian philosophy.

British colonial consolidation in India in the eighteenth century caused a decisive break in India's intellectual history, and the production of Sanskrit philosophical and literary texts never again equaled the quality or quantity of those composed in the late medieval period.[7] Yet out of the ashes of one textual tradition came a new proliferation of textual production, the writings of the Orientalists. These Westerners, such as William Jones, H. T. Colebrooke, and F. Max Müller, sought to apply the philological methods developed over hundreds of years in the study of Latin and

Greek texts to uncover truths about the Sanskrit textual tradition. Some recent critics, most notably Edward Said, have depicted these men as imperialist agents hardly involved in any meaningful way with the interpretation of foreign ideas. Saidian accounts understand the creation of the Orient as a mirroring process by which Western thinkers projected their opposite onto an Eastern Other. The understanding of essentialized binary relationships between West and East like materialism/spiritualism, this-worldly/otherworldly, science/religion, individual/community, masculine/feminine were more important than empirical investigation.[8] Said, who first polemicized the terms "Orientalist" and "Orientalism," maintains that whether Orientalists correctly or incorrectly understood the objects of their investigations is beside the point:

> The phenomenon of Orientalism as I study it here deals principally not with a correspondence between Orientalism and Orient, but with the internal consistency of Orientalism and its ideas about the Orient . . . despite or beyond any correspondence, or lack thereof, with a "real" Orient.[9]

This indifference to the actual objects of the Orientalists' study, and the bracketing of questions of truth or falsehood regarding Orientalist discourses, has hampered understanding of the Orientalist enterprise. Instead of the mirroring model that Said presents, a more complete model is suggested in the works of Charles Hallisey and Sheldon Pollock, for which Hallisey coins the phrase "intercultural mimesis."[10] "Intercultural mimesis" describes a process in which thinkers appropriate certain concepts or symbols they find in non-Western traditions and then recontextualize these concepts or symbols for ideological reasons specific to the European cultural sphere. To cite one example, Pollock points to the new way that the British Raj used Sanskrit *dharmaśāstra* texts—in particular, their concept of *varṇa* (often translated "class" or "caste")—as a tool for the uniform centralized governance of the Indian subcontinent.[11] Such cases suggest that real contact did at times take place between the Orientalists and their objects of study, however compromised by frequent recontextualizations and the distortions of imperial power. Furthermore, elites in Asian societies were often complicit in creating and sustaining Orientalist ideas, using Orientalist discourses as a means for maintaining their own elite status in the new context of colonial society.[12]

We should also approach the classificatory efforts of the nineteenth-century historians of Indian philosophy in terms of intercultural mimesis.

The earliest European scholars of Indian philosophy had a need for a means to classify the bewildering variety of philosophical doctrines and texts they found in Indian archives. They naturally sought out and privileged Sanskrit texts that would allow them to establish models for classification. In particular, the Indian doxographies of the medieval period suited their needs. These texts, frequently written by Advaita Vedāntins, tended to hierarchize philosophical schools, and these hierarchies likewise influenced the opinions of eighteenth- and nineteenth-century scholars in the West. As I discuss in chapter 8, one doxography in particular, the fourteenth-century *Sarvadarśanasaṃgraha* (Compendium of All Philosophical Systems) stood out among all others for its influence in medieval India and modern Europe. This led to the elevation of Advaita Vedānta above all other schools, especially in the writings of Paul Deussen and A. E. Gough.[13]

These Indologists' previous philosophical allegiances within the European cultural sphere also influenced the choice of the Indian philosophical system they held to be the oldest and, by their logic, therefore the most authentic. The influence of Kant's and Schopenhauer's transcendental idealism led many Orientalists to valorize the monism of Advaita Vedānta, which seemed to them closest to European idealism and which they understood as the true message of the Vedas. Richard Garbe, however, opposed this trend by championing the allegedly atheistic Sāṃkhya system as the true representative of pure philosophical inquiry in India. While Garbe's narrative did not have the widespread influence of Deussen's glorification of Advaita Vedānta, his central focus on the atheistic *Sāṃkhyasūtras* led to the widespread opinion that atheism is the true position of the Sāṃkhya school.

Many critics of Orientalism overlook the diversity of opinion among the Orientalists themselves. Although Said vilifies Orientalists for their totalizing, essentializing attitude toward Eastern cultures, he takes a similar totalizing approach by failing to differentiate between the diverse opinions of the many Orientalist thinkers.[14] Orientalists hold many assumptions in common, but they also differ greatly in the details of their interpretations. For instance, Heinrich Zimmer, who fled Nazi Germany with his Jewish wife to settle in New York, accepted the Orientalist depiction of aggressive Aryan migrants who invaded India in the second millennium BCE and conquered the Dravidian peoples they found there. Yet Zimmer insisted that ultimately it was the Dravidians who conquered the materialistic, warlike Aryans by infiltrating their religion with the Buddhist and Sāṃkhya values of pacifism, meditation, and world renunciation.[15] This contrasts, to put it mildly, with University of Munich Professor Walther Wüst, who sought to show in a 1937 lecture that Adolf Hitler's supposed insights were part of the "hereditary, long-term tradition . . . of the great Aryan personality of antiquity, the Buddha."[16] Clearly, there are meaningful differences between the Orientalists Zimmer and Wüst. Yet no one has sought to do justice to the complicated history of Orientalism itself—a definitive "history of Orientalism" has yet to be written.[17] Although that is not my project here, I hope that by applying the same intellectual-historical approach to the Orientalists that I applied earlier to premodern Indian authors, by acknowledging that Deussen and Gough, too, are part of the *Wirkungsgeschichte* of Indian philosophy, I can also do my small part to fill the lacunae in our knowledge of that history.

COLEBROOKE AND GOUGH: THE STRUGGLE FOR THE ESSENCE OF VEDĀNTA

H. T. Colebrooke, president of the Asiatic Society of Bengal and founder of the Royal Asiatic Society in London, stands next to Sir William Jones as one of the preeminent Orientalists of the late eighteenth and early nineteenth centuries.[18] Like other major figures of his time, he wrote on an enormous range of topics, from Indian mathematics to Prakrit poetry. Colebrooke's most significant contribution to the history of Indian philosophy comes in a series of lectures he gave from 1823 to 1827 at the Royal Asiatic Society, entitled "On the Philosophy of the Hindus." In his first lectures, he outlined the main attributes of the six *āstika* systems, and subsequently he covered the "heretical systems" of the Jainas and Buddhists, along with "certain other Indian sects," including the Māheśvaras, Pāśupatas, and Pāñcarātras. He describes these last five systems as exhibiting "some analogy to the *Sánc'hyas,* or followers of Capila or of Patanjali [*sic*]."[19]

Colebrooke's survey of the philosophical systems is remarkable for how much it adheres to the accounts of his Sanskrit primary sources, and how rarely he misinterprets or misrepresents the texts he was reading. A beginning student of Indian philosophy in the twenty-first century could do much worse than to start with Colebrooke's survey. In particular, he avoids the philosophical accretions of the late nineteenth-century Orientalists, many of whom find in the Indian philosophical systems identities and homologies with Greek and German philosophical systems. Unlike these later thinkers, Colebrooke is generally content to present doctrines without explicit comparison to Western philosophies, and without direct praise or disparagement. Colebrooke had read an enormous number of texts from the different systems and shows real interpretive insight with his analytical comments. It is no wonder that his reputation is so imposing among nineteenth-century scholars and that his later critics show great deference to him even while attacking his views.

H. T. Colebrooke, like other nineteenth-century Orientalists, is centrally concerned with the differentiation of philosophical doctrines. Although Colebrooke, too, depends on Mādhava's fourteenth-century doxography *Sarvadarśanasaṃgraha* for his basic enumeration of the schools, much of his work comes directly from his understanding of the primary texts of the schools in question. In his presentation of the Sāṃkhya system, for example, Colebrooke depends heavily on two texts: the *Sāṃkhyakārikā* with Gauḍapāda's commentary and the *Sāṃkhyasūtras* with Vijñānabhikṣu's commentary. He takes the *Sāṃkhyasūtras* to be an ancient treatise of the Sāṃkhya school, although he is skeptical of the claim that the text was authored by Kapila himself. He also notes that Vijñānabhikṣu must have been a relatively late commentator.[20] Nonetheless, he relies more on Vijñānabhikṣu's *Sāṃkhyapravacanabhāṣya* than on any other text for his own exposition of Sāṃkhya philosophy.

As I discussed in chapter 5, at the start of the *Sāṃkhyapravacanabhāṣya* Vijñānabhikṣu discusses a number of schools and provides his own vision of how their doctrines might be coordinated. This is doubtless one of the reasons Colebrooke found the text so valuable. Following the logic of Vijñānabhikṣu's text, Colebrooke describes the system of the Sāṃkhya as "partly heterodox, and partly conformable to the established Hindu creed."[21] Unlike later Orientalists who simply assert the "orthodoxy" of the "six schools," Colebrooke sees gradations of orthodoxy, in part determined by the degree to which each school bases its teachings on the Vedas themselves and on the degree to which each school reasons independently of the Vedas. On this basis, he describes "the two *Mímánsás* [*sic*]" as "emphatically orthodox."[22] Unlike later advocates of the Advaita Vedānta such as Deussen and Radhakrishnan, Colebrooke does not sever the close historical connection between Pūrva Mīmāṃsā and Vedānta. He emphasizes that both schools have as their primary concern scriptural interpretation and not abstract reasoning.

Although Colebrooke notes that Sāṃkhya is only "partly conformable to the established Hindu creed," if anything, this fact makes the Sāṃkhya school even more intriguing to him. He finds traces of Sāṃkhya ideas in numerous other schools and apparently non-Sāṃkhya texts, and he considers the Sāṃkhya the most influential of the philosophical schools. He divides the Sāṃkhya system into "two schools; one usually known by that name; the other commonly termed Yóga."[23] He also notes that Patañjali's *Yogasūtras* themselves bear the title *Sāṃkhyapravacana*, and that on most points the two systems are the same, "differing however upon one, which is the most important of all: the proof of existence of supreme God."[24] In presenting Kapila's disproof of the existence of God, he recapitulates Vijñānabhikṣu's arguments from *SPB* 5.2–12. He does not, however, note that Vijñānabhikṣu considers Kapila's private view to be that God does exist. Besides these two schools in the Sāṃkhya system, Colebrooke briefly describes a third, Paurāṇika Sāṃkhya, which "considers nature as an illusion. . . . In several of the *purános*, as the *Matsya, Cúrma* and *Vishnu*, in particular, the cosmogony, which is an essential part of an Indian theogony, is delivered consonantly to this system."[25]

Colebrooke offers two separate lectures on Mīmāṃsā and Vedānta and bases his summaries on numerous sources, noting Jaimini, Śabara, Kumārila Bhaṭṭa, and Prabhākara in particular. He is apparently indebted to Rāmānuja in portraying the Pūrva and Uttara Mīmāṃsā as parts of a single whole:

> The two together, then, comprise the complete system of interpretation of the precepts and doctrine of the *Védas*, both practical and theological. They are parts of one whole. The later *Mímānsā* is supplementary to the prior, and is expressly affirmed to be so: but, differing on many important points, though agreeing on others, they are essentially distinct in a religious as in a philosophical view.[26]

Colebrooke notes that Bādarāyaṇa's *Brahmasūtras* are in themselves quite cryptic and therefore lend themselves to many different interpretations. Śaṅkara is "the most distinguished scholiast of these *sutras*, in modern estimation," and for that reason Colebrooke restricts himself to explicating Śaṅkara and his school in his treatment of Vedānta. However, Colebrooke also acknowledges varying interpretations of the *Brahmasūtras* by Rāmānuja, Vallabha, Bhāskara, Madhva, and Nīlakaṇṭha.[27] In his explication of the Vedānta, he is particularly interested in Vedāntic polemics against the Sāṃkhya and in those places in the Upaniṣads where Sāṃkhya doctrines are presented.[28] His most controversial assertion regarding the Vedānta comes in the last paragraph of his treatment of the school. He criticizes the claim, widely held since its popularization by Schopenhauer, that the idea of the world as illusion is central to Vedāntic doctrines:

> The notion, that the versatile world is an illusion (*máya*), that all which passes to the apprehension of the waking individual is but a phantasy presented to his imagination, and every seeming thing is unreal and all is visionary, does not appear to be the doctrine of the text of the *Védánta.* I have remarked nothing which countenances it in the *sutras* of Vyása nor in the gloss of Śancara, but much concerning it in the minor commentaries and in elementary treatises. I take it to be no tenet of the original *Védántin* philosophy, but of another branch, from which later writers have borrowed it, and have intermixed and confounded the two systems. The doctrine of the early *Védánta* is complete and consistent, without this graft of a later growth.[29]

This minority opinion, that neither Bādarāyaṇa's *Brahmasūtras* nor the commentary by Śaṅkara contains the doctrine of *māyā,* has occasionally been repeated by other thinkers.[30] In the midst of the idealist system-building of the nineteenth-century philosophers, however, it was truly a thought out of season. Gough and Deussen, in particular, sought to put to rest any possibility that the late medieval and modern followers of Śaṅkara had fundamentally misinterpreted his works. Gough asserts that Colebrooke came to this mistaken assumption by relying on Vijñānabhikṣu's perverse and mistaken ideas about Vedānta philosophy:

> The assertion of the Orientalists that the doctrine of Māyā is a comparatively modern importation into the Vedāntic system is groundless, and the hypothesis of a primitive Vedānta in harmony with the system known as the Yogadarśana or demiurgic Sānkhya [*sic*] is untenable. . . . This brings us to the source of Colebrooke's error. His mistake arose from the acceptance of the polemical statement of an opponent of the Vedāntins, Vijñānabhikṣu, the celebrated exponent of the aphorisms of the Sānkhya, the author of the Sānkhyapravacanabhāshya. . . . In his commentary on the Sānkhya aphorisms, Vijñānabhikṣu propounds a theory that the several Darśanas or systems of Indian philosophy, are successive steps of ascent to the full truth of the demiurgic Sāmkhya or Yoga philosophy. . . . Vijñānabhikṣu's proposal to treat the several systems as progressive instalments of the truth, has no countenance in the works of Indian scholasticism. The systems are in those works exhibited on every page as in open hostility against each other. Vijñānabhikṣu's treatment of the philosophy of the Upanishads is false from

first to last; and Colebrooke's assertion falls with the fall of the assertion of Vijñānabhikṣu.[31]

There is some plausibility to Gough's charge that Colebrooke relies on Vijñānabhikṣu in his statements about the doctrine of *māyā* as a "later growth."[32] Vijñānabhikṣu follows Sanskrit commentarial convention in never referring to any individual "crypto-Buddhist" (*pracchannabauddha*) or "proponent of illusion" (*māyāvādin*) by name; instead, he refers to all of these opponents as "moderns" (*ādhunikas*). Although most readers have understood Vijñānabhikṣu's definition of "moderns" to encompass earlier thinkers including Śaṅkara, it would not be internally inconsistent to understand Vijñānabhikṣu's critique as only applying to post-Śaṅkara Advaita.[33]

While Colebrooke notes that Vijñānabhikṣu's commentary on the Sāṃkhya was written at a relatively recent date, Gough was the first to depict Vijñānabhikṣu's project as fundamentally perverse. Colebrooke observes that Vijñānabhikṣu has also written commentaries on the *Yogasūtras* and *Brahmasūtras* and is inspired by Vijñānabhikṣu to refer to Sāṃkhya as "partly heterodox." But according to Gough, Vijñānabhikṣu's affiliation is purely Sāṃkhya, and he is bent on the perversion of the true doctrine of the Upaniṣads. Like Colebrooke, Gough paraphrases the arguments against the existence of God in Vijñānabhikṣu's *Sāṃkhyapravacanabhāṣya* as the official position of the Sāṃkhya school, also failing to note that Vijñānabhikṣu himself ultimately accepts the existence of God. While Colebrooke notes the existence of numerous other Vedāntic schools besides Śaṅkara's, Gough simply fails to mention these other schools in his *Philosophy of the Upanishads.* Also remarkable is Gough's insistence that no other author besides Vijñānabhikṣu treats the systems as "progressive installments of the truth,"[34] especially as he had evidence to the contrary directly under his nose—Gough cowrote with E. B. Cowell the most widely read English translation of Mādhava's *Sarvadarśanasaṃgraha.* This Sanskrit text, as I discuss in chapter 8, shows clear affinities with the works of Vijñānabhikṣu and other medieval authors in its hierarchical organization of doctrines.

Comparing Gough's *Philosophy of the Upanishads* to Colebrooke's "On the Philosophy of the Hindus," we see the role of the Orientalist transformed: he has become an open advocate for one Indian philosophical school over another. Basing his work closely on Śaṅkara's *Brahmasūtrabhāṣya,* Gough presents the history of Indian philosophy as a fundamental conflict between Sāṃkhya dualism and Vedāntic non-dualism. Gough does not wish to complicate matters by introducing other schools. He neither remarks on a theistic school called the Yoga that is closely related to Sāṃkhya nor a school called Pūrva Mīmāṃsā that is closely related to Vedānta. Beginning with the thesis that the Upaniṣads are fundamentally Vedāntic in nature, without a trace of Sāṃkhya doctrines, Gough concludes that even "the teaching of the Śvetāśvatara Upanishad and of the Bhagavadgītā, notwithstanding their Sānkhya phrases and Sānkhya references, is as purely Vedāntic as that of any Vedāntic work whatever."[35] Traditionally, there are two particular references to Sāṃkhya in the *Śvetāśvatara Upaniṣad* that Vedāntins have found challenging: the "she-goat, who is colored red, white, and black" at *Śvet. Up.* 4.5 and a figure named "Kapila" at *Śvet. Up.* 5.2. Gough explains the former by recapitulating Śaṅkara's argument that the red, white, and black refer not to the three *guṇas* but to the triad of heat, water, and earth from the *Chāndogya Upaniṣad*.[36] He interprets the latter in a more historical way: he admits that the name "Kapila" may indeed refer to the founder of the Sāṃkhya, but he reinterprets the historical significance of the Sāṃkhya school itself. The Sāṃkhya "was originally a more precise set of terms for the enumeration of the emanations out of Prakṛiti or Māyā, and of the differences between Māyā and Purusha or Brahman."[37] In its original state, Sāṃkhya (understood etymologically as "enumeration") was in accord with the doctrine of *māyā* and was just an enumeration of its unreal transformations.[38] Only in later times did it harden into a distinctly atheist school that upheld the reality of the world and the plurality of *puruṣas*.

PAUL DEUSSEN AND THE INFLUENCE OF GERMAN IDEALISM

Paul Deussen was a disciple of Arthur Schopenhauer (1788–1860), the most notable European philosopher to claim inspiration from Indian sources. Schopenhauer was aware of his own special place in world philosophical history and wrote that "I do not believe that my doctrine could have ever been formulated before the Upanishads, Plato, and Kant were able to all cast their light simultaneously onto a human mind."[39] Deussen founded the Schopenhauer-Gesellschaft in 1911 and shared Schopenhauer's conviction that the doctrine of *māyā* was the central teaching of the Upaniṣads. His understanding of Vedānta and other Indian doctrines far exceeded Schopenhauer's, who had access to the Upaniṣads only through a Latin translation of Dārā Shikoh's Persian translation of the original Sanskrit text. It was through Deussen's writings that nineteenth-century German idealism had its most direct influence on the young discipline of Indology.

Deussen accepted many of the same premises of Gough—for instance, that the Upaniṣads are unambiguously Vedāntic in their outlook and that the Sāṃkhya was a school that later grew out of the Upaniṣads. But unlike Gough, Deussen struggled with some of the perplexing historical consequences of these ideas. He also went farther than his Indological predecessors in treating Indian philosophy in a comparative way and making normative philosophical claims based on insights from Eastern and Western philosophy. His *Allgemeine Geschichte der Philosophie* was the first history of philosophy to attempt to cover Indian philosophy alongside and as the equal of Western philosophy. His widely read translation of the Upaniṣads had an enormous effect on scholarly opinion of Vedānta in the twentieth century, and it was he more than any single thinker who was responsible for the opinion that Advaita Vedānta was the genuine representative of the Upaniṣads. However, he did at least acknowledge that other, competing interpretations existed:

> In India the influence of this perverted and pervasive spirit of our age has not yet overthrown in religion and philosophy the good traditions of the great ancient time. . . . It is true, that even here in the sanctuary of the Vedāntic metaphysics, the realistic tendencies, natural to man, have penetrated, producing the misinterpreting variations of Śaṅkara's Advaita, known under the names Viśiṣṭādvaita, Dvaita, Śuddhādvaita of Rāmānuja, Madhva, Vallabha,—but India till now has not yet been seduced by their voices, and of hundred Vedāntins . . . fifteen perhaps adhere to Rāmānuja, five to Madhva, five to Vallabha, and seventy-five to Śaṅkara.[40]

Part of Deussen's project involves a philosophy of history based on his observations from the histories of Western and Eastern philosophy. Reversing Hegel's dialectical scheme, in which history is a rational teleological progression of more and more adequate manifestations of *Geist,* Deussen sees history as a systematic regression from truth to error. Hegel depicts monistic Hinduism as being part of the "religion of nature," the first of three religious phases that culminates in absolute religion, that is, Christianity. Deussen works in the other direction, regarding monism or "idealism" as the highest doctrine, which he calls the original philosophy of both ancient Greece and ancient India. Applying his scheme of deevolution to the history of Indian philosophy, he enumerates six stages:

1. Idealism—Ātman is the only reality; plurality and change are merely illusion (*māyā*).
2. Pantheism—The world is real, and yet ātman is the only reality, since ātman is the entire universe.
3. Cosmogonism—The ātman is cause, producing the world from itself as its effect.
4. Theism—There is a distinction drawn between ātman as creator of the world and ātman entering into creation: that is, between the highest soul and the individual soul.
5. Atheism—Causal power is transferred from God to matter itself.
6. Deism—For "practical reasons" (*Opportunitätsrücksichten*), the doctrine of a personal God is attached to atheism.[41]

The first stage, according to him, corresponds to the earliest Vedānta teachings, as expressed by Yājñavalkya in the *Bṛhadāraṇyaka Upaniṣad.* The second stage is expressed in those Upaniṣads that identify the "infinitely small *ātman* within us as the infinitely large *ātman* outside of us."[42] Cosmogonism is used by those texts that try to reconcile pantheism with creation myths. Theism is expressed by the *Śvetāśvatara Upaniṣad.* Atheism exists in the doctrines of the Sāṃkhya, and deism in the doctrines of the Yoga school.

Deussen's scheme implies that each of the five subsequent stages of decline proceeds in orderly succession from the original Indian monism. They are the inevitable result of the worldly ignorance and materialism of the majority of people, who gradually reinterpret and distort the originally pure idealism until it becomes almost unrecognizable. Deussen also suggests that a similar process occurs in ancient Greece, where the monistic doctrines of Parmenides and Plato devolve into the later, post-Aristotelian schools that, like the Sāṃkhya, sought mere remedies for the suffering of existence instead of the highest truth.[43] Deussen's scheme is an attempt to systematize Schopenhauer's belief that Plato, Kant, and the Upaniṣads were all expressing the same truth.[44] However, the explicitly historical nature of Deussen's project is a departure from Schopenhauer's stance, since Schopenhauer considered any attempt to understand history as a systematic or regular process as fundamentally misguided.[45] Yet this is precisely what

Deussen does, depicting a transcultural process by which pure idealism gradually succumbs to materialistic interpretations.

The most obvious function of this sixfold scheme is as a systematic means to show that "the whole Sāṃkhya system is nothing but a result of the degeneration of the Vedānta by means of the growth of realistic tendencies."[46] Both Gough and Deussen see the conflict between Vedānta and Sāṃkhya as the fundamental conflict between the two poles of Indian philosophy: idealism versus realism, monism versus dualism, and the disinterested quest for truth versus the pessimistic flight from the pain of existence. Deussen applies his scheme of historical deevolution explicitly in his interpretation of *Śvet. Up.* 4.5, "the she-goat, who is colored red, white, and black." He is able to reconcile the differences between Sāṃkhya and Vedānta by historicizing their interpretations of the passage:

> That this verse expresses the fundamental thought of the Sāṃkhya doctrine is not open to question. . . . At the same time however these three expressions, both by the names themselves and by their order, which according to the Sāṃkhya doctrine ought to be different, point back to *Ch. Up.* 6.4, where everything in the universe is shown to consist of the three elements . . . heat, water, and food. . . . In this controversy both sides are right. The Vedāntist, inasmuch as the verse unquestionably refers back to *Ch. Up.* 6.4; and the Sāṃkhyist, inasmuch as the three constituent elements, which according to *Ch. Up.* 6.2 proceed from the "one without a second," and of a mixture of which everything in the universe consists, have been psychologically transformed into the three *guṇas.*[47]

Proceeding from his deevolutionary account of the history of Indian philosophy, Deussen is able to reconcile the obvious Sāṃkhya allusions in the *Śvetāśvatara Upaniṣad* with his commitment to the primacy of the Advaita Vedānta. Unlike Gough, Deussen does not insist that all of the Upaniṣads are a pure expression of monistic Vedānta philosophy. Instead, he reads the different Upaniṣads as representing different developmental strata. Pure, original Vedāntic ideas are expressed primarily in the *Bṛhadāraṇyaka,* the oldest of the Upaniṣads. The more recent *Śvetāśvatara,* however, contains both theistic and Sāṃkhya elements, and thus it combines elements of stages three and four in his deevolutionary scheme. This scheme is also inspired by Deussen's admiration for Śaṅkara's twofold division of ultimate and conventional truth. According to Deussen:

> [Śaṅkara] constructs out of the materials of the Upaniṣads two systems, one esoteric, philosophical (called by him *nirguṇā vidyā*, sometimes *pāramārthikā avasthā*) containing the metaphysical truth for the few ones, rare in all times and countries, who are able to understand it; and another exoteric, theological (*saguṇā vidyā, vyāvahārikī avasthā*) for the general public, who want images, not abstract truth, worship, not meditation.[48]

Inspired by his *ācārya*'s tolerance for both absolute and conventional understandings of Brahman, Deussen does not completely condemn the theistic representations of Brahman he finds in various later Upaniṣads. He does, however, continue to condemn Sāṃkhya, which he sees as possessing no redeeming qualities. Precisely because he believes that Sāṃkhya is barren and philosophically incoherent, however, he has difficulty in explaining the close affiliation between the Yoga and Sāṃkhya schools. Since Vedānta preceded Sāṃkhya and is philosophically superior, it seems impossible that Patañjali could have chosen Sāṃkhya as the philosophical basis for his system of spiritual praxis. This leads Deussen to the uneasy conclusion that "there seems to have been a time when Vedāntic thought lived only in this realistic form of the Sāṃkhya; for when the Yoga took the form of a philosophical system it was built up on the very inconvenient base of the Sāṃkhya system, probably because at that time no other base was available."[49] Deussen also writes the Yoga system into his historical scheme by placing it as the sixth and last phase of "deism." He makes the rather counterintuitive claim that the sixth phase of Yogic deism is somehow derived "from considerations of practical convenience" out of the atheistic system of Sāṃkhya. Like many historians after him, Deussen is ultimately at a loss to explain why God (*īśvara*) makes an appearance in the Yoga system, since the twenty-five Sāṃkhya principles appear to constitute a completely self-sufficient cosmology without any need for a God.

Deussen's interpretation of the history of Indian philosophy is compelling for two reasons. First, his attempt to establish the chronology of the different Upaniṣads was ambitious and largely successful; his periodization is accepted by scholars today, with a few modifications, and his translation of sixty Upaniṣads is still widely read and cited.[50] Second, unlike Colebrooke and Gough, Deussen attempted a genuinely philosophical interpretation of the Upaniṣads, and thanks to his access to primary texts in Sanskrit he was able to bring together Eastern and Western philosophy in a way that Schopenhauer could not. Deussen's project was unmistakably inspired by Schopenhauer's vision of a single perennial philosophy. Despite his recognition that India contained a multiplicity of philosophical voices, not just one, through his historical typology he was able to uphold the notion inherited from Schopenhauer of a "concordance of Indian, Greek and German metaphysics; the world is *māyā,* is illusion, says Śaṅkara;—it is a world of shadows, not of realities, says Plato;—it is 'appearance only, not the thing in itself,' says Kant."[51] This unified vision of the world's philosophies championed by Deussen became enormously popular in the twentieth century, and its influence is still felt today.

RICHARD GARBE: SĀṂKHYA AS THE FOUNDATION OF INDIAN PHILOSOPHY

Indologist Richard Garbe's name is the one most closely associated with Vijñānabhikṣu, and it was he who brought Vijñānabhikṣu's philosophy to the attention of the wider public. But Garbe considers himself a scholar of Sāṃkhya and had little or no interest in Vijñānabhikṣu's Yogic and Vedāntic works. Garbe is an apologist for the Sāṃkhya and argues against what he sees as the biases in the work of Gough and Deussen. At the same time, he seeks to save the Sāṃkhya from Vijñānabhikṣu. While Gough portrayed Vijñānabhikṣu as an inauthentic Vedāntin who sought to introduce Sāṃkhya realism into the purely idealistic doctrines of the Vedānta, Garbe sees him as an inauthentic Sāṃkhya who sought to import Vedāntic theism into the purely atheistic Sāṃkhya system. Garbe accepts it as established that Advaita Vedānta was the true representative of the Vedāntic tradition and only seeks to rehabilitate Sāṃkhya from its unsympathetic portrayals. In the process, Vijñānabhikṣu becomes a doubly marginal figure: not authentically monistic enough to be considered a true Vedāntin, and not atheistic enough to be considered a true Sāṃkhya.

Garbe was responsible for the first complete translation of one of Vijñānabhikṣu's works into a Western language, his German translation of the *Sāṃkhyapravacanabhāṣya* in 1889. This was followed by his Sanskrit edition of the *Sāṃkhyapravacanabhāṣya,* published as the second volume of the Harvard Oriental Series in 1895. Both works were based on Fitzedward Hall's 1856 edition of the text.[52] Garbe's Sanskrit edition is a work of painstaking philological detail, correcting many of the errors in Hall's text with assistance from several manuscripts and Sanskrit pandits in Benares.[53] It remains the edition on which all of the later Indian publications of the *Sāṃkhyapravacanabhāṣya* have been based. In contrast to his cool philological professionalism, however, the introduction to his Sanskrit edition of the text contains a scathing indictment of Vijñānabhikṣu's central project:

> Vijñānabhikṣu's point of view has already been set forth by A. E. Gough. . . . Gough shows the utter baselessness of the exposition which Vijñānabhikṣu gives of the contents of the Upanishads and of the relations of the philosophic systems to one another. . . . In order to bridge over the chasm between the Sānkhya system and his own theism (which he is pleased to style Vedāntic), Vijñānabhikṣu resorts to the strangest means to do away with one of the fundamental doctrines of the genuine Sānkhya, which is the denial of God. . . .
>
> The second point concerns the Upanishad doctrine of the illusory nature (*māyā*) of the world of phenomena and the Sānkhya doctrine of the reality of matter (*prakṛti*). Even this contradiction our author clears away by an appeal to what he calls "original Vedānta," which teaches, as he avers, the reality of the world. Some kindred spirit had already identified the *māyā* of the Vedānta with the *prakṛti* of the Sānkhya, namely in the Çvetāçvatara Upanishad, iv. 10; and accordingly our commentator does not scruple to make the most of this identification as a scriptural one; and repeats in divers places of his work . . . the explanation that by *māyā* in Scripture is meant nought else than real matter.
>
> Nevertheless, in spite of all of the false assumptions and the errors of which Vijñānabhikṣu is undoubtedly guilty, his Commentary on the Sānkhya Sūtras must be declared to be not only the fullest source that we have for a knowledge of the Sānkhya system, but also one of the most important of such sources [*sic*].[54]

Garbe accepts Gough's proposition that the monistic interpretation is the only true interpretation of the Upaniṣads and combines this with his own certainty, gathered from earlier scholars and from the text of the *Sāṃkhyasūtras* itself, that the true Sāṃkhya philosophy is atheistic. Although he identifies the *Sāṃkhyasūtras* as a late text and notes its borrowings from the *Brahmasūtras,* it does not occur to him to question whether the text's atheism is truly representative of the earlier Sāṃkhya school. While he notes the existence of Vijñānabhikṣu's commentary on the *Brahmasūtras* and his subcommentary on the *Yogasūtras,* he seems to have felt no need to familiarize himself with these works before undertaking a translation of the *Sāṃkhyapravacanabhāṣya,* in spite of Vijñānabhikṣu's frequent references there to his *Brahmasūtras* commentary. Unlike his colleagues, he is singularly obsessed with the Sāṃkhya system.

This obsession is revealed in Garbe's *Philosophy of Ancient India,* first published in 1897. Like many Orientalists of his era, he entertains cultural diffusionist ideas of an ancient connection between Indian and Greek philosophy. But Garbe does not even consider the possibility that Indian philosophy has its origins in Greece:

> It is a question requiring the most careful treatment to determine whether the doctrines of the Greek philosophers . . . were really first derived from the Indian world of thought, or whether they were constructed independently of each other in both India and Greece, their resemblance being caused by the natural sameness of human thought. For my part, I confess I am inclined to the first opinion.[55]

For Garbe, those ideas coalesce around the possibility that the Sāṃkhya is the source for numerous schools of Greek philosophy. After a brief nod to Deussen's assertion of the unity between Vedāntic ideas and the philosophies of Plato and Parmenides, Garbe lists the numerous philosophers he believes are either strikingly similar to, or even could have been influenced by, Sāṃkhya: Anaximander, Heraclitus, Empedocles, Democritus, Epicurus, Pythagoras, the Gnostics, Plotinus, and Porphyry.[56] While for some of these philosophers Garbe admits that the India connection is rather tenuous, with others it is absolutely clear—with Porphyry, for instance, "the Indian influence can be proved directly; for he has made use of the treatise of Bardesanes, from which he copied an important passage about the Brahmans."[57] Likewise, there is "no doubt" that Pythagoras was dependent on Indian philosophy and science, and from there the similarities to Sāṃkhya would indicate a historical influence.[58]

What is it that leads Garbe to choose Sāṃkhya, instead of Vedānta, as the school most likely to have had a meaningful impact on the many schools of philosophy in ancient Greece? He suggests that Sāṃkhya was more portable than other Indian philosophical schools, such as Vedānta, because the Sāṃkhya was more analytical and rational in nature, hence more suitable for the rationally minded Greek philosophers. Although Garbe acknowledges that the theme of the oneness of Brahman is central to the earliest Upaniṣads, he does not quite draw the conclusion that Vedānta is therefore the oldest of the Indian philosophical systems for, according to him, Sāṃkhya is "the oldest *real* system of Indian philosophy [emphasis added]."[59] Unlike Deussen and Gough, Garbe draws a sharp distinction between the primary methods of Vedānta and Sāṃkhya. While Vedānta is primarily concerned with scriptural interpretation, the Sāṃkhya alone "attempts to solve its problems solely by the means of reason. . . . In Kapila's doctrine, for the first time in the history of the world, the complete independence and freedom of the human mind, its full confidence in its own powers were exhibited."[60] Like Colebrooke but unlike Deussen and Gough, Garbe rightly stresses that Mīmāṃsakas and premodern Vedāntins consider free-floating reason aimless and destructive; they condemn freethinkers who disregard the Veda in favor of reason alone. It is this free-thinking aspect of Sāṃkhya that Garbe holds up as the Greek philosophical ideal, inherited by way of India. Orientalists seldom picked up on this observation, however, instead following Deussen in downplaying these differences of method in their quest to find an Indian analogue to the transcendental idealism of Kant. Liberated from its cultural context as a school of scriptural exegesis, twentieth-century thinkers were free to interpret Advaita Vedānta either in the idealist framework Deussen advocates or, later, in terms of an experiential model influenced by William James.[61]

Like many nineteenth-century Orientalists, Garbe notes that it is the "pessimism" of the Sāṃkhya that underlies the later teachings of the Buddhists and Jainas.[62] Unlike most of these thinkers, he also considers the Sāṃkhya logically prior, and perhaps even by extension historically prior, to the system of the Vedānta. The last paragraph of Garbe's "Outline of a History of Indian Philosophy" is a response to "those who feel inclined to look down slightingly from a monistic point of view upon the dualistic conception of the world."[63] According to Garbe, "the knowledge of the difference between body and soul is one condition, and it is also an indispensable condition, of arriving at a true monism."[64] This argument reverses the elaborate scheme of historical deevolution proposed by Deussen to explain the emergence of the philosophically untenable dualism of the Sāṃkhya system. While Garbe tactfully sidesteps the question of whether dualism or monism is philosophically superior, there is no question about where he thinks the true philosophical spirit resides among the systems of Indian philosophy.

This complex of philosophical affiliations helps to explain Garbe's conflicted relationship with Vijñānabhikṣu. On the one hand, Vijñānabhikṣu's *Sāṃkhyapravacanabhāṣya* is "the fullest source we have for a knowledge of the Sānkhya system."[65] On the other hand, Vijñānabhikṣu violates the spirit of the Sāṃkhya's reliance on reason alone by importing concepts that have nothing to do with Sāṃkhya whatsoever and that are indefensible when argued rationally. The *Sāṃkhysūtras* argue against the possibility of the existence of God, yet Vijñānabhikṣu rejects these arguments in favor of a conception of God that he borrows from the Purāṇas. Even as these theistic tendencies subtract from Vijñānabhikṣu's value as a Sāṃkhya commentator, other factors disqualify him as a commentator on Vedānta. The most significant of these is his insistence on the reality of the world—since Garbe fully accepts Gough and Deussen regarding the authentic teachings of the Vedānta school, Vijñānabhikṣu cannot be a true Vedāntin if he teaches the world is real. Failing these two tests, Garbe concludes that Vijñānabhikṣu's philosophy is unclassifiable, hence perverse. For the nineteenth-century Orientalists, who sought to tame India and its culture by means of classification, unclassifiability was perhaps the most inexcusable of all intellectual errors.

ORIENTALISM AND MODERN HINDU THOUGHT

The four thinkers I discuss in this chapter—Colebrooke, Gough, Deussen, and Garbe—had enormous influence on twentieth-century work on the history of Indian philosophy. This influence spread back to India and across the ocean to North America. For instance, the imprint of Deussen is apparent in Eliot Deutsch's attempt to read Śaṅkara as providing a transcendental argument to prove the existence of a noumenal realm called Brahman; the imprint of Garbe is apparent in Debiprasad Chattopadhyaya's attempt to champion Sāṃkhya as an authentically Indian form of critical atheism.[66] The influence of these thinkers has been on Indians and non-Indians alike. The influence of Deussen and Schopenhauer on Swami Vivekananda and Sarvepalli Radhakrishnan is unmistakable, for instance in Vivekananda's formulation of a "*tat tvam asi* ethics" of compassion closely modeled after Schopenhauer's formulation.[67] This process by which Europeans reformulated Hindu philosophy and then exported it back to India as the ancient essence of Hinduism has been described as "the pizza effect" by Agehananda Bharati.[68] Just as pizza was first exported from Italy to the United States, elaborated on by Americans, and then exported back to Italy to become the signature Italian food, the prevalent Indian understanding of Hindu philosophy and religion has been significantly influenced by European elaborations.

The danger in emphasizing the European influences in modern Hindu thought, however, is the tendency by some scholars to conclude from this that modern Hinduism is inauthentic and to posit a simplistic binary opposition between "traditional" Sanskritic and "modern" European-inspired Hindu thought.[69] This also has led to the unwarranted conclusion that Indians in the modern period have been merely passive recipients of Western ideas about the true essences of traditional Hinduism, pawns in an imperialist conspiracy to rob them of both their cultural and material riches. But just as there is no single way of being a "traditional" Hindu, there is a wide range of visions among modern Hindus about what the true essence of Hinduism is, if such an essence exists. Influential modern Hindu thinkers such as Gandhi, Vivekananda, and Radhakrishnan, acknowledged that they received inspiration from non-Hindus in forming a Hindu self-identity. But their engagement with Hindu traditions was a creative negotiation between many different Indian and non-Indian cultural influences, not a wholesale acceptance of modern European values and rejection of premodern Indian ones.

Emphasizing the heavy influence of the European Indologists in the modern period often conceals something else, the influence of premodern Indian texts and native Indian scholars on those Europeans themselves. The Saidian model, portraying Orientalism as a pure product of European imperialism with no engagement with Asian texts and ideologies, is untenable in the face of overwhelming evidence of a two-way cultural influence. Not only were modern Indians transformed by their British rulers into tea-sipping, ersatz Englishmen. In varying ways and to varying extents, European Orientalists also became "Orientalized" through their engagement with Asian cultures and ideas.[70] The pro-Advaita biases that Deussen and Gough inscribed into their interpretations of the history of Indian philosophy were themselves borrowed from the Sanskrit texts that they relied on for their understanding of the relation between the systems of Indian philosophy. Medieval doxographies such as Mādhava's *Sarvadarśanasaṃgraha* contain within them the seeds of these reductive understandings of the diversity of philosophical doctrines within India. Deussen accepted Mādhava's portrayal of the hierarchy of schools and rejected Vijñānabhikṣu's portrayal because only the former served Deussen's ideological agenda. To better understand this process of intercultural mimesis, it is also necessary to understand the way in which Indian doxographers themselves dealt with the problem of doctrinal diversity in premodern India.

[8] DOXOGRAPHY, CLASSIFICATORY SCHEMES, AND CONTESTED HISTORIES

DOXOGRAPHY AS A GENRE

The history of the classification of doctrines in premodern India is complex, and only recently have historians of Indian philosophy begun to see the study of doctrinal classification as being a worthwhile topic of investigation in itself. Indian doxographies were first translated into Western languages in the nineteenth and twentieth centuries, and they helped earlier generations of Orientalists sort through the overabundance of texts and doctrines they found in Indian archives. The same characteristics that made doxographies attractive to Western scholars, their simplicity and willingness to generalize, also created difficulties. Because doxographies were written by practicing philosophers with their own strong doctrinal affiliations, they were also vehicles used to subordinate some schools and elevate others. For this reason, some scholars have railed against the doxographers for the unreliability of their portrayals of the different schools. However, when understood as documents written at a certain place and time by authors who were pursuing specific ideological ends through their writing, these texts function as important evidence for the historian of ideas. Because of the centrality of these texts in delimiting doctrinal boundaries in medieval India, to understand the heresiological attitudes of late medieval authors like Vijñānabhikṣu one must understand the doxographical problematic that they inherited from the classifiers of Indian philosophical traditions who preceded them. In this chapter, I present some of the major features of texts important for an understanding of the history of doxography in India. These include Cāttaṉār's *Maṇimēkalai* (sixth century CE?), Bhāviveka's *Madhyamakahṛdayakārikā* (sixth century CE), Haribhadra's *Ṣaḍdarśanasamuccaya* (eighth century CE), Mādhava's *Sarvadarśanasaṃgraha* (fourteenth century CE), and Madhusūdana Sarasvatī's *Prasthānabheda* (sixteenth century CE).

The term "doxography" is a neologism, coined by the nineteenth-century philologist Hermann Diels for his enormous volume in 1879 entitled *Doxographi Graeci*. Recently this word has gained currency among Sanskritists to describe a similar type of writing that summarizes and classifies the schools of Indian philosophy. The most well known among these are probably Haribhadra's *Ṣaḍdarśanasamuccaya* (Collection of the Six Philosophical Systems) and Mādhava's *Sarvadarśanasaṃgraha* (Compendium of All Philosophical Systems).[1] Like the Latin and Greek doxographers, Haribhadra and Mādhava are not historians of philosophy. They represent the systems of Indian philosophy as completely static, and in most cases they refrain from naming any actual philosopher. Most often, a philosopher's doctrines are subsumed under a general philosophical category, like "Vaiśeṣika," "Sāṃkhya," or "Mīmāṃsā," and presented completely impersonally. Tensions between thinkers in the same school or developments in a single author's own intellectual development are typically glossed over or ignored.[2] Although some doxographers in premodern Europe also provide biographical information on the thinkers they present, this perspective is absent in Indian doxography. Traditional Indian hagiographies, by contrast, recount the lives and miraculous activities of a given philosopher in colorful detail, along with accounts of his most famous triumphs in philosophical debate. These works come closer to portraying philosophy as a human practice, complete with institutional and interpersonal dynamics.[3] Of course, the accretions of myth surrounding the famous philosophers portrayed in these texts cannot be treated as reliable accounts of those philosophers' lives. Yet Indian hagiographies are themselves valuable historical records reflecting attitudes toward a philosopher in the centuries after his death and can function as a corrective to some of the impersonal aspects of Indian doxography.

In the European context, Diels invented the term *doxographus*, "writer of opinions," to contrast with another neologism, *biographus*, "writer of lives." Diels sought to make a distinction between the two modes of writing, yet in practice we find numerous premodern European works combining biographical and doxographical features.[4] For this reason, only a handful of texts written in Greek and Latin meet Diels's narrow definition of doxography. Others, such as Diogenes Laërtius's *Lives of Eminent Philosophers* and Cicero's *The Nature of the Gods*, combine doxographical features with biography and polemic, respectively. For Diels, the tradition of Greek doxography must be traced to Theophrastus (fourth century BCE), and his work *Tenets in Natural Philosophy*. More recently, David Runia and Jaap Mansfeld have argued that Theophrastus and later Greek doxography have their origins in the dialectical method of Aristotle. According to Aristotle's *On the Soul* (*De Anima*), one should begin an inquiry by first recounting the opinions of others:

> In our inquiry about the soul we shall have to raise problems for which we must find a solution, and in our progress we must take with us for comparison the theories expounded by our predecessors, in order that we may adopt those which are well stated, and be on our guard against any which are unsatisfactory. But our inquiry must begin by laying down in advance those things which seem most certainly to belong to the soul by nature.[5]

This practice of briefly summarizing the opinions of others before setting out on one's own inquiry was eventually developed by a few authors, such as Theophrastus and Aëtius, into free-standing texts that collect opinions of the natural philosophers.[6] Although these works are not primarily polemical in content, they nonetheless contain occasional critical judgments from their authors.[7]

While there are few Greek and Latin works that can be simply classified as doxography in Diels's narrow sense, there are many that contain doxographical sections or can be said to contain doxographical information. The argument among classicists over what should and should not be counted as doxography sheds light on the younger debate among Indologists. David Runia, for instance, differs from Diels in calling Diogenes Laertius a doxographer, although he also remarks that *Lives of Eminent Philosophers* is more of a hybrid text due to Diogenes' biographical inclinations. Runia is unwilling to call the works of Cicero doxography, although he describes *The Nature of the Gods* as beginning with "a long doxographical survey of theological opinions inserted in a piece of Epicurean polemic."[8]

When we turn to the situation in premodern India, we find more examples of "pure" doxography than in Greece and Rome. This is especially the case in the late medieval period, by which time doxography seems to have dislodged itself from earlier narrative and polemical contexts, much as Theophrastus did from Aristotle. While there are no hybrid biographical-doxographical works along the lines of that by Diogenes Laërtius in India, there are other similarities in structure between his *Lives of Eminent Philosophers* and Indian doxographies. Diogenes Laërtius bases his presentation of the Greek philosophers around the definition each philosopher gives of "the good."[9] Haribhadra's *Ṣaḍdarśanasamuccaya* orders its account of the six Indian systems based on the deity each accepts and on the means each school adopts to achieve liberation (*mokṣa*).[10] Such concerns are obviously imposed on each of the philosophical schools in order to present a cohesive overview of the different schools' views. In the Indian context, for instance, it is clear that the question of deity does not apply to schools that do not accept any deity (Bauddha, Lokāyata, Jaina, Mīmāṃsā), nor does the question of means to liberation apply to schools that do not accept liberation as a goal of human life (Lokāyata, Mīmāṃsā). Nonetheless, Haribhadra does his best to assign a deity and a means to liberation to the schools that lack them.

Both Diogenes and Haribhadra work from accepted parameters. The schools of philosophy are already defined; only minor variations of emphasis and organization are open to the doxographers. Clearly, the organizational tool Haribhadra chooses to employ is one that is extrinsic to the schools he is required to cover. For this reason, Richard Rorty's trenchant description of doxography is just as applicable to the Indian as it is to the European situation. According to Rorty, doxography is "the attempt to impose a problematic on a canon drawn up without reference to that problematic, or, conversely, to impose a canon on a problematic constructed without reference to that canon."[11] Although Greek doxographers were more prone to discuss biographical details of thinkers' lives while Indian doxographers repeated stock philosophical arguments and tended to avoid personal names entirely, both types of doxographers were presented with a previous canon, then were asked to somehow make sense of the doctrines therein to create a cohesive account of the schools' differences on a handful of philosophical topics.

The Jaina doxographer Haribhadra is the author of the earliest doxography in India to be widely edited and translated in the modern period, the *Ṣaḍdarśanasamuccaya*. Whether it should be considered the oldest extant doxography depends largely on how doxography in India is defined. Because premodern Sanskrit intellectuals, like their European counterparts, did not identify the features of a distinct genre known as doxography, it is difficult to know how exactly to approach the issue. Olle Qvarnström, the only scholar to write at length on the structure of doxography in India, describes doxographers as writers who "endeavoured in their writings to furnish a comprehensive and impartial account of an opponent's placita."[12]

He classifies Indian doxographies into three types. The first two involve a prima facie viewpoint (*pūrvapakṣa*) followed by the author's own critique (*uttarapakṣa*). In the first type, there is a back-and-forth dialogue between author and opponent; in the second type, the *pūrvapakṣa* takes up the first half of a chapter and the *uttarapakṣa* is presented in the second half. Qvarnström's third type "consists of texts that simply outline one system after the other in separate chapters" without explicit refutation of these systems.[13]

I choose to restrict Qvarnström's definition somewhat and use the word "doxography" only for the third type he presents. My reasons for doing this are threefold. First, I think that if we wish to retain a meaning of the word "doxography" close to the sense used by contemporary historians of Western philosophy, it makes the most sense to count only those texts that provide a relatively neutral overview of the opinions of multiple schools. While these texts often contain subtle criticism of the schools presented, their primary function is to summarize, not to critique. Second, my interest in the study of Indian doxography arises primarily from the value these texts provide in helping us understand the underlying logic behind systems of doctrinal classification in premodern India. Qvarnström's interest, by contrast, appears to be the data that Buddhist and Jaina authors can provide about the early doctrines of their opponents.[14] Many texts can be said to contain "doxographical information" interesting to the modern historian, but not all of these texts are doxographies. Third, if we construe the word "doxography" too broadly, it will not be useful as a descriptive term. The majority of philosophical authors in premodern India write texts using the convention of *pūrvapakṣa* and *uttarapakṣa,* and by accepting Qvarnström's first and second types of doxography, every text containing multiple *pūrvapakṣas* might qualify as doxography. Texts such as Haribhadra's *Ṣaḍdarśanasamuccaya* and Mādhava's *Sarvadarśanasaṃgraha* form a genre distinct from Rāmānuja's *Śrībhāṣya* and Jayanta Bhaṭṭa's *Nyāyamañjarī* and therefore deserve a designation all their own.[15]

EARLY MODELS FOR DOXOGRAPHY IN INDIA: CĀTTAṈĀR AND BHĀVIVEKA

Accounts of the doctrines of one or several philosophical schools are common in texts that are not normally considered philosophy, as readers of Vyāsa's *Mahābhārata* and Aśvaghoṣa's *Buddhacarita* will be aware. Another example of this, remarkable in its comprehensive treatment of multiple schools of thought, comes from Cāttaṉār's Tamil poem *Maṇimēkalai* (sixth century CE?).[16] *Maṇimēkalai* is the story of a South Indian temple dancer and courtesan who seeks to give up her profession in order to pursue the Buddhist virtues of charity and philosophical study and to eventually become a Buddhist nun. The text is extraordinary insofar as it is the only extant Buddhist narrative written in Tamil. For this reason, it was widely neglected and only rediscovered by scholars in the nineteenth century. It is also a text that defies easy genre classification. Although large parts of the text follow Tamil literary conventions, the last sections comprise a lengthy compendium of the teachings of the various philosophical systems, culminating with a discussion of Buddhist logic. Just as this text was overlooked by scholars of Tamil because of its Buddhist content, it has been overlooked by historians of Indian philosophy because it was written in Tamil, not Sanskrit. However, chapters 27–29 of the poem have numerous characteristics in common with later Sanskrit doxography. Therefore, *Maṇimēkalai* can be described as an Indian doxographical source that predates Haribhadra's *Ṣaḍdarśanasamuccaya.*[17]

In its sections on the philosophical systems, *Maṇimēkalai* follows several conventions of later Sanskrit doxography. For instance, it begins its typology of the schools according to the number of means of valid knowledge (*pramāṇas*) that each accepts. And, like many texts that followed it, it lists the schools of philosophy (*darśanas*) as being six. Also like later doxographies, this number seems purely conventional. Although Cāttaṉār lists six systems, he does so in the midst of a discussion of many systems and thinkers that do not find their way onto this official list. It seems that the notion of the "six systems" predated both Cāttaṉār and Haribhadra, and both are working from an earlier template. Both thinkers are clearly aware that there are more than six schools total, but both also feel compelled to include this number.

Cāttaṉār's text begins with a discussion of the number of means of valid knowledge (*pramāṇas*). This method of structuring a text is common in Indian doxography; what is unfamiliar are the number and kinds of *pramāṇas* that Cāttaṉār presents. He describes three different thinkers who are followers of the Vedas: Vedavyāsa, Kṛtakoṭi, and Jaimini. According to Cāttaṉār, Vedavyāsa accepts ten *pramāṇas,* Kṛtakoṭi eight, and Jaimini six.[18] Although Vedavyāsa, author of the *Mahābhārata,* was in later times identified with Bādarāyaṇa, author of the *Brahmasūtras,* there is no reason to assume this is what Cāttaṉār had in mind; the enumeration of ten *pramāṇas* would also set him at odds with all of the known schools of Vedānta.[19] Kṛtakoṭi is a relatively obscure Mīmāṃsā commentator, and there is no record of any Mīmāṃsā school accepting eight *pramāṇas.* Jaimini, of course, is the author of the *Mīmāṃsāsūtras,* but he does not give any particular number of *pramāṇas.* Their first enumeration in the Mīmāṃsā school comes in Śabara's commentary on Jaimini's text, where Śabara accepts six.[20]

After this rather unfamiliar enumeration of *pramāṇas,* Cāttaṉār provides a more familiar list of the six schools:

1. The Lokāyata school of Bṛhaspati (one *pramāṇa*)
2. The Bauddha school of Jina (two *pramāṇas*)[21]
3. The Sāṃkhya school of Kapila (three *pramāṇas*)
4. The Nyāya school of Akṣapāda (four *pramāṇas*)
5. The Vaiśeṣika school of Kaṇāda (five *pramāṇas*)
6. The Mīmāṃsā school of Jaimini (six *pramāṇas*)[22]

The list of the six schools presented by Cāttaṉār is extremely tidy, too tidy, in fact. Although Jaimini might plausibly (though anachronistically) be said to accept six *pramāṇas,* Kaṇāda, the founder of the Vaiśeṣika school, accepted only two *pramāṇas.*[23] Nonetheless, the logic behind the claim regarding Kaṇāda is clear—each school accepts one more *pramāṇa* than the last, for a total of six schools and six *pramāṇas.* In this account of the six schools, symmetry is as much a concern as fidelity to the teachings of each of the six thinkers.

The information presented in the doxographical chapters of *Maṇimēkalai* is in the form of encounters between the temple dancer Maṇimēkalai and the representatives of various philosophical schools. Cāttaṉār presents the basic information about the ten *pramāṇas* and the six schools in Maṇimēkalai's encounter with a logician (*pramāṇavādin*). After her introduction to a few logical categories, Maṇimēkalai encounters representatives of sects that are found nowhere in the logician's list of the six systems. In order, she meets a Śaiva (*śaivavādin*), a Brahmā worshipper (*brahmavādin*), a follower of the Veda (*vedavādin*), an Ājīvika, a Digambara Jaina (*nigaṇṭhavādin*), a Sāṃkhya, a Vaiśeṣika, a Materialist (*bhūtavādin*), and finally the Buddhist teacher Aravaṇa Aḍigal. Maṇimēkalai expresses distaste at the doctrines of the Ājīvikas and Materialists, in particular. Other systems, such as the Sāṃkhyas and Jainas, are depicted with some sympathy.[24] But the text represents Buddhism as the highest teaching, and other teachings are depicted as worthwhile only insofar as they point toward Buddhist truths.[25] In this way, the structure of chapters 27 through 29 of *Maṇimēkalai* anticipates later doxographies such as Mādhava's *Sarvadarśanasaṃgraha*, which also proceeds in graduated steps from lower doctrines to the highest truth. Only when Maṇimēkalai listens to the Buddhist doctrines presented by Aravana Aḍigal does she find "the truth . . . free from all inconsistency."[26] Cāttaṉār's story culminates with Maṇimēkalai's full acceptance of Buddhist teachings and of "the life of austerity . . . that is indispensable for attaining wisdom and being free of the burden of faults that bind us to the interminable cycle of rebirth."[27]

Another Buddhist text that has received recent scholarly attention for its doxographical content is the *Madhyamakahṛdayakārikā* (Verses on the Heart of the Middle Way). It was written by the sixth-century philosopher Bhāviveka, also known as Bhāvaviveka and Bhavya.[28] Bhāviveka is primarily known for his Svātantrika reading of the Mādhyamika Buddhist philosopher Nāgārjuna. Unlike many other followers of Nāgārjuna who claim that the proper technique for a Mādhyamika is simply to show the error inherent in any philosophical view, Bhāviveka seeks to provide independent arguments (*svatantra*) in order to convince opponents of the cogency of the Madhyamaka school. This orientation encouraged Bhāviveka to engage with other philosophical schools in philosophical debate and instilled in him an interest in understanding opponents' views that Prāsaṅgika Mādhyamikas often did not share. Furthermore, Bhāviveka was inclined to accept those tenets of other schools that he believed conformed to Mādhyamika doctrine. This led him to some extraordinary assertions regarding the Vedānta tradition's proximity to Mahāyāna Buddhism.

Bhāviveka's *Madhyamakahṛdayakārikā* is divided into eleven chapters of widely varying lengths and purposes. Although chapters 4 through 9 take their titles from the names of rival philosophical schools, the other chapters are devoted to proving major tenets of Madhyamaka Buddhism. This is especially the case in the lengthy third chapter, which deals with the nature of the Buddhist *dharmas*, the purely conventional nature of causality, suffering, the two truths, the bodies of the Buddha, and so forth.[29] Only after he has laid out these positive arguments in support of Madhyamaka philosophy does he engage his opponents' arguments. These opponents appear in chapters 4 through 9: Hīnayāna Buddhism, Yogācāra Buddhism, Sāṃkhya, Vaiśeṣika, Vedānta, and Mīmāṃsā. Bhāviveka concludes in chapters 10 through 11 with a proof of the Buddha's omniscience and a recapitulation of the main points of Madhyamaka philosophy.

Although this text contains a great deal of information about other schools besides Madhyamaka Buddhism, it straddles the line between doxography and philosophical polemic. The *Madhyamakahṛdayakārikā* presents each of the opponents' arguments as objects of refutation, and each chapter is arranged in the form of a prima facie argument (*pūrvapakṣa*), followed by a lengthy refutation (*uttarapakṣa*). So the Yogācārin only has seven verses and the Sāṃkhya only four verses before they are refuted by Bhāviveka in responses over ten times as long as the original *pūrvapakṣin*'s argument. Bhāviveka's responses often show a real knowledge of and engagement with the systems that he is critiquing. As informative as these critiques are to historians who seek to excavate the doctrines of sixth-century Sāṃkhya, Vedānta, and Mīmāṃsā, however, these are polemics, not attempts to compile a number of viewpoints in a systematic and orderly fashion.[30] In fact, there is no apparent order in the sequence of doctrines he refutes. Bhāviveka begins with the two schools that he elsewhere maintained do have some soteriological usefulness, the Hīnayāna and Yogācāra schools.[31] Like most Indian polemicists, his portrayal of his opponents is not always reliable as a historical source. For instance, he ascribes to Mīmāṃsā the belief that a God created the world, when in fact most recorded schools of Mīmāṃsā are atheistic.[32]

Bhāviveka's portrayal of Vedānta is particularly intriguing, if somewhat difficult to pin down. Some features of his portrayal of Vedānta are familiar, such as the metaphor of space and the space inside of different pots to explain the non-dual relation between the Brahman and the individual souls.[33] At other times, the Vedānta he describes seems to advocate a type of difference and non-difference relation, or even a theory of Brahman as "person" similar to the views of some later Śaiva sects.[34] This diversity serves as the basis for one of his arguments against the Vedānta: Vedānta is a hodgepodge of ideas, borrowed from many different sources including the Buddha himself, and therefore its internal inconsistency rules it out as a doctrine accepted by reasonable people.[35]

Another aspect of this text foreshadows the inclusivist attitudes of the medieval doxographers, as well as Vijñānabhikṣu's project of reading Sāṃkhya and Yoga in such a way that they will be in concord with Bhedābheda Vedāntic teachings (see chapter 5 in this volume). In the *Madhyamakahṛdayakārikā,* Bhāviveka redefines Vedāntic concepts in order to show how they might fit into the conceptual universe of Madhyamaka Buddhism. In chapter 4, a Hīnayāna interlocutor accuses the Mahāyāna Buddhist of being a crypto-Vedāntin, paralleling later Vedāntins who accuse the Advaita Vedānta of crypto-Buddhism. This may be the earliest acknowledgment in a Sanskrit text of the similarity between the two schools. According to the Hīnayāna opponent, "the Mahāyāna is not the word of the Buddha, because it is not included in the Sūtrāntas, etc., or because it is a teaching of another path [than the Buddha's], similar to the Vedānta system."[36] Bhāviveka responds to this opponent by conceding the similarity, but then he traces this similarity to the Buddha's influence: "Everything that has been well said in the Vedānta was spoken by the Buddha."[37] Again at the end of his rather scathing critique of the Vedānta doctrine in chapter 8 of the *Madhyamakahṛdayakārikā*, Bhāviveka remarks: "Accepting that this splendid teaching of the Buddha is free from fault, the Vedāntins, full of desire, have claimed it as their own."[38]

But what in the pre–Śaṅkara Vedānta of the sixth century does Bhāviveka see as overlapping with Madhyamaka Buddhism? In spite of their many differences, he observes that they appear to share the doctrine of non-origination (*ajātivāda*), which states that nothing really ever comes into or passes out of existence. Nāgārjuna attempts to prove in his *Mūlamadhyamakakārikā* that causality is only a conventional truth and cannot be part of the ultimate nature of things. Something similar appears in the *Māṇḍūkyakārikā* of Gauḍapāda (sixth century CE). For Gauḍapāda, non-origination means that all that is originated must be ultimately unreal (*mithyā*), since real things do not change. As a proto-Advaitin, Gauḍapāda concludes that the only reality is the absolute and beginningless self (*ātman*) described in the Upaniṣads.[39] This is certainly too much for Bhāviveka to concede. Instead of re-reading Mādhyamika denials of causation in terms of an Upaniṣadic ultimate self, as Gauḍapāda does, Bhāviveka turns the tables in rereading the self not as an absolute entity but as the abstract concept of non-origination:

> Non-origination is the nature (*svabhāva*) of beings. Because it is not produced and does not perish, it is also called the "self" (*ātman*). . . . If it is just this sort of self that you [the Vedāntin] mean, then that [concept of self] is proper and without error, because of the many common properties it shares, such as its name.[40]

This is an extremely reductive, and perhaps even a sarcastic, understanding of the Advaita concept of selfhood. Nonetheless, it is evidence that inclusivistic strategies of co-option were present in Buddhist engagements with rival schools, much as they were in later Vedānta doxographies. It also shows how inclusivism, sometimes championed by modern scholars as a form of philosophical nonviolence, can be more akin to a hostile takeover of another school's most cherished ideas.[41]

Cāttaṉār's *Maṇimēkalai* and Bhāviveka's *Madhyamakahṛdayakārikā* offer invaluable clues for the origins of doxography in India. While Bhāviveka does depict a number of different schools in a fair amount of depth, these numerous schools are presented as prima facie arguments (*pūrvapakṣas*) to be refuted point by point in debate.[42] For this reason, I have refrained from labeling the *Madhyamakahṛdayakārikā* as a doxography, in spite of its obvious importance to historians.[43] While it is possible that the Indian doxographical genre grew out of the *pūrvapakṣa/uttarapakṣa* form so familiar in Indian philosophical texts, the structure of doxography offers greater freedom to portray the schools of philosophy as subtle progressions from lower to higher truth. The refutation of a *pūrvapakṣa,* in contrast, portrays *mano-a-mano* conflict, in which one doctrine triumphs over another. *Maṇimēkalai* is remarkable because it is one of a kind, a glimpse of roads not taken by later doxographers. For example, the list of ten *pramāṇas* expands the normal list to include *pramāṇas* only accepted by followers of the Purāṇas (*paurāṇikas*).[44] Cāttaṉār is happy to make room for schools such as followers of the god Brahmā, followers of the Veda (*vedavādins*), and the Ājīvikas. These classifications are forgotten by the later doxographers, even those that identify themselves as exhaustive lists of all of the schools. At the same time, *Maṇimēkalai* uses classificatory strategies that become more familiar with the late medieval doxographies. In this way, *Maṇimēkalai* gives us a glimpse of what pre-sixth-century Indian doxography may have looked like, while foreshadowing the structure and content of the later, more familiar Sanskrit doxographies. It is also the only doxography presented explicitly as a narrative, with an inquisitive main character meeting each of the proponents of various schools.[45] This presents the intriguing possibility that Indian doxography has its origins in storytelling instead of philosophical debate. *Maṇimēkalai,* whether or not its format reflects an earlier stratum of Indian doxography, helps provide a fresh perspective as we go on to approach later, more familiar texts.

HARIBHADRA, JAINISM, AND THE SIX SYSTEMS

The Jaina author Haribhadra's *Ṣaḍdarśanasamuccaya* is the earliest extant Sanskrit doxography in India. He uses the enumeration of the schools as six as an ordering principle, in a way similar to the enumeration of six doctrines in *Maṇimēkalai.* According to traditional sources, Haribhadra lived in approximately the eighth century, not far from the town of Chitrakoot (currently in northern Madhya Pradesh). While Cāttaṉār acknowledges other schools as existing outside of the classification of six, Haribhadra initially suggests that his list of six is exhaustive.[46] In both texts, the six schools enumerated differ from the list of the six orthodox schools usually cited in the modern period. For the Jaina Haribhadra, the six schools are Buddhism, Nyāya, Sāṃkhya, Jainism, Vaiśeṣika, and Mīmāṃsā. In *Maṇimēkalai,* they are Lokāyata, Buddhism, Sāṃkhya, Nyāya, Vaiśeṣika, and Mīmāṃsā.[47] While Cāttaṉār almost treats Jainism as a preliminary or subdoctrine of Buddhism, Haribhadra gives it a separate place of its own, at the expense of Lokāyata materialism.[48]

These Jaina and Buddhist lists differ from later Advaita accounts in that they include Buddhism and Jainism among the six schools. Haribhadra does this by defining the term *āstika* ("affirmer") differently than it is understood by medieval Vedāntins such as Vijñānabhikṣu and Madhusūdana Sarasvatī. He says that his enumeration of the six schools, including Buddhism and Jainism, is a "summary of all the *āstika* views." His commentator Maṇibhadra elucidates this by defining the *āstika* views as those that affirm the existence of another world (*paraloka*), transmigration (*gati*), virtue (*puṇya*), and vice (*pāpa*).[49] Jainism and Buddhism qualify under this definition just as much as Nyāya, Vaiśeṣika, Sāṃkhya, and Mīmāṃsā. Here and elsewhere, *āstika* does not mean "theist," or "affirming the existence of a world-creating God." If it did, the only one of Haribhadra's six systems to qualify would arguably be Nyāya.

The label *āstika* would be meaningless without the existence of its antithesis, *nāstika* ("denier"). Haribhadra only identifies one school, the Lokāyata, as *nāstika.* After he lists the six *āstika* schools, he appends a mention of the Lokāyata school:

> 78. Others do not accept that there is a difference between the Naiyāyika doctrine and the Vaiśeṣikas. In their opinion, there are only five *āstika* schools.
>
> 79. In their opinion, the number of the six schools of philosophy is completed by adding the doctrine of the Lokāyatas. Therefore, that doctrine will be described.[50]

This passage helps clarify just how the enumeration of the six schools functions. Haribhadra is not simply adding up all of the schools that he can find and then presenting this number as the total. Rather, the number six is an established total for the number of possible schools. Haribhadra's job is to look at all of the possible candidates and to see how they can be most reasonably categorized to number six.[51] Like Cāttaṉār, Haribhadra was familiar with many more than six schools. Perhaps because the Lokāyata was frequently mentioned as one of the six schools, he cannot simply pass over the materialist school in silence. Instead, he offers an acknowledgment that there are other possible ways of counting the schools—not as numbering five or seven but as adding up to six in some different combination. And he suggests one possible way of doing so: by combining two closely related schools such as the Nyāya and Vaiśeṣika into one. But Haribhadra personally prefers to leave the Lokāyata out of his enumeration.

The doctrine that Haribhadra considers the best is, of course, Jainism. He describes it in terms that he uses for none of the other schools: it is "free from fault" (*anagha*) and completely devoid of contradictions.[52] But he does not portray the Jaina doctrine last or imply that it is a culmination of all other schools. In his text it comes fourth, between Sāṃkhya and Vaiśeṣika. Haribhadra's ordering of the six schools appears to be arbitrary. For instance, he presents the closely related schools of Nyāya and Vaiśeṣika apart from one another. Nor is there presentation in order of the number of *pramāṇas* accepted by each school. Although the *Ṣaḍdarśanasamuccaya* mentions the *pramāṇas* accepted by each school, it has a method for categorizing each of the schools that is different from Cāttaṉār's enumeration of *pramāṇas.* Haribhadra writes that there are two fundamental criteria for differentiating each of the six systems of philosophy:

> 2. Taking into account their fundamental differences, there are only six philosophies. They should be known by the wise according to differences in deity (*devatā*) and principle (*tattva*).[53]

The first means of classifying the different schools, deity, seems fairly self-evident. Different schools have different sorts of gods, although some others do not acknowledge the existence of any god at all. By "principle" (*tattva*), Haribhadra might mean the number of fundamental entities each system acknowledges as existing in the world. For Sāṃkhya, of course, the number is twenty-five; Haribhadra also describes the Naiyāyikas as having sixteen *tattvas.*[54] The commentator Maṇibhadra proposes another way of understanding Haribhadra's word *tattva.* According to him, *tattvas* are "the secrets that bring about liberation" (*mokṣasādhakāni rahasyāni*).[55] This soteriological reading of the term suggests that each school offers a distinctive teaching that leads to liberation and that along with the school's deity, it is possible to organize schools in terms of their means to liberation.

The problem with this way of classifying schools, like classifying in terms of deity, is that it imposes an extrinsic set of issues on each of the schools and then searches within each school for a teaching that will fit this problematic. The Mīmāṃsā school, for instance, takes heaven (*svarga*) rather than liberation (*mokṣa*) as the ultimate human end. Therefore, it offers no doctrine or secret teaching that will lead to liberation. Nonetheless, Maṇibhadra claims that the study of the Veda as the means of liberation is taught by the Mīmāṃsā school. The Mīmāṃsā is especially problematic among the *āstika* schools, since in its early forms it accepts neither the existence of a deity nor the possibility of liberation from the cycle of death and rebirth. Nonetheless, it is presented by all premodern doxographers as an *āstika* school.

It is worthy of notice that Vedānta and Yoga, two schools that came to assume enormous importance in the medieval and modern periods, are absent from Cāttaṉār and Haribhadra.[56] The Vedānta's absence is further confirmation of Nakamura's thesis that the Vedānta was not widely known or acknowledged by the other philosophical schools in the seventh to tenth centuries CE.[57] In his commentary on the *Ṣaḍdarśanasamuccaya*, Maṇibhadra maintains that the Vedānta, or Uttara Mīmāṃsā, is considered in Haribhadra's text as a subdivision of Jaimini's Mīmāṃsā school. Haribhadra seems to have in mind the school of Mīmāṃsā of Kumārila Bhaṭṭa, based on his inclusion of nonexistence (*abhāva*) as one of the *pramāṇas* accepted by the Mīmāṃsā and by his description of the Mīmāṃsā as denying the existence of God.[58] The inclusion of nonexistence as a *pramāṇa* excludes the school of Prabhākara from Haribhadra's account of Mīmāṃsā. His description of the nonexistence of God would also seem to exclude all of the Vedānta schools from possibly being understood as subschools of Mīmāṃsā.

Remarkably, Mīmāṃsā and Lokāyata are the only two schools that Haribhadra describes as having no god; according to Haribhadra, the deity (*devatā*) of the Buddhists is Sugata (i.e., the Buddha), and the god of the Jainas is Jinendra (the supreme Jaina patriarch). The concept of "deity" (*devatā*) is especially fluid for Haribhadra, as attested by the problems his commentator Maṇibhadra has in trying to gloss the term. Maṇibhadra writes after Haribhadra's introduction of the concept that deities are those "who superintend each of the systems."[59] Yet it is unclear how either the Buddha or Jinendra can fit this definition, since according to many Indian Buddhist schools and most Jaina schools, these two great sages ceased to have any concern with the phenomenal world after they were liberated.

Therefore, in the cases of the Buddhist and Jaina schools, Maṇibhadra gives a slightly different interpretation of deity. In his treatment of the Buddha, he writes that "the Buddha is the deity, i.e. the original creator of the [Buddhist] system."[60] Jinendra is "the deity, the originator of the [Jaina] system, the original person."[61] This interpretation of the word "deity" is problematic, however, since virtually every system can claim an originator. At other places, therefore, Maṇibhadra gives a different interpretation of *devatā*. Haribhadra divides the Sāṃkhya into two camps: "Some Sāṃkhyas are atheists (*nirīśvara*), while others have Īśvara as their God. But for all of them, there are twenty-five principles."[62] Taking the meaning of "deity" as "originator of the system," it would seem logical to say that all Sāṃkhyas accept Kapila as their deity. However, here Maṇibhadra once again understands the meaning of deity as superintendent (*adhiṣṭhātṛ*).[63]

An alternative definition of deity that the commentator Maṇibhadra does not suggest, but which might make better sense of Haribhadra's assertion that both Buddhism and Jainism are theistic, is the notion that a deity is a being whose speech is infallible, who in himself functions as a *pramāṇa*.[64] Haribhadra describes the Mīmāṃsā school in these terms: "The followers of Jaimini say that there is no deity (*deva*) who has qualities such as omniscience, and whose speech would be a means of knowledge (*māna*)."[65] In Buddhism and Jainism, the words of the Buddha and Jinendra, respectively, function as a means of knowledge. They are also objects of devotion for practitioners of the respective schools. In this way, we might make a more plausible claim that these two schools accept a "deity." Although it is challenging to come up with a single, consistent definition of this word that will be suitable to each of the schools Haribhadra surveys, it is not difficult to understand why he was inclined to argue that Buddhism and Jainism were not godless, as often claimed. Rejection of god is a well-known characteristic of the Lokāyata school, a school that Haribhadra wanted to disassociate from Jainism at all costs. By understanding the Jainas as accepting a god, he moves them closer to schools like the Nyāya and farther from the Lokāyatas.[66]

MĀDHAVA AND THE INFLUENCE OF ADVAITA DOXOGRAPHY

The *Sarvadarśanasaṃgraha* is the most influential and widely read of all of the Indian doxographies. There are a number of reasons for this. The first is the depth of its presentations of the various schools. Unlike the two doxographies just described, the *Sarvadarśanasaṃgraha* presents actual arguments of the various philosophical schools and presents them with a fair degree of detail. Besides its depth, the *Sarvadarśanasaṃgraha* also offers more breadth in the number of schools that it covers. Unlike the *Ṣaḍdarśanasamuccaya,* which treats only six schools (plus an appendix on Cārvāka), the *Sarvadarśanasaṃgraha* offers chapters on sixteen different schools. The *Sarvadarśanasaṃgraha* is traditionally ascribed to the Advaita Vedānta philosopher Mādhava, who lived in the fourteenth century as a minister of the Vijayanagara empire and eventually became the head of the Advaita monastery at Śṛṅgeri reputedly founded by Śaṅkara.[67] Mādhava's text is more than simply a complete and objective description of all of the philosophical schools. It is an idealized representation of the state of philosophical affairs according to the worldview of one of the most famous exponents of Advaita, according to tradition also the author of enormously popular Advaita texts such as the *Pañcadaśī* and the *Śaṅkaradigvijaya.* Although it has been praised in the past for the clarity with which it presents philosophical doctrines, for my purposes it is most interesting for its ideological slant, and the techniques it employs to subordinate its fifteen other schools to Advaita Vedānta. It is a testament to the seamlessness of these techniques and the dominance of Advaita philosophy in the modern period that the *Sarvadarśanasaṃgraha* has often been considered an accurate depiction of the Indian philosophical schools, so much so that Deussen's volume on India in his *Allgemeine Geschichte der Philosophie* is largely based on Mādhava's text.[68]

Like many other Indian doxographies, the *Sarvadarśanasaṃgraha* begins with lesser philosophical schools, progressing in order of their acceptability, until it finally culminates in the highest philosophy, Advaita Vedānta.[69] Mādhava presents each philosophical school as a corrective to the one that came before it. So, for instance, the Cārvāka school presents the view in chapter 1 that there is only one valid means of knowledge, perception. Immediately at the beginning of chapter 2, the Buddhists challenge this view, offering arguments in support of an additional means of knowledge, rational inference. Mādhava continues with this conceit for approximately the first eight chapters of his work, but he uses it less and less as its artificiality becomes increasingly apparent. How does Vaiśeṣika atomism function as the logical corrective to the Raseśvara Śaiva sect, for instance? Nonetheless, the overall impression of his text is that the schools function together in a dialectical process—although most of the central doctrines of the Buddhists are unacceptable to Advaita Vedānta, the

Buddhists' refutation of Cārvāka views can be accepted without reservation. This process is sometimes problematic, since the grounds by which the Buddhist disproves some Cārvāka theories are not acceptable to an Advaitin. A refutation of Cārvāka hedonism on the basis of the Buddhist doctrine of momentariness, for instance, is unacceptable, since Advaita does not accept that all entities in the world only exist for a moment before they pass out of existence. In other cases, however, Buddhist arguments are acceptable—such as the Buddhist arguments about the validity of rational inference (*anumāna*), a means of knowledge accepted by both the Buddhists and Vedāntins but rejected by the Cārvākas.

Although the category of the Vedānta does appear in Mādhava's *Sarvadarśanasaṃgraha,* it does not appear on the same terms that it appears in most modern histories of Indian philosophy. Mādhava only accepts the existence of one school of Vedānta, the Advaita. Other schools that self-identify as Vedānta—most obviously, the schools of Rāmānuja (Viśiṣṭādvaita Vedānta) and Madhva (Dvaita Vedānta)—are not listed as such in Mādhava's enumeration. Instead, they are included at almost the bottom of Mādhava's hierarchy, just above the Cārvākas, Buddhists, and Jainas and below the Pāśupatas and Śaivas. The reason to group them there is to imply that they are logically inadequate even among their peers, the theistic systems of the Śaivas and Vaiṣṇavas. Mādhava's only nod to their status as alternative systems of Vedānta is the statement that "Madhva established a new system under the pretext of an interpretation of the Brahma Mīmāṃsā."[70] The *Sarvadarśanasaṃgraha* does not even acknowledge that Rāmānuja, too, has pretensions of belonging to the Brahma Mīmāṃsā, or Vedānta, school.

The reason for the subordination of Dvaita and Viśiṣṭādvaita Vedānta in the *Sarvadarśanasaṃgraha* is fairly obvious. These two schools represented the greatest threat to the Advaita Vedānta in the fourteenth century when Mādhava was writing, and hence their dismissal as minor theistic schools is an effective rhetorical strategy for defending Advaita as the only true school of Vedānta philosophy. This strategy has been a great success. An earlier generation of Indologists who relied on texts like the *Sarvadarśanasaṃgraha* too uncritically came to regard Advaita as the real and most historically accurate interpretation of the intention of the Upaniṣads' authors, and this view still persists in Neo-Vedāntic religious circles in spite of ample evidence to the contrary. Following the well-known verse at *Manu.* 2.11 where the *nāstika* is defined as a "reviler of the Veda" (*vedanindaka*), Mādhava and other medieval Vedāntins understood Buddhists and Jainas as being included with Cārvākas in the category of *nāstika*. Therefore, Mādhava could not put Dvaita and Viśiṣṭādvaita at the very bottom of his hierarchy. Instead, he lists them directly after the *nāstika* schools, signifying, according to the internal logic of the *Sarvadarśanasaṃgraha*, that the views of Rāmānuja and Madhva represent the lowest of the *āstika* teachings. The views of Bhedābheda thinkers such as Bhāskara and Nimbārka are omitted from the *Sarvadarśanasaṃgraha* and from other Advaita doxographies. Bhedābheda was literally written out of the history of Indian philosophy; indeed, in part because of the decision of Mādhava and other Advaita doxographers that Bhedābheda was not even worth mentioning, it remains relatively unknown among scholars in Europe and North America today.[71]

The two schools that Mādhava elevates to the penultimate and antepenultimate positions in his doxography, just below the Advaita, are the systems of Patañjali and of the Sāṃkhyas. This choice, too, has some historical logic. Neither the Sāṃkhya nor the system of Patañjali represented an actual challenge to the Advaita by the fourteenth century. Both systems were no longer considered alternatives to the Advaita Vedānta at all. To the extent they still existed, they existed as complementary systems to the various Vedānta schools of the medieval period. Central concepts from Sāṃkhya had been appropriated and altered to do the work of the Advaita Vedānta. So, for instance, the term *prakṛti* in medieval Advaita eventually became a synonym for *māyā*. As long as it was understood that *prakṛti* was not ultimately real, and was not set into motion by itself, there was no serious contradiction in adopting the notion of a *prakṛti* divided into three *guṇas*.

Six centuries earlier, Śaṅkara steadfastly refused such relatively benign acceptance of Sāṃkhya categories. So, for instance, a Sāṃkhya *pūrvapakṣin* in Śaṅkara's *Brahmasūtrabhāṣya* suggests that when the Upaniṣad refers to the "many offspring" colored red, white, and black (*Śvet. Up.* 4.5), it was in fact referring to the three *guṇas*, agitation (*rajas*), purity (*sattva*), and lethargy (*tamas*). Śaṅkara rejects this interpretation of the passage completely in his commentary on *BS* 1.4.9. According to him, the primary meaning of the "red, white, and black" offspring are the three elements of fire, water, and earth. The passage could only be taken to refer in a secondary sense to the Sāṃkhya *guṇas*.[72] While early Vedāntins such as Śaṅkara and Bhāskara refuse to cede a single argument or Upaniṣadic interpretation to the Sāṃkhyas, later Vedāntins took a much softer line and in some cases were quite eager to show how Sāṃkhya could be sympathetically reinterpreted. Vijñānabhikṣu is the most extreme example of this trend in medieval Vedānta, but he is not anomalous in his general acceptance of Sāṃkhya teachings on a conventional (*vyāvahārika*) level.

Another reason for Mādhava to place the Sāṃkhya and Yoga just under Advaita Vedānta in Mādhava's text is that it is rather plausible to see the Advaita of Śaṅkara as a direct response to the mistaken views of Sāṃkhya. Advaita Vedānta presents a critique of and an elaboration on Sāṃkhya theories such as *satkāryavāda* (the theory that the effect preexists in the cause).[73] Although Sāṃkhya was not still a viable and discrete philosophical system in the fourteenth century, when Mādhava wrote the *Sarvadarśanasaṃgraha*, at earlier times it was a thriving school of philosophy and a real threat to Vedānta.[74] Many of Bādarāyaṇa's *Brahmasūtras* are themselves responses to a Sāṃkhya interlocutor, and the Vedānta commentators Śaṅkara and Bhāskara explicate these passages as rejections of fundamental Sāṃkhya concepts, like the existence of an autonomous *prakṛti*.[75] Unlike later Vedāntins, they are not even willing to adopt Sāṃkhya philosophical terms as synonyms for familiar Vedānta concepts—for example, *prakṛti* as a synonym for *māyā*, or *puruṣa* as a synonym for *jīva*.

There is some controversy regarding the authenticity of the sixteenth and final chapter of the *Sarvadarśanasaṃgraha*, which deals with Advaita Vedānta. Some manuscripts of the *Sarvadarśanasaṃgraha* end abruptly after dealing with Patañjali's Seśvara Sāṃkhya system with the statement that "the system of Śaṅkara, which comes next in succession, and which is the crest-gem of all systems, has been explained by us elsewhere; it is therefore left untouched here."[76] Although undoubtedly there are texts ascribed to Mādhava that do treat Advaita at some length (e.g., the *Pañcadaśī*), such an ending would be anomalous among doxographies. Advaita doxographies generally end with an exposition of Advaita philosophy, complete with Advaita critiques of the other systems.[77] Recent editions of the *Sarvadarśanasaṃgraha* do include such a chapter, which begins with a critique of Sāṃkhya that is reminiscent of the critique in Śaṅkara's *Brahmasūtrabhāṣya*, specifically of *prakṛti* as an independent causal agent.[78] Although it is not certain, Hajime Nakamura and Klaus Klostermaier have observed that stylistically, chapter 16 could very well be Mādhava's work and that perhaps Mādhava wrote the chapter slightly later than the rest of the text.[79]

MADHUSŪDANA SARASVATĪ: FOREIGNNESS AND THE PHILOSOPHICAL OTHER

Even later in the medieval period are the *Prasthānabheda* (The Various Religious Sources) and the *Vedāntakalpalatikā* (The Creeper Vine of Vedāntic Views), two works written by the influential Advaita Vedāntin Madhusūdana Sarasvatī (sixteenth century).[80] The latter is a lengthy point-by-point refutation of the views of the non-Advaita schools, enumerated in a way similar to their presentation in Mādhava's *Sarvasiddhāntasaṃgraha*.[81] The former, the *Prasthānabheda*, is remarkable because instead of enumerating six, ten, or sixteen philosophical schools (*darśanas*), Madhusūdana organizes his text around the eighteen "sciences" (*vidyās*) or "sources" (*prasthānas*). This was an alternative scheme employed by some Advaita doxographies, including the *Sarvamatasaṃgraha* and the *Sarvasiddhāntasaṃgraha*, and it is an expansion from older lists that speak of fourteen "sciences."[82]

One of the important differences between the analytical terms *darśana* and *vidyā* is that "sciences" are not inherently at odds in the way that "philosophical schools" are often depicted. Instead, they can represent different, and often complementary, branches of knowledge, much in the way that modern biology, chemistry, and physics are understood as complementary. Furthermore, in Madhusūdana's works, *prasthānas* are primarily understood as different varieties of texts, not different philosophical positions.[83] Madhusūdana divides the *vidyās* into four Vedas, six Vedic limbs (*vedāṅgas*), four additional limbs (*upāṅgas*), and four additional Vedas (*upavedas*). He helpfully explains that the Vedānta and Mīmāṃsā fit under the *upāṅga* known as exegesis (*mīmāṃsā*); the Nyāya and Vaiśeṣika under the *upāṅga* of logic (*nyāya*); Sāṃkhya and Yoga, along with the *Mahābhārata, Rāmāyaṇa,* and the texts of the Śaivas and Vaiṣṇavas, fit under the broad *upāṅga* of legal texts (*dharmaśāstra*).

The *nāstikas,* writes Madhusūdana, have their own six sources (*prasthānas*): the four sects of Buddhists, the Cārvākas, and the Digambara [Jainas]. Although when speaking of the *āstikas,* Madhusūdana takes *prasthāna* to mean "foundational text," the word *prasthāna*'s semantic fluidity allows him to understand it simply as a synonym for *darśana* when he refers to *nāstika* schools. Indeed, his standard enumeration of Cārvākas, Jainas, and four schools of Buddhists (Madhyamaka, Yogācāra, Sautrāntika, and Vaibhāṣika) seems to be based on Mādhava's *Sarvadarśanasaṃgraha* and Pseudo-Śaṅkara's *Sarvasiddhāntasaṃgraha,* not on original works from these schools. Likely because they do not fit into the overarching classification of the eighteen schools, Madhusūdana gives them brief treatment in the *Prasthānabheda.* He is also the first doxographer to explicitly associate the beliefs of the *nāstikas* with those of foreigners (*mlecchas*): "To sum up, the *nāstikas* have six sources (*prasthānas*). We disregard them because, like the teachings of the barbarians, they are external to the Vedas (*vedabāhya*), and because they are useless even for the indirect attainment of human moral ends."[84] Madhusūdana's criteria for classifying a text as *nāstika* are pragmatic in part: while the texts of foreigners and *nāstikas* are wholly useless for any human end (*puruṣārtha*), he claims that all *āstika* texts do lead to these ends, either directly or indirectly.

Madhusūdana concludes the *Prasthānabheda* by organizing the *āstika* schools into three hierarchical categories, based on their theories of the creation of the world. The Nyāya, Vaiśeṣika, and Mīmāṃsā belong to the *ārambhavāda,* an atomistic theory of creation.[85] The Sāṃkhya, Yoga, and the theistic schools belong to the *pariṇāmavāda,* the theory of the real transformation of primal matter. The highest of the three cosmogonies is the *vivartavāda,* the theory of the unreal manifestation of Brahman. This theory is held only by the Vedāntins:

> According to the third viewpoint, that of the *brahmavādins,* Brahman, which is self-luminous, supreme bliss, and without a second, arranges itself by means of its own illusory power (*māyā*) in the form of the world in a way that is ultimately false (*mithyā*). The true purpose of all the sages who have created the systems is in the central purport, the unique, highest Lord, since all the systems ultimately issue into the *vivartavāda.* Those sages cannot just be confused, since they are omniscient. However, the access to human moral ends is not immediately possible for those who are preoccupied with external objects. The sages teach the various systems so that such people will not become *nāstikas.* Not knowing the true purport (*tātparya*) of the sages, people follow those various paths, grasping for ends that are contrary to the Vedas and overlooking the true purport of the Vedas.[86]

The fourteenth-century Advaita doxographies *Sarvadarśanasaṃgraha* and *Sarvasiddhāntasaṃgraha* hint at a possible union of all *āstika* philosophical schools by portraying the schools as a dialectical progression culminating in the Advaita school. In the sixteenth century, Madhusūdana goes further by claiming that all of the great sages of the *āstika* schools outside of the Advaita knew that some of the doctrines they taught were false. They taught what they did in order to keep humans from gravitating toward *nāstika* doctrines and instead taught systems designed to gradually lead these people to the ultimate truths in the Advaita Vedānta. His claim is remarkably similar to Vijñānabhikṣu's strategy for rationalizing Kapila's apparent atheism in the *Sāṃkhyapravacanabhāṣya.* Just as Vijñānabhikṣu maintains that Kapila was aware that he taught an untruth when teaching the nonexistence of God, Madhusūdana believes that all *āstika* sages outside of the Vedānta knew that their teachings were partial and flawed. In both cases, sages saw their teachings as useful in helping an audience with limited understanding avoid more serious pitfalls. Such a strategy is one possible way of solving a vexing problem to any thinker who sought to value the *āstika* schools over the *nāstikas* in an unambiguous way. For Śaṅkara and thinkers of his era who had no particular concern with showing that the *nāstika* schools were inferior to all of the *āstika* schools, the simple solution was simply to deny that Kapila, the sage of the Sāṃkhyas, was truly a reliable source. For Madhusūdana approximately eight hundred years later, discrediting Kapila, Patañjali, and the other *āstika* sages was not a viable alternative. Instead, he adopted an explanatory strategy commonly found in the Purāṇas by which these sages could both be said to be omniscient and to be the originators of schools that were flawed in some way.

We can regard Madhusūdana Sarasvatī and Vijñānabhikṣu as the culminating points at the end of a long tradition of discourse about the "other" in Indian philosophy. Most often for Vedāntins, whether Advaita, Bhedābheda, or some other branch, the word used to describe such an outsider is *nāstika.* By the late medieval period, the word *nāstika* had become little more than a vague pejorative. As discussed here, Jainas and Buddhists rejected the epithet *nāstika* as applicable to themselves and, instead, claimed that the Cārvāka materialists were the true *nāstikas.* Madhusūdana Sarasvatī expands the semantic rage of *nāstika* even further when he blurs this concept with the concept of "foreigner" or even "barbarian" (*mleccha*). According to him in the *Prasthānabheda,* there is a practical equivalence of both groups, as both are extra-Vedic. In chapter 9, I present a history of the word pair *āstika* and *nāstika.*

[9] AFFIRMERS (*ĀSTIKAS*) AND DENIERS (*NĀSTIKAS*) IN INDIAN HISTORY

TOWARD A COMPARATIVE HERESIOLOGY

While it is widely acknowledged that heresiography, "writing about heresy," was one of the central preoccupations of ancient and medieval Christian authors, little work has been done to reflect on the conceptual analogues to the categories of "heresy" and "heretic" in premodern India.[1] This has not stopped scholars from using Christian heresiological terms as translations for indigenous Indian concepts, however. Authors in India used two terms in particular, *āstika* and *nāstika,* to classify insiders and outsiders among philosophical and theological traditions. These Sanskrit terms have been translated variously, and the arbitrariness of these translations is an indication of how unsophisticated Indologists have been on heresiological matters in general. The pair of terms does not mean "theist" and "atheist," although some have translated them this way, perhaps under the influence of the modern Hindi words *āstik* and *nāstik.*[2] A simple glance at the lists of *āstika* schools makes this point clear: among the commonly enumerated *āstika* schools, Vaiśeṣika, Mīmāṃsā, and Sāṃkhya have all propounded atheism of one form or another.[3] The most common translations of *āstika* and *nāstika* are "orthodox" and "heterodox." Although this is an improvement, use of these two terms transposes Indian discourses of the Other into a Christian heresiological context that inevitably obscures as much as it elucidates. Because of the different heresiological presuppositions in Indian doxography and in Christian heresiography, it is best to avoid as much as possible such terms drawn from Christian traditions.

The pluralistic and polycentric relation of the many Greek and Roman philosophical schools is closer to the situation in premodern India. Historians of Indian philosophy have tended to draw on Western religious categories when approaching Indian philosophy because of the oft-repeated view that, unlike Western philosophy, all Indian philosophers have a religious or soteriological focus.[4] Whatever the merits of this interpretation, for most of the history of Indian philosophy up until the modern period, the institutional relationships of the schools of Indian philosophy have been much closer to the structure of the Greek and Roman philosophical schools than the centralized, apostolic magisterium of the Christian church. This does not mean that Indian or Greek schools were "secular" or uninterested in theological matters. The Epicureans, like early Vaiśeṣika philosophers in India, gave the gods little role to play in their atomistic cosmogony. But other Greeks, such as the Stoics, had a more robust understanding of God's place in the creation of the universe, and the precise nature of the gods was a common point of debate among Greek schools. According to Marcel Simon, among the Greek philosophical sects "there existed no universally recognized criterion of authority by which to classify them in two opposing categories and to distinguish truth and error."[5] Simon's observation could apply equally well to Indian philosophy for most of its history. Up until the late medieval period, there was no single uniform understanding of the meaning of *āstika* or a universally agreed-on list of the *āstika* and *nāstika* schools.

The classifications *āstika* and *nāstika* were of central significance to the late medieval doxographers discussed in chapter 8, who sought to provide a system of classification that unambiguously distinguished insiders and outsiders. While the fourteenth-century *Sarvadarśanasaṃgraha* and *Sarvasiddhāntasaṃgraha* used the terms sparingly, the concepts are nonetheless fundamental to the texts' organization, as the Cārvāka, Buddhist, and Jaina systems always appear at the lowest end of the Advaita hierarchies.[6] Hierarchically arranged texts like the *Sarvadarśanasaṃgraha* and *Sarvasiddhāntasaṃgraha* have a fundamental tension to deal with, since the binary *āstika/nāstika* classification is implicitly at odds with a gradual, hierarchical progression of truths. In the sixteenth century, Madhusūdana Sarasvatī and Vijñānabhikṣu endeavored to show that the differences between *āstika* and *nāstika* were real and unbridgeable, while differences among the *āstika* schools themselves were small or nonexistent. Before the medieval period, this systematic attempt to unify all *āstika* doctrines was hinted at but never fully enunciated as the goal of a systematic philosophical project.

THE MEANING OF *ĀSTIKA* AND *NĀSTIKA*

How is it that a school qualifies as *āstika*? What essential property must it have to avoid falling into *nāstikatva*? The etymology of these terms is important: the *āstika* is someone who says that "there is" (*asti*), while the *nāstika* says "there is not" (*nāsti*). The central question, then, is what precisely is being affirmed or denied. Historically, commentators have given a number of different answers to this question. When attempting to justify their own use of these terms, modern introductory texts on Indian philosophy generally cite *Manu.* 2.11: "Any twice-born who disregards these two roots [*śruti* and *smṛti*] on the basis of the science of logic should be excluded by the righteous as a *nāstika,* a reviler of the Veda."[7] This definition, however simple it may appear, requires analysis.

The southern Indian commentator Medhātithi (ninth century) provides a revealing gloss on some of the terms in Manu's famous verse. He is concerned to identify precisely what it means to scorn the Veda on the basis of the science of logic (*tarkaśāstra*). Should this imply that those who follow the injunctions of the Veda are being illogical?[8] He understands the "science of logic" just to refer to "the works on logic written by *nāstikas,* namely the works of the Buddhists, Cārvākas, and so forth, in which it is proclaimed again and again that the Veda is contrary to *dharma.*"[9] Medhātithi understands Manu's injunction primarily in the context of ritual action. If someone does something forbidden by the Vedas and the *smṛti,* and even when warned that it is prohibited by the Veda he says that he does not care since the Vedas lack authority, then he should be excluded (e.g., excluded from officiating at sacrifices). It is important to note here that "the reviler of the Veda" is not someone who says that the Veda is untrue, but someone who says that the Veda is immoral. Medhātithi's gloss of the word *nāstika* itself also reflects his preoccupation with ritual action. Commenting on *Manu.* 8.309, he writes that "a *nāstika* is one who says, 'there is no other world; there is no [purpose in] gift-giving; there is no [purpose in] sacrificing.'"[10] For Medhātithi, a *nāstika* is someone who refuses to participate in Vedic rituals because he sees them as pointless or even immoral.

Medhātithi seems to have in mind in particular the Buddhist and Jaina critiques of Vedic ritual on the basis of the doctrine of nonviolence (*ahiṃsā*). Elsewhere in his commentary on Manu, he explicitly argues for the necessity of violence in certain contexts.[11] Yet it was not only the Buddhists and Jainas who opposed the tradition of Vedic ritualism and its practice of animal sacrifice; the Sāṃkhya and Yoga schools were also at the forefront of this debate.[12] The most well-known expression of the Sāṃkhya rejection of Vedic sacrifice, and, by extension, the rejection of the sanctity of the Vedas, comes at *Sāṃkhyakārikā* 2: "Scripture, like perception, [is ineffective in relieving suffering] since it is associated with impurity, destruction, and excess. The best means is the one that is the opposite to those two, since it is the knowledge of the manifest, the unmanifest, and the knower."[13] From an early period, *āstika* schools were split on the question of animal sacrifice. While the Sāṃkhya position on nonviolence may have originally been the minority opinion among the *āstika* schools, it eventually gained credence, even among Brahmins who specialize in ritual performance. The acceptance of the principle of nonviolence has been so thorough that animal sacrifice among Hindus today is uncommon, and many Indians are of the opinion that such things as cow slaughter were never practiced in ancient India.[14]

Although *SK* 4 admits that there are three means of valid knowledge—perception (*dṛṣṭa*), rational inference (*anumāna*), and reliable testimony (*āptavacana*)—Īśvarakṛṣṇa is unambiguous that rational inference is the preferred method, since of the three only it is pure and free from destruction and excess.[15] In this, the Sāṃkhya and Yoga schools are opposed to Mīmāṃsā and Vedānta, which argue that scriptural authority is the primary means of knowledge, and all others are subordinate to these.[16] This priority of rational inference in Sāṃkhya explains why appeals to scriptural authority are relatively rare in Sāṃkhya literature. There are certainly many passages in the Upaniṣads that the Sāṃkhya could employ in defense of its central concepts. The choice not to do so has enabled Vedāntic commentators to portray the Upaniṣads as uniformly contrary to Sāṃkhya teachings.[17]

Late medieval Advaita doxographies typically rank Sāṃkhya and Yoga high on the list of *āstika* doctrines, likely because Sāṃkhya and Yoga, conceived by then as two separate but related schools, had been thoroughly tamed and their terminology co-opted as part of a larger Vedāntic cosmology. Yet of all systems later listed as *āstika*, it is Sāṃkhya and Yoga that come closest to Manu's description of a "reviler of the Veda." Certainly, Sāṃkhya accepts scriptural authority as one of the means of valid knowledge, and if the minimum requirement for being an *āstika* is only this, Sāṃkhya qualifies.[18] But Sāṃkhya is unlike Vedānta, which saw reason as only able to function properly when anchored to the truths revealed by scripture.[19] Sāṃkhya denies that reason by itself is inherently aimless and unstable. On the contrary, for Sāṃkhya it is scriptural authority that needs to be checked by reason, since blind adherence to Vedic injunctions without critical evaluation leads to immorality and demerit. Therefore, Medhātithi's description of a *nāstika* text as one "in which it is proclaimed again and again that the Veda is contrary to *dharma*" fits the *Sāṃkhyakārikā* and its early commentaries perfectly. By the standards of the Vedic ritualist tradition, the tradition whose principles the authors of the *Manusmṛti* had internalized, the Sāṃkhya and Yoga are *nāstika* traditions.

The heresiological writings of the influential Mīmāṃsaka Kumārila Bhaṭṭa (seventh century CE) fully corroborate the idea that during his time there was no general conception of the *āstika darśanas* over and against the *nāstika* Buddhist and Jaina schools. In the *Tantravarttika,* Kumārila writes that "the treatises on righteousness and unrighteousness that have been adopted in Sāṃkhya, Yoga, Pāñcarātra, Pāśupata, and Buddhist works . . . are not accepted by those who know the Veda."[20] As Vincent Eltschinger remarks:

> Kumārila is far from attempting to federate all the denominations which post-classical Indian and Western scholarship have been used to classify as "hinduistic" and even "orthodox." According to him, Sāṃkhya, Yoga, Pāñcarātra, and Pāśupata are no less heterodox than Buddhism and Jainism. . . . Moreover, most of the *clichés* that had long been associated with heretics recur in Kumārila's description, the most significant one having them resort to autonomous, non-scripturally based reasoning and argumentation. As Kumārila says, these are the revilers of the Veda (*vedanindaka*), the "sophists" (*haituka*) and the deniers (*nāstika*) who according to Manu should be carefully avoided by righteous Brahmins.[21]

It should be no surprise that, in the worldview of the Pūrva Mīmāṃsā school, a "reviler of the Vedas" is simply a synonym for a ritual skeptic, someone who refused to perform rituals or acknowledge their efficacy. According to the Mīmāṃsakas, we do not listen to the Vedas for information about the world; rather, the essence of the Vedas is injunction (*vidhi*). Of course, some passages in the Veda appear to impart factual information about the world, for instance, statements such as "Vāyu is the swiftest deity." In fact, the sole function of these "statements of praise" (*arthavāda*) is to encourage ritual action,[22] not to impart knowledge about time-bound states of affairs in the world. The Vedas cannot do this because they are eternal. Since the Vedas would already have had to exist before any particular state of affairs came to pass, it is a logical impossibility that they should give information about any event in time.[23] Instead, the only function of the Vedas is to prescribe action. A "reviler of the Veda," then, can only mean someone who refuses to do the things that the Veda prescribes.

Although the Vedānta school's interpretive techniques were themselves grounded in the techniques of the Pūrva Mīmāṃsā (and hence the Vedānta was also known as Uttara Mīmāṃsā, "Later Mīmāṃsā"), they had some substantial differences.[24] One of these differences was the abandonment of the idea that the Veda is primarily about ritual injunctions and does not impart knowledge about the world. Instead, the Vedāntins divided the Veda into two parts, the section on ritual action (*karmakāṇḍa*) and the section on Brahman (*brahmakāṇḍa*). Although the injunctions to ritual action in the *karmakāṇḍa* are important, they are only a prerequisite to higher knowledge. For Vedāntins, the Veda—and the Upaniṣads in particular—should be understood as a text that imparts information about highest truths, epitomized by great statements such as "You are that." When interpreted properly, these statements are instrumental for achieving liberation, the ultimate end of human existence. The different schools of Vedānta have differing understandings of the meaning of the great statements and the precise role of ritual activity in relation to knowledge of highest truths. But all Vedāntins agree that the most important function of the Veda is as a vehicle for knowledge of the highest truth.[25]

The earlier meaning of *nāstika,* the reviler of the Veda, was primarily an issue of orthopraxy (correct ritual performance) instead of orthodoxy (correct opinion). Over time, however, the second issue displaced the first. This coincided, I believe, with the gradual rise of the Vedānta school and decline of the Pūrva Mīmāṃsā. We see evidence of the lack of general acknowledgment of a school known as "Vedānta" in the Jaina *Ṣaḍdarśanasamuccaya* and the Buddhist *Maṇimēkalai.* This corroborates Hajime Nakamura's observations that before the tenth century, Vedānta was rarely acknowledged by Jainas, Buddhists, and other Brahmanical schools. When Vedānta was acknowledged, it was not Śaṅkara's Vedānta but often some pre-Advaita version of Vedānta that subscribed to the theory of real transformation (*pariṇāmavāda*) to explain the nature of reality.[26] By the late medieval period, this situation had changed completely.

The Mīmāṃsā weakened and lost influence, although it never lost its fundamental interpretive importance. To the extent that it did survive, it took on theistic ideas from the other schools.[27] However, the Vedāntic understanding of the Veda as imparting information about ultimate truths became the primary model for scriptural interpretation, just as Nyāya logical principles became common currency for any school that sought to engage in rigorous logical argumentation. By this period, the word *nāstika* was understood in terms of orthodoxy rather than orthopraxy. Thus, a reviler of the Veda was someone who denied that the Vedas' depiction of ultimate reality was accurate.

PERSPECTIVES FROM THE JAINAS, BUDDHISTS, AND GRAMMARIANS

In the previous chapter I highlighted another understanding of the word pair *āstika/nāstika,* from the Jaina doxographer Haribhadra and his commentator Maṇibhadra. Haribhadra's understanding of the terms seems worlds apart from the *Manusmṛti,* since he does not consider reverence for the Veda to be the marker of an *āstika.* Yet Maṇibhadra's commentary shows the same concern with orthopraxy that we find in Medhātithi, the commentator on the *Manusmṛti.* It is in the context of this earlier, orthoprax sense of "reviler of the Veda" that we can best make sense of the term *nāstika* as presented by the Jainas Haribhadra and Maṇibhadra. Medhātithi defines a *nāstika* as one who says, "there is no other world; there is no [purpose in] gift-giving; there is no [purpose in] sacrificing."[28] Compare this with Maṇibhadra's understanding of *āstika* views as those that affirm the existence of another world (*paraloka*), transmigration (*gati*), virtue (*puṇya*), and vice (*pāpa*).[29] For both Haribhadra and Maṇibhadra, these two designations have to do with ritual/ethical action (*karman*). They agree that some actions lead to merit and that others result in demerit. Differences arise when each school begins to categorize various actions according to their karmic results. This is most obvious in the case of violence (*hiṃsā*), which always leads to demerit according to Jainas, whereas Mīmāṃsakas hold that in certain ritual contexts, violence can have positive results. The significance in belief in "other worlds" (*paraloka*) is also in the context of ritual/ethical action: other worlds are important because only by recognizing the existence of other worlds can we acknowledge that actions in this life have future consequences.

Besides the two interpretations of the word *nāstika* represented by Medhātithi and Maṇibhadra, a third definition from the Sanskrit grammatical tradition complicates our understanding. The words *āstika* and *nāstika* are derived from Pāṇini's rule at *Aṣṭādhyāyī* 4.4.60.[30] Pāṇini simply provides the derivation of the two words (along with a third, *daiṣṭika*) without suggesting what exactly is being accepted by the *āstika* or rejected by the *nāstika*. The first substantive definition of the two words in the Pāṇinian tradition comes in the *Kāśikāvṛtti*, a commentary by the seventh-century authors Jayāditya and Vāmana. They write, "The *āstika* is the one who believes that 'there exists another world.' The opposite of him is the *nāstika*."[31] This definition has obvious similarities to Maṇibhadra's and Medhātithi's interpretations, since both include existence of another world (*paraloka*) as one of the affirmations of the *āstika*. But the stripped-down definition from the grammatical tradition omits the belief in the efficacy of ritual action found in Medhātithi, as well as the belief in merit and demerit found in both Maṇibhadra and Medhātithi.

We should not conclude from a single seventh-century passage that the grammarians' definition was the original understanding of the two words and that Maṇibhadra's and Medhātithi's interpretations were further developments. But the passage does offer proof that there were multiple and related but competing definitions of these terms and that Maṇibhadra's definition was not simply a bastardization of *Manusmṛti* 2.11 or an example of wishful thinking among the Jainas.[32] Although there is no conclusive evidence to rule in favor of any of these three interpretations as the oldest meaning of the term *nāstika*, these ambiguities should lead historians to reexamine the certainty with which they proclaim *Manusmṛti* 2.11 to be the original and authentic source for the meaning of the term *nāstika*. For Sanskrit grammarians in the seventh through the seventeenth centuries, an *āstika* is simply one who believes in a life hereafter, and a *nāstika* is one who does not.[33] While the existence of a life hereafter usually implies the existence of an ethical system rewarding virtue and punishing vice, this is not always the case.[34]

The Jainas Maṇibhadra and Haribhadra consider themselves representatives of an *āstika* philosophy and apply the epithet *nāstika* exclusively to the materialist Lokāyata school. Textual evidence suggests a similar situation among the Buddhists, specifically that the word *nāstika* was a pejorative that no Buddhist wanted to be associated with. This comes across clearly in the *Bodhisattvabhūmi* (Stages of the Bodhisattva Path), a section of the encyclopedic *Yogācārabhūmi* traditionally ascribed to the Yogācara Buddhist philosopher Asaṅga (4th c. CE).[35] In this text's "Chapter on Knowing Reality" (*Tattvārthapaṭalam*), the *Bodhisattvabhūmi* critiques two types of Buddhists, both of whom distort the Buddha's teachings. In doing so, it recapitulates the understanding of the Yogācāra mind-only doctrine as a middle way between two extreme Buddhist viewpoints. The text first criticizes those who are guilty of undernegation, affirming the existence of that which does not exist. Although it does not give names, this presumably refers to the Hīnayāna Abhidharma schools' acceptance of constituent elements (*dharmas*) as having a real existence independent of the mind. The text's harshest critique, however, is aimed at the Buddhists who are guilty of universal negation (*sarvavaināśika*), those who say that nothing whatsoever exists. According to the *Bodhisattvabhūmi,* this is the "worst kind of denier" (*pradhāno nāstikaḥ*):

> When some people hear the difficult and profound Mahāyāna sūtras that deal with emptiness and convey a meaning that needs to be interpreted, they do not discern the correct meaning, they develop false concepts, they have unreasonable views based only on logic (*tarka*), and they say: "All of reality is nothing but a designation; whoever sees it this way, sees correctly." For these people there is no real thing to serve as the basis of designation. This means that there cannot be any designation at all. How can reality be nothing but designation? By saying this they deny both designation and reality. Someone who denies designation and reality should be known as the worst kind of *nāstika.* Those who are wise and practice a religious life should not speak or share living quarters with this kind of *nāstika.* He causes himself to fall, and those who agree with his false views fall as well.[36]

This passage of the *Bodhisattvabhūmi* is remarkable for how much it adopts from *Manusmṛti* 2.11. Like the passage in the *Manusmṛti,* it criticizes the *nāstika* for his reliance on logic (*tarka*) alone. For Manu, the *nāstika*'s reasoning is flawed because he ignores the teachings of the Vedas. In the *Bodhisattvabhūmi,* this "worst kind of *nāstika*" is presumably guilty of using his own reasoning independent of the teachings of the Buddha. Both passages also suggest that *nāstikas* should be subject to a complete social isolation so that others will not be infected by their dangerous and potentially damning beliefs. For Brahminical ritualists following the *Manusmṛti,* this meant exclusion from sacrifice; for Buddhists who accepted the words of the *Bodhisattvabhūmi,* this would have entailed shunning by other monks or even expulsion from the monastic community. In both cases, the charge of being a *nāstika* was a real threat to social standing and livelihood.

Although the worst sort of *nāstika* is nowhere identified by name in the *Bodhisattvabhūmi,* later Buddhists clearly understood the text to be attacking Madhyamaka Buddhism. The eighth-century Mādhyamika philosopher Bhāviveka took quite seriously this injunction by the Yogācāra Buddhists calling for the monastic expulsion of Mādhyamikas. After quoting this passage from the *Bodhisattvabhūmi* in his *MHK,* Bhāviveka responds: "These angry words are like vomit: they show undigested pride."[37] He elaborates on this simile in the text's autocommentary:

> Your angry words show pride just as vomit shows undigested food. Here anger is compared to vomit, your words are compared to the act of vomiting, and pride is compared to undigested food. Someone who vomits shows undigested food. When you express your anger, you show your pride in exactly the same way. But you do not refute our view.[38]

This dyspeptic dispute between Buddhists leaves no doubt that the charge of being a *nāstika* was quite severe, suggesting not only lapses of doctrine but also severe defects of ethical character serious enough to warrant social ostracism.[39] Buddhists and Jainas were no more willing to accept this label applied to them than were other groups, and the *Bodhisattvabhūmi*'s use of the term suggests that Buddhists, too, were concerned about erecting symbolic boundaries between communities. Modern historiographers of Indian philosophy have largely been blind to the numerous intertextually related definitions of the terms *āstika* and *nāstika.* This oversight is further evidence of our own credulity and overreliance on a handful of texts for our understanding of a complex situation in the history of ideas. An engagement with the entire Indian intellectual tradition—including the writings of the grammarians, Jainas, and Buddhists—is necessary for an adequate understanding of the history of Indian philosophy.

The pre-tenth-century history of the word *nāstika* shows hidden continuities among commentators in the Jaina, Buddhist, and *dharmaśāstric* traditions. Manu's definition of *nāstika* as "reviler of the Veda" seems at first to have nothing to do with a Jaina definition of a *nāstika* as one who rejects the existence of other worlds, transmigration, virtue, and vice. Yet when analyzed further, these two thinkers generally agree that the distinction between *āstika* and *nāstika* is primarily ethical and not doctrinal.[40] This explains why the distinction was so fundamental. Brahmins, and particularly the intellectual elites who had the most access to textual production, naturally had a great deal of interest in upholding the ritual/ethical order, since the alternative was chaos and social dislocation. Yet in later periods, when acceptance or rejection of the Veda was understood primarily in terms of affirming or negating its assertions about fundamental philosophical truths, the logic underpinning the importance of the categories also began to fall away. Why should the mere affirmation of the Veda's authority have any great significance? The Sāṃkhya school technically affirms the Veda but at the same time belittles its contents as impure, so as to undercut the claims of other schools that rely on the Veda as their primary source of knowledge. From the standpoint of a Vedāntin, schools like the Sāṃkhya that profess to base their teachings on the Veda yet rely on false interpretations should in many ways be *more* dangerous, since they claim true teachings as their own and then insidiously pervert them. Buddhists and Jainas, who do not threaten the integrity of the message of the Veda, are a minor threat in this regard. Then why do late medieval Vedāntins take such pains to discredit Buddhists and Jainas, while giving Sāṃkhyas, originally their worst enemies, a free pass?[41]

BEYOND ORTHODOXY AND HETERODOXY

The words *āstika* and *nāstika* are difficult to translate. One reason for this is the fluctuations in the meanings of the terms themselves between different periods of time and different social contexts in India. This difficulty becomes even worse when we look at those words in English that have been used to translate these two terms. Despite the best efforts of historians of Indian philosophy, the terms used to translate Sanskrit philosophical concepts are imbued with Eurocentic (and specifically Christian-centric) meanings. The two words most commonly used to translate *āstika/nāstika,* "orthodox" and "heterodox," come out of the Christian theological tradition and hence carry historical connotations that distort the understanding of native Indian categories of thought.

For late medieval Vedāntins, the word *āstika* denotes schools that nowadays are often described as "Hindu," and the *nāstikas* correspond to the non-Hindu schools of the Jainas, Buddhists, and materialists. Yet the terms *orthodoxia* and *heterodoxia* in their early Christian usages did not simply correspond to Christian versus non-Christian doctrines. Rather, *orthodoxia* referred to true Christian doctrine, and *heterodoxia,* to both false teachings within the church (e.g., Gnosticism and Arianism) and the teachings of pagan philosophical schools. By the medieval period, a third term, *hairesis* (heresy), came to be understood as distinct from heterodoxy: heresy denoted false Christian teachings, heterodoxy false teachings outside the church.[42] Yet throughout Christian history, *orthodoxia* referred to not just any Christian teaching but to the one Christian system that was considered theologically impeccable.[43] This contrasts with the Sanskrit term *āstika*, which can refer to any school within certain sectarian boundaries, even if some of its teachings are flawed. It is this stricter definition of orthodoxy that the early Indologist H. T. Colebrooke had in mind when he referred to the Vedānta and Mīmāṃsā as "emphatically orthodox," whereas the Sāṃkhya's reservations about Vedic authority made it "partly heterodox, and partly conformable to the established Hindu creed."[44]

For Christian heresiology, heresy is by far a larger threat than heterodoxy (in the medieval sense of heterodoxy: a false teaching external to the church). Augustine remarks in *The City of God* that "it is worse to be a deserter from the faith and, by reason of desertion, an enemy of the faith than to be one who has never lost what he never had."[45] The logic behind this view suggests that it is precisely those who misinterpret scripture that are the most dangerous to the stability and coherence of orthodoxy. There are hints of this attitude in early Vedānta's attitude toward Sāṃkhya. But the late medieval doxographers turn this attitude on its head. It is those schools that deny the authority of scripture that are the most worthy of contempt, whereas any school that accepts scripture must have at least some sort of preliminary value toward a complete understanding of the doctrines of the highest school.

The instability of this position among late medieval thinkers is a direct consequence of the shift of the meaning of *nāstika* described earlier. If the *nāstika* is one who says "there is no purpose in ritual/ethical action," he is an obvious threat to the social order. In this worldview, characteristic of the Brahmanical ritual specialists, divergences in doctrine can be overlooked as long as there is complete agreement about the efficacy of ritual action. However, late medieval Vedāntins inherited the structure of this earlier scheme even as the meaning of the central *āstika/nāstika* dyad had shifted. Although it is clear that *āstikas* were praiseworthy and *nāstikas* were a threat, it is not clear why the *nāstikas'* mere lack of interest in the Veda as a scriptural source should cause so much consternation. The sixteenth-century authors Appaya Dīkṣita, Madhusūdana Sarasvatī, and Vijñānabhikṣu shared a need to emphasize the similarities among the *āstika* schools and to overemphasize the differences between *nāstikas* and *āstikas.* Vijñānabhikṣu is the most extreme example of this tendency, arguing that whereas all differences of opinion among *āstika* schools are illusory, differences between *āstikas* and *nāstikas* (especially the crypto-*nāstika* Advaita school) are profound and unbridgeable. One way of looking at Vijñānabhikṣu's move to unify these schools is as an attempt to resolve this new understanding that the essence of the Vedas are their philosophical doctrines and not the practices they enjoin.[46]

The word heresy, often used by Christians to refer to erroneous theological positions within Christianity, is derived from the Greek term *hairesis,* "choice." In non-Christian contexts, this word had no negative connotation. So, for instance, during his reign Marcus Aurelius endowed four chairs of philosophy in Athens corresponding to the four great philosophical "sects" (*haireseis*): Platonism, Aristotelianism, Stoicism, and Epicureanism. In the context of the philosophical sects, *hairesis* was not counterposed with *orthodoxia,* a word rarely employed to describe Greek and Roman philosophy until the nineteenth century. The Epicurean or Stoic was making a "choice" after using his or her reason to discriminate among the competing tenets of the different schools of philosophy. For Diogenes Laërtius, *hairesis* was even a term of esteem, since only systems of thought that met certain criteria were allowed this designation.[47] But Christians saw the Christian heretic's "choice" in a more sinister light. The heretic chooses to turn away from the fullness of the Christian revelation, sometimes by following a heresiarch away from orthodox teachings or, in other cases, distorting Christianity by emphasizing some parts of the Christian message over and against other parts. These were some of the reasons that Irenaeus, Augustine, and Epiphanius were so much harder on Christian heretics than they were on pagans. Of course, Christian heresiology has the benefit of hindsight, while those Christians making their theological choices did not. Arianism, for instance, the majority position among Christians in the mid-fourth century, is today categorized as heresy.[48] Had historical circumstances been different, Arianism would today be understood as the true teaching of the gospels, and Athanasianism just a popular early heresy.

Ultimately, no single English word can do justice to the richness and complexity of the Sanskrit terms *āstika* and *nāstika.* This is not to say that the two terms must remain untranslated. Any candidate must retain the inherent ambiguity in the two terms. The *āstika* says "there is" and the *nāstika* says "there is not," so the object of affirmation or negation is unclear. It could be the efficacy of ritual/ethical action, as in Medhātithi's earlier gloss, or simply the epistemic authority of the Veda as understood by the late medieval doxographers. "Believer" and "infidel," though tempting, are also too fraught with Western connotations of right theological opinion (and the latter too closely associated with medieval struggles between Christians and Muslims).[49] The terms "affirmer" and "denier" are better, since these are neutral with regard to the question of right opinion versus right practice. An affirmer (*āstika*) might be one who "affirms the value of ritual" (Medhātithi), one who "affirms the existence of virtue and vice" (Maṇibhadra), one who "affirms the existence of another world after death" (the grammarians), or one who "affirms the Vedas as the source of ultimate truth" (Vijñānabhikṣu, Mādhava, etc.). The typical translations for the terms *āstika* and *nāstika,* "orthodox" and "heterodox," succeed to a certain extent in expressing the Sanskrit terms in question. The more detailed analysis of history of the two concepts presented here points to the impossibility of fully capturing the ambiguity of the original Sanskrit words. This should be no surprise, of course, since any act of translation strips the original words of some meanings and introduces new connotations in their place. Keeping this in mind, I suggest the English expressions "affirmer" and "denier" as better approximations of *āstika* and *nāstika.*

ĀSTIKA AND *NĀSTIKA* IN THE LATE MEDIEVAL PERIOD

Unlike Mādhava and Madhusūdana Sarasvatī, Vijñānabhikṣu never attempted to write a doxography. Yet his systematic attempt to unify all *āstika* systems contains strategies for limiting and ranking the truths of various systems of philosophy that exhibit what might be called "doxographic concern." The late medieval doxographies of the Advaita Vedāntins, structured in hierarchical fashion from the Cārvākas at the bottom to the Advaita Vedānta at the top, display an unresolved tension. The gradualist, hierarchical format of these texts conflicts with the binary *āstika/nāstika* distinction. In these texts, we see two different strata of ordering principles. The hierarchical progression of schools appears in the sixth-century *Maṇimēkalai* of Cāttaṉār and likely has its origins in earlier doxographical models. Although the *āstika/nāstika* distinction is probably even older, its origins are not in doxography but in Vedic ritualists' concerns about normative behavior. Even though they heap scorn on the *nāstikas* (even associating them in the *Prasthānabheda* with foreign barbarians), the late medieval doxographies ultimately cannot justify the qualitative break between the highest of the *nāstika* schools (typically the Jainas) and the lowest of the *āstikas.* Attempts at justification for this break are sometimes based on the *āstikas* being "external to the Vedas" (*vedabāhya*). More typically, no explanation is given. By the sixteenth century, the term *nāstika* had become a frozen category denoting materialists, Buddhists, and Jainas. Authors avoid exploring the logic behind this distinction. But as Mādhava suggests, the Buddhist and Jaina doctrines are superior to the materialists and can be understood as the beginning of a dialectical process in which each lower doctrine is sublated by the next.[50] Contrary to Madhusūdana's assertion in the *Prasthānabheda,* then, some of the *nāstika* doctrines do serve a human end, as they act as preliminary stages on the way to the ultimate truth.

Vijñānabhikṣu's project of the unification of *āstika* doctrinal systems holds out the possibility of resolving this conflict if it can illustrate why *nāstika* doctrines have no place in the human effort to reach ultimate truth and liberation. Vijñānabhikṣu frequently deploys the terms *āstika* and *nāstika* in his writings, often at critical moments when he must distinguish between insiders and outsiders in his general scheme. The *nāstikas* he is most concerned with refuting are the Buddhists, especially the schools he calls Śūnyavāda (Madhyamaka, also known as the school of emptiness) and Vijñānavāda (Yogācāra, also known as Mind-only).[51] His interest in the Vijñānavāda is especially interesting, since he associates the Buddhist school's position of the illusory nature of the world (*māyāvāda*) with the school of the Advaita. Refuting one, he says, refutes the other.[52] It is this identification between the Advaita Vedānta and a Buddhist school that allows him to vilify the Advaitins so thoroughly. If the Advaitins were real *āstikas,* logic would force Vijñānabhikṣu to admit that their teachings possess some kind of preliminary value, like the Naiyāyikas. Advaita Vedānta is the only school that Vijñānabhikṣu singles out as *nāstikas* masquerading as *āstikas,* an indication of his extreme antipathy toward that school.[53]

Vijñānabhikṣu does not use the word *āstika* as often as *nāstika,* and he uses it mainly when acknowledging that despite appearances, all the *āstika* schools' views can be reconciled and none lack authority when understood as limited to their proper scope of inquiry. In this way, Vijñānabhikṣu tries to make sense of a very troubling passage from the *Padma Purāṇa* that lumps numerous *āstika* systems in with the *nāstikas,* labeling them all as teachings of "darkness" (*tāmasa*), which by merely hearing this can destroy the wise.[54] It makes sense that the Buddhists, Jainas, and Cārvākas are included in this list. But the inclusion of Sāṃkhya, Nyāya-Vaiśeṣika, and Pūrva Mīmāṃsā creates difficulties for Vijñānabhikṣu's project of unifying the *āstika* schools. In this regard, the *Padma Purāṇa's* presentation of schools is more reminiscent of the Vedāntins' Śaṅkara and Bhāskara's take-no-prisoners approach to the refutation of Sāṃkhya in the eighth century. In order to frame this quotation from the *Padma Purāṇa* properly, Vijñānabhikṣu declares,

> Or it may be that in order to impede the knowledge of those who are wicked, in certain parts of the believers' systems (*āstikadarśana*), teachings have been set down that are contrary to scripture. These systems lack authority just in those parts. But on their main topics, which are not opposed to revealed scripture or traditional texts, they are authoritative. Only on this ground is the *Padma Purāṇa* justified in its criticism of all schools other than Vedānta and Yoga.[55]

Vijñānabhikṣu depicts each of the *āstika* systems other than Vedānta and Yoga as performing a double function. Their teachings are designed both to aid the good in their quest toward liberation and to hinder the wicked in whatever their goals might be. For example, Nyāya's teaching of the soul as experiencing pleasure and pain and Sāṃkhya's teaching of the nonexistence of God are designed to aid the practitioner who is not yet fully advanced enough for the complete *āstika* teachings. These teachings should instead be understood as a "temporary concession" (*abhyupagamavāda*) used to keep the good but confused from straying farther from the path.[56] False teachings also serve the function of deluding the wicked, much as Viṣṇu deluded the demons by disguising himself as the Buddha.[57] It is unclear whether a single false doctrine can simultaneously function in both ways for different groups. For instance, could the Buddha's teaching of no-self (*anātman*), which had such dire consequences for the demons of the *Viṣṇu Purāṇa,* also have a productive function for other listeners? It is conceivable that it would help the egotistical let go of their attachment to an ephemeral, false self and instead pave the way toward a complete understanding of the true, eternal self. These speculations are academic, given the simple way to avoid relying on the potentially misleading teachings of the *āstika* schools. By becoming familiar with the proper scope of each system's authority, it is easy to ignore those statements that fall outside each system's proper purview. This requires the guidance of an exegete such as Vijñānabhikṣu, who can instruct his audience as to which interpretations of scripture are valid and which are erroneous. It is remarkable that even in his commentary on the *Sāṃkhyasūtras,* Vijñānabhikṣu evaluates doctrines primarily by whether they contradict revealed and traditional texts (*śruti* and *smṛti*). Vijñānabhikṣu shows his Vedāntic roots by repeatedly returning to the idea that truth is a matter of correct scriptural interpretation.

I have argued that "orthodox" and "heterodox" are poor translations of *āstika* and *nāstika*. Nonetheless, it can be a useful thought-experiment to apply the three Christian heresiological terms "orthodox," "heterodox," and "heretical" to the premodern Indian situation. For Vijñānabhikṣu, the only completely "heretical" school is Advaita Vedānta. It is an *āstika* school, a school that claims the Veda as its source but completely misinterprets scripture and therefore leads to the destruction of those who choose it. The other *āstika* schools contain teachings that might be described as heretical, but Vijñānabhikṣu chooses to de-emphasize this, instead stressing their positive uses. The major difference between Indian and Christian heresiology in this regard is that whereas medieval Vedāntins were likely to focus on the parts of Nyāya and Sāṃkhya that were free from error, Christian heresiologists maintained that a single drop of doctrinal error would irrevocably taint an entire school. Followers of the lesser *āstika* schools might still obtain liberation in this or future lives, but a member of a heretical Christian sect squanders his or her only opportunity to reach the kingdom of heaven. For Vijñānabhikṣu, "heterodoxy" corresponds to the *nāstika* views he outlines. Although he is dismissive of these views, Vijñānabhikṣu regards the error of the Advaitins' heresy as far more urgent than the mistakes of the heterodox Buddhists. As applied to the Indian context, "orthodoxy" does not refer to any school that calls the Vedas a valid means of knowledge but to only those schools that correctly interpret the Vedas. For Vijñānabhikṣu, the only fully orthodox *āstika* schools are the Vedānta and Yoga. Although he is heavily influenced by the Sāṃkhya and Nyāya schools, they contain elements of "heresy" and thus cannot be called completely orthodox.

Although the terms "orthodoxy," "heterodoxy," and "heresy" are not native Indian categories, they can be used in such a thought-experiment. Together, these terms offer a slightly more nuanced conceptual scheme that can be used to reanalyze some of the instabilities in the binary pair *āstika/nāstika* as it is conceptualized in the works of Vijñānabhikṣu, Mādhava, and Madhusūdana Sarasvatī. Although Vijñānabhikṣu's argument of the unity of all *āstika* schools holds out the promise of resolving the ambiguities arising in Mādhava's and Madhusūdana's explicitly hierarchical schemes, ultimately he too relies on hierarchical classification to reconcile explicit contradictions among the *āstika* schools. For Mādhava and

Madhusūdana, only the Advaita Vedānta school can properly be described as "orthodox," yet for Vijñānabhikṣu both Bhedābheda Vedānta and Yoga are free from interpretive error. These two schools each address different topics. Vedānta is the only school that completely reveals the highest knowledge, the nature of Brahman, whereas the practices outlined in the Yoga school are the most immediate means to liberation from the cycle of birth and death. Since neither school impinges on the other or makes erroneous claims beyond its proper scope, both qualify as orthodox, that is, as non-heretical *āstika* schools.

Madhusūdana's and Mādhava's concern with excluding *nāstikas* dates back to an earlier stage of Vedic ritualism. Although they uphold the structure of the *āstika/nāstika* distinction, the logic behind the distinction disappeared with the Vedāntic reinterpretation of the Vedas' function. Hence, Madhusūdana and Mādhava struggle to explain why the threat from *nāstikas* is so grave. Furthermore, the hierarchical structure of their doxographies undermines the binary separation they strive to maintain. Despite their denigration of the Buddhists, this structure inevitably makes Buddhism a preliminary step toward ultimate truth, and therefore Buddhism cannot be depicted as completely useless. Vijñānabhikṣu primarily relies on the category of *nāstika* as a polemical tool against a heretical school that portrays itself as *āstika* while secretly propagating Buddhist views. His arguments in the *Sāṃkhyapravacanabhāṣya* against Buddhism are an extension of his polemics against Advaita Vedānta. While he avoids the instabilities inherent in the doxographic genre, he too uses hierarchical categories to subordinate the Nyāya and Sāṃkhya to Vedānta and Yoga. For Vijñānabhikṣu, the differences between Nyāya, an *āstika* school, and Buddhism, a *nāstika* school, are quantitative, not qualitative. Both schools contain misleading teachings, and although Buddhism contains many more, he is forced to admit that even it is not totally corrupt. Therefore, the door remains open to argue that Buddhism, Jainism, and even the schools of the barbarians (*mlecchas*) function as a preliminary step toward the highest truth of Vedānta.

None of the premodern doxographers is bold enough to walk through that door, to suggest that the barbarian sects, such as Christianity, Judaism, and Islam, are useful on the path toward knowledge of Brahman. But these three late medieval thinkers paved the way for nineteenth- and twentieth-century innovators such as Vivekananda, Aurobindo, and Radhakrishnan, who transformed Vedānta into a global philosophy. Radhakrishnan portrays it as the essence of Hinduism or even as the essence of religion: "Vedānta is not a religion, but religion itself in its most universal and deepest significance."[58] Many recent studies have pointed to an "invention of Hinduism" during the nineteenth century. These studies typically portray Radhakrishnan and other Neo-Vedāntins as alienated from the past, inauthentic representatives of a Sanskritic intellectual tradition to which they had little access. While there is some truth in this depiction, this thesis exaggerates the role of colonialism in the creation of a unified Hindu philosophical message. It is to these modern heirs of Vedāntic doxography that I turn in chapter 10.

[10] HINDU UNITY AND THE NON-HINDU OTHER

INCLUSIVISM AND HINDU TOLERATION

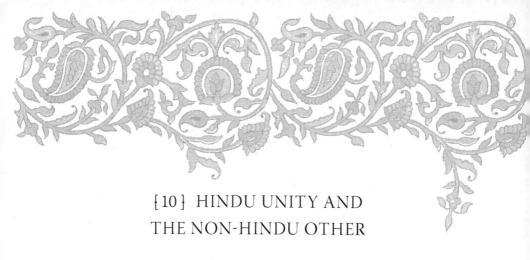

The tendency of thinkers in India to create hierarchies of systems of belief, with their own afforded the highest position, was not specific to the late medieval period. Many scholars have remarked on this tendency toward assimilation throughout Indian history, such as in the Purāṇas' attempts to portray the Buddha as an avatar of Viṣṇu.[1] Sri Aurobindo writes candidly that "[Hinduism] is in the first place a non-dogmatic *inclusive* religion and would have taken even Islam and Christianity into itself, if they had tolerated the process [my emphasis]."[2] This tendency to absorb philosophical, theological, and cultic diversity as part of a larger whole is substantially different from the "toleration" sometimes cited as one of Hinduism's essential features. As presented by European liberal traditions following John Locke, toleration involves the privatization of theological claims. Each sect is treated equally and allowed to thrive or wither on its own without either the support or censure of a laissez-faire state.[3] The citizens of the state are likewise expected to tolerate the private religious convictions of others, with the understanding that these others will also allow them freedom of worship.[4] Vivekananda, for instance, was a modern Hindu reformer who recognized the limitations of the discourse of toleration and taught that the true Hindu attitude is an active embrace of other religions and gods.[5] The word "inclusivism," popularized in Hindu studies by Paul Hacker, is a better approximation of the process in India by which a multitude of various sects, philosophies, gods, and modes of worship are united under a single overarching concept, whether the late medieval idea of six *āstika darśanas* or the modern term Hinduism. The phenomenon of inclusivism was also a way of establishing a hierarchy of gods in a polytheistic society. In the *Bhagavad Gītā,* Kṛṣṇa explains that he is the primordial God (*ādideva*) and the God of the gods (*devadeva*).[6] He is the recipient of all sacrifices:

> When devoted men sacrifice
> to other deities with faith,
> they sacrifice to me, Arjuna,
> however aberrant the rites.
> I am the enjoyer
> and the lord of all sacrifices;
> they do not know me in reality,
> and so they fail.[7]

When Kṛṣṇa later reveals his true form to Arjuna, Arjuna sees that Kṛṣṇa is the whole and the other gods are his parts:

> I see the gods
> in your body, O God,
> and hordes
> of varied creatures:
> Brahmā, the cosmic creator, on his lotus throne,
> all the seers
> and celestial serpents.[8]

Kṛṣṇa is the supreme God insofar as all the other gods depend on him for their existence. In this scheme, the other gods do exist, albeit merely as parts of Kṛṣṇa. Seen in its sociohistorical context, the strategy of inclusivism allowed worshippers in an extremely pluralistic theological environment to coexist and acknowledge one another's gods, though typically not as equals. For the Vaiṣṇava, all the benefits bestowed on the worshipper of Śiva come ultimately from Viṣṇu. And for the Śaiva, the fruits of devotion to Viṣṇu have their ultimate origin in Śiva. The *Īśvara Gītā* (Song of Lord Śiva), a later text that reworks central themes of the *Bhagavad Gītā* from a Śaiva point of view, illustrates inclusivism's reciprocality. In this text Śiva proclaims, "I am the enjoyer of all sacrifices and the one who bestows their fruits. Taking the form of all the Gods, I am everywhere, the self of everyone."[9] Using many of the same words and concepts, Śiva and Kṛṣṇa each announce that the other god is just a manifestation of himself.

Paul Hacker, a scholar of Vedānta and apologist for Roman Catholicism, argues that the rhetoric of "Hindu tolerance" is little more than a disingenuous attempt to subordinate Western religions to Hinduism. He sees exclusivism as admirably straightforward and free from the type of rhetorical ploys found in modern Hindu apologetics. Because "toleration" is a misnomer, Hacker proposes the alternative term "inclusivism," which he defines as "claiming for, and thus including in, one's own religion what really belongs to an alien sect."[10] Hacker makes particular historical claims about inclusivism, asserting that it is a uniquely Indian form of *Auseinandersetzung* and typically the result of feelings of inferiority.[11] According to Hacker, "the most outstanding example" of inclusivism comes from Tulsīdās, the sixteenth-century author of the *Rāmcaritmānas:*

> In Banaras, a city in which the cult of Śiva was predominant, he proclaimed devotion to Rāma. His ingenious safeguard against possible hostility from the alien sect was his teaching that worship of Śiva was all right, because Śiva himself was the foremost and noblest worshipper of Rāma. In this way Tulsīdās did not encroach on the religion of Śiva but claimed it in its entirety for his own. It seems that this method was employed especially by such religious groups as felt themselves inferior to their environment.[12]

Like some other modern Indologists, Hacker sees the concept of Hinduism as a recent phenomenon, and modern claims of Hindu unity as a "fiction."[13] Hinduism is nothing more than a "collective label" (*Sammelbezeichnung*) created by Western scholars to find a convenient way of describing "the innumerable, partly related, partly divergent religious phenomena of one geographical and historical region."[14] In many of these claims, Hacker is guilty of generalizing features of modern Hindu-Christian polemics to premodern Indian history. But the term "inclusivism" is useful despite his use of the term to criticize Hinduism in general and what he labels "Neo-Hinduism" in particular. Hacker may be correct that in the modern period, Hindus used inclusivistic strategies to defend their religion from missionaries' attempts to prove Christianity's superiority. But throughout Indian history, such strategies also were used as a tool for assimilation from a position of strength, such as in ongoing attempts to absorb Jainism, Buddhism, and even Sikhism into Hinduism.[15]

Hacker coined the problematic term "Neo-Hinduism" to distinguish thinkers such as Vivekananda, Aurobindo, Radhakrishnan, and Gandhi from "surviving traditional Hinduism." He makes little attempt to conceal his dislike of Neo-Hinduism, which he describes as "stillborn" and as having lost all continuity with earlier forms of Hinduism.[16] Although both "Neo-Hindus" and "traditional Hindus" practice inclusivism, Hacker maintains that only traditional Hindus were able to do so while retaining Hinduism's previous vitality.[17] If, as Hacker insists, "Hinduism" is an invention of modern scholars without any premodern equivalent, then the label "Neo-Hinduism" is doubly misleading. While "Neo-Vedānta" may be useful to call attention to important differences between modern Vedānta thinkers such as Vivekananda and Radhakrishnan and their premodern precursors, "Neo-Hindu" serves as little more than a pejorative. A more serious problem is Hacker's definition of the term "inclusivism," as "claiming for, and thus including in, one's own religion what really belongs to an alien sect."[18] His definition presupposes that the actual boundaries between religions are clear and self-evident and that historians are the proper adjudicators of each religion's true belongings. Does this apply equally to the Christian theology's illicit borrowing of the theological concepts of the immortal soul and the infinity of God from Greek philosophy? Such concepts are not found in Christianity in its pure, Semitic, pre-Hellenized form. The widespread tendency of "claiming for one's own what really belongs to another" is a primary means of change, growth, and innovation in all philosophical and theological traditions, not just in Hinduism. Hacker's definition of inclusivism thus shows his deep historicist biases, which lead him to condemn Hindu innovations of the modern period as inauthentic.

Moreover, Hacker's portrayal of inclusivism as a uniquely Indian phenomenon is the work of a Christian polemicist, not an impartial scholar of Indian religions. Inclusivism is a tendency more widespread in Hinduism than in Judaism, Christianity, or Islam. But it appears in the religions of the book as well, for example, in the Christian inclusivism of Nicholas of Cusa and Karl Rahner.[19] Hacker's myopic focus on Hindu inclusivism also obscures widespread exclusivist trends in pre-twelfth-century Hinduism, such as Kumārila Bhaṭṭa's rejection of Sāṃkhya, Yoga, Pāñcarātra, Pāśupata, and Buddhist interpretations of *dharma.* It is best to think of exclusivism and inclusivism as existing side by side in a variety of different traditions. The late medieval thinkers discussed in this book exhibit marked inclusivist tendencies, but none is a thoroughgoing inclusivist. In all the examples from premodern India that I have cited, ultimately a line is drawn between insiders and outsiders, *āstikas* and *nāstikas.*

The reverse side of Vijñānabhikṣu's inclusivistic attitude toward the schools of the affirmers (*āstikas*) is his exclusivistic rejection of the schools of the deniers (*nāstikas*). Vijñānabhikṣu's exclusivism regarding one school in particular, the Advaita Vedānta, has earned him even more notoriety than his views on the God of Sāṃkhya and Yoga.[20] In contrast, Vijñānabhikṣu's critiques of Buddhists and Jainas have hardly merited any comment, since his negative attitude was widely shared by the other *āstika* schools.[21] When discussing the Buddhists and Jainas, Vijñānabhikṣu relies heavily on the distinction between *āstika* and *nāstika.* In spite of his "difference and non-difference" stance toward the multiple *āstika* schools, non-difference does not come into play when discussing the *nāstikas.* Vijñānabhikṣu's charge that Advaita Vedāntins are "crypto-Buddhists" (*pracchannabauddhas*) assimilates Advaita to Buddhism and, by extension, argues that the Advaita is actually a *nāstika* school. Vijñānabhikṣu's primary need for the category of *nāstika* is as a way of denigrating Advaita. He spends little time in polemics against the other groups of deniers. Although Vijñānabhikṣu nowhere theorizes about the basis or origins of the distinction between *āstika* and *nāstika,* it is nonetheless central to his project: the category of *āstika* is ultimately meaningless without an opposite. He believes that certain doctrines are simply beyond all acceptability and serve no positive function. The category of *nāstika* is essential to him in finding a place for such groups as Advaita Vedānta.

Vijñānabhikṣu's near-contemporary Madhusūdana Sarasvatī clearly articulates the connection between the project of the inclusion of *āstikas* and the exclusion of *nāstikas.* He implicitly draws on *Manusmṛti* 2.11, which defines a *nāstika* as a "reviler of the Veda." For the late medieval Vedāntins, "reviler of the Veda" had come to mean a reviler of the doctrines taught in the Veda. The understanding of a "reviler of the Veda" as one who reviles the practices of the Veda had been eclipsed, just as the norms of practice enjoined by the Veda had been eclipsed by later modes of worship and as the Mīmāṃsā had been eclipsed by the Vedānta. According to Madhusūdana,

> Those [*āstika*] sages cannot just be confused, since they are omniscient. However, the access to human moral ends is not immediately possible for those who are preoccupied with external objects. The sages teach the various systems so that such people will not become deniers (*nāstikas*). Not knowing the true purport (*tātparya*) of the sages, people follow those various paths, grasping for ends that are contrary to the Vedas and overlooking the true purport of the Vedas.[22]

Sanskrit doxographers in the late medieval period were concerned with the concordance of the *āstika* systems in a way that pre-twelfth-century authors were not. The corollary of this was an increasing concern with and systematization of the category of *nāstika*. According to both Madhusūdana and Vijñānabhikṣu, merely acknowledging the Vedas' authority is not enough; one must also interpret the Vedas correctly, without "overlooking the true purport." Vijñānabhikṣu's critique of the Advaitins is that they do just this, misinterpreting the Upaniṣads to say that the phenomenal world is an illusion.

DECODING LATE MEDIEVAL DOXOGRAPHY

By the late medieval period, of course, Buddhism was virtually nonexistent in India, and Jainism hardly a threat. Therefore, the need to use inclusivistic or syncretic means to unify *āstika* doctrines would have been less, not more, urgent. So why would thinkers of the late medieval period have been more concerned with defining the boundaries of orthodoxy than their predecessors had been in the classical period? Vijñānabhikṣu is often labeled by his modern detractors as a "syncretist." Although "syncretism" in modern English usage refers to the merging of religions or philosophies that are properly separate, the original Greek term *synkrētismós* used by Plutarch meant something different. It referred to a custom of people on the isle of Crete to overcome local feuds and to form a sacred alliance in order to withstand foreign aggression.[23] Could this putting aside of intramural differences in the face of an external threat have been the fundamental impulse that led to attempts to unify *āstika knowledge*-systems and find principled reasons to reject the *nāstikas*? If so, what was the particular threat that led to the *synkrētismós* in the medieval Indian example?

The obvious answer to this question—the single most pronounced historical change between the eighth and sixteenth centuries—was the migration of Muslims into India that led to the eventual political domination of northern India, first by the Delhi Sultanate (1206–1526) and later by the Mughal Empire (1526–1707). Living in late medieval northern India as subjects of the Mughal Empire, Vijñānabhikṣu and Madhusūdana Sarasvatī must have encountered Islam. There is even a widely disseminated story of Madhusūdana's visit to Akbar's court at Fatehpur Sikri.[24] Yet in Madhusūdana's *Prasthānabheda* (The Various Religious Sources), ostensibly an exhaustive catalog of all doctrines, Islam is never mentioned.[25] Among Islamic intellectuals, Akbar and Dārā Shikoh went to great efforts to try to understand the systems of Indian philosophy, going so far as to translate the *Mahābhārata, Rāmāyaṇa,* Purāṇas, and Upaniṣads into

Persian.[26] But those on the other side made no attempt to translate philosophical and theological works from Persian and Arabic into Sanskrit, indicative of a worldview that did not see any value or purpose in intercultural or interreligious understanding.[27] For Akbar and other like-minded rulers, there was obvious practical benefit from creating a court religion that combined Hinduism and Islam. By creating a distinctively Indian religion incorporating symbols that resonated with all his subjects, Akbar might have been able to strengthen allegiances and solidify his support among groups that might have been uneasy submitting to a Muslim ruler. No similar utility existed from the standpoint of the śāstric scholars of that era. The traditions of Sanskrit grammar, Mīmāṃsā, and Dharmaśāstra would have convinced them of the a priori uselessness of all extra-Vedic traditions. At the same time, though, among Sanskrit authors there was no explicit ideological resistance to Islam. Unlike later Hindu nationalist intellectuals, who sometimes recorded their fantasies of heroic and violent resistance to Muslim oppression, Sanskrit intellectuals of the sixteenth and seventeenth centuries responded with silence.[28]

Is it possible that the Cārvākas, Jainas, and Buddhists functioned as placeholders for Islam in late medieval Sanskrit doxographies? After all, five hundred years before Madhusūdana and Vijñānabhikṣu wrote, the Buddhist philosophers had ceased to offer any meaningful competition to the school of Vedānta. What could possibly have been the use of vilifying a school that had disappeared almost completely from the Indian subcontinent?[29] The answer to this question requires an understanding of doxography as a genre and as part of the larger *śāstric* imaginary. The frustration of many modern scholars in dealing with the Indian doxographies comes from misunderstanding their purpose. The doxographies were not empirical accounts of a state of affairs on which we can base reliable and comprehensive accounts of the Indian philosophical schools. Rather, they were an idealized vision of the doctrines: clear, unambiguous, distinct, and progressing inevitably from lower to higher. This is evident in the earliest known doxographies. We see it, for instance, in the logical progression of schools in *Maṇimēkalai* from one *pramāṇa* (Lokāyata), to two (Buddhists), to six (Mīmāṃsā), with only a passing concern with fidelity to each school's actual position on the issue. In the classical period Buddhist *pūrvapakṣins* had been etched into the collective śāstric memory, and for that reason Buddhism was given a part to play on lists of doctrines long after the Buddhists themselves had left the stage. In this textual universe, the question "how was it the Buddhists remained in the doxographic record long after they had ceased to exist on the ground?" is based on a foreign understanding of doxography. A more relevant question might be, "Under what conditions might Buddhism be removed from the doxographic record, and another doctrine (e.g., Islam) take its place?"

The purpose of doxography in India was clearly not the cataloging of all existing schools of philosophical thought, or all the schools that had existed throughout history. Despite Haribhadra's assertion that "there are only six schools of philosophy"[30] and the apparent promise of some doxographies' titles to survey "all systems," these doxographers knew quite well that there were other systems that fell outside their descriptive purview. The late medieval doxographers naturalized a state of affairs that was many centuries beyond their own historical situation, in what amounted to a suppression of historical change.[31] Only a fundamental shift in the understanding of the purpose of doxography could have removed the Buddhists from their fixed place among *nāstika* schools. They served an important function in doxography as the prototypical *nāstika* school, allowing *āstikas* to define themselves over and against the Buddhists.

THE ABSENCE OF ISLAM

The nearly total lack of mention of Muslims in Sanskrit texts has led some historians to suggest that there was little contact between Sanskrit intellectuals and Muslims, or if there was contact, there was no awareness of Islam as a religion or system of belief. Sanskrit texts were very late to adopt the word *musulmāna,* instead often describing Muslims with the names of other foreigners who had arrived more than a millennium earlier: *yavanas* (Ionians) or *śakas* (Scythians).[32] In other cases, the Sanskrit authors were more accurate, labeling the foreigners they encountered as *turuṣkas* (Turks), yet they still did not acknowledge that many of these foreigners shared a single religious identity. Sanskrit intellectuals focused on their (imagined) place of origin, not their beliefs. The logic of medieval Indian xenology followed the patterns of doxography and *śāstra* generally, applying categories from a millennium earlier to changing sociocultural conditions without concern for their descriptive adequacy.

Medieval texts in Indian vernacular languages, however, offer ample evidence to refute the idea that most medieval Indians were unaware of the general tenets of a religion shared by the group of people known as Muslims. That this conventional wisdom has persisted for so long is an indication of a heavy reliance on Sanskrit texts, accompanied by ignorance or a lack of interest in works in other Indian languages. In particular, the evidence from medieval *bhakti* texts suggests that Hindus and Muslims were quite aware of their mutual differences and even indicates a lively tradition of theological debate between the two groups. One remarkable text was written by the Marathi poet Eknāth (1553–1599). In this work, *Hindu-Turk Saṃvād* (Dialogue Between Hindu and Turk), Eknāth expresses an awareness of the Muslims' and Vaiṣṇavas' differences in both practice and theology. His goal, like that of many other late medieval *bhakti* poets, was to transcend sectarian differences in order to realize the truth of the one universal God worshipped by all people, Hindu and Muslim alike.

Eknāth begins his work by proclaiming the oneness of all religions: "The goal is one; the ways of worship are different. / Listen to the dialogue between these two!"[33] The middle section of the text depicts two characters, a Brahmin and a Turk, dwelling on their mutual differences and mocking each other. The Turk suggests, predictably, that Hindus engage in idolatry and demean God by portraying him as a keeper of cows. The Brahmin responds: If God is omnipresent, why does He not exist in statues?

> Turk: O Brahmin, listen to what I have to say:
> Your scripture is a mystery to everyone.
> God has hands and feet, you say—
> This is really impossible!
>
> Brahmin: Listen, you great fool of a Turk!
> See God in all living things.
> You haven't grasped this point
> And so you have become a nihilist (*śūnyavādka*).[34]

The Brahmin labels his opponent with the remarkable Marathi epithet "nihilist" (*śūnyavādka*). This pejorative term hints a vestigial cultural memory of a much earlier debate between Vedāntins and Mādhyamika Buddhists. The Mādhyamikas, also known in Sanskrit as *śūnyavādins,* maintained the doctrine of emptiness (*śūnyatā*), teaching that there is no ultimately existent reality, no God or ultimate principle serving as the foundation of the world's existence. This passage should not be interpreted as indicating that Eknāth really believes the Muslims subscribe to the same atheist doctrines as the Mādhyamika Buddhists do. Rather, this word is another example of the extraordinary adaptability of Indian terms used for othering. These words, emptied of all historical and doctrinal specificity, in time become little more than vague pejoratives. This is what also happens to the term *nāstika,* whose meaning varied widely across historical epochs, eventually becoming associated with foreigners as well. Even a Muslim, who affirms the existence of a supreme God, a life after death, and a specific path of ethical behavior, can be put in the same category as Buddhists.

In Sheldon Pollock's article "Rāmāyaṇa and Political Imagination in India," he illustrates another way that medieval Hindus employed cultural memory to categorize Muslims. He points out that in numerous medieval commentaries and retellings of the story of Rāma, the demons (*rākṣasas*) of the story are identified with Muslims.[35] For instance, in the *Rāmāyaṇa* section in which the demon Virādha asks to be buried in a pit after his death rather than cremated, two eighteenth-century commentators remark that the Muslims, "who are the *rākṣasas* of the Kali age, still follow this custom."[36] Pollock is particularly interested in medieval kings who fashioned their public image in the likeness of Lord Rāma, using the text's narrative logic to portray Muslim opponents as demons. But demonization can be found in other contexts as well. Cynthia Talbot notes that although there is little explicit use of royal symbols from the Rāmāyaṇa in the medieval inscriptions of Andhra Pradesh, Muslims are demonized in a similar way.[37] I would add that that the motif of one's adversaries as demons has very early roots in India. In particular, the portrayal of philosophical opponents as demons dates back at least as far as the *Chāndogya Upaniṣad.* The story of the God Indra, his *asura* rival Virocana, and their teacher Prajāpati appears at *Ch. Up.* 8.7.1–8.12.6. In order to test the pupils, Prajāpati teaches Indra and Virocana that the true self (*ātman*) is nothing other than the body. While Indra rejects this teaching and comes back again and again to Prajāpati to eventually receive the truth, Virocana, delighted, shares this flawed teaching with the other demons.

> Now, Virocana, his heart totally content, went back to the demons (*asuras*) and announced to them this correspondence (*upaniṣad*): "It is the body (*ātman*) that one should extol in this world. It is the body that one should care for. . . . Therefore, even today people here say of a man who gives no gifts, has no faith, and offers no sacrifices: "What a demonic (*āsura*) fellow!"[38]

This theory of the self corresponds roughly to the recorded views of the Cārvāka materialists, who maintain that the self is identical to the body and perishes when the body perishes.[39] The materialist school was widely reviled by other Indian philosophers, including Jainas and Buddhists. But Buddhists and Jainas were not immune from demonization; the *Rāmāyaṇa* and Purāṇas depict Buddhists and Jainas in demonic form. *Viṣ. Pu.* 3.18 traces the origin of Buddhism and Jainism to the false doctrines taught by Lord Viṣṇu to the *asuras* who threatened the gods in battle. Once they had given up their sacrifices and embraced the false tenets of one of the two religions, they lost the powers they had gained through their austerities and were massacred by the gods.[40] Remarkably, this version of the story of Viṣṇu's Buddha avatar has been all but erased from the cultural memory of modern Hindus. It has been replaced with a vague acceptance of the basic validity of the Buddha's teaching, and especially his teaching of nonviolence, as a positive philosophical contribution.

Vijñānabhikṣu's works are not free from the language of demonization. His favorite myth is the tale of the churning of the ocean of milk to acquire the nectar of immortality. He begins three of his works with allusions to the myth, and of course his commentary on the *Brahmasūtras,* the *Vijñānāmṛtabhāṣya* (Commentary on the Nectar of Knowledge), takes its name from the story. It, too, is a tale of struggle between the gods and demons. After the demons steal the nectar for themselves, Viṣṇu assumes the seductive female form Mohinī to trick the demons and keep the nectar among the gods. This is followed by a great battle in which the gods prevail.[41] In the benedictory verses of his commentary on the *Brahmasūtras,* Vijñānabhikṣu metaphorically identifies his activity as a commentator with the churning of the ocean of milk:

3. This nectar of knowledge, drawn out by churning of the sea of milk that is the speech of revealed texts, remembered texts, and reasoning, I offer to Brahmins to please the teacher.

4. Having distributed the nectar and used the Mohinī that is discriminative wisdom to cheat the demons who are bad arguments, let those who desire nectar drink this.

5. After Brahmins have drunk this and become strong, conquering the leaders of the troops of demons who are the infidels (*pākhaṇḍa*), may they reach the abode of the great teacher through knowledge and ritual action.[42]

By the logic of this metaphor, Vijñānabhikṣu's text is itself the nectar of immortality. The original telling of this particular story in the Purāṇas does not code the *asuras* as Buddhists, Jainas, or infidels generally. But this type of demonization is so common that when Vijñānabhikṣu follows the logic of his extended metaphor, demons are alternatively "bad arguments" (*kutarkas*) or the infidels (*pākhaṇḍas*) whom the Brahmins will have to face in debate.[43] Like many terms used for othering in medieval Sanskrit, the identity of the infidel is kept extremely vague, and in the Purāṇic and śāstric context in which Vijñanabhikṣu is working, the Buddhists and Jainas are the most obvious groups that might fit this definition. Divining the intention behind Vijñānabhikṣu's words is ultimately impossible. But there is every reason to suspect that his readers in the sixteenth and seventeenth centuries did not confine the category of demonic Other to Buddhists and Jainas alone. Because of the adaptability and vagueness of such categories, many readers would have understood the category of *pākhaṇḍa* to apply equally to Muslims, whose military and ideological threat was a much more pressing concern than imagined verbal assaults from Buddhist philosophers.

HINDUISM: A MODERN INVENTION?

"Hindu" was not originally a Sanskrit word but a Persian term used by Muslims to describe a regional or ethnic identity: the people living near the Indus, or Sindhu, river.[44] Only at a relatively late date was the term adopted by Indians to refer to themselves, typically as distinguished from outsider groups known as *turuṣkas* (Turks) or *mlecchas* (barbarians). Cynthia Talbot has recorded the earliest usage of the word "Hindu" in an Indian language from inscriptions in mid-fourteenth-century Andhra, in which some Vijayanagara kings were described with the epithet "Sultan among Hindu kings" (*Hindu-raya-suratrana*).[45] Talbot cautions, though, that in these inscriptions, "Hindu meant Indic as opposed to Turkish, not 'of the Hindu religion' as opposed to 'of the Islamic religion.'"[46] In Gauḍīya Vaiṣṇava texts written in Bengali in the sixteenth and seventeenth centuries, "Hindu" was occasionally used to distinguish natives from *yavanas* or *mlecchas*.[47] Although the context makes clear that these foreigners were Muslims, Gauḍīya Vaiṣṇava writers did not state this explicitly until the eighteenth century, when the term *musulmāna* finally became common usage in Bengali. In this case too, the word may have designated ethnicity generally and not a specific set of religious beliefs.

The rarity of words such as "Hindu" and "Muslim" has led a number of historians to conclude that Hindus were not aware of fundamental religious differences between the two groups. Even more remarkably, some historians claim that before the nineteenth century, there was no native understanding of a single unified Hindu religion. Perhaps the most forceful exponent of this view is Heinrich von Stietencron. In an article entitled "Religious Configurations in Pre-Muslim India and the Modern Concept of Hinduism," he states his thesis:

> It has been shown that the term "Hinduism" is a relatively recent one. Not only is the term modern, as I hope to show in this paper, but also the whole concept of the oneness of Hindu religion was introduced by missionaries and scholars from the West. . . . Historically, the concept of Hindu religious unity is questionable when applied to any period prior to the nineteenth century. Both the religious practice and the theological doctrine of important Hindu religious traditions go against it.[48]

Few scholars dispute that the word "Hinduism" was coined in the modern period.[49] Stietencron, however, is arguing a much stronger thesis: before the nineteenth century, there was no idea of a unity of practice or doctrine among the groups labeled in the modern era as "Hindus." In his article, he seeks to prove this alleged lack of unity through his analysis of the *Somaśambhupaddhati,* a work on Śaiva ritual compiled by the late eleventh-century author Somaśambhu. This work portrays all the religious subsects today included under the umbrella of Hinduism as being distinct and even antagonistic. Somaśambhu says that if a person wishes to achieve liberation (*mukti*), he must be a member of one Śaiva sect. For other groups—including Buddhists, Jainas, Bhāgavatas, Pāśupatas, Naiyāyikas, Sāṃkhyas, Pūrva Mīmāṃsakas, and Vedāntins—the only opportunity for the highest liberation is conversion to Śaivism.[50] To this end, the *Somaśambhupaddhati* describes a ritual that removes the invisible mark (*liṅga*) on the person who follows one of these other groups, allowing him to start over again, his karmic slate wiped clean, and able to earn ritual merit (*puṇya*) as a Śaiva.

Stietencron's analysis of the *Somaśambhupaddhati* proves that in at least one eleventh-century textual community, there was little or no conception of a unified Hindu religious identity. But Stietencron suggests that the attitude of this text can be generalized to all groups of people in India in all epochs until the nineteenth-century invention of a unified Hindu religion by Europeans. To substantiate this very broad assertion, Stietencron would need to cite a number of other texts, both earlier and later, that persuasively reflect this same understanding of the disunity of "Hindu" religious groups. More important, he would need to show that pre-nineteenth-century texts that have been seen by others as postulating a unified Hindu or proto-Hindu identity do not actually do so. Without much more evidence from a range of texts in other time periods, the description of religious conversion to Śaivism in the *Somaśambhupaddhati* lends itself to various historical interpretations, some of which directly contradict Stietencron's assertion that "the whole concept of the oneness of Hindu religion was introduced by missionaries and scholars from the West."

The historian David Lorenzen has questioned the modern invention of Hinduism hypothesis. In his article "Who Invented Hinduism?" Lorenzen challenges Stietencron:

> This essay argues that the claim that Hinduism was invented or constructed by European colonizers, mostly British, sometime after 1800 is false. The evidence instead suggests that a Hindu religion theologically and devotionally grounded in texts such as the *Bhagavad Gītā,* the Purāṇas, and philosophical commentaries on the six *darśanas,* gradually acquired a much sharper self-conscious identity through the rivalry between Muslims and Hindus in the period between 1200 and 1500, and was firmly established long before 1800.[51]

To defend this thesis, Lorenzen cites examples from a number of late medieval texts that do show a sense of self-conscious religious identity among groups we now call Hindu. While these authors did not use any equivalent of the term "Hinduism" (*hindutā* and *hindutva* are, of course, modern neologisms), they do show a clear understanding that those people known as Hindus shared religious practices that differed from those of other groups, particularly Muslims. Lorenzen draws his evidence from late medieval vernacular literature, including the poetry of Eknāth, Anantadās, Kabīr, and Vidyāpati. Vidyāpati (early 15th c.) understands that there are differences between Hindus and Turks, and that these differences have their basis in religion. He even uses the Apabhraṃśa term *dhamme* in the sense of "religion," much as the word *dharma* functions in modern Indian languages:

> The Hindus and Turks live close together.
> Each makes fun of the other's religion (*dhamme*).
> One calls the faithful to prayer. The other recites the Vedas.
> One butchers animals by bleeding.
> The other cuts (off their heads) . . .
> The Turks coerce passers by into doing forced labor.

Grabbing hold of a Brahmin boy, they put a cow's vagina on his head.
They rub out his *tilak* and break his sacred thread.
They want to ride on horses. They use rice to make liquor.
They destroy temples and construct mosques.[52]

In this passage we see a kind of vilification of Muslims similar to the "demonization" of Muslims described by Pollock and Talbot. More important, here this vilification is coupled with a distinct sense of a Hindu religious identity, a sense that most Hindus share a set of practices and that these practices contrast with those of the Turks. Although these late medieval works most often identify religious similarity or difference on the basis of practice, they also acknowledge differences of belief. Many *bhakti* poets contrast the Hindu belief that God exists in all living things, animate and inanimate, with Islam's emphasis on iconoclasm and God's transcendence.

The celebrated fifteenth-century poet Kabīr also composed numerous poems that depict two distinct religious groups, Hindus and Muslims, engaged in theological disagreement. Like many other *nirguṇa bhakti* poets, Kabīr ridicules both sects, faulting them for their pettiness and possessive attitude toward God:

If the mosque is the place where God resides,
then who owns the rest of the land?
Ram lives in images and holy locations?—
Then why has no one ever found him there?
Hindus, Muslims—Where did they come from?
Who got them started down this road?[53]

Kabīr's neither-nor attitude toward the two religions is possible only if he and his readers perceive two sects that should be rejected, each presenting a distinct and unified set of religious claims. Kabīr has been claimed by both modern Muslims and modern Hindus to be one of their own, whereas modern secularists regard him as a proto-secular advocate of Hindu-Muslim harmony. But perhaps it is better to see him as an equal-opportunity vilifier of the two dominant religions of late medieval northern India. Kabīr's object was not to demonize Muslims but to mock all the manifestations of organized religion that he saw in these two competing groups, both of which fail to bring worshippers any closer to God.[54]

The increasing availability of translations of vernacular texts from the late medieval period should finally put to rest the notion that there was no conception of a specifically Hindu religious identity that differed from the beliefs and practices of Muslims. Although early uses of the word "Hindu" in fourteenth-century inscriptions seem to use the word in a geographical or ethnic sense, Cynthia Talbot acknowledges that ethnicity is a composite of many factors—including "language, costume, marriage customs and fighting styles"—some of which have their basis in religious practice.[55] Just as observation led the authors of vernacular texts to remark on differences of food or dress, eventually it led to an appreciation of the principled religious differences underlying some of the more superficial differences in custom. "Hindu" was originally an ethnic designator. But the ample evidence from fifteenth- and sixteenth-century writers shows that by that time, the word "Hindu" had been adopted by vernacular-language authors and had in some contexts taken on a more specifically religious sense.

Although Stietencron would surely resist this idea, his analysis of the eleventh-century *Somaśambhupaddhati* is accidental evidence in support of Lorenzen's thesis. Both Lorenzen and Pollock mark the period shortly after the *Somaśambhupaddhati* century as a time of important shifts in Hindu self-representation. For Pollock, the twelfth century was the beginning of the invention of a new tradition in which kings became Rāma by adopting his symbols and applying them to their own historical circumstances.[56] For Lorenzen, the period between 1200 and 1500 was the time in which rivalry between Hindu and Muslim created a newly self-conscious identity of Hindu or proto-Hindu unity. In this book I have focused on a group of texts from the same time period: philosophical works written in Sanskrit. The evidence from medieval philosophy and doxography corroborates the thesis that Lorenzen has advanced. Before the twelfth century, the category of "affirmer" (*āstika*) is a blurry one, potentially admitting groups such as the Buddhists and Jainas, who affirm the existence of worlds after death. But sometime during a critical period between the twelfth and fourteenth centuries, the category of *āstika* began to harden into the classification of the "six systems" as they are recognized today. At the same time, Buddhists and Jainas became permanently classified as "deniers" (*nāstikas*) in influential Advaita doxographies. Also in the late medieval period, the category of *nāstika* underwent a subtle blurring with categories like "barbarian" (*mleccha*), allowing foreigners to be classed together with Buddhists and Jainas.[57] This blurring also allowed the epic and Purāṇic strategies of "demonization," once applied solely to Buddhists, Jainas, and Cārvākas, to extend to foreigners, and especially to Muslims. Philosophical authors writing in Sanskrit do not acknowledge Islam explicitly. But the perceived threat of Islam motivated them to create a strictly defined category of *āstika* philosophical systems, systems that professed belief in the authority of the Veda. This category was later reformulated according to further developments in the nineteenth century, and the medieval list of *āstika darśanas* became known as the "schools of Hindu philosophy."

COMMUNALISM, UNIVERSALISM, AND HINDU IDENTITY

There are dangers in recognizing the existence of Hindu-Muslim divisions in medieval India. My greatest concern is that my thesis might be taken out of context to support a Hindu communalist political agenda. Romila Thapar, among others, has pointed out the communalists' need to present a unified, homogenous group identity:

> "Communal" . . . in the Indian context has a specific meaning and primarily perceives Indian society as constituted of a number of religious communities. Communalism in the Indian sense therefore is a consciousness which draws on a supposed religious identity and uses this as the basis for an ideology. It then demands political allegiance to a religious community and supports a programme of political action designed to further the interests of that religious community. . . . Such identity tends to iron out diversity and insists on conformity, for it is only through a uniform acceptance of the religion that it can best be used for political ends.[58]

The rather arcane historical controversy over philosophical and theological identities in medieval India has ramifications for contemporary Indian political debates. Arguments for a Hindu self-identity or a unified Hindu theological voice in the medieval period can be co-opted by Hindu communalist political actors.[59] Accordingly, I suspect that a part of the motivation of Stietencron and others to assert that Hindu identity is purely a nineteenth-century colonial construction is to weaken Hindu communalism. For if "Hinduism" is merely an artificial construction that outsiders imposed on Indians in the nineteenth century, simplistic historical narratives of medieval Hindu unity in the face of Muslim oppression would be proved false. By acknowledging a process of *synkrētismós* by which late medieval Hindus formulated a new religious identity over and against a Muslim Other, seeing medieval history through a religious, communal lens once again becomes possible.

The evidence presented in this book suggests that there was no single understanding of what it meant to be a Hindu in medieval India. "Hindu unity" was not a structure created in the late medieval period that has existed unchanged from that point to the present day. "Unifying Hinduism" is a process, not an entity. Indian intellectuals have been engaged in this process for at least seven hundred years. Although they often have agreed that this unity exists, the demon has always been in the details. We see a debate over the details of this unity in the confrontation between Advaita Vedāntins and their Bhedābhedavāda opponents in sixteenth-century India. Although both groups provided hierarchical accounts of the *āstika* schools, their understandings of the metaphysical ground of *āstika* unity were very different. One vision of Hindu unity, the Advaita Vedānta view, has come to dominate modern Hinduism. But Hindu philosophical minorities refuse to be silenced and continue to assert alternative interpretations of what it means to be a Hindu.

This evidence of a gradually developing and deeply contested Hindu identity in the medieval period cannot be used to reduce regional political struggles in medieval India to a global Muslim-versus-Hindu clash of civilizations. Nor can it be adduced as evidence for Hindu communalist arguments that Muslims were engaged in religious genocide against Hindus for explicitly theological reasons. As Thapar notes regarding medieval religious identities,

> Even the recognition of a religious identity does not automatically establish a religious community. . . . Clashes which on the face of it would now be interpreted as between Hindus and Muslims, would require a deeper investigation to ascertain how far they were clashes between specific castes and sects and to what degree did they involve support and sympathy from other castes and sects identifying with the same religion or seeking such idenity.[60]

Religious motivations for violent behavior by Muslims against Hindus and Hindus against Muslims in the medieval period cannot be ruled out, as Stietencron might wish, on the grounds that Hinduism did not exist. But for most incidents of violence between Hindus and other groups, the evidence points to motives more political than theological. This applies to the widely publicized destruction of Hindu temples by Muslims[61] and also to the history of Śaiva violence against Jainas and Buddhists, often elided by those who seek to emphasize Hinduism's superior history of religious toleration.[62] Despite textual evidence possibly suggesting that Hindus saw it as their duty to wage holy war against demonic followers of the Buddha and Mahāvīra, those struggles too were grounded more often in *realpolitik* than in religious principle.[63]

The first way of classifying the Other in Sanskrit doxography is binary and exclusivist. It denies that the doctrines of the Other have any value, even preliminary value, in achieving the goal of liberation from the cycle of death and rebirth. This logic underlies either-or distinctions such as "affirmers" (*āstikas*) and "deniers" (*nāstikas*). In extreme instances, this same logic has led to the literal demonization of opposing groups, as in Vijñānabhikṣu's coding of his philosophical opponents as the *asuras* who attempted to steal the nectar of immortality. The second way of categorizing the Other is hierarchical and inclusivist. It is the impulse leading Mādhava to portray all doctrines besides Advaita as preliminary means to a higher truth or leading Vijñānabhikṣu to suggest that Kapila taught Sāṃkhya to help those who were not ready for the truth of God's existence. Typically, these two modes, binary and hierarchical, coexist in late medieval Indian doxographies in a complex and unstable relationship, both asserting and denying that the Other is completely different from the insiders in one's home community.

The inclusivistic logic of hierarchization has led to some remarkable developments in modern Hinduism, particularly among Hacker's so-called Neo-Hindus.[64] Writers like Vivekananda and Radhakrishnan, often criticized for their Westernized, inauthentic understanding of Indian philosophical traditions, drew in large part on the hierarchical, inclusivistic tendencies exhibited in medieval Indian doxographies. Radhakrishnan's enunciation of Vedānta's relation to the other branches of Hinduism is a modern reformulation of Mādhava's and Madhusūdana Sarasvatī's hierarchies:

> All sects of Hinduism attempt to interpret the Vedānta texts in accordance with their own religious views. The Vedānta is not a religion, but religion itself in its most universal and deepest significance. . . . While no creeds and no scruples were forced to disappear as unsuitable or out of date, every one of them developed on account of the influence of the spirit of the Vedānta, which is by no means sectarian.[65]

Vedānta is the essence of Hinduism. But it is more than this for Radhakrishnan. It is the essence of religion itself, and the most promising foundation for "a universal religion of which the historical faiths are but branches."[66] The religions of the book, despite their exclusivistic tendencies, are for Radhakrishnan also branches of this universal faith. He follows the logic of inclusivism to its absolute conclusion, extending and universalizing Vedānta as a path for all human beings. Unlike Vijñānabhikṣu, whose inclusivism ends abruptly with a binary division between the *āstikas* and *nāstikas* such as Buddhists (and crypto-Buddhist Advaitins), for Radhakrishnan truth and liberation are open to all the world's major religions. Paul Hacker and Heinrich von Stietencron are correct to point out that this type of universalism was never embraced by any school of Vedānta in premodern India. Yet the critics fail to acknowledge Radhakrishnan's fidelity to the underlying logic of inclusivism, which at its most abstract level is a privileging of unity over difference, seeing all apparent contradictions as part of a higher synthesis.

From this historical perspective, both the universalizing tendencies of Neo-Vedāntic reformers and the demonizing tendencies of Hindu communalists have their roots in medieval discourses of self and Other, of unity and difference. The unification of Hinduism is a continuing process as different groups struggle to define a Hindu essence and to tame the unruly excess of beliefs and practices today grouped together as Hindu. Hindu communalism has at its ideological foundation the need to completely elide differences within specifically circumscribed Hindu parameters. At the same time, it exaggerates differences between Hindu and non-Hindu, particularly with regard to the Muslims and Christians who have replaced Buddhists and Jainas in the discourses that enable Hindu self-identity.[67] Yet contemporary Hinduism also contains universalizing, globalizing tendencies: the global Hinduism of the heirs of Radhakrishnan and Vivekananda is one that transcends national boundaries and that understands Hindu philosophical truth as a legacy that belongs to all nations equally.[68] As Vivekananda wrote, "No man, no nation, my son, can hate others and live; India's doom was sealed the very day they invented the word *mlechchha* [*sic*] and stopped from communion with others."[69] Perhaps there are even stirrings of a third way, one that acknowledges differences between religions as real (unlike the universalists) but sees these differences as potentially enriching Hinduism, rather than threatening to destroy it (as the communalists do).

The process of the unification of Hinduism continues today. Some modern Hindus have found strength and sustenance in diversity, acknowledging that differences within Hinduism ultimately frustrate all systematic attempts to portray it as reducible to any single philosophical system. Others have denied this diversity, rewriting India's history in an effort to present Hinduism as a timeless, univocal indigenous tradition threatened by foreign intruders. The dynamic tension between unity and difference has existed since the beginning of philosophical speculation in India. Understanding the current state of Hinduism and its future possibilities requires us to delve more deeply into this past. Most of all, as scholars we must fight against the projection of contemporary political ideologies onto Indian history in order to fully appreciate the riches of the intellectual traditions known today as Hinduism.

NOTES

1. INTRODUCTION

1. For example, "There is a mighty law of life, a great principle of human evolution, a body of spiritual knowledge and experience of which India has always been destined to be guardian, exemplar and missionary. This is the *sanatana dharma*, the eternal religion" (Aurobindo Ghose 2005[1909]:219).
2. Mishra (2009:20). Pankaj Mishra gives this summary of the hypothesis of the modern invention of Hinduism in a review of Wendy Doniger's *The Hindus: An Alternative History*, failing to note that Doniger herself has criticized this hypothesis as too simplistic (Doniger 1991a).
3. For more, see Hobsbawm and Ranger (1983).
4. This thesis, which I develop at greater length in chapter 10, is largely an elaboration on and restatement of David Lorenzen's thesis in the article "Who Invented Hinduism?" (Lorenzen 2005:53).
5. *yāny etāni trayīvidbhir na parigṛhītāni . . . sāṃkhyayogapāñcarātrapāśupataśākhya-granthaparigṛhītadharmādharmanibandhanāni.* Kumārila Bhaṭṭa's *Tantravārttika*, commentary on *MS* 1.3.4, in Abhyaṅkara and Jośī (1970, 2:112). For an in-depth discussion of this passage, see Eltschinger (forthcoming).
6. For instance, Vyāsa's commentary on *YS* 2.33 states that Vedic ritual specialists (e.g., Mīmāṃsakas) will accrue demerit for their performance of animal sacrifices. In this regard, followers of Yoga and Sāṃkhya are closer to the nonviolent traditions of Buddhism and Jainism than to Vedic ritualism. For more, see Halbfass (1983).
7. Stietencron (1995:60). As Stietencron points out, such exclusivist texts contradict the oft-repeated idea that Hinduism believes all spiritual paths are valid.
8. In introduction to Garbe (1895:xiii).
9. Ibid., xiv.
10. For example, Rukmani (1981).
11. On Vijñānabhikṣu as a Vedāntin, see Ram (1995).
12. I prefer "affirmer" and "denier" as translations for *āstika* and *nāstika*, respectively (see chapter 9).
13. Marx (1969[1853]:89). On the question of historical consciousness and premodern India, see Pollock (1989) and Halbfass (1988:349–50).

14. Vedāntins of the eighth century and earlier were especially concerned with the refutation of Sāṃkhya, a school widely regarded as *āstika* by later doxographers (Nakamura 1989:473–74).
15. Only one scholar disputes this, Udayavīra Śāstrī, who claims Vijñānabhikṣu lived in the fourteenth century (Rukmani 1981).
16. P. K. Gode attempts to identify Bhāvāgaṇeśa as Bhāvagaṇeśa Dīkṣita, a Citpāvan Brahmin who lived in Varanasi in the late sixteenth century (Gode 1944). While this argument is plausible, it is also based on several conjectures. Names of two other students of Vijñānabhikṣu have been recorded: Prasāda Mādhava and Divyasiṃha Miśra (Upādhyāya 1994:36).
17. Gode puts Bhāvāgaṇeśa's dates between 1550 and 1600 (Gode 1944:28); Śrīvāstavya claims 1583–1623 (Śrīvāstavya 1969:44).
18. Śrīvāstavya (1969:43); Rukmani (1981).
19. Śrīvāstavya (1969:24). Suspiciously, Śrīvāstavya, a professor at the University of Allahabad, claims that Vijñānabhikṣu lived in Allahabad.
20. For a chronology of Vijñānabhikṣu's works, see Rukmani (1981:6–7). She does not list Vijñānabhikṣu's commentary on the *Bṛhadāraṇyaka Upaniṣad*, which has been recently edited by Noriaki Hosoda but does not appear in manuscript catalogues (Hosoda 1998). Vijñānabhikṣu also claims to have written a treatise on Nyāya, but it has never been found (Jha 1995:125).
21. *etena bhagavadgītāvyākhyāpekṣā 'pi yāsyati / śabdādibhedamātreṇa gītāyā arthasāmyataḥ //* See the edition in Nicholson (2005:300).
22. The published work is the *Vijñānāmṛtabhāṣya*, which has been published both by the Chowkhamba Sanskrit Series Office (1901) and more recently by the Benares Hindu University Press (1979).
23. Although sometimes he cannot avoid these issues, such as his assertion of the existence of God in his commentary on the atheistic *Sāṃkhyasūtras.*
24. *Bh. Pu.* 3.25.1–3.33.37.
25. Madhusūdana Sarasvatī ([16th c. CE]1850:23–24).
26. In particular, see Halbfass (1988:349–68) and Qvarnström (1999).
27. For a concise definition and summary of different types of Western doxographies, see Runia (1998) and Mansfeld (2004).
28. Rorty (1984:62).
29. Runia (1999:34).
30. Cowell and Gough (1978) and Śaṅkara (1983[14th c. CE?]). One such link is Paul Deussen's presentation of Indian philosophical schools in his *Allgemeine Geschichte der Philosophie* (Deussen 1899). The *Sarvasiddhāntasaṃgraha*, a doxography once attributed to Śaṅkara, is now generally accepted to be a product of an anonymous author between the fourteenth and sixteenth centuries (Halbfass 1988:535; Pande 1998:99–130).
31. On the category of "the mystical," see King (1999:7–34).
32. Dyson (2006:309).
33. For one history of such mix-and-match comparisons, see Tuck (1990).
34. Donald Davidson (2001) argues against the coherence of the idea of "radically different conceptual schemes" between cultures or languages. For a critique of Davidson, see Forster (1998).
35. The early list of the "six schools" enumerated by Cāttaṉār and Haribhadra differs from the list of six schools made popular by historians in the modern period.

36. Krishna (1991:14).
37. The exception to this is the school of Advaita Vedānta. Although generally classified as an *āstika* school, Vijñānabhikṣu understands it in reality as a form of Buddhism and therefore at odds with the *āstikas*.
38. Rorty (1984:69).
39. Besides references to him by his disciples, Vijñānabhikṣu is also cited by Puruṣottama, a Vedāntin in the Vallabha commentarial tradition (Smith 2005:436). Vallabha himself wrote a doxographical work, the *Bālabodha*, that shares some features with Advaita doxographies (Smith 2005:422–24).
40. For example, "My contention is that without examining Orientalism as a discourse one cannot possibly understand the enormously systematic discipline by which European culture was able to manage—and even produce—the Orient politically, sociologically, militarily, ideologically, scientifically, and imaginatively during the post-Enlightenment period" (Said 1978:3).
41. One such statement from Said acknowledges a real place, yet argues for its irrelevance for the study of Orientalism: "There were—and are—cultures and nations whose location is in the East, and their lives, histories, and customs have a brute reality obviously greater than anything that could be said about them in the West. About that fact this study of Orientalism has very little to contribute, except to acknowledge it tacitly. But the phenomenon of Orientalism as I study it here deals principally, not with a correspondence between Orientalism and Orient, but with the internal consistency of Orientalism and its ideas about the Orient (the East as career) despite or beyond any correspondence, or lack thereof, with a 'real' Orient" (Said 1978:5).
42. Dirlik (1996:99).
43. This trend includes the recent closing of two of the oldest Sanskrit programs in the Western world, at Cambridge and Berlin. While South Asian Studies continues at both universities, there is a clear effort to recast their programs in terms of modern South Asian studies.
44. Cohen (2000:3).
45. On the dyad of religious/secular and its vexed place in Said's thought, see Anidjar (2006).
46. Burckhardt (1990[1860]:98).
47. On the allegedly "dividual" nature of Indian subjectivity, see Marriott (1976).
48. Davis (2008). On the reading of Indian history in terms of such a lack of the features of modern European consciousness, see Chakrabarty (2000:32).
49. See Paul Hacker's typology in Halbfass (1995:229–52).
50. On the Orientalists' periodization of Indian history, see Prakash (2000).
51. The most serious recent attempts to do constructive philosophy by looking for inspiration from outside the European philosophical canon come not from continental philosophy or postcolonial theory but from analytical philosophers such as Mark Siderits, Derek Parfit, and Jonardon Ganeri.
52. Chakrabarty (2000:5–6).
53. One such idea is "difference and non-difference" (*bhedābheda*), discussed at length in chapters 2 and 3.
54. For instance, Smith (2004:241).
55. This is the crux of Donald Davidson's argument against radically different conceptual schemes (Davidson 2001:195–98).

56. Richard King suggests that Buddhist philosophy, with its simultaneous insistence on the fragmentary and impermanent nature of the self and its universal message of escape from suffering, offers one possibility for a way out of this theoretical impasse (King 1999:198–99).

2. AN ALTERNATIVE HISTORY OF VEDĀNTA

1. For more, see Prakash (1990:388).
2. Paul Deussen was perhaps the most influential advocate of this model of Indian cultural degeneration (see chapter 7).
3. For one presentation and defense of this Naiyāyika "common-sense realism," see Matilal (1986).
4. Deussen (1912). On the variety of philosophical teachings on the self presented in the early Upaniṣads, see Black (2007:29–44).
5. For example, Dasgupta (1922, 3:105).
6. "Bādarāyaṇa's philosophy was some kind of *bhedābheda-vāda* or a theory of the transcendence and immanence of God (Brahman)" (Dasgupta 1922, 2:42). See also Nakamura (1989:500).
7. Nakamura (1989:432–36).
8. *BS* 1.3.34–39 argues that only twice-borns are allowed to study Vedānta.
9. Dasgupta (1922, 2:42); Nakamura (1989:489–90).
10. *aṃśo nānāvyapadeśād anyathā cāpi.* For more, see Nakamura's analysis of Śaṅkara (Nakamura 1989:450).
11. *aṃśa ivāṃśo nahi niravayavasya mukhyo 'ṃśaḥ saṃbhavati* (Śaṅkara 1996 [8th c. CE?], 1:829).
12. Nakamura (2004:137).
13. *bhedābhedātmakaṃ sarvaṃ vastu* (Nakamura 2004:137).
14. Nakamura (2004:139). Nakamura takes this list from Ānandagiri's summary of Bhartṛprapañca.
15. *te nāmarūpe avyākṛte satī vyākriyamāṇe tasmād etasmād ātmana ākāśanāmākṛtī saṃvṛtte. tac cākāśākhyaṃ bhūtaṃ anena prakāreṇa paramātmanaḥ saṃbhūtaṃ prasannād iva salilān malam iva phenam. na salilaṃ na ca salilād atyantaṃ bhinnaṃ phenaṃ salilavyatirekeṇādarśanāt salilaṃ tu svacchaṃ anyac ca phenān malarūpāt* (*Upadeśasāhasrī* 2.1.19 in Śaṅkara 1978[8th c. CE]:127); my translation is based on Hacker's (1949) German translation.
16. With regard to the depiction of the process of world-creation in Śaṅkara's *Upadeśasāhasrī,* Hacker writes: "Dieses Bild veranschaulicht das Übergangstadium, in dem sich Śaṅkara zwischen der realistischen Auffassung der B.S. (nach der Brahman 'materielle Ursache' der Welt ist) und dem ausgeprägten Illusionismus des späteren Advaita (welches das Brahman als das reale Substrat einer Scheinmanifestation, vivarta, lehrt) befindet" (Hacker 1949:19).
17. Rao (1996).
18. On Bhāskara's dates, see Nakamura (1989:65–72) and Ingalls (1967:61).
19. *sūtrābhiprāyasaṃvṛtyā svābhiprāyaprakāśanāt / vyākhyātaṃ yair idaṃ śāstraṃ vyākhyeyaṃ tannivṛttaye //* (Dvivedin 1903:1).
20. For instance, Rāmānuja criticizes Advaita by saying that if one person is liberated, all should be liberated, since Advaitins believe the self is one, not many. This argument also appears in Bhāskara's commentary on the *Brahmasūtras.*

21. Tapasyananda (1996):174–83). The Mādhava who wrote this hagiography is probably not the same person who wrote the *Sarvadarśanasaṃgraha.*
22. *sarvāpekṣā ca yajñādiśruter.* Śaṅkara interprets this in a way diametrically opposed to those outside the Advaita tradition, including Rāmānuja, Vijñānabhikṣu, and the like.
23. For example, *BhG* 2.47, 3.8.
24. For example, Śaṅkara's commentary on *BhG* 3.3–9 in Sadhale (1985:269–87).
25. I have in mind the sorts of differences in social convention between Smārta and Mādhva Brahmins as depicted in U. R. Anantha Murty's novel *Samskara* (Anantha Murty 1978).
26. Dasgupta (1922, 3:108).
27. This is an illustration of the phenomenon of "proximate difference," in which small differences between closely related groups are often exaggerated in order to make social distinctions (Cohen 1985).
28. Dasgupta (1922, 3:101); Carman (1974:28–30).
29. This is the project Gerhard Oberhammer undertakes in his excellent study of Yādavaprakāśa (Oberhammer 1997).
30. Oberhammer (1997:10).
31. Ibid., 14.
32. Smith (1998) and (2005).
33. Gupta (2007).
34. Nicholson (2002:578–83).
35. It might make sense to understand "Bhedābhedavāda" as a wider category than "Bhedābheda Vedānta," since a thinker such as Kumārila seems to fall under the former rubric, but clearly not the latter (since he had no particular interest in Brahman). However, since in normal usage these two terms are synonyms, I use them interchangeably to refer to a particular group of Vedāntins.
36. Dasgupta (1922, 3:194).
37. Most of these recent studies have been on late medieval theistic Bhedābheda Vedānta, such as Frederick Smith's work on Vallabha (Smith 1998, 2005) and Ravi Gupta's on Jīva Gosvāmī (Gupta 2007).

3. VIJÑĀNABHIKṢU'S "DIFFERENCE" AND "NON-DIFFERENCE" VEDĀNTA

1. Alternatively, the word *bhedābheda* can be analyzed as a *madhyamapadalopin,* a compound in which the middle term has been omitted: "non-difference [that does not exclude] difference." Philosophically, however, it makes little difference whether the compound is a *dvandva* or a *madhyamapadalopin.*
2. Even if we take *bhedābheda* as a *saptamī tatpuruṣa* compound rather than as a *dvandva* or *madhyamapadalopin,* the meaning of the compound would be "identity-in-difference" rather than "difference-in-identity." I take it that the Western tradition is called "difference-in-identity" because difference is ultimately subsumed by identity, as a multiplicity of phenomena are ultimately shown to be aspects of a larger whole. Therefore, "identity-in-difference" would mean something substantially different.
3. Vedānta Deśika (1974[14th c. CE]:11).
4. For a defense from critics who claim that Jainas violate the law of contradiction, see Matilal (1981:59–61).
5. Bhāvāgaṇeśa (1969[16th c. CE]).

6. A notable exception to this are so-called Neo-Vedāntins such as Vivekananda, who rank inference and "immediate experience" (*anubhava*) above scripture.
7. Nakamura argues that, contrary to common assumption, the "prior" Mīmāṃsā school is not meant as chronologically earlier than the Uttara Mīmāṃsā. Rather, the Pūrva Mīmāṃsā is logically prior to the Uttara Mīmāṃsā: all Vedāntins agree that mastery of ritual is a prerequisite for study of the sections of the Veda concerning Brahman (Nakamura 1989:412).
8. This refers to the Advaita doctrine of limitationism (*avacchedavāda*), typically ascribed to the Bhāmatī school of Advaita. On this model, Brahman is likened to space (*ākāśa*) generally and the individual self to a space located inside a pot. The pot is an artificial limiting condition (*upādhi*) that has no real effect on the space that is located inside of it, since in reality there is no difference with the space inside or outside of a pot.
9. *ādhunikās tu jīvabrahmaṇor akhaṇḍatayā jīve 'pi brahmaśabdo mukhya eva ākāśaśabda iva ghaṭākāśe. jīvasyābrahmatvaṃ tv ajñānakalpitam. tathā hi tat tvam asi ahaṃ brahmāsmi anena jīvenātmanā 'nupraviśya nāmarūpe vyākaravāṇi nānyad ato 'sti draṣṭā ity ādy abhedaśrutiśatebhyo jīvo 'pi brahmaiva cinmātratvāviśeṣāt. aiśvaryabandhayoś copādhidvayadharmatvāt. na ca dvā suparṇā sayujā sakhāyā samānaṃ vṛkṣaṃ pariṣasvajāte nityo nityānāṃ cetanaś cetanānām eko bahūnāṃ yo vidadhāti kāmān. tam ātmasthaṃ ye 'nupaśyanti dhīrās teṣāṃ śāntiḥ śāśvato netareṣām ātmani tiṣṭhan ātmano 'ntaraḥ sa me ātmeti vidyāt triṣu dhāmasu yad bhogyaṃ bhoktā bhogaś ca yad bhavet. tebhyo vilakṣaṇaḥ sākṣī cinmatro 'ham sadāśivaḥ. ityādibhedaśrutiśatānupapattir iti vācyam aupādhikabhedānuvādakatvena tādṛśavākyopapatteḥ* (Tripāṭhī 1979:20).
10. *tatrocyate abhedavākyānurodhena bhedavākyānām aupādhikabhedaparatvaṃ yathā kalpyate tathā bhedavākyānurodhenābhedavākyānām avibhāgādilakṣaṇābhedap aratvaṃ kathaṃ na kalpyate. avirodhasyobhayathaiva sambhavāt* (Tripāṭhī 1979:21).
11. Potter (1977:51–53).
12. *śrūyate cāvibhāgādirūpābhedo 'pi yathodakaṃ śuddhe śuddham ākṣiptaṃ tādṛg eva bhavati evaṃ muner vijānata ātmā bhavati gautama na tu tad dvitīyam asti tato 'nyad vibhaktam ityādiśrutiṣu. smṛtiṣu ca—avibhaktaṃ ca bhūteṣu vibhaktam iva ca sthitam / vyaktaṃ sa eva vā 'vyakta sa eva puruṣaḥ paraḥ // ityādiṣu. pratyutāvibhā gādilakṣaṇābhedasya pāramārthikatayā tatparatvam evocitam. aupādhikabhedasya tu mithyātvena tatparatvaṃ nocitam iti* (Tripāṭhī 1979:21).
13. *na cāvibhāgaparatve satyabhedaśabde lakṣaṇā 'sti bhidir vidāraṇe iti vibhāge 'pi bhididhātor anuśāsanāt* (Tripāṭhī 1979:21).
14. *nanu ya etasminn udaram antaraṃ kurute 'tha tasya bhayaṃ bhavatītyādiśrutau. tasyātmaparadeheṣu sato 'py ekamayaṃ hi yat / vijñānaṃ paramārtho 'sau dvaitino 'tathyadarśinaḥ // ityādismṛtau ca bhedanindāśravaṇān na bhedaparatvaṃ śrutīnāṃ sambhavatīti cen na abhedavākyānām avibhāgaparatayā bhedanindāvākyānām api vibhāgalakṣaṇamedaparatvāt pratipādyaviparītasyaiva nindārhatvāt. anyathā manasaivedam āptavyaṃ neha nānāsti kiṃcana mṛtyoḥ sa mṛtyum āpnoti ya iha nāneva paśyatītyādiśrutiṣu jaḍavargeṣv api bhedanindanādabhedaḥ syāt* (Tripāṭhī 1979:22).
15. Using the strategy of relativizing difference and non-difference to refer to different times is logically independent of Vijñānabhikṣu's primary strategy for reconciling the two. In some ways it appears to be an afterthought in his discussion of difference and non-difference in *VAB* 1.1.2 and is likely borrowed from earlier Bhedābheda thinkers.

16. "Part" and "whole" refer to the self and Brahman. *aṃśāṃśinoś ca bhedābhedau vibhāgāvibhāgarūpau kālabhedenāviruddhau. anyonyābhāvaś ca jīvabrahmaṇor ātyantika eva tathā śaktiśaktimadavibhāgo 'pi nitya eveti mantavyam* (Tripāṭhī 1979:26).
17. On identity and mutual absence in Navya-Nyāya, see Potter and Bhattacharyya (1993:18).
18. Tripāṭhī (1979:26).
19. See Vijñānabhikṣu's explanation in Garbe 1895:1.
20. *tasmād siddhau jīveśvarayor aṃśāṃśibhāvena bhedābhedau vibhāgāvibhāgarūpau. tatrāpy avibhāga eva ādyantayor anugatatvāt svābhāvikatvāt nityatvāc ca satyaḥ. vibhāgas tu madhye svalpāvacchedena naimittiko vikārāntaravad vācārambhaṇamātram iti viśeṣaḥ. tad evam ātmādvaitaṃ vyākhyātaṃ sāmānyato brahmādvaitavākyāni ca tṛtīyasūtre vyākhyāsyāmaḥ. tad evam anyonyābhāvalakṣaṇabhedena jīvād atyantabhinna eveśvaro brahmaśabdārtha iti siddham* (Tripāṭhī 1979:32).
21. *aṃśo nānāvyapadeśāt anayathā cāpi dāśakitavāditvam adhīyata eke.*
22. Nakamura (1989:500). However, Nakamura claims that, based on internal evidence from the *Brahmasūtras* themselves, Bādarāyaṇa was not the author of the *Brahmasūtras* (Nakamura 1989:405–7).
23. Śaṅkara (1996[8th c. CE]:728–29).
24. These views are traditionally ascribed to the two major divisions of post-Śaṅkara Advaitins, the Bhāmatī school holding limitationism and the Vivaraṇa school reflectionism. For further discussion, see Potter (1963:172–82).
25. *kiṃ cākhaṇḍaikātmye sati muktasya punarbandhāpattiḥ ekāntaḥkaraṇaviyoge 'pi muktāṃśa evāntaḥkaraṇāntarasambhavāt. yathaikaghaṭāvacchinnākāśasya tadghaṭabhaṅge 'pi ghaṭāntareṇa punaḥ sambandho bhavati tadvat* (Tripāṭhī 1979:23). Advaitins can counter by arguing that although both ignorance and the self are omnipresent, the union (*saṃyoga*) of the liberated self with ignorance is noneffective, whereas the union of the bound self with ignorance is an effective union (Shree Narayan Mishra, personal communication). Mishra offers the example of the relationship between a recently retired professor (the *jīva*) and his former vice chancellor (*ajñāna*). Although the retired professor may once again come into contact with the vice chancellor at occasional social functions, the vice chancellor will no longer have any power over him!
26. *api ca candrajalacandrākāśaghaṭākāśāgnivisphuliṅgacchāyātapastrīpuruṣādidṛṣṭā ntaiḥ pratibimbāvacchedāṃśādivādāḥ parasparavirodhena sarve na sambhavantīty eka eva vāda āśrayaṇīyaḥ. itarās tu vivakṣitatattadaṃśamātre dṛṣṭāntā ity abhyupeyam. tathā ca sati aṃśavāda evāśrayituṃ yuktaḥ* (Tripāṭhī 1979:26).
27. *aṃśatvaṃ ca sajātīyatve sati avibhāgapratiyogitvam tadanuyogitvaṃ cāṃśitvam. yena ca rūpeṇāṃśatā yatra vivakṣyate tenaiva rūpeṇa sājātyaṃ tatra grāhyaṃ yathā ātmāṃśalakṣaṇe ātmatvenaiva sājātyaṃ sadaṃśādilakṣaṇeṣu ca sattvādirūpeṇaivety ato nātiprasaṅgaḥ* (Tripāṭhī 1979:26).
28. I borrow the translations "adjunct" (*pratiyogin*) and "subjunct" (*anuyogin*) from Matilal (1968:32).
29. Explanation provided by Shree Narayan Mishra (personal communication). See also Potter (1993:18) and Matilal (1968:31–34).
30. In a following statement, however, Vijñānabhikṣu seems to suggest that, strictly speaking, only *ātmatva* should be considered the common property of Brahman

and the selves: "Or, more precisely, it should be understood as having the same class by means of a class that is directly pervaded by the property of being a substance (*dravyatvasākṣādvyāpyajāti*)" (Tripāṭhī 1979:16). This refers to the nine substances (*dravyas*) of the Nyāya-Vaiśeṣika school. Being pervaded directly by the property of being a substance, in this case, would mean that both the self and Brahman are pervaded by *ātmatva*, since *ātman* is one of the nine substances.

31. Tripāṭhī (1979:34). Vijñānabhikṣu frequently cites the *Sāṃkhyasūtras* and the *Yogasūtras* in his commentary on the *Brahmasūtras*, an indication that even in his earliest works he frequently saw the doctrines of these separate schools as complimentary. Nevertheless, he opines in the *Vijñānāmṛtabhāṣyam* that Vedānta is superior to Sāṃkhya, since Sāṃkhya concerns itself with the conventional (*vyāvahārika*) self while Vedānta concerns itself with the ultimate (*pāramārthika*) self.
32. Ram (1995:33).
33. Tripāṭhī (1979:27).
34. Accepting the manuscripts' reading of *vetanāḥ* ("possessions") instead of Tripathi's substitution *cetanāḥ* ("consciousnesses").
35. During the period of dissolution, the *jīva*'s consciousness is latent: that is, not in use. At the time of creation, its consciousness becomes effective (Shree Narayan Mishra, personal communication).
36. *nanu niravayavasya brahmaṇaḥ kathaṃ mukhyo 'ṃśaḥ syād iti cen na yathoktal akṣaṇāṃśatvasyāvayavatvābhāve 'pi darśanāt. yathā śarīrasya keśādir aṃśo rāśeś caikadeśo 'ṃśaḥ pituś ca putra iti. sarve ca jīvāḥ pitari putravetanā (putracetanā) iva cinmātre brahmaṇi nityasarvāvabhāsake viṣayabhāsanarūpaṃ svalakṣaṇaṃ vihāya pralaye lakṣaṇānanyatvaṃ gacchanti. sargakāle ca tadicchayā tata eva labdhacaitanyaphalopadhānā āvirbhavanti pitur iva putrāḥ. ato jīvā brahmāṃśā bhavanti. ātmā vai jāyate putraḥ iti śrutyā putre pitur avibhāgalakṣaṇābhedavaj jīve 'pi brahmaṇo 'vibhāgalakṣaṇābhedasya bahu syāṃ prajāyeyetyādiśrutyā siddher iti. ato jīvā brahmāṃśā mukhyā eva bhavanti* (Tripāṭhī 1979:27).
37. Most commentators use the threefold division, although Vijñānabhikṣu actually writes in his commentary on *BS* 1.1.2 that "origin, etc." refers to a sixfold set of world-stages: arising, existence, growth, development, decline, and passing away. *jāyate 'sti vardhate vipariṇamate 'pakṣīyate vinaśyatīty evaṃ rūpaṃ janmādiṣaṭkaṃ* (Tripāṭhī 1979:19).
38. Srinivasa Rao claims that Śaṅkara did not actually subscribe to *vivartavāda* (Rao 1996). He does not dispute that this position of the unreality of the phenomenal world was taken by virtually all subsequent Advaitins.
39. This is the standard position of the Bhāmatī and Vivaraṇa schools.
40. In the case of the Advaitins, one central aporia is the ontological status of ignorance itself: Is it real? Is it unreal? Where did it originate? What is its locus? The Advaitins attempt to resolve this problem by positing a third category of entities that are *anirvacanīya*, neither totally real nor totally unreal. For more, see Ingalls (1953) and Potter (1963:163–67).
41. Translated by Olivelle (1998:247).
42. The depiction of difference and non-difference as difference of effect and non-difference of cause is especially characteristic of Bhāskara's thought (Dasgupta 1922, 4:329).
43. Although the two different groups share the epithet *satkāryavādin*, their views lead them to construe the Sanskrit compound *satkārya* in two different ways. While

Sāṃkhyas and realist Vedāntins understand it to be a *karmadhāraya* compound expressing "an effect that is real," Advaitins take it to be a *ṣaṣṭhī tatpuruṣa* compound, "the effect of that which is real." "That which is real," of course, refers to Brahman.

44. Unless otherwise stated, I use the word *prakṛti* to refer to the original *prakṛti* (that is, *mūlaprakṛti, pradhāna*), although technically it can refer to any of the eight *tattvas* which themselves cause another *tattva*. In this sense, *mūlaprakṛti, buddhi, ahaṃkāra,* and the five *tanmātras* are the *prakṛtis.* The remaining sixteen evolutes of *mūlaprakṛti* are termed *vikāras.*
45. Tripāṭhī (1979:17).
46. *kāryāvibhāgādhāratvasyaivopādānasāmānyalakṣaṇatvāt* (Tripāṭhī 1979:17).
47. *tad evādhiṣṭhānakāraṇaṃ yatrāvibhaktaṃ yenopaṣṭabdhaṃ ca sadupādānakāraṇaṃ* (Tripāṭhī 1979:17).
48. *yathā sargādau jalāvibhaktāḥ pārthivasūkṣmāṃśās tanmātrākhyāḥ jalenaivopaṣṭambhāt pṛthivyākāreṇa pariṇamanta ity ato jalaṃ mahāpṛthivyā adhiṣṭhānakāraṇam iti* (Tripāṭhī 1979:17).
49. Rao (1996:272–77).
50. Tripāṭhī (1979:18).
51. In this regard, Bhāskara was closer to Śaṅkara, who also maintained that Brahman could be material cause of the world without undergoing any essential change. It is possible that early Vedāntins only understood "unchanging" to mean "unchanging in essence." For more, see Rao (1996:275).
52. In later Advaita, the terms *māyā* and *avidyā* are closely connected, though not interchangeable. Typically, *avidyā* is the cause of concealment, while *māyā* is the cause of projection.
53. Karl Potter, for instance, opines that Śaṅkara made a "deliberate decision to avoid" the causal conundrums with which his successors occupied themselves (Potter 1963:165). Srinivasa Rao takes a more positive attitude toward what he sees as Śaṅkara's clear and logical account of Brahman's causality, and he faults later Advaitins for diverging from Śaṅkara's views (Rao 1996). But both Potter and Rao agree that later Advaitins had quite a different take on such questions than Śaṅkara did.
54. This is summarized from Shastri (1989:72–79).
55. See Arthur Venis's discussion of Prakāśānanda's dates in his introduction to *Vedāntasiddhāntamuktāvalī* (Venis 1975:vii–xii).
56. *tad etad brahmāpūrvam anaparam anantaram abāhyam* (*Bṛh. Up.* 2.5.19). I translate *apūrvam* and *anaparam* as having "no cause, no effect," since Prakāśānanda understands these words causally, and not merely temporally.
57. *yad uktaṃ jagatkāraṇatvaviṣayaśrutyor ajñānabrahmagocarayor mitho virodha iti tan na. brahmājñānāj jagajjanma brahmaṇo 'kāraṇatvataḥ / adhiṣṭhānatvamātreṇa kāraṇaṃ brahma gīyate // 38 // dṛśyatvādyanumānasiddhānirvacanīyasya jagato 'nādyanirvacanīyā avidyaiva kāraṇaṃ na brahma tasya kūṭasthasya kāryakāraṇavilakṣaṇatvāt tad etad brahmāpūrvam anaparam anantaram abāhyam ayam ātmā brahma sarvānubhūr iti śruteḥ. kathaṃ tarhi brahmaṇo jagatkāraṇatvaṃ śrutau prasiddhaṃ jagattatkāraṇādhiṣṭhānatvena kāraṇatvopacārāt* (Venis 1975: 116–17). Although this passage is the likely source of Appaya Dīkṣita's summary of Prakāśānanda's view on causality, it is not Prakāśānanda's last word on the subject but only a provisional view. He later writes that speaking precisely, ignorance is also not the cause of the world. The very notion of cause and effect is erroneous and outside the scope of the Upaniṣads. Therefore, an Advaitin only says that ignorance

is the cause of the world to put an end to the awkward silence that results when asked, "What is the cause of the world?" (*kiṃ jagataḥ kāraṇam iti pṛṣṭe prāptāprat ibhānivṛttimātraprayojanatayā ajñānaṃ kāraṇam iti abhihitatvāc ca*) (Venis 1975: 117–18).

58. In his colophon, Prakāśānanda himself acknowledges his doctrinal differences with other Advaitins of the same time period and implies that he is somehow recovering the true teachings of an earlier era of Advaita: "This entire essence of Vedānta taught by me is unknown to modern thinkers" (*vedāntasārasarvasvam ajñeyam adhunātanaiḥ / aśeṣeṇa mayoktaṃ*) (Venis 1975:186).
59. Dasgupta (1922, 2:221); Timalsina (2006:115–27).
60. Dasgupta (1922, 2:224).
61. The later Advaitins list six entities as being *anādi*: the self (*jīva*), the Lord (*īśa*), pure consciousness (*viśuddhacitta*), the difference between the self and the Lord (*jīveśvarabheda*), ignorance (*avidyā*), and the relation between ignorance and consciousness (*avidyācittasaṃyoga*).
62. I would add that if it is legitimate to say that something is "changeless" simply because it does not change its essential nature, then for satkāryavādins everything is changeless. Sāṃkhya-Yoga can easily say that *prakṛti*, too, is as changeless as the Brahman of the Vedāntins.
63. For more, see Nakamura (1989).
64. See Śaṅkara's interpretation of *Śvet. Up.* 4.5 in his commentary on *BS* 1.4.9 (Śaṅkara 1996[8th c. CE?]:477–78).
65. *kālārkabhakṣitaṃ sāṃkhyaśāstraṃ* (Garbe 1895:1).

4. A HISTORY OF GOD IN SĀṂKHYA AND YOGA

1. Garbe (1895:xii).
2. Ibid., xiii–xiv.
3. Larson, for example, is typical in understanding the "classical Sāṃkhya" as beginning with the *Sāṃkhyakārikā*; the middle Upaniṣads, *Buddhacarita*, and *Bhagavad Gītā* for him represent "proto-Sāṃkhya" (Larson 1998:75).
4. *ajām ekāṃ lohitaśuklakṛṣṇāṃ bahvīḥ prajāḥ sṛjamānāṃ sarūpāḥ / ajo hy eko juṣamāṇo 'nuśete jahāty enāṃ bhuktabhogām ajo 'nyaḥ // Śvet. Up.* 4.5 (Olivelle (1998: 424), my translation.
5. *BSB* 1.4.9 in Śaṅkara (1996[8th c. CE], 1:55).
6. *Śvet. Up.* 5.2 (Olivelle 1998:426).
7. *BSB* 2.1.1 in Śaṅkara (1996[8th c. CE], 1:533–39).
8. *BSB* 2.1.1 in Bhāskara (1903[8th c. CE]:87–88).
9. For example, *BS* 2.1.4–6 (Śaṅkara 1996[8th c. CE], 1:545–52).
10. For example, *Śvet. Up.* 4.1–7 (Olivelle 1998:422–24).
11. For example, Johnston (1974:85).
12. For example, Sen Gupta (1981:75).
13. *pradhānaṃ purūṣaṃ caiva praviśyātmecchayā hariḥ / kṣobhayām āsa samprāpte sargakāle vyayāvyayau //* (*Viṣ. Pu.* 1.2.29), quoted in Tripāṭhī (1979:18).
14. On the character of proofs for God's existence situated within theistic traditions, see Clayton (2006).

15. Chattopadhyaya (1969).
16. Franklin Edgerton examines at length passages in the *Mokṣadharma Parvan* that Hopkins and Oldenburg have claimed express an atheistic position. Edgerton concludes his examination of these passages by asserting, "Where, then, do we find that 'original' atheistic view expressed? I believe: nowhere. A study of the epic and other early materials (mostly collected by Hopkins) has convinced me that there is not a single passage in which disbelief in Brahman or God is attributed to Sāṃkhya" (Edgerton 1924:8). In particular, the meaning of the word *anīśvara* at *Mbh.* 12.289.3a has been the site of controversy (see Edgerton 1924:8–14). Most recently, James Fitzgerald has argued that the correct translation is "How can one who is not a powerful Lord become Absolutely Free?" (Fitzgerald forthcoming).
17. On the precise meaning of *anvīkṣikī*, see Halbfass (1988:275–86). Jacobi and other Indologists understood it as the Sanskrit word closest to the Western concept of "philosophy."
18. On the precise meaning of *BhG* 5.4 and its relation to other usages of *sāṃkhya* and *yoga* in the *Bhagavad Gītā*, see Malinar (1996:194). She considers it a later interpolation (ibid., 405).
19. This point is argued at length in Edgerton (1924).
20. *loke 'smin dvividhā niṣṭhā purā proktā mayānagha / jñānayogena sāṃkhyānāṃ karmayogena yoginām // BhG* 3.3 in Sargeant and Chapple (2009:160), my translation. See also Malinar (1996:155).
21. Edgerton (1924:6): "The term *Sāṃkhya* did not, in and of itself, imply any 'teaching' at all in the sense of any speculative formulation of metaphysical truth, but merely the opinion that man could gain salvation by knowing the supreme truth, however formulated."
22. For the diversity of meanings of *sāṃkhya* and *yoga* in the *Bhagavad Gītā* itself, see Malinar (1996:155, 194, 405).
23. Quoted in K. Chattopadhyaya (1927:854).
24. Ibid. The same passage is cited in Bronkhorst (1981:310). Bronkhorst also argues that Kumārila used the word *yoga* to refer to Nyāya-Vaiśeṣika (ibid., 312).
25. Bimal Matilal writes in a footnote when discussing this passage from Vātsyāyana that "according to some, yoga refers to the dual school of Nyāya and Vaiśeṣika. . . . The term Yoga does not mean here the Yoga school of Patañjali. It might have meant logic—the science of reasoning (yukti)" (Matilal 1977:77).
26. Besides Śaṅkara, only a handful of premodern commentators, including Mādhavasarasvatī and Vijñānabhikṣu, use "yoga" as a designation for Patañjali's philosophy. See Bronkhorst (1981:311, 315).
27. Bronkhorst (1981:311).
28. Olivelle, following Böhtlingk, translates the phrase as "the application of Sāṃkhya" (Olivelle 1998:628).
29. Larson and Bhattacharya (1987:317–18).
30. Exceptions to this tendency to refuse to take the Purāṇas seriously as philosophical texts include Sheridan (1986) and Dasgupta (1922, 3:496–511, 4:1–50).
31. *Bh. Pu.* 3.25.1–3.33.37 in Goswami (1971:247–83).
32. Dasgupta (1922, 3:496).
33. Bronkhorst (1983:149–64).
34. Wezler and Motegi (1998:160).

35. *iṃ cānyat śruteḥ śrutir api cāsya mūrtim ācaṣṭe kṛttivāsāḥ pinākahasto vitatadhanvā nīlaśikhaṇḍī ityādi. tadabhyupagamāt svapakṣahānir iti cet. syān matam. yadi tarhi śrutivacanān mūrtimān īśvaraḥ parigṛhyate tena siddham asyāstitvam. kasmāt. na hy asato mūrtimattvam upapadyata iti kṛtvā. etad apy ayuktam [kasmāt]. abhiprāyānavabodhāt. na hy ekāntena vayaṃ bhagavataḥ śaktiviśeṣaṃ pratyācakṣmahe māhātmyaśarīrādiparigrahāt. yathā [tu] bhavatocyate. pradhānapuruṣavyatiriktas tayoḥ prayoktā nāstīty ayam asmadabhiprāyaḥ. tasmād etasya bādhakam. ato na pradhānapuruṣayor abhisambandho 'nyakṛtaḥ.* Wezler and Motegi (1998:159), my translation.
36. *kleśakarmavipākāśayair aparāmṛṣṭaḥ puruṣaviśeṣa īśvaraḥ* (Maas 2006:35), my translation.
37. Bronkhorst understands the expression *īśvaramaharṣi* (Wezler and Motegi 1998:100, lines 4–6) as expressing "a great seer, who is an incorporation of God." This interpretation would be in line with the idea, frequently stated in Sāṃkhya, that Kapila is himself an incarnation of God (Bronkhorst 1983:152–53)
38. Gauḍapāda (1964:153).
39. Jha (1965:93).
40. For example, Miller (1998:36): "For Patañjali, the Lord is not a creator God who grants grace; rather, he is a representation of the omniscient spirit (puruṣa) as the archetypical yogi."
41. Commentary on *SK* 23 in M. Jha (1965:93).
42. Bronkhorst (1981:316). I am deeply indebted to Bronkhorst's work for most of my arguments in this chapter regarding the relationship between Sāṃkhya and Yoga.
43. Translated in Bronkhorst (1981:309). The colophon of the first section of the *Yogasūtras* reads: *iti pātañjale yogaśāstre sāṃkhyapravacane samādhipādaḥ prathamaḥ* (Maas 2006:87).
44. In the introduction of the new critical edition of the first *pāda* of the *Yogasūtras,* Philipp Maas claims that the commentary ascribed to Vyāsa was in its original form an autocommentary by the author of the *Yogasūtras* himself (Maas 2006:xii–xix). If true, this is even stronger evidence that the text was considered a Sāṃkhya work from its inception.
45. *atha yogānuśāsanaṃ* (Maas 2006:1).
46. *athāto dharmajijñāsā* (Abhyaṅkara and Jośī (1970:25).
47. *athāto brahmajijñāsā* (Śaṅkara 1996[8th c. CE]:55).
48. Quoted in Bronkhorst (1981:309).
49. *sāṃkhyā nirīśvarāḥ kecit kecid īśvaradevatāḥ / sarveṣām api teṣāṃ syāt tattvānāṃ pañcaviṃśatiḥ //* (Murty 1957:46).
50. Quoted in Bronkhorst (1981:316–17).
51. Ibid., 315.

5. READING AGAINST THE GRAIN OF THE *SĀṂKHYASŪTRAS*

1. Garbe (1895:xi).
2. *tat tvam eva tvam evaitad evaṃ śrutiśatoditam / sarvātmanāṃ avaidharmyaṃ śāstrasyāsyaiva gocaraḥ //* (Garbe 1895:1).

3. This is not the only difference Vijñānabhikṣu identifies. For instance, in the *Yogavārttika,* he writes that the precise philosophical meaning of the word *avidyā* differs between the two schools (Rukmani 1981:26).
4. *kālārkabhakṣitaṃ sāṃkhyaśāstraṃ jñānasudhākaram / kalāvaśiṣṭam bhūyo 'pi pūrayiśye vacomṛtaiḥ //* (Garbe 1895:1). This is obviously an allusion to the myth of Rāhu, the demon responsible for eclipses. *Kālārka* might also be translated as "black sun."
5. *nārāyaṇaḥ kapilamūrtir* (Garbe 1895:1).
6. G. Jha (1995:125).
7. *nanu nyāyavaiśeṣikābhyām apy eteṣv artheṣu nyāyaḥ pradarśita iti tābhyām asya gatārthatvam saguṇanirguṇatvādiviruddharūpair ātmasādhakatayā tadyuktibhir atratyayuktīnāṃ virodheno 'bhayor eva durghaṭaṃ prāmāṇyam iti. maivam. vyāvahārikapāramārthikarūpaviṣayabhedena gatārthatvavirodhayor abhāvāt. nyāyavaiśeṣikābhyāṃ hi sukhiduḥkhyādyanuvādato dehādimātravivekenātmā prathamabhūmikāyām anumāpitaḥ ekadā parasūkṣme praveśāsambhavāt. tadīyaṃ ca jñānaṃ dehādyātmatānirasanena vyāvahārikaṃ tattvajñānaṃ bhavaty eva . . . vivakṣitārthe . . . bādhābhāvāt, yatparaḥ śabdaḥ sa śabdhārtha iti nyāyāt* (Garbe 1895:1–2).
8. *atrāpi vyavahāraparamārthabhāvenaiva vyavasthā sambhavati. asatyam apratiṣṭhaṃ te jagad āhur anīśvaram ityādiśāstrair nirīśvaravādasya ninditatvād asminn eva śāstre vyāvahārikasyaiveśvarapratiṣedhasyaiśvaryavairāgyādyarthaṃ na pratiṣidhyeta tadā paripūrṇanityanirdoṣaiṣvaryadarṣanena tatra cittāveṣato vivekābhyāsapratibandhaḥ syād iti sāṃkhyācāryāṇām āśayaḥ* (Garbe 1895:2).
9. For example, Gadamer's critique of psychological hermeneutics (Gadamer 1989:186–97) and Wimsatt's critique of the "intentional fallacy" (Wimsatt 1954:3–20).
10. On this criticism of the Mīmāṃsā interpretive theory, and Kumārila Bhaṭṭa's reply, see Chari (1990:168).
11. The importance of indifference to godlike powers is emphasized at *YS* 3.50. In the *Tattvakaumudī,* Vācaspati enumerates the *aiśvaryas* as eight: *aṇiman* (ability to become extremely small), *laghiman* (ability to become extremely light), *gariman* (ability to become extremely heavy), *mahiman* (ability to become extremely large), *prāpti* (ability to acquire any object), *prākāmya* (the fulfillment of all desires), *īśitva* (lordship over all material things), and *kāmāvasāyitā* (infallibility of purpose) (commentary on *SK* 23 in M. G. Jha 1965:15). Lists of *aiśvaryas* vary slightly in different texts.
12. *nāsti sāṃkhyasamaṃ jñānaṃ nāsti yogasamaṃ balam / atra te saṃśayo mā bhūj jñānaṃ sāṃkhyaṃ paraṃ matam // ityādi vākyaṃ tad vivekāṃśa eva sāṃkhyajñānasya darśanāntarebhya utkarṣaṃ pratipādayati na tv īśvarapratiṣedhāṃśe 'pi* (Garbe 1895:3).
13. Austin (1975:94–120).
14. *tasmād abhyupagamavādapraudhivādādinaiva sāṃkhyasya vyāvahārikeśvaraprati ṣedhaparatayā brahmamīmāṃsāyogābhyāṃ saha na virodhaḥ. abhyupagamavādaś ca śāstre dṛṣṭo yathā viṣṇupurāṇe ete bhinnadṛśaṃ daityā vikalpāḥ kathitā mayā / kṛtvābhyupagamaṃ tathā. saṃkṣepaḥ śrūyatāṃ mameti. astu vā pāpināṃ jñānapratibandhārtham āstikadarśaneṣv apy aṃśataḥ śrutiviruddhārthavyavasth āpanam. teṣu teṣv aṃśeṣv aprāmāṇyaṃ ca śrutismṛtyaviruddheṣu tu mukhyaviṣayeṣu prāmāṇyam asty eva. ata eva padmapurāṇe brahmayogadarśanātiriktānāṃ darśanānāṃ nindā 'py upapadyate* (Garbe 1895:4).

15. The word *prauḍhivāda* appears twice in the *Sāṃkhyapravacanabhāṣya;* the variant spelling *prauḍhavāda* appears once.
16. Raghavan and Thakur (1969). Jayanta's understanding of *abhyupagamasiddhānta,* in its basic outlines, was also accepted by Pakṣilasvāmin. The other major interpreter of *abhyupagamasiddhānta,* Uddyotakara, understood this type of tenet not as something only temporarily accepted for the sake of argument but, rather, as something that is already implicitly accepted by one's own school, although not explicitly stated in the school's sūtras. I recount Jayanta's position because it is more relevant to Vijñānabhikṣu's understanding of "temporary concession" (*abhyupagamavāda*). For a much more detailed analysis of *abhyupagamsiddhānta,* see Marui (forthcoming).
17. I borrow the details of this scenario from Marui (forthcoming). Jaina logicians sometimes used less plausible, more playful examples for their temporary tenets, such as "the fire is cold," "there is a herd of elephants sitting on a blade of grass," and "the donkey has a horn." These examples come from Parśvadeva's *Nyāyapraveśavṛttipañjikā* (in Dignāga 1930[5th c. CE]:44, line 26). See also Ingalls (1955:164).
18. *tasmāt tadviśeṣaparīkṣaṇārthaḥ aparīkṣitābhyupagamaḥ prauḍhavādinā kriyamāṇaḥ abhyupagamasiddhānta iti sūtrārthaḥ. ittham eva ca tatra tatra pravādukānoāṃ vyavahāraḥ* (Raghavan and Thakur 1969, 2:550).
19. Unlike Western logic, Indian logic is not a formal logic. Therefore it does not distinguish validity from truth in the way that most Western logicians do. For more, see Matilal (1998:16–17).
20. Garbe (1895:119).
21. Quoted in Schroeder (2001:15–16).
22. Ibid., 9–19.
23. Lamotte (1988[1949]:16–23).
24. Lamotte (1988[1949]:21); King (1995:120–26).
25. Garbe (1895:2).
26. Bronkhorst (1983:157).
27. Although Vijñānabhikṣu did have knowledge of the *Sāṃkhyakārikā,* he quotes from it far less than from the Purāṇas and the Upaniṣads.
28. *astu vā pāpināṃ jñānapratibandhārtham āstikadarśaneṣv apy aṃśataḥ śrutivirud dhārthavyavasthāpanam* (Garbe 1895:4). See Garbe's reaction to this passage in his introduction to this work (ibid., xii).
29. For a thoughtful discussion of Viṣṇu's Buddha avatar, see O'Flaherty (1976:187–211).
30. For variations on and precedents of this myth, see Eltschinger (forthcoming).
31. *yeṣāṃ śravaṇamātreṇa pātityaṃ jñāninām api* (Garbe 1895:4).
32. Obviously, Buddhists are here conflated with Jainas.
33. Summary of Garbe (1895:4).
34. *śrutismṛtyaviruddheṣu tu mukhyaviṣayeṣu prāmāṇyam asty eva. ata eva padmapurāṇe brahmayogadarśanātiriktānāṃ darśanānāṃ nindā 'py upapadyate* (ibid.).
35. Ibid.
36. *adhikaṃ tu brahmamīmāṃsābhāṣye prapañcitam asmābhir iti* (ibid.).
37. *idaṃ brahmātmajñānaṃ viviktajīvajñānāt sāṃkhyoktād api śreṣṭhaṃ nāto 'dhikaṃ jñānam asti* (Tripāṭhī 1979:28).
38. *viśeṣas tv atrocyate prakṛtisvātantryavādibhyāṃ sāṃkhyayogibhyāṃ puruṣārthaprayuktā pravṛttiḥ svayam eva puruṣeṇa ādyajīvena saṃyujyata ity abhyupagamyate*

ayaskāntena lohavat. asmābhis tu prakṛtipuruṣasaṃyoga īśvareṇa kriyata ity abhyupagamyate (ibid., 18).

39. *āstikaśāstrasya na kasyāpy aprāmāṇyaṃ virodho vā svasvaviṣayeṣu sarveṣām abādhād avirodhāc ceti* (Garbe 1895:4).
40. *yogadarśane tv ābhyām abhyupagamavādapratiṣiddhasyeśvarasya nirūpaṇena nyūnatāpariharo 'pīti* (ibid., 5).
41. The Mīmāṃsā and the early Vaiśeṣika system also seem to have excluded God. All of the remaining *āstika* systems, however, are theistic.
42. It is for this reason that the Mīmāṃsā, an atheistic system, posits the existence of *apūrva*. It functions as an invisible causal link connecting the original act and its eventual effect. It is necessary because the entire Indian philosophical tradition agrees that an effect must immediately follow its cause in time. If God existed, however, he could take note of a person's actions and create positive or negative results whenever he deems it suitable, just as a parent might sometimes defer punishment of his or her child.
43. *īśvarāsiddher iti yad uktaṃ tan nopapadyate karmaphaladātṛtayā tatsiddher iti ye pūrvapakṣiṇas tān nirākaroti neśvarādhiṣṭhite phalaniṣpattiḥ karmaṇā tatsiddheḥ (SS 5.2). īśvarādhiṣṭhite kāraṇe karmaphalarūpapariṇāmasya niṣpattir na yuktā āvaśyakena karmaṇaiva phalaniṣpattisambhavād ity arthaḥ* (Garbe 1895:117).
44. For instance, in his commentary on *SS* 5.2, Vijñānabhikṣu indicates that the thing that the sūtra calls "superintended by God" (*īśvarādhiṣṭhite*) is the cause (*kāraṇe*).
45. The translator Nandalal Sinha claims that the *Sāṃkhyasūtras* do not argue that God does not exist but only that God's existence cannot be proven. In his terminology, Sāṃkhya is *nirīśvara,* but not *nāstika:* "It is nirīśvara, lit. god-less, as it explains all and every fact of experience without reference to, and without invoking the intervention of, a divine agency. Those who imagine that, in the Sāṃkhya, there is a denial of God, obviously fail to recognize the distinction between the two words, nāstika and nirīśvara" (Sinha 1979:xiv). Sinha's reading introduces confusing and historically arbitrary new meanings of these two terms (*nāstika* simply means "atheist" for him, while *nirīśvara* means "one who believes in God but denies the possibility of proving his existence"). It also ignores the disproofs of God presented in *SS* 5.2–9.
46. *īśvarasyāpy upakārasvīkāre laukikeśvaravad eva so 'pi saṃsārī syāt apūrṇakāmatayā duḥkhādiprasaṅgād* (Garbe 1895:117).
47. *pradhānaśaktiyogāc cet saṅgāpattiḥ* (ibid., 118).
48. *kiṃ ca prakṛtiṃ praty aiśvaryaṃ prakṛtipariṇāmabhūtecchādinā na sambhavati anyonyāśrayāt icchotpattyanantaraṃ prakṛtipravartanaṃ prakṛtipravṛttyanantaraṃ cecchādir iti. nityecchādikaṃ ca prakṛtau na yuktaṃ śrutismṛtisiddhasāmyāvasthān upapatteḥ* (ibid.).
49. For example, Miller's interpretation of *YS* 1.24 in Miller (1998), or Eliade's conception of the "metaphysical sympathy" between Īśvara and the yogin (1970[1958]:73–76).
50. *ayaṃ ceśvarapratiṣedha aiśvarye vairāgyārtham īśvarajñānaṃ vināpi mokṣapratipādanārthaṃ ca prauḍhivādamātram iti prāg eva vyākhyātam. anyathā jīvavyāvṛttasyeśvaranityatvāder gauṇatvakalpanāgauravam. aupādhikānāṃ nityajñānecchādīnāṃ mahadādipariṇāmānāṃ cāṅgīkāreṇa kauṭasthyādyupapatter ityādikaṃ brahmamīmāṃsāyāṃ draṣṭavyam iti* (Garbe 1895:119).
51. Garbe (1889:271) and Sinha (1979:397) offer two different interpretations. Garbe's interpretation, suggested to him by the Varanasi pandit Rāmmiśra, seems the more plausible.

6. YOGA, PRAXIS, AND LIBERATION

1. Rukmani (1981:8, 13–14).
2. *pātañjalasāṃkhyapravacanayogaśāstra* (Bronkhorst 1981:309).
3. *śrīpātañjalabhāṣyadugdhajaladhir vijñanaratnākaro vedavyāsamunīndrabuddhikhanito yogīndrapeyāmṛtaḥ / bhūdevair amṛtaṃ tad atra mathituṃ vijñānavijñair iha śrīmadvārttikamandaro gurutaro manthānadaṇḍo 'rpyate // sarvavedārthasāro 'tra vedavyāsena bhāṣitaḥ / yogabhāṣyamiṣeṇāto mumukṣūṇām idaṃ gatiḥ // gaṅgādyāḥ sarito yadvad abdher aṃśeṣu saṃsthitāḥ / sāṃkhyādidarśanāny evam asyaivāṃśeṣu kṛtsnaśaḥ //* (Rukmani 1981:20).
4. *Mbh* 1.16.1–40, 1.17.1–30; *Viṣ. Pu.* 1.9 (among many other Purāṇic sources).
5. *śrutismṛtinyāyavacaḥkṣīrābdhimathanoddhṛtam / jñānāmṛtaṃ guroḥ prītyai bhūdevebhyo nu dīyate // pariviṣayya sadbuddhyā mohinyevātha dānavān / kutarkān vañcayitvedaṃ pīyatām amṛtepsubhiḥ // pītvaitad balavantas te pākhaṇḍāsurayūthapān / vijitya jñānakarmabhyāṃ yāntu śrīmadguroḥ padam //* (Tripāṭhī 1979:1). The reference to "knowledge and ritual action" is a rejection of the Advaita view that knowledge alone, separate from action, leads to liberation.
6. *brahmavid āpnoti paraṃ brahma veda brahmaiva bhavati tam eva viditvāti mṛtyum eti ityādiśrutisiddhaparamapuruṣārthasādhanatāke brahmajñāne vidhiḥ śrūyate ātmety evopāsīta sa ma ātmeti vidyāt tam eva dhīro vijñāya prajñāṃ kurvīta brāhmaṇaḥ ityādirūpaḥ. tatra kiṃ brahma kiṃ vā tasya brahmatānirvāhakaṃ guṇajātam kīdṛśaṃ vā tasya jñānam kīdṛśaṃ vā tasya phalam ityādikaṃ viśiṣya mumukṣūṇāṃ jijñāsitaṃ bhavati śrutiṣv āpātato 'nyonyaviruddhārthatāyāḥ śākhābhedena pratibhāsanād iti. atas tannirṇayāya brahmamīmāṃsāśāstram apekṣitam* (Tripāṭhī 1979).
7. Rukmani (1981:6).
8. *tatra yogaḥ kiṃsvarūpaḥ kimupāyaḥ kena vā dvāreṇa jñānamokṣayoḥ kāraṇam ityādikaṃ mumukṣūṇāṃ vividiṣitaṃ bhavati brahmamīmāṃsāsāṃkhyādiṣu ca jñānam eva vicāritaṃ bāhulyena jñānasādhanamātras tu yogaḥ saṃkṣepataḥ jñānajanyayogas tu saṃkṣepato 'pi teṣu nokto 'tivistareṇa dvividhaṃ yogaṃ pratipipādayiṣur bhagavān patañjaliḥ ṣiṣyāvadhānāyādau yogānuśāsanaṃ śāstram ārabhyatayā pratijñātavān atha yogānuśāsanam* (Rukmani 1981:22).
9. On *samprajñātasamādhi*, see *YS* 1.17; on *asamprajñātasamādhi*, see *YS* 1.18. For a close reading of Vijñānabhikṣu's analysis of the two terms, see Fort (2006:273–87).
10. For an in-depth discussion of *jīvanmukti* in Indian philosophical traditions, see Fort (1998).
11. *tathā ca karmakṣayadvārā jñānasyevāsamprajñātayogasyāpi mokṣahetutvaṃ siddhaṃ. tatra cāsamprajñātayogenākhilasaṃskāradāhakena prārabdhakarmāpy atikramyata iti jñānādviśeṣaḥ. jñānasya hi prārabdhanāśakatve bādhikāsti tasya tāvad eva ciram ityādiśrutir jīvanmuktiśrutismṛtayaś ca. yogasya prārabdhanāśakatve bādhakaṃ nāsti pratyuta dagdhakarmacayo 'cirād ity eva smaryate ataḥ prārabdham api karma karmavipākoktaprāyaścittādivad evātikramya jhaṭiti mocanam eva yogasya phalam. anyac ca yogadvayenākhilasaṃskārakṣaye bhogasaṃskārākhyasahak āryabhāvāt prārabdhaṃ karmāpi yat phalākṣamaṃ bhavati idam api yogaphalam. tad uktaṃ mokṣadharme nāsti sāṃkhyasamaṃ jñānaṃ nāsti yogasamaṃ balam iti. balaṃ prārabdhasyāpy atikrameṇa svecchayā śīghramokṣahetuḥ* (Rukmani 1981:29).
12. *nāsti sāṃkhyasamaṃ jñānaṃ nāsti yogasamaṃ balam* (*Mbh* 12.304.2, cited in Garbe 1895:3).

13. It might be suggested that Vedānta has its own problems with this dualism of insentient (*jaḍa*) matter and conscious (*cetana*) selves. Specifically, how is it that something insentient, like *prakṛti*, could have arisen from Brahman, which is pure consciousness? This is an old problem, one that is posed by the Sāṃkhya interlocutor in *BS* 2.1.4.
14. Most of the Indian philosophical systems were also forms of "spiritual exercise" in the sense that Pierre Hadot (1995) has described the philosophies of ancient Greece and Rome.
15. Feuerstein (1989:197), for instance, at times sides with Vijñānabhikṣu and against Vācaspati Miśra because he believes the former was a more advanced practitioner of yoga than the latter. I see no clear indication that one was more spiritually advanced than the other simply based on their writings. Furthermore, philosophical arguments from private experience are virtually impossible to verify. Medieval commentators appear to have recognized this and thus argue primarily from scriptural authority and rational inference.
16. *pradhānaṃ puruṣaṃ caiva praviśyātmecchayā hariḥ / kṣobhayām āsa samprāpte sargakāle vyayāvyayau //* (*Kūrma Pu.* 1.4.13).
17. On the chronology of Vijñānabhikṣu's works, see Rukmani (1981:6–7).
18. *vārttikācaladaṇḍena mathitvā yogasāgaram / uddhatyāmṛtasāro 'yaṃ granthakumbhe nidhīyate //* (Jha 1995:1). Vijñānabhikṣu alludes to the story of the churning of the ocean of the milk by the gods in the introduction of numerous works.
19. Vijñānabhikṣu also reiterates in the fourth section of the *Yogasārasaṃgraha* that Nyāya and Vaiśeṣika are part of this larger concordance. For more detail, he refers readers back to a treatise he has written on Nyāya (Jha 1995:125). Unfortunately, that work has never been found.
20. *puruṣārthaśūnyānāṃ guṇānāṃ pratiprasavaḥ kaivalyaṃ svarūpapratiṣṭhā vā citiśaktir iti.*
21. *kṛtārthaṃ prati naṣṭam apy anaṣṭaṃ tad anyasādhāraṇatvāt.*
22. *vedāntinas tu paramātmani jīvātmalayo mokṣa iti vadanti taiḥ sahāsmākaṃ na virodhaḥ. samudre nadīnām iva brahmaṇi jīvānām upādhilayenāvibhāgasyaiva layaśabdārthatvāt tasya ca pararūpeṇa apratiṣṭhatva eva paryavasānāt* (Jha 1995:119). The final sentence of this passage has been mistranslated in the only English edition of the *Yogasārasaṃgraha* as "And this return finally leads to the non-existence (of the Human Self) in the form of something other (than the Supreme Self)" (Jha 1995:121). This translation implies that Vijñānabhikṣu believes that dissolution leads to complete identity between individual self and Brahman. But Vijñānabhikṣu has made clear in the *Vijñānāmṛtabhāṣyam* that non-separation (*avibhāga*) is something different from the complete identity (*tādātmya*) advocated by Advaitins.
23. For the former interpretation, see Garbe (1895). For the latter, see Rukmani (1981:1–17).

7. VEDĀNTA AND SĀṂKHYA IN THE ORIENTALIST IMAGINATION

1. Pollock (2001a, 2001b).
2. Upādhyāya (1994:36).
3. Sanskrit text in Bhāvāgaṇeśa (1969[16th c. CE]). See also Larson and Bhattacharya (1987:413–16).

4. Larson and Bhattacharya (1987:429).
5. This citation is discussed in Smith (2005:436). Puruṣottama's dates are either 1657 or 1668 to 1725 CE, making him a contemporary of Nāgojī Bhaṭṭa (ibid., 425).
6. Colebrooke (1977[1837]:143–269).
7. Pollock (2001a:393–94).
8. For one such Saidian critique of Indology, see Inden (1990).
9. Said (1978:5).
10. Hallisey (1995:33), Pollock (1993a:97–98).
11. Pollock (1993a:98).
12. Arif Dirlik (1996:112–17) suggests that it is by analyzing these "contact zones" between Orientalists and their Asian informants that we can begin to understand the extent to which Asians themselves contributed to Orientalist discourses.
13. Gough cotranslated the most influential of these Advaita doxographies, Mādhava's *Sarvadarśanasaṃgraha* (Cowell and Gough 1978). Deussen's *Allgemeine Geschichte der Philosophie* (1899) draws heavily on Mādhava in its account of Indian philosophical systems.
14. Wilhelm Halbfass makes this point eloquently: "In his polemical zeal against Orientalist constructions and essentializations, [Said] overlooks completely the extent of essentialist constructions in his own presentation. . . . On the one hand, he disregards internal differences *within* cultures; on the other hand, he overlooks common denominators *between* cultures . . . he does not want to recognize the realm of shared meanings in which even some of the more distorted views of the Orient took place, and without which neither understanding nor misunderstanding would be possible" (Halbfass 1997:8–9).
15. Zimmer (1969:378–80).
16. Quoted in Pollock (1993a:90).
17. Said largely ignores German Orientalism because it violates some of his central theses—among them that Orientalism is inseparable from imperial domination and that all Orientalists posit the Orient as the ontological "Other." Germany had no colonies in Asia, and German Orientalists often sought to identify themselves as the true heirs to "Aryan" intellectual traditions, denying India's otherness. More recently, German Orientalism has been examined from a variety of angles by Halbfass (1988), Pollock (1993a), and Kontje (2004).
18. For more detailed biographies of H. T. Colebrooke, see Müller (1890) and Rocher and Rocher (forthcoming).
19. Colebrooke (1977[1837]:378). Of course, Sanskrit transliteration schemes had not yet been standardized at the time Colebrooke was writing.
20. Colebrooke (1977[1837]:231–32).
21. Ibid., 228.
22. Ibid., 227.
23. Ibid., 228.
24. Ibid., 236.
25. Ibid.
26. Ibid., 324.
27. Ibid., 334.
28. Ibid., 348–50.
29. Ibid., 377.
30. Most recently by Rao (1996).

31. Gough (1882:258–60).
32. Another possibility, although slight, is that Colebrooke was aware of the sixteenth-century author Prakāśānanda, one of the few premodern Advaitins who actually held that the phenomenal world has the same ontological status as a hallucination or dream (Dasgupta 1922, 2:221).
33. In my opinion, this reading is incorrect since earlier Bhedābhedavādins who clearly have Śaṅkara in mind also refrain from naming him directly (e.g., Bhāskara in Dvivedin 1903). It would be understandable, however, if Colebrooke was not aware of this convention.
34. Gough (1882:258–59).
35. Ibid., 200–201.
36. Ibid., 223.
37. Ibid., 228.
38. For a critique of the commonly held view that *sāṃkhya* should be understood to mean "enumeration," see Edgerton (1924:35–37).
39. Quoted in Halbfass (1988:107).
40. Deussen (1907:45–46).
41. Summarized from Deussen (1899:213–15).
42. Ibid., 214.
43. Ibid., 230.
44. Ibid., 44.
45. Schopenhauer (1958[1856]:439–46).
46. Deussen (1907:39).
47. Ibid., 251–53.
48. Ibid., 47–48.
49. Ibid., 40.
50. For example, Olivelle (1998:12–13).
51. Deussen (1907:227).
52. The full title of Hall's edition is remarkable, given the theistic character of Vijñānabhikṣu's text: *The Sankhya-pravachana-bhashya: A Commentary on the Aphorisms of the Hindu Atheistic Philosophy* (Hall 1856).
53. Garbe tactfully alludes to these errors in his introduction to Vijñānabhikṣu (1895:x).
54. Ibid., xii–xiv.
55. Garbe (1897:37).
56. Ibid., 33–52.
57. Ibid., 51.
58. The "analogies between the Sāṃkhya systems and the Pythagorean philosophy" begin with "the name of the Indian system, which is derived from the word *saṃkhyā*, 'number,' and from the fundamental importance attached to number by Pythagoras" (Garbe 1897:39).
59. Garbe (1897:10).
60. Ibid., 30.
61. On Jamesian "experiential" interpretations of Indian philosophy, see Halbfass (1988:395).
62. Garbe (1897:11).
63. Ibid., 30.
64. Ibid., 30–31.
65. Garbe (1895:xiv).

66. Deutsch (1969); D. Chattopadhyaya (1969).
67. For more, see Hacker (1978:554).
68. Bharati (1970:273–77).
69. For instance, Hacker in Halbfass (1995:231–32). Also see chapter 10.
70. On this process of "Orientalization," see Dirlik (1996:101–3). In some cases that Said refused to acknowledge, the Orientalization process even included the political awakening of those European Orientalists who, in sympathy with the objects of their studies, spoke out against the European imperial project in Asia (e.g., James Legge, E. G. Browne, and W. S Blunt). In the context of the history of Indian philosophy, the process of Orientalization I am concerned with is not one of politics, dress, or cultural mores. It is one in which Indologists unwittingly picked up and transmitted the biases of the Sanskrit texts that they relied on, representing the biases as disinterested scientific truths about non-Western cultures and philosophies.

8. DOXOGRAPHY, CLASSIFICATORY SCHEMES, AND CONTESTED HISTORIES

1. Other Indian works that Halbfass (1988:350–51) classifies as doxography include *Prasthānabheda* of Madhusūdana Sarasvatī (1850[16th c. CE]), *Sarvasiddhāntasaṃgraha* of Śaṅkara (1983) [14th c. CE?], *Sarvamatasaṃgraha* (anonymous), *Sarvadarśanakaumudī* of Mādhava Sarasvatī, *Ṣaḍdarśanasamuccaya* of Rājaśekhara, *Ṣaḍdarśananirṇaya* of Merutuṅga, *Ṣaḍdarśanīsiddhāntasaṃgraha* of Rāmabhadra Dīkṣita, and *Sarvasiddhāntapraveśaka* (anonymous). On other Buddhist and Jaina doxographers, see Qvarnstöm (1999:176–79); on Bhāviveka as a Buddhist doxographer, see Eckel (2009); and on Jaina doxography, see Folkert (1993).
2. There are, of course, exceptions to this tendency. For instance, while Haribhadra conflates the Prabhākara and Bhāṭṭa schools of Mīmāṃsā, Mādhava does briefly acknowledge one of the differences between the schools (Abhyankar:286–87).
3. Sometimes a single author would write both a doxography and a hagiography, covering similar material from two different angles. This is the case with Mādhava; in addition to his *Sarvadarśanasaṃgraha, Śaṅkaradigvijaya* is traditionally, though probably incorrectly, ascribed to the same author (Tapasyananda 1996).
4. Cited in Runia (1998).
5. Aristotle *De anima* 1.2, 403b 20–25 (1936[4th c. BCE]:19).
6. Mansfeld (2004), Runia (1999:49–51).
7. Runia (1999:46).
8. Runia (1998); see also Runia (1999:52).
9. Diogenes Laertius (1925[3rd c. CE]).
10. D. Goswami (1905:3).
11. Rorty (1984:62). Rorty's definition of doxography occurs in a polemic against the doxographical genre itself. Unlike three other genres in the history of philosophy—which Rorty labels as historical reconstruction, *Geistesgeschichte,* and intellectual history—he claims that doxography simply serves no legitimate purpose. By "doxography," Rorty seems to have in mind widely read modern works such Bertrand Russell's *A History of Western Philosophy* and Frederick Copleston's *History of Philosophy.* He castigates this genre as being intellectually timid, and as the "genre that inspires boredom and despair" (ibid.). David Runia takes exception to

this pejorative redefinition of doxography (Runia 1999:34). I contend that although Rorty perhaps overextends the term "doxography" in applying it to Copelston and Russell, nonetheless his analysis of their structural similarities is an important observation. As students of Indian philosophy are well aware, modern histories of Indian philosophy are guilty of precisely the same tedious treatment of their topic, with the added drawback that the authors are often writing in their second or third language, not their native tongue.

12. Qvarnström (1999:173–74). Other notable treatments of Indian doxography are Folkert (for Jaina doxography) (1993:113–45, 341–409) and Halbfass (1988:349–68).
13. Qvarnström (1999:174).
14. See, for instance, his excellent account of Bhāviveka's critique of the Vedānta school. He describes Bhāviveka's *Madhyamakahṛdayakārikā* (6th c.) as "the earliest Sanskrit doxographical work that has come down to us" (Qvarnström 1989:98). Presumably he understands this text to be a doxography of the second type, since each chapter begins with a *pūrvapakṣa,* followed by an *uttarapakṣa.*
15. Rāmānuja's text includes a lengthy Advaita Vedānta *pūrvapakṣa,* and Jayanta's a lengthy Buddhist *pūrvapakṣa.* Both might plausibly be labeled "doxography" using Qvarnstöm's typology. As far as I know, Halbfass (1988:349–68) was the first to apply the word "doxography" to Indian texts. I believe his intention was precisely to highlight this distinct genre, which had generated little interest before his work. In Folkert's work on Jaina doxographies, he uses the word "compendia" (Folkert 1993:113–46).
16. On the difficult question of *Maṇimēkalai's* dates, see Richman (1988:160–61).
17. In the context of his work on Bhāviveka's *Madhyamakahṛdayakārikā,* see Eckel's discussion of *Maṇimēkalai* (Eckel 2009:15–17).
18. Cāttaṉār's ten *pramāṇas* are *pratyakṣa, anumāna, upamāna, āgama, arthāpatti, svabhāva, aitihya, abhāva, pariśeṣa,* and *sambhava.* The first five and the eighth, *abhāva,* are familiar and together make up the *pramāṇas* accepted by the Bhāṭṭa Mīmāṃsakas. Although *svabhāva* (inherent nature), *aitihya* (traditional belief), *pariśeṣa* (implication by correlation), and *sambhava* (probability) are unfamiliar in later doxographical accounts, some do occur as *pramāṇas* in earlier contexts. See for instance *Bh. Pu.* 11.19.17: *śrutiḥ pratyakṣam aitihyam anumānaṃ catuṣṭayam / pramāṇeṣv anavasthānād vikalpāt sa virajyate.*
19. The theory that Vedavyāsa and Bādarāyaṇa are the same author appears for the first time in Vācaspati Miśra's *Bhāmatī* and probably came about long after *Maṇimēkalai* was written (Nakamura 1989:404–5). Vedāntic schools either accept three *pramāṇas* (e.g., Viśiṣṭādvaita, Dvaita) or six (Advaita).
20. Śabara, commentary on Jaimini 1.1.4 (Jha 1933).
21. Jina, "victorious," here seems to be a generic epithet referring to the Buddha, who was victorious over Māra's attempts to thwart his enlightenment.
22. My account of chapter 27 of *Maṇimēkalai* relies on the summary in Varadachari (1971). Unfortunately, there are no reliable translations of the poem in print.
23. Kaṇāda, *Vaiśeṣikasūtra* 9.2.5, in K. Sharma (1972:210–11).
24. After the Sāṃkhya teaching, Cāttaṉār says that "Maṇimēkalai listened to this account with lively interest" (Daniélou and Iyer 1993:135, 139). Maṇimekalai's Buddhist teacher remarks that Buddhist logic is itself based on the teachings of the Jaina teacher Jinendra, who was the first to establish that the two means of knowledge are perception (*pratyakṣa*) and deduction (*anumāna*) (ibid., 152).

25. Monius (2001:66).
26. Daniélou and Iyer (1993:172), Alain Daniélou's translation.
27. Ibid.
28. On the question of the name of Bhāviveka/Bhāvaviveka/Bhavya, see Eckel (2009). Recent scholarship suggests that "Bhāviveka" was the original name of the author of the *Madhyamakahṛdayakārikā*.
29. On Bhāviveka's interpretations of Madhyamaka in the third chapter of the *Madhyamakahṛdayakārikā*, see Eckel (1978).
30. On Bhāviveka's portrayal of Vedānta in the *Madhyamakahṛdayakārikā*, see Nakamura (1989:206–17) and Qvarnström (1989).
31. In another text, *Madhyamakaratnapradīpa*, Bhāviveka establishes a three-tiered hierarchy of truths. At the bottom is erroneous conventional truth (*mithyāsaṃvṛtisatya*), exemplified by schools such as Vedānta and Mīmāṃsā. Next comes the correct conventional truth (*tathyasaṃvṛtisatya*) of the Hīnayāna and Yogācāra Buddhists. The highest level, the ultimate truth (*paramārthasatya*), is solely the province of Madhyamaka Buddhism (Qvarnström 1989:100–101).
32. Lindtner (2001:102–5). The schools of Kumārila Bhaṭṭa and Prabhākara are atheistic to the extent that they reject the idea of a creator god and arguably reject the idea of any god at all as a type of linguistic fiction. We find theistic influences in some of the late medieval Mīmāṃsakas, such as Laugākṣi Bhāskara.
33. On the significance of this "limitationist" metaphor in Advaita Vedānta, see chapter 3 in this volume.
34. Nakamura (1989:208–12).
35. Qvarnström (1989:91, 101–4).
36. *na buddhoktir mahāyānaṃ sūtrāntādāv asaṃgrahāt / mārgāntaropadeśād vā yathā vedāntadarśanam //* (*MHK* 4.7, in Lindtner 2001:50).
37. *vedānte ca hi yat sūktaṃ tat sarvaṃ buddhabhāṣitam* (*MHK* 4.56, in Lindtner 2001:55).
38. *tāthāgatīm avitathāṃ matvā nītim imāṃ śubhām / tasmāj jātaspṛhais tīrthaiḥ kṛtaṃ tatra mamāpi tat //* (*MHK* 8.86, in Lindtner 2001:89).
39. King (1995:138–40). The Gauḍapāda who composed the *Māṇḍūkyakārikā* is most likely not the same person who wrote the *Gauḍapādabhāṣya*, a commentary on the *Sāṃkhyakārikā*.
40. *ajātatā hi bhāvānāṃ svabhāvo 'kṛtrimatvataḥ / anapāyitvataś cāsāv ātmety api nigadyate // īdṛśo yady abhipreta ātmā hi bhavatām api / nāmādibahusādharmyān nirdoṣaḥ sopapattikaḥ //* (*MHK* 89, 95, in Lindtner 2001:89–90).
41. On Bhāviveka's hierarchy of systems and the question of his "inclusivism," see Eckel (2009).
42. Qvarnström (1989).
43. It is essential to remember that premodern doxographers were not historians of philosophy and should not be evaluated by their success or failure in accurately preserving a historical record of the situation in a given era.
44. Varadachari (1971:13).
45. Although Aśvaghoṣa's *Buddhacarita* depicts Siddhārtha Gautama's meeting with *śramaṇa* teachers before his awakening, the only teachers whose doctrines are presented at length are those of Ārāḍa Kālāma, whose views are similar to the views ascribed to the Sāṃkhya school in the *Mahābhārata* (Kent 1982). Obviously,

Maṇimēkalai's quest for ultimate truth parallels Siddhārtha's quest, although not necessarily the version presented in the *Buddhacarita.*

46. *darśanāni ṣaḍ eva.* The commentator Maṇibhadra clarifies that the word *eva* is in the sense of limitation (*avadhāraṇa*): there are only six systems of philosophy, although they can be further subdivided, for instance, into the eighteen schools of Buddhism or the many disciples of Jaimini's Mīmāṃsā (Goswami 1905:3).
47. Another list of six is provided by the Naiyāyika Jayanta Bhaṭṭa's play *Āgamaḍambara,* also known as *Ṣaṇmatanāṭaka.* The play's six schools are Buddhism, Jainism, Cārvāka, Mīmāṃsā, Nyāya, and Pañcarātra (Raghavan and Thakur 1964). Like Cāttaṉār's *Maṇimēkalai,* Jayanta Bhaṭṭa's play illustrates the possible connections between doxography and storytelling.
48. Daniélou and Iyer (1993:130–31); D. Goswami (1905).
49. D. Goswami (1905:70).
50. *naiyāyikamatād anye bhedaṃ vaiśeṣikaiḥ saha / na manyante mate teṣāṃ pañcaivāstikavādinaḥ // ṣaḍdarśanasaṃkhyā tu pūryate tanmate kila / lokāyatamatakṣepāt kathyate tena tanmatam //* (D. Goswami 1905:71).
51. This tendency to first establish the number of doctrines or sects and then fit known sects into this scheme was a widespread technique in the premodern world. For instance, Islamic scholars used the number of the seventy-two heretical sects as established by the prophet in the *hadith* as the principle for evaluating the sects of their own eras. To do this, in some cases, they double-counted the same sect by using two different names; in other cases, they excluded sects on the rationale that these sects were so heretical that they no longer could be considered Muslims (Henderson 1998:125–26).
52. D. Goswami (1905:59).
53. *darśanāni ṣaḍ evātra mūlabhedavyapekṣayā / devatātattvabhedena jñātavyāni manīṣibhiḥ //* (D. Goswami 1905:3).
54. Ibid., (1905:13–14).
55. Ibid., 4.
56. Bhāviveka is the exception to this trend. He acknowledges Vedānta as a philosophical school of its own and is therefore of great interest to historians of early Vedānta (Nakamura 1989:206–19).
57. Nakamura sees occasional acknowledgment of Vedānta among Buddhists and Jainas from 600 to 900 CE as a peripheral school of thought, although they had no apparent knowledge of Advaita Vedānta. Only after the tenth century does Advaita become a central target of Jaina polemics. Rather, "for some centuries after the demise of Śaṅkara the influence of Bhāskara was stronger than that of Śaṅkara" (Nakamura 1989:263, 294–95).
58. D. Goswami (1905:64).
59. *devatā darśanādhiṣṭhāyakāḥ* (ibid., 3).
60. *buddho devatā . . . darśanādikaraḥ* (ibid., 5).
61. *devatā darśanapravartaka ādipuruṣaḥ* (ibid., 39).
62. *sāṃkhyā nirīśvarāḥ kecit kecid īśvaradevatāḥ / sarveṣām api teṣāṃ syāt tattvānāṃ pañca viṃśatiḥ //* (ibid., 32).
63. Ibid.
64. Folkert (1993:125–26) argues along similar lines when he identifies *devatā* in Haribhadra with *āptatva.* In this book he also compares Haribhadra to the later Jaina doxographers Rājaśekhara, Merutuṅga, and Jinadatta.

65. *jaiminīyāḥ punaḥ prāhuḥ sarvajñādiviśeṣaṇaḥ / devo na vidyate ko 'pi yasya mānaṃ vaco bhavet //* (D. Goswami 1905:64).
66. Yet for Haribhadra, not all *āstika* schools have a *devatā,* even by his broad understanding of the word. He identifies both the *nirīśvara* Sāṃkhya and the Mīmāṃsā as being devoid of a *devatā.*
67. Some recent scholars dispute Mādhava's authorship of the *Sarvadarśanasaṃgraha.* The fourteenth-century date of the text, however, is not disputed. See preface to Klostermaier's edition of the *Sarvadarśanasaṃgraha* (Klostermaier 1999:v–vi). On the question of who founded the Śṛṅgeri maṭha, see Clark (2006).
68. Strictly speaking, of course, Mādhava's text is not historical at all, as it presents Indian philosophical doctrines as existing side by side in static and unchanging forms.
69. The *Sarvasiddhāntasaṃgraha,* ascribed to Śaṅkara, is similar to Mādhava's *Sarvadarśanasaṃgraha* in its structure. However, it abandons any explicit claim that each later system refutes the former in its fifth chapter (out of twelve) (Śaṅkara 1983 [14th c. CE?]).
70. *brahmamīmāṃsāvivaraṇavyājena ānandatīrthaḥ prasthānāntaram āsthiṣata* (Abhyankar 1978:128). One must avoid confusing the philosophers Mādhava (the fourteenth-century Advaita Vedāntin) and Madhva (the thirteenth-century founder of the Dvaita Vedānta school).
71. Yet Mādhava, if he was also author of the *Śaṅkaradigvijaya,* knew the Bhedābhedavādin Bhāskara and the basic Bhedābhedavāda viewpoint. Mādhava portrays Bhāskara in debate with Śaṅkara in that work (Tapasyananda 1996:174–83).
72. Śaṅkara (1996 [8th c. CE?]:477–78).
73. Mayeda even argues that Śaṅkara's notion of "unevolved name-and-form" is modeled on the Sāṃkhya notion of *prakṛti* (Mayeda 1992:19–22).
74. On the strength of the Sāṃkhya school in the eighth century, see Nakamura (1989).
75. Even Rāmānuja, less than two centuries earlier than Mādhava, follows Bhāskara's and Śaṅkara's interpretations, rejecting Sāṃkhya in his commentary on the *Brahmasūtras.* In this case, Rāmānuja followed closely to earlier commentaries in crafting his own, leaving little room for the wholesale reinterpretation of the relationship between Vedānta and Sāṃkhya that we find in the works of medieval Advaitins. For a close comparison of Śaṅkara, Bhāskara, and Rāmānuja's interpretations of the *Brahmasūtras,* see Nakamura (1989:451–65).
76. Cowell and Gough (1978:273).
77. Halbfass (1988:353–54).
78. Abhyankar (1978:389).
79. Nakamura (1989:242); Klostermaier (1999:1).
80. *Prasthānabheda* is part of Madhusūdana Sarasvatī's much longer *Mahimnastotraṭīkā,* but it is often treated as a stand-alone work. For a complete list and chronology of his works, see S. Gupta (2006).
81. Madhusūdana actually enumerates twenty-one viewpoints, including the Advaita Vedānta. Although opponents' views are first presented in brief, most of Madhusūdana's text is devoted to lengthy refutations of some of these views, including rejection of Bhedābheda arguments (Karmarkar 1962:36).
82. Halbfass (1988:353–54).
83. Śaṅkara's *Sarvasiddhāntasaṃgraha* also includes a list of the eighteen sciences. Unlike Madhusūdana, though, Śaṅkara does not show how the different *darśanas* fit into the categories of *vidyās.*

84. *evaṃ militvā nāstikānāṃ ṣaṭ prasthānāni. tāni kasmān nocyante. satyam. vedabāhyatvāt teṣāṃ mlecchādiprasthānavat paramparayāpi puruṣārthānupayogitvād upekṣaṇīyam eva* (Madhusūdana 1850[16th c. CE]:13). It is not clear whether Madhusūdana also considers *mleccha* teachings as completely useless for any human end. He might possibly acknowledge, as the Mīmāṃsaka Śabara does, that foreigners' knowledge is often useful in some instrumental way, such as their skill in the breeding and capturing of birds (Śābarabhāṣya 1.3.10, in Abhyaṅkara and Jośī 1970:149–54).
85. Of course, most Mīmāṃsakas would be surprised to find that they subscribe to *ārambhavāda.*
86. *svaprakāśaparamānandādvitīyaṃ brahma svamāyāvaśān mithyaiva jagadākāreṇa kalpata iti tṛtīyaḥ pakṣo brahmavādinām. sarveṣāṃ prasthānakartṝṇāṃ munīnāṃ vivartavādaparyavasānenādvitīye parameśvara eva pratipādye tātparyaṃ na hi te munayo bhrāntāḥ sarvajñatvāt teṣāṃ kiṃtu bahirviṣayapravaṇānām āpātataḥ puruṣārthe praveśo na saṃbhavatīti nāstikyavāraṇāya taiḥ prakārabhedāḥ pradarśitāḥ. tatra teṣāṃ tātparyam abuddhvā vedaviruddhe 'py arthe tātparyam utprekṣamāṇās tanmatam evopādeyatvena gṛhṇanto janā nānāpathajuṣo bhavanti* (Madhusūdana 1850[16th c. CE]:23–24).

9. AFFIRMERS (*ĀSTIKAS*) AND DENIERS (*NĀSTIKAS*) IN INDIAN HISTORY

1. John B. Henderson's useful comparative study is silent about Indian heresiology, perhaps because he was aware of its complexity (Henderson 1998:3).
2. For example, Doniger (1991b:18); Sharma (1987:63–64). The Sanskrit terms *seśvara* and *nirīśvara* are a better approximation of "theist" and "atheist."
3. As I discuss in chapter 4, however, *nirīśvara* Sāṃkhya has not been nearly as common as most historians suggest.
4. For a reexamination of the supposed soteriological character of Indian philosophy, see Krishna (1991:16–34).
5. Simon (1979:104).
6. Mādhava's *Sarvadarśanasaṃgraha* only uses the term *nāstika* twice, both times as an epithet for the Cārvāka school, "the crest-gem of the *nāstikas*" (*nāstikaśiromaṇin*) (Abhyankar 1978, 2:255). *Āstika* does not occur in the text. Śaṅkara begins the Vaiśeṣika chapter of the *Sarvasiddhāntasaṃgraha* by emphatically marking a break from the doctrines that came before: "Now the Vaiśeṣika, who accepts the teachings of the Vedas, refutes the Buddhist, Lokāyata, and Jain schools, who are *nāstikas,* external to the Vedas" (*nāstikān vedabāhyāṃs tān bauddhalokāyatārhatān / nirākaroti vedārthavādī vaiśeṣiko 'dhunā //*) (Śaṅkara 1983[14th c. CE?]:19).
7. *yo 'vamanyeta te mūle hetuśāstrāśrayād dvijaḥ / sa sādhubhir bahiṣkāryo nāstiko vedanindakaḥ // Manu.* 2.11 (Olivelle 2006:404).
8. For an analysis of this passage and the dangers of reason "ungrounded" and functioning as an end in itself, see Ganeri (2001:7–9).
9. *nāstikatarkaśāstraṃ bauddhacārvākādiśāstraṃ yatra vedo 'dharmāyeti punaḥ punar uddhuṣyate* (Jha 1999, 1:72).
10. *nāsti paraloko nāsti dattaṃ nāsti hutam iti nāstikaḥ* (Jha 1999, 2:203).
11. For Medhātithi on Manu 4.162 and 8.349–51, see Jha (1999, 4:430–31 and 6:374–79).
12. Halbfass (1983:1–26).

13. *dṛṣṭavad ānuśravikaḥ sa hy aviśuddhaḥ kṣayātiśayayuktaḥ / tadviparītaḥ śreyān vyaktāvyaktajñavijñānāt // SK* 2, in Wezler and Motegi (1998:47).
14. One indication of this is the furor surrounding D. N. Jha's *Myth of the Holy Cow* (D. Jha 2002), a book banned by a court in Hyderabad for its thesis that ancient Indians slaughtered and ate cows.
15. See *Yuktidīpikā* commentary on *SK* 2 (Wezler and Motegi 1998:47).
16. The locus classicus of Yoga's rejection of the violence enjoined by the Vedas is Vyāsa's commentary on *YS* 2.33. He writes that there are three motivations for killing: greed, as in the case of one who kills an animal for its meat and skin; anger, as in the case of one who has been harmed by another; and delusion, as in the case of one who believes that merit will accrue by killing an animal in sacrifice. Vyāsa's commentary is in G. Śāstrī (1989:255).
17. For example, Śaṅkara and Paul Deussen.
18. According to Sāṃkhya commentators, "reliable testimony" (*āptavacana*) refers both to the testimony of reliable persons and to the testimony of scripture (e.g., M. Jha 1965).
19. Clooney (2001:29); Ganeri (2001:7).
20. *yāny etāni trayīvidbhir na parigṛhītāni . . . sāṃkhyayogapāñcarātrapāśupataśākhyagranthaparigṛhītadharmādharmanibandhanāni.* See Kumārila Bhaṭṭa's *Tantravārttika,* commentary on *MS* 1.3.4, in Abhyaṅkara and Jośī (1970, 2:112).
21. Eltschinger (forthcoming).
22. *PMS* 2.1.1, 2.1.7, in Abhyaṅkara and Jośī (1970, 2:333–54, 2:380).
23. Ibid., 2.1.6 (2:379–80).
24. On Vedānta as "Uttara Mīmāṃsā," see Clooney (1993:23–29).
25. While some schools of Vedānta believe that the path to liberation requires a combination of knowledge and ritual action (*jñānakarmasamuccayavāda*), Advaitins might be described as somewhat hostile to ritual, since they maintain that at a certain stage, ritual activity can be abandoned completely.
26. Nakamura (1989:206–16).
27. By the fifteenth century, this process of adaptation had gone so far that some Mīmāṃsakas even accepted the existence of God (e.g., Laugākṣi Bhāskara in Gajendragadkar and Karmarkar 1998:69).
28. *nāsti paraloko nāsti dattaṃ nāsti hutam iti nāstikaḥ* (G. Jha 1999, 2:203).
29. *āstikavādinām iha paralokagatipuṇyapāpāstikyavādināṃ* (D. Goswami 1905:70).
30. *āstināstidiṣṭaṃ matiḥ* (Tripathi and Malaviya 1985, 5:265).
31. *paraloko 'sti iti yasya matiḥ sa āstikaḥ. tadviparīto nāstikaḥ. Kāśikā* 1801 (Tripathi and Malaviya 1985, 5:265).
32. Possible scriptural evidence for the grammarians' understanding occurs at *Kaṭha Up.* 1.20: "There is this doubt about a man who is dead. 'He exists' (*asti*), say some, others, 'He exists not' (*nāyam asti*)" (translation in Olivelle 1998:379). To the best of my knowledge, no premodern commentator has cited this passage as justification for the definition of *nāstika* and *āstika.*
33. This understanding is reiterated in the grammarian Bhaṭṭoji Dīkṣita's *Siddhānta Kaumudī* (Vasu 1962).
34. The Ājīvika school, for instance, accepts rebirth while denying that good or bad actions have any consequences.
35. Whether or not Asaṅga was the author of *Yogācārabhūmi,* this text was likely composed in the fourth or fifth century CE.

36. Asaṅga (Dutt 1966:31); this translation is by Eckel (2009:65–66).
37. Eckel's translation (2009:282). For the original Sanskrit and Tibetan of this passage, see ibid., 432.
38. Eckel (2009:432).
39. The *Bodhisattvabhūmi*'s concern with the overnegation of the Madhyamaka and relative lack of concern with the undernegation of Hīnayāna is itself an indication of the importance of ethical action among Buddhists. A Hīnayāna Buddhist, although he may not understand the ultimate truths of Buddhism, will continue to believe in karma and to follow the Buddhist eightfold path. But a nihilistic interpretation of Madhymaka Buddhism will entail the complete nonexistence of agent, action, and effect and will likely lead to the abandonment of Buddhist practice. This is why Nāgārjuna acknowledges at *MMK* 24.11 that the misperception of emptiness can lead to complete destruction, the same way a snake when mishandled can lead to the death of the handler: *vināśayati durdṛṣṭā śūnyatā mandamedhasam / sarpo yathā durgṛhīto vidyā vā duṣprasādhitā //* (Kalupahana 1986:335).
40. Of course, at a second-order level, both of the assertions that "there are consequences for our actions" and "there are no consequences for our actions" can be understood as statements of doctrine. But the real significance of these statements is on the practical level.
41. Nakamura (1989:473) argues that the Sāṃkhya school was the main target of Bādarāyaṇa's *Brahmasūtras,* as well as of its early commentators Śaṅkara and Bhāskara.
42. Henderson (1998:17).
43. Ibid.
44. Colebrooke (1977[1837]:117–228).
45. Henderson (1998:138).
46. By the sixteenth century, many of the *śrauta* rites enjoined in the *Ṛg Veda* and the *Brāhmaṇas* had fallen partly or completely out of practice, and newer rituals described in the *Āgamas* and *Tantras* had taken their place. It would have been hard to maintain that the essence of the Vedas were their ritual injunctions when, in fact, few of these rituals were being performed.
47. For instance, there was some debate as to whether the skepticism of Sextus Empiricus should be recognized as a hairesis; Sextus argued that it should, since although the skeptics do not rely on dogmatic propositions, they do follow a certain method of reasoning (Simon 1979:110–11).
48. Henderson (1998:43–44).
49. The polemical usage of these two Sanskrit words show some similarities to the way the words "optimist" and "pessimist" are used in contemporary political discourse in the United States. Every politician declares himself an "optimist" and labels his opponent a "pessimist." Yet devoid of context, "optimist" and "pessimist" are empty terms, every bit as underdetermined as *āstika* and *nāstika.*
50. Mādhava in Abhyankar (1978). By "sublation," I have in mind something similar to the Hegelian *Aufhebung*—not merely a negation but also a fulfillment of the doctrines that came before. In an explicitly Advaita context, also cf. Eliot Deutsch's notion of "subration" (Deutsch 1969:15–36).
51. Garbe (1895:20–22).
52. *etenādhunikānāṃ vedāntibruvāṇām api mataṃ vijñānavādatulyayogakṣematayā nirastam* (ibid., 21).

53. Bhedābheda Vedāntins have also been negatively associated with a *nāstika* school. The Viśiṣṭādvaitin Vedānta Deśika called Yādavaprakāśa "a Vedāntin who smells like a Jaina" (*vedāntijainagandhin*) (Vedānta Deśika (1974)[14th c. CE]:11).
54. Garbe (1895:4).
55. *astu vā pāpināṃ jñānapratibandhārtham āstikadarśaneṣv apy aṃśataḥ śrutivirud dhārthavyavasthāpanam. teṣu teṣv aṃśeṣv aprāmāṇyaṃ ca śrutismṛtyaviruddheṣu tu mukhyaviṣayeṣu prāmāṇyam asty eva. ata eva padmapurāṇe brahmayogadarśanātiriktānāṃ darśanānāṃ nindāpy upapadyate* (ibid., 4).
56. This is similar to Madhusūdana's argument in the final section of the *Prasthānabheda* (Madhusūdana 1850[16th c. CE]:23–24).
57. *Viṣ. Pu.* 4.18. On variations of this story, see O'Flaherty (1976:187–211).
58. Radhakrishnan (1927:23).

10. HINDU UNITY AND THE NON-HINDU OTHER

1. For example, Biardeau (1989:160).
2. Ghose (2000:143).
3. Following this logic, the first amendment of the U.S. Constitution states that "Congress shall make no law respecting an establishment of religion or prohibiting the free exercise thereof." For a contrast of this "Jeffersonian project" of the privatization of religion with the public debate (*vāda*) of the Indian philosophical schools, see Clayton (2006).
4. "No private person has any right in any manner to prejudice another person in his civil enjoyments because he is of another church or religion. All the rights and franchises that belong to him as a man, or as a denizen, are inviolably to be preserved to him. These are not the business of religion. No violence nor injury is to be offered him, whether he be Christian or Pagan" (Locke 2004[1689]:10).
5. "Why should I tolerate? Toleration means that I think that you are wrong and I am just allowing you to live. Is it not a blasphemy to think that you and I are allowing others to live? I accept all religions that were in the past, and worship with them all; I worship God with every one of them, in whatever form they worship Him. I shall go to the mosque of the Mohammedan; I shall enter the Christian's church and kneel before the crucifix; I shall enter the Buddhistic temple, where I shall take refuge in Buddha and in his Law" (Vivekananda 1970–1972, 2:374).
6. For instance, at *BhG* 10.12 and 10.15 (respectively).
7. *BhG* 9.23–24, translated in Miller (1986:86): *ye 'py anyadevatābhaktā yajante śraddhayānvitāḥ / te 'pi mām eva kaunteya yajanty avidhipūrvakam // ahaṃ hi sarvayajñānāṃ bhoktā ca prabhur eva ca / na tu mām abhijānanti tattvenātaś cyavanti te //*
8. *BhG* 11.15, translated in Miller (1986:99): *paśyāmi devāṃs tava deva dehe sarvāṃs tathā bhūtaviśeṣasaṃghān / brahmāṇam īśaṃ kamalāsanastham ṛṣīṃś ca sarvān uragāṃś ca divyān //*
9. *Kūrma Pu.* 2.4.8, my translation. (The Īśvaragīta makes up the first eleven chapters of the second section of the *Kūrma Purāṇa*). *ahaṃ hi sarvahaviṣāṃ bhoktā caiva phalapradaḥ / sarvadevatanurbhūtvā sarvātmā sarvasaṃsthitaḥ //* (A. Gupta 1971:389). Cf. *BhG* 9.24.
10. Hacker (1978:599).
11. Hacker (1983:21; 1978:600).
12. Hacker (1978:600).

13. Ibid., 239.
14. Ibid., 480.
15. In the modern period, V. S. Savarkar has argued that Jainism, Buddhism, and Sikhism are facets of Hinduism (Savarkar 1989[1928]:123–26).
16. Hacker in Halbfass (1995:231–32).
17. Hacker in Halbfass (1995:232).
18. Hacker (1978:599).
19. In Nicholas of Cusa's fifteenth-century *De Pace Fidei,* for instance, Cusa portrays all faiths, including Hinduism and Islam, as imperfect but genuine expressions of the Christian gospel (Hopkins 1995). Hacker is a critic of inclusivist trends in twentieth-century Catholicism, exemplified particularly by Karl Rahner's concept of the "anonymous Christian" (for more, see Hacker 1978:793–819).
20. Larson and Bhattacharya write that Vijñānabhikṣu's "syncretism is hardly complete, for it is quite clear that Vijñānabhikṣu has very little patience with the māyāvāda or Advaita Vedānta of Śaṅkara and his followers" (Larson and Bhattacharya 1987:375).
21. Indeed, the Advaitins frequently manufacture superficial differences between their views and those of the Buddhists, even on issues where their position is closer to the Buddhists than to other *āstika* schools. For instance, on Maṇḍana Miśra's anti-Buddhist polemics in the *Brahmasiddhi,* see H. Nicholson (2002:577–78).
22. *na hi te munayo bhrāntāḥ sarvajñatvāt teṣāṃ kiṃtu bahirviṣayapravaṇānām āpātataḥ puruṣārthe praveśo na saṃbhavatīti nāstikyavāraṇāya taiḥ prakārabhedāḥ pradarśitāḥ. tatra teṣāṃ tātparyam abuddhvā vedaviruddhe 'py arthe tātparyam utprekṣamāṇās tanmatam evopādeyatvena gṛhṇanto janā nānāpathajuṣo bhavanti* (Madhusūdana 1850[16th c. CE]:23).
23. Assmann (1996:34).
24. Halbfass (1988:186–87).
25. Ibid.
26. Ahmad (1999:167–81, 191–96, 218–23).
27. For a review of texts translated from Sanskrit into Persian during the Mughal period, see Ernst (2003:178–87).
28. The main exception to this silence seems in to be in Jaina texts such as *Hīrasaubhāgya,* a biography of Hīravijaya Sūri (1527–1595) (Dundas 1999). In the modern period, Bankimcandra Chatterji's *Ānandamaṭh* (2005 [1882]) tells a story of violent *saṃnyāsin* resistance against Muslim soldiers working for the British East India Company. "Vande Mātaram," now the national song of India, appeared for the first time in this work.
29. The question of the doxographers' portrayals of Jainas is in some ways even more vexing than their portrayal of Buddhists. Mādhava, for instance, would have had close acquaintance with Jainas and Jainism in his position as a minister in the Vijayanagara courts. Yet his treatment of Jainism in the *SDS* shows no more insight than his summaries of the Buddhists or Cārvākas. This again highlights the restraints that the genre of doxography put on its authors.
30. *darśanāni ṣaḍ eva* (D. Goswami 1905:3).
31. On the logic of śāstra, see Pollock (1985:516).
32. Thapar (1989:223). Obviously, *yavana* came to be regarded as a generic term for "foreigner" or "barbarian." On *yavana* and *śaka,* see Halbfass (1988:176–77). Cases where Muslims are recognized as such in Sanskrit texts are often nineteenth-century interpolations. For instance, the *Bhaviṣya Purāṇa* refers to *mahāmada* (Mohammedans) and alludes to the story of Adam and Eve (Halbfass 1988:194).

33. Zelliot (1982:177).
34. Ibid., 178.
35. There are different classes of demons in Hindu mythology. In particular, we should distinguish between *rākṣasas,* flesh-eating creatures of the night, and *asuras,* a class of celestial beings who were created before the *devas* and who antagonized them. Pollock shows that Muslims are described as both *asuras* and *rākṣasas.* In the demonization of Buddhists and Jainas, they are generally described as *asuras.* For a typology of demons in India, see Sutherland (1991:49–61).
36. Pollock (1993b:287).
37. Talbot (1995:696–97).
38. *Ch. Up.* 8.8.4–8.8.5; translation from Olivelle (1998:283–84).
39. One important difference, however, is that while Virocana believes that caring for the body leads to the attainment of the next world, Cārvākas deny that such a world exists.
40. Mādhava alludes to this story in his hagiography of Śaṅkara, the *Śaṅkaradigvijaya.* He depicts the Advaita philosopher as an incarnation of Śiva sent to earth to counteract all of the false views caused by Viṣṇu's own incarnation as the Buddha (Tapasyananda 1996:4).
41. For example, *Viṣ. Pu.* 1.9, *Mbh* 1.15–17.
42. *śrutismṛtinyāyavacaḥkṣīrābdhimathanoddhṛtam / jñānāmṛtaṃ guroḥ prītyai bhūdevebhyo nu dīyate // pariviṣayya sadbuddhyā mohinyevātha dānavān / kutarkān vañcayitvedaṃ pīyatām amṛtepsubhiḥ // pītvaitad balavantas te pākhaṇḍāsurayūthapān / vijitya jñānakarmabhyāṃ yāntu śrīmadguroḥ padam //* (Tripāṭhī 1979:1).
43. On the definition and changing meaning of *pāṣaṇḍa* (and *pākhaṇḍa,* which is a variant spelling), see Thapar (1978:66) and Eltschinger (forthcoming).
44. Halbfass (1988:192–93); Thapar (1989:222). The only authors to deny this are Hindu nationalists such as Savarkar, Golwalkar, and their followers.
45. Talbot (1995:700).
46. Ibid.
47. O'Connell (1973:341).
48. Stietencron (1995:51).
49. Dermot Killingley traces the word "Hindooism" to a text by the Bengali religious reformer Rammohan Roy in 1816 (Killingley 1993:62). Geoffrey Oddie has pointed out earlier usage of the word in the writings of eighth-century British missionaries (Oddie 2006:70–72).
50. Stietencron (1995:60).
51. Lorenzen (2005:53).
52. Ibid., 73.
53. Hawley and Juergensmeyer (1988:41).
54. For evidence of Kabīr as an equal-opportunity reviler of Islam and Hinduism, see complaints against him recorded by the sixteenth-century author Anantadās: "He has abandoned the customs of the Muslims and has broken the touchability rules of the Hindus" (quoted in Lorenzen 2005:71).
55. Talbot (1995:720).
56. Pollock (1993b:263).

57. At *Manusmṛti* 2.11, *nāstikas* are defined as twice-borns who revile the Veda. Since twice-borns (members of the three highest *varṇas*) are only indigenous to India, this excludes foreigners from the category of *nāstika*. In later definitions, this stipulation seems to have been dropped. On the Sanskrit term *mleccha*, see Thapar (1971) and Halbfass (1988:175–89).
58. Thapar (1989:209–210).
59. For instance, Cynthia's Talbot's painstaking work on fourteenth-century Vijayanagara inscriptions has already been taken out of its historical context and co-opted by the RSS (*Rashtriya Swayamsevak Sangh*): "The word 'Hindu' has an inspiring historical background. It has been the motivating concept for our independence struggle for the last one thousand years. . . . The proud epithet applied to the great emperors who founded the Vijayanagar empire was 'Hindu raya suratrana,' i.e., the protectors of the Hindus and their values of life" (Sheshadri 2009).
60. Thapar (1989:225).
61. Eaton (2000:314–15); Talbot (1995:718).
62. For example, "in India there never was any religious persecution by the Hindus, but only that wonderful reverence, which they have for all religions of the world" (Vivekananda 1970–1972, 1:391). On the destruction of Jaina and Buddhist monasteries by Śaivas, see Thapar (1989:219–20).
63. Thapar (1989:219–20).
64. On the terms "Neo-Hindu" and "Neo-Vedāntin," see Halbfass (1995:8).
65. Radhakrishnan (1927:23).
66. Radhakrishnan (1940:347).
67. V. S. Savarkar, founder of the hindutva ideology, ignores the precedent of the *Purāṇas* by arguing that Jainas, Buddhists, and Sikhs are Hindus, insofar as their religions are native to India (Savarkar 1989[1928]:123–26). Other formative thinkers for Hindu nationalism, such as Dayananda Saraswati, were less embracing of these groups.
68. For instance, the global, transnational phenomenon of modern postural yoga threatens the idea of yoga as a legacy belonging to Hinduism or to the nation of India alone (for more, see Alter 2004).
69. Vivekananda (1970–1972, 5:52).

BIBLIOGRAPHY

Abhyankar, V. S., ed. (1978). *Sarva-darśana-saṃgraha,* by Mādhava [14th c. CE]. Poona: Bhandarkar Oriental Research Institute.

Abhyaṅkara, K. V., and G. Jośī (1970). *Śrīmajjaiminipraṇīte Mīmāṃsādarśane,* vols. 1–2, by Jaimini [1st c. CE?]. Puṇya: Ānandāśrama.

Ahmad, Aziz (1999). *Studies in Islamic Culture in the Indian Environment.* New Delhi: Oxford University Press.

Alter, Joseph S. (2004). *Yoga in Modern India: The Body Between Science and Philosophy.* Princeton, N.J.: Princeton University Press.

Anantha Murthy, U. R. (1978). *Samskara: A Rite for a Dead Man.* Translated by A. K. Ramanujan. New York: Oxford University Press.

Anidjar, Gil (2006). "Secularism." *Critical Inquiry* 33: 52–77.

Aristotle [4th c. BCE] (1936). *On the Soul.* Translated by W. S. Hett. Cambridge, Mass.: Harvard University Press, Loeb Classical Library.

Assman, Jan (1996). "Translating Gods." In *The Translatability of Cultures,* edited by Sanford Budick and Wolfgang Iser, 25–36. Stanford, Calif.: Stanford University Press.

Austin, J. L. (1975). *How to Do Things with Words.* Cambridge, Mass.: Harvard University Press.

Baird, Robert (1971). *Category Formation and the History of Religions.* Religion and Reason Series, no. 1. The Hague: Mouton.

Berling, Judith A. (1980). *The Syncretic Religion of Lin Chao-en.* New York: Columbia University Press.

Bharati, Agehananda (1970). "The Hindu Renaissance and Its Apologetic Patterns." *Journal of Asian Studies* 29(2): 267–87.

Bhāvāgaṇeśa [16th c. CE] (1969). "Sāṃkhyatattvayāthārthyadīpana." In *Sāṃkhyasaṃgraha,* edited by V. P. Dvivedin, 33–58. Varanasi: Chowkhamba Sanskrit Series Office.

Biardeau, Madeleine (1989). *Hinduism: The Anthropology of a Civilization.* New Delhi: Oxford University Press.

Bilimoria, Purushottama (1993). "Is *Adhikāra* Good Enough for 'Rights'?" *Asian Philosophy* 3(1): 3–14.

Black, Brian (2007). *The Character of the Self in Ancient India: Priests, Kings, and Women in the Early Upaniṣads.* Albany: State University of New York Press.

Borelli, John (1976). "The Theology of Vijñānabhikṣu: A Translation of His Commentary on Brahma Sūtras 1.1.2 and an Exposition of His Difference-in-Identity Theology." PhD diss., Fordham University.

Bronkhorst, Johannes (1981). "Yoga and Seśvara Sāṃkhya." *Journal of Indian Philosophy* 9: 309–20.

—— (1983). "God in Sāṃkhya." *Wiener Zeitschrift für die Kunde Südasiens* 27: 149–64.

—— (2008). "Innovation in Seventeenth Century Grammatical Philosophy: Appearance or Reality?" *Journal of Indian Philosophy* 35(5/6): 543–50.

Burckhardt, Jacob (1990) [1860]. *The Civilization of the Renaissance in Italy.* Translated by S. G. C. Middlemore. London: Penguin.

Carman, J. B. (1974). *The Theology of Rāmānuja: An Essay in Religious Understanding.* New Haven, Conn.: Yale University Press.

Chakrabarty, Dipesh (2000). *Provincializing Europe: Postcolonial Thought and Historical Difference.* Princeton, N.J.: Princeton University Press.

Chari, V. K. (1990). *Sanskrit Criticism.* Honolulu: University of Hawai'i Press.

Chatterji, Bankimcandra (2005) [1882]. *Ānandamaṭh, or The Sacred Brotherhood.* Edited and Translated by Julius J. Lipner. New York: Oxford University Press.

Chattopadhyaya, Brajadulal (1998). *Representing the Other? Sanskrit Sources and the Muslims (Eighth to Fourteenth Century).* New Delhi: Manohar.

Chattopadhyaya, Debiprasad (1969). *Indian Atheism: A Marxist Analysis.* Calcutta: Manisha.

Chattopadhyaya, K. (1927). "A Peculiar Meaning of 'Yoga.'" *Journal of the Royal Asiatic Society of Great Britain and Ireland,* 854–58.

Chemparathy, George (1972). *An Indian Rational Theology: Introduction to Udayana's Nyāyakusumāñjali.* Vienna: Gerold.

Cicero [45 BCE] (1997). *The Nature of the Gods.* Edited and translated by P. G. Walsh. New York: Oxford University Press.

Clark, Matthew (2006). *The Dasanami-Samnyasis: The Integration of Ascetic Lineages into an Order.* Leiden: Brill.

Clayton, John (2006). *Religions, Reasons, and Gods: Essays in Cross-Cultural Philosophy of Religion.* Cambridge: Cambridge University Press.

Clooney, Francis X. (1993). *Theology After Vedānta: An Experiment in Comparative Theology.* Albany: State University of New York Press.

—— (2001). *Hindu God, Christian God: How Reason Helps Break Down the Boundaries Between Religions.* New York: Oxford University Press.

Cohen, Anthony P. (1985). *The Symbolic Construction of Community.* London: Routledge.

Cohen, Jeffrey Jerome, ed. (2000). *The Postcolonial Middle Ages.* New York: St. Martin's Press.

Colebrooke, H. T. (1977) [1837]. *Essays on the History, Literature, and Religions of Ancient India.* New Delhi: Cosmo.

Consul, Sadhna (1993). *Vijñānabhikṣu ke Vedānt-Siddhāntoṃ kā Samīkṣātmak Adhyayan.* Jaipur: Classic.

Cowell, E. B., and A. E. Gough, trans. (1978). *Sarvadarśanasaṃgraha,* by Mādhava [14th c. CE]. Varanasi: Chowkhamba Sanskrit Series Office.

Daniélou, Alain, and T. V. Gopala Iyer, trans. (1993). *Manimekhalaï,* by Cāttaṉār [6th c. CE?]. New Delhi: Penguin.

Dasgupta, Surendranath (1922). *A History of Indian Philosophy.* Vols. 1–4. New Delhi: Motilal Banarsidass.

Davidson, Donald (2001). "On the Very Idea of a Conceptual Scheme." In *Inquiries into Truth and Interpretation,* 183–98. Oxford: Clarendon Press.

Deussen, Paul (1899). *Allgemeine Geschichte der Philosophie.* Vol. 1, part 3. Leipzig: F. A. Brockhaus.

—— (1907). *Outlines of Indian Philosophy.* Berlin: Karl Curtius.

—— (1912). *System of the Vedānta.* Translated by Charles Johnston. Chicago: Open Court.

Deutsch, Eliot (1969). *Advaita Vedānta: A Philosophical Reconstruction.* Honolulu: University of Hawai'i Press.

Diels, Hermann (1879). *Doxographi Graeci.* Berolini: G. Reimer.

Dignāga [5th c. CE] (1930). *The Nyāyapraveśa.* Edited by Anandshankar B. Dhruva. Baroda: Oriental Institute.

Diogenes Laertius [3rd c. CE] (1925). *Lives of Eminent Philosophers.* Vols. 1 and 2. Translated by R. D. Hicks. Loeb Classical Library. Cambridge, Mass.: Harvard University Press.

Dirlik, Arif (1996). "Chinese History and the Question of Orientalism." *History and Theory* 35(4): 96–118.

Doniger, Wendy (1991a). "Hinduism by Any Other Name." *Wilson Quarterly* 15(3): 35–41.

——, ed. and trans. (1991b). *The Laws of Manu.* New York: Penguin.

Dumont, P.-E. (1933). *L'Īśvaragītā: Le chant de Śiva.* Baltimore: Johns Hopkins University Press.

Dundas, Paul (1999). "Jain Perceptions of Islam in the Early Modern Period." *Indo-Iranian Journal* 42: 35–46.

Dutt, Nalinaksha, ed. (1966). *Bodhisattvabhūmi,* by Asaṅga [4th c. CE]. Tibetan Sanskrit Works Series, no. 7. Patna: K. P. Jayaswal Research Institute.

Dvivedin, Vindhyeshvari Prasada, ed. (1903). *Brahmasūtrabhāṣyam,* by Bhāskara [8th c. CE]. Benares: Chowkhamba Sanskrit Book Depot.

Dyson, Freeman (2006). "Is God in the Lab?" In *The Scientist as Rebel,* 305–14. New York: New York Review of Books.

Eaton, Richard M. (2000). "Temple Desecration and Indo-Muslim States." *Journal of Islamic Studies* 11(3): 283–319.

Eckel, Malcolm D. (1978). "Bhāvaviveka and the Early Mādhyamika Theories of Language." *Philosophy East and West* 28(3): 323–37.

—— (2009). *Bhāviveka and His Buddhist Opponents.* Harvard Oriental Series, vol. 70. Cambridge, Mass.: Harvard University Press.

Edgerton, Franklin (1924). "The Meaning of Sānkhya and Yoga." *American Journal of Philology* 45: 1–46.

Eliade, Mircea (1970) [1958]. *Yoga, Immortality and Freedom.* Translated by Willard R. Trask. Princeton, N.J.: Princeton University Press.

Eltschinger, Vincent (forthcoming). "Apocalypticism, Heresy, and Philosophy: Toward a Sociohistorically Grounded Account of Sixth Century Indian Philosophy." In *Papers of the International Conference "Doctrine and World-View in Indian Philosophy,"* edited by Piotr Balcerowicz. New Delhi: Motilal Banarsidass.

Ernst, Carl W. (2003). "Muslim Studies of Hinduism? A Reconsideration of Arabic and Persian Translation from Indian Languages." *Iranian Studies* 36(2): 173–95.

Feuerstein, Georg (1989). *Yoga: The Technology of Ecstasy.* Los Angeles: Jeremy P. Tarcher.

Fitzgerald, James L. (forthcoming). "The Sāṃkhya-Yoga 'Manifesto' at Mbh 12.289–290." In *Battles, Bards, Brahmans. Papers from the Epics Section of the 13th World Sanskrit Conference. Edinburgh, 10th-14th July 2006,* edited by John Brockington, 185–212. Delhi: Motilal Banarsidass.

Folkert, Kendall W. (1993). *Scripture and Community: Collected Essays on the Jains.* Atlanta: Scholars Press.

Forster, Michael N. (1998). "On the Very Idea of Denying the Existence of Radically Different Conceptual Schemes." *Inquiry* 41(2): 133–85.

Fort, Andrew O. (1998). *Jīvanmukti in Transformation: Embodied Liberation in Advaita and Neo-Vedānta.* Albany: State University of New York Press.

—— (2006). "Vijñānabhikṣu on Two Forms of *Samādhi.*" *International Journal of Hindu Studies* 10(3): 271–94.

Gadamer, Hans-Georg (1989). *Truth and Method.* New York: Continuum.

Gajendragadkar, A. B., and R. D. Karmarkar, eds. (1998). *The Arthasaṃgraha,* by Laugākṣi Bhāskara [17th c. CE]. New Delhi: Motilal Banarsidass.

Ganeri, Jonardon (2001). *Philosophy in Classical India.* London: Routledge.

Garbe, Richard, trans. and introduction (1889). *Sāṃkhya-pravacana-bhāṣya: Vijñānabhikshu's Commentar zu den Sāṃkhyasūtras,* by Vijñānabhikṣu [16th c. CE]. Leipzig: F. A. Brockhaus.

——, ed. (1895). *Sāṃkhya-pravacana-bhāṣya,* by Vijñānabhikṣu [16th c. CE]. Harvard Oriental Series, vol. 2. Cambridge, Mass.: Harvard University Press.

—— (1897). *The Philosophy of Ancient India.* Chicago: Open Court.

Gauḍapāda (1964). *The Sāṃkhyakārikā of Īśvarakṛṣṇa with the Commentary of Gauḍapāda.* Edited and translated by T. G. Mainkar. Poona: Oriental Book Agency.

Ghose, Aurobindo (2000). *India's Rebirth.* Edited by Sujata Nahar. Paris and Mysore: Institut de recherches évolutives and Mira Aditi.

—— (2005). *Nationalism, Religion, and Beyond: Writings on Politics, Society, and Culture.* Edited by Peter Heehs. Delhi: Permanent Black.

Gode, P. K. (1944). "The Chronology of Vijñānabhikṣu and His Disciple Bhāvagaṇeśa, the Leader of the Citpāvan Brahmins of Benares." *Adyar Library Bulletin* 8(1): 20–28.

Gombrich, Richard (1971). *Precept and Practice: Traditional Buddhism in the Rural Highlands of Ceylon.* Oxford: Clarendon.

Goswami, C. L. (1971). *Śrīmad Bhāgavata Mahāpurāṇa: Part One.* Gorakhpur: Gita Press.

Goswami, Damodara Lal, ed. (1905). *Ṣaḍdarśanasamuccaya, with a Commentary Called Laghuvṛtti by Maṇibhadra,* by Haribhadra [8th c. CE]. Benares: Chowkhamba Sanskrit Book Depot.

Gough, Archibald Edward (1882). *The Philosophy of the Upanishads.* London: Trübner.

Gupta, Anand Swarup, ed. (1971). *The Kūrma Purāṇa.* Varanasi: All-India Kashiraj Trust.

Gupta, Ravi (2007). *The Chaitanya Vaishnava Vedanta of Jiva Gosvami: When Knowledge Meets Devotion.* London: Routledge.

Gupta, Sanjukta (2006). *Advaita Vedānta and Vaiṣṇavism: The Philosophy of Madhusūdana Sarasvatī.* London: Routledge.

Hacker, Paul, ed. and trans. (1949). *Upadeshasāhasrī: Unterweisung in der All-Einheits-Lehre der Inder von Meister Shankara.* Bonn: Ludwig Röhrscheid.

—— (1978). *Kleine Schriften.* Edited by Lambert Schmidthausen. Wiesbaden: Franz Steiner.

—— (1983). *Inklusivismus: Eine indische Denkform.* Vienna: Gerold.

Hadot, Pierre (1995). *Philosophy as a Way of Life: Spiritual Exercises from Socrates to Foucault.* Translated by Michael Chase. Oxford: Blackwell.

Halbfass, Wilhelm (1983). *Studies in Kumārila and Śaṅkara.* Reinbek: Orientalistische Fachpublikationen.

—— (1988). *India and Europe.* Albany: State University of New York Press.

——, ed. (1995). *Philology and Confrontation: Paul Hacker on Traditional and Modern Vedānta.* Albany: State University of New York Press.

—— (1997). *Beyond Orientalism: The Work of Wilhelm Halbfass and Its Impact on Indian and Cross-Cultural Studies.* Edited by Eli Franco and Karin Preisendanz. Amsterdam: Rodopi.

Hall, Fitzedward, ed. (1856). *The Sankhya-pravachana-bhashya: A Commentary on the Aphorisms of the Hindu Atheistic Philosophy,* by Vijñānabhikṣu [16th c. CE]. Calcutta: Baptist Mission Press.

Hallisey, Charles (1995). "Roads Taken and Not Taken in the Study of Theravāda Buddhism." In *Curators of the Buddha,* edited by Donald S. Lopez, 31–62. Chicago: University of Chicago Press.

Hatcher, Brian A. (1999). *Eclecticism and Modern Hindu Discourse.* New York: Oxford University Press.

Hawley, John Stratton, and Mark Juergensmeyer (1988). *Songs of the Saints of India.* New York: Oxford University Press.

Henderson, John B. (1998). *The Construction of Orthodoxy and Heresy.* Albany: State University of New York Press.

Hiriyanna, Mysore (1957). *Indian Philosophical Studies.* Vols. 1–2. Mysore: Kavyalaya.

Hobsbawm, Eric, and Terence Ranger, eds. (1983). *The Invention of Tradition.* Cambridge: Cambridge University Press.

Hopkins, Jasper, trans. (1995). *Nicholas of Cusa's* De pace fidei *and* Cribratio Alkorani. Minneapolis: A. J. Banning.

Hosoda, Noriaki, ed. and introduction (1998). "Bṛhadāraṇyakāloka: Vijñānabhikṣu's Commentary on the Bṛhadāraṇyakopaniṣad," by Vijñānabhikṣu [16th c. CE]. In *Ko Upanishaddo kara genshi bukkyō ni itaru rinne shishō no mondai ni kansuru kenkyū,* 3–102. Tokyo: National Diet Library.

Houben, Jan E. M. (1997). "*Sūtra* and *Bhāṣyasūtra* in Bhartṛhari's Mahābhāṣya Dīpikā: On the Theory and Practice of a Scientific and Philosophical Genre." In *India and Beyond: Aspects of Literature, Meaning, Ritual, and Thought,* edited by Dick van der Meij, 271–305. London: Kegan Paul.

—— (1999). "Why Did Rationality Thrive but Hardly Survive in Kapila's 'System'? On the *Pramāṇas,* Rationality, and Irrationality in Sāṃkhya (Part I)." *Asiatische Studien* 53(3): 491–512.

—— (2001). "'Verschriftlichung' and the Relation Between the *Pramāṇas* in the History of Sāṃkhya (Why Did Rationality Thrive but Hardly Survive in Kapila's 'System'? Part II)." In *Etudes de lettres: La rationalité en Asie,* edited by Johannes Brokhorst, 165–94. Lausanne: University of Lausanne Press.

Inden, Ronald (1990). *Imagining India.* Oxford: Blackwell.

Ingalls, Daniel H. H. (1953). "Śaṃkara on the Question: Whose Is Avidyā?" *Philosophy East and West* 3: 69–72.

—— (1955). "A Reply to Bhattacharya." *Philosophy East and West* 5: 163–66.

—— (1967). "Bhāskara the Vedāntin." *Philosophy East and West* 17: 61–67.

Jackson, Roger R. (1989). "Matching Concepts: Deconstructive and Foundationalist Tendencies in Buddhist Thought." *Journal of the American Academy of Religion* 62(3): 561–87.

Jha, D. N. (2002). *The Myth of the Holy Cow.* New York: Verso.

Jha, Ganganatha, trans. (1933). *Śābara-bhāṣya,* by Śabara [2nd c. CE?]. Baroda: Oriental Institute.

——, ed. and trans. (1995). *Yogasārasaṃgraha of Vijñānabhikṣu,* by Vijñānabhikṣu [16th c. CE]. Delhi: Parimal.

——, ed. and trans. (1999). *Manusmṛti with the 'Manubhāṣya of Medhātithi.* Vols. 1–10. New Delhi: Motilal Banarsidass.

Jha, Mahāmahopādhyāya Ganganath, trans. and ed. (1965). *Tattvakaumudī,* by Vācaspati Miśra [10th c. CE]. Poona: Oriental Book Agency.

Johnston, E. H. (1974). *Early Sāṃkhya.* New Delhi: Motilal Banarsidass.

Kalupahana, David J., ed. and trans. (1986). *The Philosophy of the Middle Way: Mūlamadhyamakakārikā,* by Nāgārjuna [2nd c. CE?]. Albany: State University of New York Press.

Kapstein, Matthew T. (2001). *Reason's Traces: Identity and Interpretation in Indian and Tibetan Buddhist Thought.* Boston: Wisdom.

Karmarkar, R. D., ed. and trans. (1962). *Vedāntakalpalatikā,* by Madhusūdana Sarasvatī [16th c. CE]. Poona: Bhandarkar Institute Press.

Kent, Stephen A. (1982). "Early Sāṃkhya in the Buddhacarita." *Philosophy East and West* 32(3): 259–78.

Killingley, Dermot (1993). *Rammohun Roy in Hindu and Christian Tradition: The Teape Lectures 1990.* Newcastle upon Tyne: Grevatt and Grevatt.

King, Richard (1995). *Early Advaita Vedānta and Buddhism.* Albany: State University of New York Press.

—— (1999). *Orientalism and Religion: Postcolonial Theory, India, and "the Mystic East."* London: Routledge.

Klostermaier, Klaus K., trans. and ed. (1999). *Sarvadarśanasaṃgraha: Chapter 16: Śaṅkaradarśanam,* by Mādhava [14th c. CE]. Chennai: Adyar Library and Research Centre.

Kontje, Todd (2004). *German Orientalisms.* Ann Arbor: University of Michigan Press.

Krishna, Daya (1991). *Indian Philosophy: A Counter-Perspective.* New Delhi: Oxford University Press.

—— (2001). *New Perspectives in Indian Philosophy.* Jaipur: Rawat.

Kumar, Shiv, ed. and trans. (1988). *Sāṃkhyasāra of Vijñānabhikṣu,* by Vijñānabhikṣu [16th c. CE]. Delhi: Eastern Book Linkers.

Lamotte, Étienne (1998) [1949]. "The Assessment of Textual Interpretation in Buddhism." In *Buddhist Hermeneutics,* edited by Donald S. Lopez, 11–27. Honolulu: University of Hawai'i Press.

Larson, Gerald (1998). *Classical Sāṃkhya.* New Delhi: Motilal Banarsidass.

Larson, Gerald, and R. S. Bhattacharya, eds. (1987). *Encyclopedia of Indian Philosophies.* Vol. 4, *Sāṃkhya: A Dualist Tradition in Indian Philosophy.* Princeton, N.J.: Princeton University Press.

Lindtner, Christian, ed. (2001). *Madhyamakahṛdayam of Bhavya,* by Bhāviveka (aka Bhavya) [6th c. CE]. Adyar: Adyar Library and Research Center.

Locke, John (2004) [1689]. *A Letter Concerning Toleration.* Edited by Hilaire Belloc. Whitefish, Mont.: Kessinger.

Lorenzen, David, ed. (1994). *Bhakti Religion in North India: Community, Identity, and Political Action.* Albany: State University of New York Press.

—— (2005). "Who Invented Hinduism?" In *Defining Hinduism: A Reader,* edited by J. E. Llewellyn, 52–80. New York: Routledge.

Maas, Philipp André (2006). *Samādhipāda: Das erste Kapitel des* Pātañjalayogaśāstra *zum ersten Mal kritisch Ediert.* Aachen: Shaker.

Madhusūdana Sarasvatī [16th c. CE] (1850). *Prasthānabheda.* Sanskrit text and German translation in *Indische Studien. Beiträge für die Kunde des Indischen Altertums,* edited by Albrecht Weber, 1–24. Berlin: F. Dümmler.

Malinar, Angelika (1996). *Rājavidyā: Das königliche Wissen um Herrschaft und Verzicht.* Wiesbaden: Otto Harrassowitz.

Mansfeld, Jaap (2004). "Doxography of Ancient Philosophy." *Stanford Encyclopedia of Philosophy.* Available at http://plato.stanford.edu/entries/doxography-ancient/ (accessed June 12, 2007).

Marriott, McKim (1976). "Hindu Transactions: Diversity Without Dualism." In *Transaction and Meaning,* edited by Bruce Kapferer, 109–42. Philadelphia: Institute for the Study of Human Issues.

Marui, Hiroshi (forthcoming). "The Meaning of a Diversity of Established World Views or Tenets (*siddhānta*) in Debate." In *Papers of the International Conference "Doctrine and World-View in Indian Philosophy,"* edited by Piotr Balcerowicz. New Delhi: Motilal Banarsidass.

Matilal, Bimal Krishna (1968). *The Navya-Nyāya Doctrine of Negation.* Cambridge, Mass.: Harvard University Press.

—— (1977). *Nyāya-Vaiśeṣika.* In *A History of Indian Literature,* vol. 6, fasc. 2, edited by Jan Gonda. Wiesbaden: Otto Harassowitz.

—— (1981). *The Central Philosophy of Jainism.* Ahmadabad: L. D. Institute of Indology.

—— (1986). *Perception: An Essay on Classical Indian Theories of Knowledge.* Oxford: Clarendon.

—— (1998). *The Character of Logic in India.* Edited by Jonardon Ganeri and Heeraman Tiwari. Albany: State University of New York Press.

Miller, Barbara Stoler, trans. (1986). *The Bhagavad Gita: Krishna's Counsel in Time of War.* New York: Columbia University Press.

——, trans. (1998). *Yoga: Discipline of Freedom,* by Patañjali [4th c. CE?]. New York: Bantam.

Mishra, Pankaj (2009). Review of *The Hindus: An Alternative History,* by Wendy Doniger. *New York Times Book Review,* April 26, p. 20.

Monius, Anne E. (2001). *Imagining a Place for Buddhism.* New York: Oxford University Press.

Müller, Friedrich Max (1890). "Life of Colebrooke." In *Chips from a German Workshop,* vol. 4, 359–99. New York: Scribner.

Murty, K. Satchidananda, ed. and trans. (1957). *Ṣaḍdarśanasamuccaya,* by Haribhadra [8th c. CE]. Delhi: Eastern Book Linkers.

Nakamura, Hajime (1989). *A History of Early Vedānta Philosophy: Part 1.* New Delhi: Motilal Banarsidass.

—— (2004). *A History of Early Vedānta Philosophy: Part 2.* New Delhi: Motilal Banarsidass.

Nicholson, Andrew J. (2005). "Doctrine and Boundary-Formation: The Philosophy of Vijñānabhikṣu in Indian Intellectual History." PhD diss., University of Chicago.

Nicholson, Hugh (2002). "Apologetics and Philosophy in Maṇḍana Miśra's *Brahmasiddhi.*" *Journal of Indian Philosophy* 30: 575–96.

Oberhammer, Gerhard (1997). *Materialien zur Geschichte der Rāmānuja-Schule III: Yādavaprakāśa, der vergessene Lehrer Rāmānujas.* Vienna: Österreichischen Akademie der Wissenschaften.

O'Connell, Joseph T. (1973). "The Word 'Hindu' in Gauḍīya Vaiṣṇava Texts." *Journal of the American Oriental Society* 93(3): 340–44.

Oddie, Geoffrey A. (2006). *Imagined Hinduism: British Protestant Missionary Constructions of Hinduism, 1793–1900.* New Delhi: Sage.

O'Flaherty, Wendy Doniger (1976). *The Origins of Evil in Hindu Mythology.* New Delhi: Motilal Banarsidass.

Olivelle, Patrick, ed. and trans. (1998). *The Early Upaniṣads: Annotated Text and Translation.* New York: Oxford University Press.

——, ed. and trans. (2006). *Manu's Code of Law: A Critical Edition and Translation of the* Mānava-Dharmaśāstra. New Delhi: Oxford University Press.

Padmarajiah, Y. J. (1986). *A Comparative Study of Jaina Theories of Reality and Knowledge.* New Delhi: Motilal Banarsidass.

Pande, Govind Chandra (1998). *Life and Thought of Śaṅkarācarya.* New Delhi: Motilal Banarsidass.

Passmore, John (1965). *The Historiography of the History of Philosophy.* Gravenhage: Mouton.

Pollock, Sheldon (1985). "The Theory of Practice and the Practice of Theory in Indian Intellectual History." *Journal of the American Oriental Society* 105(3): 499–519.

—— (1989). "Mīmāṃsā and the Problem of History in Traditional India." *Journal of the American Oriental Society* 109(4): 603–10.

—— (1993a). "Deep Orientalism? Notes on Sanskrit and Power Beyond the Raj." In *Orientalism and the Postcolonial Predicament,* edited by Carol A. Breckenridge and Peter van der Veer, 76–133. Philadelphia: University of Pennsylvania Press.

—— (1993b). "Rāmāyaṇa and Political Imagination in India." *Journal of Asian Studies* 52(2): 261–97.

—— (2001a). "The Death of Sanskrit." *Comparative Studies in Society and History* 43(2): 392–426.

—— (2001b). "New Intellectuals in Seventeenth-Century India." *Indian Economic and Social History Review* 38(1): 3–31.

—— (2006). *The Language of the Gods in the World of Men: Sanskrit, Culture, and Power in Premodern India.* Berkeley: University of California Press.

Potter, Karl H. (1963). *Presuppositions of India's Philosophies.* Englewood Cliffs, N.J.: Prentice Hall.

—— (1977). *Encyclopedia of Indian Philosophies.* Vol. 2, *The Tradition of Nyāya-Vaiśeṣika up to Gaṅgeśa.* New Delhi: Motilal Banarsidass.

Potter, Karl H., and Sibajiban Bhattacharyya (1993). *Encyclopedia of Indian Philosophies.* Vol. 6, *Indian Philosophical Analysis of Nyāya-Vaiśeṣika from Gaṅgeśa to Raghunātha Śiromaṇi.* New Delhi: Motilal Banarsidass.

Prakash, Gyan (1990). "Writing Post-Orientalist Histories of the Third World: Perspectives from Indian Historiography." *Comparative Studies in Society in History* 32(2): 383–408.

Qvarnström, Olle (1989). *Hindu Philosophy in Buddhist Perspective.* Lund Studies in African and Asian Religions, vol. 4. Lund: Plus Ultra.

—— (1999). "Haribhadra and the Beginnings of Doxography in India." In *Approaches to Jaina Studies: Philosophy, Logic, Rituals, and Symbols,* edited by N. K. Wagle and Olle Qvarnström, 169–210. Toronto: Center for South Asian Studies.

Radhakrishnan, Sarvepalli (1927). *The Hindu View of Life.* New York: Macmillan.

—— (1940). *Eastern Religions and Western Thought.* Oxford: Oxford University Press.

Raghavan, V., and Anantalal Thakur, eds. (1964). *Āgamaḍambara,* by Jayanta Bhaṭṭa [9th c. CE]. Darbhanga: Mithila Institute.

Ram, Kanshi (1995). Integral Non-Dualism: A Critical Exposition of Vijñānabhikṣu's System of Philosophy. New Delhi: Motilal Banarsidass.

Ram-Prasad, Chakravarthi (2002). *Advaita Epistemology and Metaphysics: An Outline of Indian Non-Realism.* London: Routledge Curzon.

Rao, Srinivasa (1996). "Two 'Myths' in Advaita." *Journal of Indian Philosophy* 24: 265–79.

Richman, Paula (1988). *Women, Branch Stories, and Religious Rhetoric in a Tamil Buddhist Text.* Syracuse, N.Y.: Maxwell School of Citizenship and Public Affairs.

Rocher, Ludo (1986). *The Purāṇas.* In *History of Indian Literature,* vol. 2, fasc. 3. Wiesbaden: Otto Harrassowitz.

Rocher, Ludo, and Rosane Rocher (forthcoming). *The Making of Western Indology: Henry Thomas Colebrooke and the East India Company.* London: Routledge.

Rorty, Richard (1984). "The Historiography of Philosophy: Four Genres." In *Philosophy in History: Essays on the Historiography of Philosophy,* edited by Richard Rorty, J. B. Schneewind, and Quentin Skinner, 49–75. Cambridge: Cambridge University Press.

Rukmani, T. S. (1970). *A Critical Study of the Bhāgavata Purāṇa.* Varanasi: Chowkhamba Sanskrit Series Office.

——, ed., trans., and introduction (1981). *Yogavārttika of Vijñānabhikṣu,* by Vijñānabhikṣu [16th c. CE]. Vol. 1. New Delhi: Munshiram Manoharlal.

Runia, David T. (1998). "Doxography." *Routledge Encyclopedia of Philosophy.* Available at http://www.rep.routledge.com/article/A045 (accessed June 12, 2007).

—— (1999). "What Is Doxography?" In *Ancient Histories of Medicine: Essays in Medical Doxography and Historiography in Classical Antiquity,* edited by Philip J. van der Eijk, 33–55. Leiden: Brill.

Sadhale, S. G. S., ed. (1985). *The Bhagavad-Gita with Eleven Commentaries.* Vol. 1. Delhi: Parimal Publications.

Said, Edward W. (1978). *Orientalism.* New York: Random House.

Śaṅkara [8th c. CE] (1978). *Upadeśasāhasrī.* Edited by S. Subrahmanyasastri. Mount Abu: Mahesh Research Institute.

—— [8th c. CE] (1992). *A Thousand Teachings: The Upadeśasāhasrī of Śaṅkara.* Edited and translated by Sengaku Mayeda. Albany: State University of New York Press.

—— [8th c. CE] (1996). *Brahmasūtrabhāṣyam,* with *Bhāmatī* and *Bhāmatīvyākhyā.* Vols. 1 and 2. Varanasi: Chaukhambha Vidyā Bhavan.

Śaṅkara [14th c. CE?] (1983). *Sarvasiddhāntasaṃgraha.* Edited and translated by M. Rangācārya. New Delhi: Ajay Book Service.

Sargeant, Winthrop, and Christopher Key Chapple, eds. and trans. (2009). *The Bhagavad Gītā.* Albany: State University of New York Press.

Śāstrī, Gosvāmī Dāmodara (ed.) (1989). *Sāṃkhya Yogadarśanam arthāt Pātañjaladarśanam.* Varanasi: Chaukhambha Saṃskṛta Saṃsthān.

Śāstrī, Mukunda, ed. (1901). *Brahmasūtrabhāṣyam,* by Vijñānabhikṣu [16th c. CE]. Chowkhamba Sanskrit Series, no. 8. Benares: Chowkhamba Sanskrit Series Office.

Savarkar, Vinayak Damodar (1989) [1928]. *Hindutva: Who Is a Hindu?* Poona City: S. P. Gokhale.

Schopenhauer, Arthur (1958) [1856]. *The World as Will and Representation,* Vol. 2. Translated by E. F. J. Payne. New York: Dover.

Schroeder, John W. (2001). *Skillful Means: The Heart of Buddhist Compassion.* Honolulu: University of Hawai'i Press.

Sen Gupta, Anima (1981). *Classical Sāṃkhya: A Critical Study.* New Delhi: Munshiram Manoharlal.

Sharma, Kashi Nath, ed. (1972). *Vaisheshikadarshana: with Vedabhaskara Commentary and an Appendix with the Hindi Gloss of the Sutras.* Hoshiarpur: V.V.R.I. Press.

Sharma, Krishna (1987). *Bhakti and the Bhakti Movement: A New Perspective.* New Delhi: Munshiram Manoharlal.

Shastri, Bhao, ed. (1989). *Siddhāntaleśasaṃgraha,* by Appaya Dīkṣita [16th c. CE]. Varanasi: Chaukhambha Sanskrit Sansthan.

Sheridan, Daniel P. (1986). *The Advaitic Theism of the Bhāgavata Purāṇa.* New Delhi: Motilal Banarsidass.

Sheshadri, H. V. (2009). "Universal Spirit of Hindu Nationalism." *Archives of RSS [Rashtriya Swayamsevak Sangh].* Available at http://www.archivesofrss.org/index.php?option=com_book&task=showFile&bookid=4 (accessed August 29, 2009).

Shikoh, Dara [17th c. CE] (1982). *Majma'-ul-Baḥrain or the Mingling of the Two Oceans.* Translated by M. Mahfuz-ul-Haq. Calcutta: Asiatic Society.

Simon, Marcel (1979). "From Greek Hairesis to Christian Heresy." In *Early Christian Literature and the Classical Intellectual Tradition,* edited by William R. Schoedel and Robert L. Wilken, 101–16. Paris: Éditions Beauchesne.

Sinha, Nandalal, trans. (1979). *The Samkhya Philosophy.* New Delhi: Oriental Books Reprint.

Smith, Frederick M. (1998). "*Nirodha* and the *Nirodhalakṣaṇa* of Vallabhācārya." *Journal of Indian Philosophy* 26: 489–551.

—— (2005). "The Hierarchy of Philosophical Systems According to Vallabhācārya." *Journal of Indian Philosophy* 33: 421–53.

Smith, Jonathan Z. (2004). *Relating Religion: Essays in the Study of Religion.* Chicago: University of Chicago Press.

Srinivasachari, P. N. (1972). *The Philosophy of Bhedābheda.* Madras: Adyar Library.

Srīvāstavya, Sureś Cāndra (1969). *Ācārya Vijñānabhikṣu aur Bhāratīya Darśan meṃ unkā Sthān.* Allahabad: Lokabharati Prakashan.

Stietencron, Heinrich von (1995). "Religious Configurations in Pre-Muslim India and the Modern Concept of Hinduism." In *Representing Hinduism: The Construction of Religious Traditions and National Identity,* edited by Vasudha Dalmia and Heinrich von Stietencron, 51–81. New Delhi: Sage.

Sutherland, Gail Hinich (1991). *The Disguises of the Demon: The Development of the Yakṣa in Hinduism and Buddhism.* Albany: State University of New York Press.

Tagare, G. V., trans. (1982). *The Kūrma-Purāṇa, Part 2.* New Delhi: Motilal Banarsidass.

Talbot, Cynthia (1995). "Inscribing the Other, Inscribing the Self: Hindu-Muslim Identities in Pre-colonial India." *Comparative Studies in Society and History* 37(4): 692–722.

Tapasyananda, Swami, trans. (1996). *Śaṅkaradigvijaya: The Traditional Life of Śri Śaṅkarācarya,* by Mādhava [14th c. CE]. Madras: Sri Ramakrishna Math.

Thapar, Romila (1971). "The Image of the Barbarian in Early India." *Comparative Studies in Society and History* 13(4): 408–36.

—— (1978). "Renunciation: The Making of a Counter-culture?" In *Ancient Indian Social History: Some Interpretations,* 63–104. New Delhi: Orient Longman.

—— (1989). "Imagined Religious Communities? Ancient History and the Modern Search for a Hindu Identity." *Modern Asian Studies* 23(2): 209–31.

Theophrastus [4th c. BCE] (1995). *Theophrastus of Eresus: Sources for His Life, Writings, Thought and Influence.* Edited by R. W. Sharples. Leiden: Brill.

Timalsina, Sthaneshwar (2006). *Seeing and Appearance.* Aachen: Shaker.

Tripathi, Jaya Shankar Lal, and Sudhakar Malaviya, eds. (1985). *Kāśikā: A Commentary on Pāṇini's Grammar, Volumes 1–10,* by Vāmana and Jayāditya [7th c. CE]. Varanasi: Tara Printing Works.

Tripāṭhī, Pandit Kedāranātha (1979). *Brahmasūtra: Vijñānāmṛtabhāṣyam,* by Vijñānabhikṣu [16th c. CE]. Varanasi: Banaras Hindu University Press.

Tuck, Andrew (1990). *Comparative Philosophy and the Philosophy of Scholarship: On the Western Interpretation of Nāgārjuna.* New York: Oxford University Press.

Upādhyāya, Baladeva (1994). *Kāśī kī Pāṇḍitya Paramparā.* Varanasi: Viśvavidyālaya Prakāśan.

Varadacarya, K. S., ed. (1969). *Nyāyamañjarī,* vols. 1–2, by Jayanta Bhaṭṭa [9th c. CE]. Mysore: Oriental Research Institute.

Varadachari, V. (1971). "Treatment of the Schools of Religion and Philosophy in the Manimekhalai." *Sri Venkateswara University Oriental Journal* 14: 9–26.

Vasu, S. C., ed. (1962). *Siddhānta Kaumudī,* by Bhaṭṭoji Dīkṣita [17th c. CE]. New Delhi: Motilal Banarsidass.

Vedānta Deśika [14th c. CE] (1974). *Śatadūṣaṇī.* Madras: V. D. Ramaswami.

Venis, Arthur, ed., trans., and introduction. (1975). *Vedāntasiddhāntamuktāvalī,* by Prakāśānanda [16th c. CE]. Varanasi: Chaukhamba Orientalia.

Vivekananda, Swami (1970–1972). *The Complete Works of Swami Vivekananda.* Vols. 1–8. Calcutta: Advaita Ashrama.

Wezler, Albrecht, and Shujun Motegi, eds. (1998). *Yuktidīpikā: The Most Significant Commentary on the Sāṃkhyakārikā.* Alt- und Neu-Indische Studien, no. 44. Stuttgart: Franz Steiner.

Wilson, H. H., trans. (1972). *Vishnu Purana.* Calcutta: Punthi Pustak.

Wimsatt, William (1954). *The Verbal Icon: Studies in the Meaning of Poetry.* Lexington: University of Kentucky Press.

Zelliot, Eleanor (1982). "A Medieval Encounter Between Hindu and Muslim: Eknath's Drama-Poem Hindu-Turk Samvad." In *Images of Man: Religious and Historical Process in South Asia,* edited by Fred W. Clothey, 171–95. Madras: New Era.

Zimmer, Heinrich (1969). *Philosophies of India.* Princeton, N.J.: Princeton University Press.

INDEX

abbreviations, xi–xii
ābhiprāyika (intentional), 95
abhyupagamasiddhānta. *See* tenets
abhyupagamavāda. *See* temporary concession (abhyupagamavāda)
absence, mutual. *See* identity and mutual absence (tādātmya and anyonyābhāva)
abstentions and observances (yamas and niyamas), 77, 78
Acintyabhedābheda (Inconceivable Difference and Non-Difference) school, 35
acintyatva (inconceivability), 35
ad hominem arguments, 3
adhiṣṭhānakāraṇa. *See* locus cause (adhiṣṭhānakāraṇa)
adhiṣṭhātṛ (superintendent), 71 101; as synonym for deity (devatā), 158
ādhunikas ("moderns"), 86, 132
advaita. *See* duality and non-duality (dvaita and advaita)
Advaita (Non-Dualist) Vedānta school, 5, 8, 25, 100, 182; attack on, 85; Brahman, causality of, 56–58, 60–61, 63–65; Buddhist school, likened to, 63, 98, 119, 132, 152, 180, 189, 204; as "crypto-nāstika," 119, 178, 180, 189; development of, 25; doxographies, 179; God and, 36; idealist school, 17; as Illusionism, 98; institutionalization, 36; liberation and, 52; limitationism, 51; Orientalism and, 17, 68, 127; *Padma Purāṇa,* whipping-boy of the, 98; Purāṇas and, 75; reflectionism, 51; scripture, false statements of, 44; superiority of, 159; threats to, 160; views, 29, 35, 61; vivarta and, 27, 30. *See also* Śaṅkara; duality and non-duality (dvaita and advaita); *Sarvadarśanasaṃgraha; Sarvasiddhāntasaṃgrah;* Vivaraṇa sub-school; Bhāmatī sub-school
Aëtius, 146
"affirmers." *See* āstikas
agent (kartṛ), 87
ahiṃsā (nonviolence), 168–69
aiśvarya. *See* lordliness (aiśvarya)
ajātivāda, 153
ākāśa. *See* space (ākāśa)
Akbar, Emperor, 190-91
akhaṇḍatā. *See* undividedness (akhaṇḍatā)
Allgemeine Geschichte der Philosophie, 134, 159
aloneness (kaivalya), 118, 119–20, 121–22
aṃśa and aṃśin. *See* part and whole (aṃśa and aṃśin)
anādi ("beginningless"), 64
Ānandagiri, 28
ānanda (bliss), 54
anātman ("no-self"), 181
anekāntavāda. *See* perspectivism (anekāntavāda)
animal sacrifice, opposition to, 3, 25, 97, 169

Lokāyata school, 147, 155, 156, 157, 173. *See also* Cārvāka school
lordliness (aiśvarya), 36, 42: distraction by, 89; indifference to, 88, 106; prakṛti and, 103. *See also* God (*īśvara*); "worldly lord" (laukikeśvara)
Lorenzen, David, 198, 200

Mādhava, 5, 9, 10, 32, 82, 158–62, 179, 180, 182–83. *See also Sarvadarśanasaṃgraha (Compendium of All Philosophical Systems)*
Madhusūdana Sarasvatī, 5, 163–65, 177, 179, 180, 182–83; āstika concordance, position on, 9. *See also Prasthānabheda (The Various Religious Sources)*
Madhva, 32, 160, 161. *See also* Dvaita (Dualist) Vedānta school
Madhyamaka (Emptiness) Buddhist school, 152–53, 180; Islam and, 193
Madhyamakahṛdayakārikā, 144–45, 151–54. *See also* Bhāviveka
Mahābhārata, 69, 71, 89, 96, 110, 115, 148; author of, 26, 149; classified as dharmaśāstra, 163; Sāṃkhya concepts and, 70, 71; translations, 190. *See also Mokṣadharma Parvan*
mahātmyaśarīra ("body of dignity"), 105
mahāvākyas. *See* "great statements" (mahāvākyas)
Mahāvīra, 97. *See also* Jinendra
Māṇḍūkyakārikā, 153
Maṇibhadra, 156, 157, 158; nāstika, understanding of, 172
Maṇimēkalai, 144, 149–51, 154, 171; āstika/nāstika hierarchy, 179, 191
Mansfeld, Jaap, 10, 146
Manusmṛti, 172, 173
Marcus Aurelius, 178
Marx, Karl, 5
material cause (upādānakāraṇa), 8, 27, 57, 60; changing versus unchanging, 58–59, 63–64; locus as, 62
Māṭharavṛtti, 76, 77, 78, 95
maṭhas (monasteries), 36
matter (prakṛti), 7, 8, 56, 65, 67, 69, 76, 139; consciousness and, 58, 70, 71, 104, 117, 120; God, mutual dependence with, 103; māyā, synonymous with, 161, 162; insentience of, 101; lordliness and, 103. *See also* Sāṃkhya school
māyā. *See* illusion (māyā)
"means of valid knowledge" (pramāṇa), 191; enumeration of, 149–50
Medhātithi, 172–173, 178–179
medievalism, 19
meditation: types of, 113. *See also* objectless meditation (asamprajñātasamādhi)
metaphors, 31, 36, 110–11, 195–96; Brahman and self, 48, 51–52, 54–56
metaphysics, 7, 202; with conceptual objects (samprajñātasamādhi), 113
Mill, James, 19
Mīmāṃsā (Exegesis) school, 3, 92, 158, 163, 191; atheism of, 152, 157; focus, 14; influence on Vendānta, 33, 40; ritual action and, 33. *See also* Pūrva Mīmāṃsā (Prior Exegesis) school; Kumārila Bhaṭṭa
Mīmāṃsāsūtras, 80, 150
miṣa ("disguise"), 110
mithyā. *See* ultimately false (mithyā)
mlecchas. *See* foreigners (mlecchas)
"moderns" (ādhunikas), 86, 132
mokṣa. *See* liberation (mokṣa)
Mokṣadharma Parvan, 70
monasteries (maṭhas), 36
monism: dualism, historical deevolution to, 135–36, 141; as "highest doctrine," 134–35; *Upaniṣads*, 25
Mughal Empire, 14, 190–91
mūlakāraṇa ("root cause"), 59
Mūlamadhyamakakārikā, 153. *See also* Madhyamaka (Emptiness) Buddhist school; Nāgārjuna
Müller, F. Max, 125
Muslims. *See* Islam
mutual absence. *See* identity and mutual absence (tādātmya and anyonyābhāva)
mutual dependence (anyonyāśraya), 103